Children's Medical Care Needs and Treatments

HARVARD CHILD HEALTH PROJECT

VOLUME II

1977

This is the second volume of a three-volume series. Under the direction of David S. Mundel, Associate Professor of Public Policy at Harvard University, a team of researchers studied the current state of children's health care under a grant to the Harvard Graduate School of Education by the Robert Wood Johnson Foundation. In volume I, *Toward a Primary Medical Care System Responsive to Children's Needs*, the Harvard Child Health Project Task Force summarizes the project's findings and conclusions. Both this volume and volume III, *Developing a Better Health Care System for Children*, contain the background reports of the project researchers, from which the summary was derived. All three volumes are published by Ballinger.

Children's Medical Care Needs and Treatments

Report of the Harvard Child Health Project

1977

Ballinger Publishing Company • Cambridge, Massachusetts
A Subsidiary of J.B. Lippincott Company

This book is printed on recycled paper.

International Standard Book Number: 0−88410−508−3

Library of Congress Catalog Card Number: 77−3365

Printed in the United States of America

Library of Congress Cataloging in Publication Data

Harvard Child Health Project.
  Children's medical care needs and treatments.

  (Its Harvard Child Health Project ; v. 2)
  1. Child health services—United States. 2. Children—Diseases.
3. Children—Hospital care. I. Title. [DNLM: 1. Child health
services—United States. 2. Child care. 3. Primary health care—
In infancy and childhood. WA320 H339h]
RJ102.H37a vol. 2 362.7'8'0973s [362.7'8'0973]
ISBN 0−88410−508−3   77−3365

Contents

List of Figures

List of Tables

Harvard Child Health Project
Advisory Committee

William M. Capron (Chairman)

Associate Dean
John F. Kennedy School of Government
Harvard University
Cambridge, Massachusetts

Robert J. Blendon

Vice President
The Robert Wood Johnson Foundation
Princeton, New Jersey

Marian Wright Edelman

Children's Defense Fund
Cambridge, Massachusetts

Peter Edelman

Director
New York State Division for Youth
Albany, New York

Dr. Leon Eisenberg

Maude and Lillian Presley Professor; and
Chairman of the Executive Committee of
    the Department of Psychiatry
Harvard Medical School
and
Senior Associate in Psychiatry
Children's Hospital Medical Center
Boston, Massachusetts

Dr. Howard Hiatt

Dean
Harvard School of Public Health
Cambridge, Massachusetts

Gilbert Steiner

The Brookings Institution
Washington, D.C.

Homer Wadsworth

The Cleveland Foundation
Greater Cleveland Associated Foundation
Cleveland, Ohio

Dr. Kerr White

School of Hygiene and Public Health
Johns Hopkins University
Baltimore, Maryland

Paul N. Ylvisaker

Dean
Harvard Graduate School of Education
Cambridge, Massachusetts

Part I

The Primary Care Focus
of Children's Medical Needs

Chapter 1

Controversial Issues in
Health Care for Children

Leon Eisenberg, M.D.

Today the need for a national health policy is acknowledged by both major political parties, as a result of perva-
sive public concern with what is perceived as a "crisis in
health care." That the crisis is chronic rather than acute is evident
from the establishment in 1927 of a National Committee on the
Costs of Medical Care and from the long succession of legislative acts
that have attempted to deal with medical care and its costs on a
piecemeal basis (Richmond, 1969). After fifty years of heated public
debate, we have almost universal agreement that there is a problem,
but no evident consensus on its solution. In part, the difficulty in
achieving agreement stems from value choices. Is a free market preferable to government regulation? Is medical care primarily physician
centered and technological or does it include support, counseling,
and advocacy? Should the fundamental decisions be made by "experts" or "consumers"? To what extent and in what areas should
authority rest with one, the other, or both? In part, the difficulty
stems from the ambiguity of the evidence or its sheer absence. Under
what circumstances and for what conditions does medical care make
a difference? What constitutes a "difference" that matters? Are more
doctors better (or worse) for the health of the public? And what
kind of doctors for what goals?

I shall attempt to set out some of the key issues, and the elements
that enter into their analysis, as a basis for evaluating the decisions
that will have to be made as our nation enters a new presidential
term. First, let us stipulate some of the major contemporary dissatis-
factions with medical care:

Costs are High, Continuously Rising and Increasingly Visible. By 1975, the annual health bill for the average American had risen to $547 from $78 in 1950. The aggregate cost totalled $118.5 billion, equivalent to 8 percent of the gross national product, a higher proportion than that allocated to health services in any other country (Mueller and Gibson, 1975). By comparison, the cost of the national health service in the United Kingdom in 1975 was about 5.4 percent of the GNP. (The problem, however, is no less severe in the U.K. than in the U.S. because British health expenditures have been increasing more rapidly than national productivity in a country experiencing severe economic constraints (Office of Health Economics, 1976).) In the United States, tax dollars meet about 40 percent of the total cost and premiums from health insurance another 25 percent. Thus, two-thirds of the payments come from sources with high *public* visibility, in contrast to out-of-pocket private payments (Chart Book, 1975). In addition, the cost of health benefits for industrial workers plays an increasingly prominent role in labor-management negotiations. Thus, government, insurance-carriers, and industry join consumers in expressing major concerns about health costs.

Our National Health Record is Unsatisfactory. Despite a steady decline in infant mortality in the United States over the past decade, the infant mortality of 16.5 deaths per 1000 live births in 1974 was higher than the rate for fifteen other developed countries. (In that same year, it was less than ten in Sweden.) Moreover, the rate for black infants was almost twice as high as that for white, and the maternal mortality rate for black mothers was four times as high as that for whites! Perhaps the most telling single figure is that not until 1973 did nonwhite infants attain the neonatal mortality rate (26.8) achieved for whites in 1950. That it is not beyond our capacity to alter ethnic and class differentials is evident from the success of federally funded maternal and infant care programs. For example, over a five-year period, a program in Denver lowered the mortality rate from 34.2 to 21.5 in the target area; the corresponding figures for Birmingham were 25.4 to 14.3, and for Omaha, from 33.4 to 13.4 (Bronfenbrenner, 1976). The population groups without care or with at most limited care are at greatest risk. Pregnant teenagers are twice as likely as older women to give birth to low birth weight (LBW) infants (under 2500 grams). The LBW rate for all births is 8.7 percent as compared to 18 percent in women under fifteen and 11 percent for those between fifteen and nineteen (Richmond, 1977).

Access to Medical Care is Inequitable. Despite the evidence for the effectiveness of prenatal care, more than 30 percent of all pregnant women have no such care in the first trimester of pregnancy. (The figure for black women is 47 percent.) Despite the unequivocal evidence that polio immunization is effective, nearly 5 million America children (one-third of those between ages one and four) were not fully immunized against polio in 1974. Days in bed as the result of illness and injury were *twice* as high for young children from low-income families as for those from high-income families. Whereas 97.4 percent of youngsters under seventeen from families with incomes over $15,000 were rated by their families as being in excellent or good health, the corresponding figure for youngsters from families with incomes under $5000 was only 90.5 percent. Yet the percentage of under-seventeen-year-olds from poor families who had not seen a physician within the past two years was 18.7 percent versus 11.9 percent for "nonpoor" children (Chart Book, 1975).

There is No Agreement and No Clear Basis for Determining Health Personnel Needs. In the late 1950s, there was a widespread belief that we suffered from a shortage of physicians. Government funding for an expansion in the capacity of medical schools has resulted in an increase in the annual number of graduates by two-thirds over the past decade. The physician-population ratio, which was 140 per 100,000 in 1960, is projected to increase to 237 per 100,000 by 1990 (Chart Book, 1975). National averages conceal wide regional disparities. In 1970, the fifteen counties with the highest per capita incomes had seven times as many practicing doctors per capita as did the fifteen counties with the lowest per capita incomes (Davis, 1972). The problem is complex. Meaningful estimates of a desirable physician-to-population ratio cannot be made without a firm decision on which tasks require a physician and which can be carried out competently by other health personnel. For example, if it is decided that nurse midwives are capable of performing normal deliveries, then the estimate for the number of obstetricians required is sharply reduced. If specified aspects of child health care can be managed effectively by pediatric nurse-clinicians, we would revise downward our estimate for the number of pediatricians needed. Similar issues are at stake for the family physician as well as a range of other specialists.

Nor is the number of persons per physician clearly correlated with health status. For example, Sweden, with its better neonatal mortality figures and its greater life expectancy (77.4 years for women and 70.2 years for men in contrast to 75.2 and 67.4, respectively, for the United States), had *720* persons per physician in contrast to 574 for our country in the index year 1972 (Chart Book, 1975). Indeed, the United Kingdom, with a slightly better life expectancy for its citizens than the United States, had *790* persons per physician.

There is Widespread Dissatisfaction With the Quality of Care. Patient complaints about poor quality reflect concerns with inadequacies in the caring or "Samaritan" aspects of the physician encounter (McDermott, 1974). In contrast, physician evaluations of quality focus on more technical aspects, such as deficits in diagnosis, treatment, and recordkeeping. Methods to assure quality face major design problems: physicians are reluctant to be monitored; surveillance jeopardizes the preservation of patient confidentiality. It is essential to establish that differences in outcome are related to the process measures chosen for examination and that the system produces changes in physician behaviors in keeping with its costs; biomedical definition of quality care is not possible for conditions where there is no evidence that one method of treatment is better than another (Greene, 1976); quality assurance for the caring aspects of health services requires consumer evaluation over and above professional assessment of technological performance. Beyond the choice between process and outcome measures in assessing the *individual* patient-physician transaction, it is an even more imposing task to attempt to demonstrate that the introduction of a modern medical care system has a significant impact on the health of the *population* served unless social conditions are modified as well (McDermott et al., 1972).

Traditional Principles of Medical Ethics Have Been Called into Question. As a profession, medicine has established a set of rules to govern its practitioners, broadly encompassed in the Hippocratic Oath. These tenets are directed *at* the physician *in behalf of* the patient; the direct assertion of patient rights has stemmed from common law and is not directly embedded in the medical oath. This ancient medical covenant has been challenged as paternalistic. A much greater emphasis is now being placed upon full disclosure and upon patient rights (Academy Forum, 1975). Moreover, recent court decisions have suggested that professional restrictions on advertising may be in restraint of trade. Maximizing choice for the consumer is a clearly admirable principle, but should that include the choice of incompetent or fraudulent providers? The issue is far from trivial. There is good reason to be suspicious of a physician monopoly upon the market of health care personnel; yet abolishing that "monopoly" by allowing free rein to less competent personnel is not necessarily in the public interest. The assertion of patient rights is a necessary emphasis, but it does not mean that the patient is always "right." If parents ask for or demand a treatment for their child (for example, a tonsillectomy), should it be incumbent on the provider to supply that treatment if the evidence indicates that the risks outweigh the benefits? Demands for quality assurance necessitate better data about which medical treatments are most effective for what conditions. Yet so much attention has been given to the possibility of harm from medical experimentation that it has become increasingly difficult to conduct precisely those controlled clinical trials necessary to distinguish effective from ineffective and harmful procedures. Many procedures labelled "treatment" have been sanctified by decades of use. Some contend that it would be unethical to withhold traditional treatments from patients allocated to the control group. The argument is unconvincing. Who is being deprived when something of uncertain value is withheld (Eisenberg, 1975a)?

This brief epitome of the generally acknowledged problem areas in health care may suffice to provide a general background against which we can turn to the more specific studies which comprise this volume.

EVALUATING THE IMPACT OF MEDICAL CARE

There is an almost universal motivation to avoid illness and a corresponding readiness to embrace remedies that promise health (Eisenberg, 1977). Medical care is generally regarded as the means for its attainment. But is this true? There is no evidence that medical advances have led to a significant increase in life expectancy in industrialized countries for the past several decades; it is likely that the major improvements in the early part of this century resulted from improvements in social conditions rather than medical innovations per se (McKeown, 1966). Yet there are specific health problems for which medical interventions do make a decisive difference (immunizations, neonatal care, antibiotic treatment, certain surgical procedures, etc.).

The apparent contradiction is in part reconciled by the realization that medical care is not the only, and not necessarily the major, influence on morbidity and mortality; its impact can be overridden by the force of social and economic conditions. For example, in the developing world, measles is one of the leading causes of death in infancy, with case mortality rates as high as 6 to 12 percent reported from tropical Africa (Editorial, 1976). Preexisting malnutrition, together with traditional folk healing practices which restrict fluid and protein intake during the acute phase of infection, contribute to the high mortality. In contrast, in the United States, *prior* to vaccination, though the *case* rate per 100,000 remained relatively constant from

1912 to 1959 (with epidemics in the late winter season every two to three years), the *death* rate declined fiftyfold, from more than 10 to less than 0.2 per 100,000. (Langmuir, 1962). In the decade after the introduction of measles vaccination in the U.S., it is estimated that 24,000,000 cases were prevented, with the savings of 2400 lives and 8000 cases of mental retardation (Bass et al., 1976). Surely this is a triumph of medical science. Yet it is one with a relatively small effect on national mortality data in the United States (given the low pre-existing death rate for measles because of favorable general health conditions) compared with the massive impact the same measure would produce were it introduced on a population-wide scale in Africa or India! (The barriers are formidable; they include limited resources and severe logistical problems: the lack of a comprehensive health visitor system for infants and the rapid inactivation of vaccine in tropical climates in the absence of adequate means for cold storage. Nonetheless, this is clearly not beyond the capacity of a nation that can send an automated laboratory to Mars. All that is lacking is a commitment to child care of the same magnitude as that to space exploration and weapons development.)

As general factors associated with better health improve (nutrition, sanitation, housing, education, working conditions, and the like), they have led to secular declines in mortality from pneumonia, gastro-enteritis, tuberculosis and rheumatic fever, once the major causes of death in infancy and childhood in the United States. Under these conditions, specific preventive and therapeutic techniques, though still of vital importance to individual patients, produce only marginal changes in the trends in morbidity and mortality statistics. Moreover, the remaining prominent causes of death and disability in childhood are far more refractory to medical interventions in the technological sphere; they are chronic in nature (the care required may be life-long); they are multifactorial in origin (congenital malformations and malignant diseases have genetic, toxic, dietary, viral, and still uniden-tified roots); they are socially determined (pollution, work conditions in industry, food additives, unwise drug prescribing, all are beyond control by the individual). The leading causes of death (and the ones chiefly responsible for the differential between the United States and Sweden) for males between fifteen and twenty-four are behavioral: motor accidents, homicide, and suicide. If we are to design effective interventions, we will have to develop a model for health and disease that goes well beyond the magic bullet model that has dominated the views of public and profession alike.

Because we count what is easily countable, like mortality rates, we end up by overstating medical impotence. It *is* true that physicians lack *specific* remedies for the majority of complaints brought into their offices (Dingle et al., 1964; White, 1973). But they *can* and *do* bring relief to most of their patients (Eisenberg, 1977; McDermott, 1977). It is more difficult to measure the comfort and the improved function produced for the patient with rheumatoid arthritis or mental retardation and his family than to record the abolition of smallpox or the lowered mortality from pneumococcal pneumonia. The arthritic or retarded child is not cured; his family may have to cope with lifelong disability; but it is surely not trivial if suffering is diminished and performance is enhanced. Even in the case of self-limited illness with a good prognosis for recovery, medical reassurance to worried parents and their children is no unimportant contribution to family welfare.

None of this argues against the need for a detailed and rigorous assessment of the effectiveness of medical procedures—quite to the contrary, that is precisely what is undertaken in the first several chapters that follow—but it is a necessary corrective to an excessively technological focus which could well be the misleading view of health care derived from a literal reading of those chapters out of context. Five conditions—iron-deficiency anemia, middle ear infection, lead poisoning, appendicitis and streptococcal throat infection—have been chosen for analysis because they are common disorders, have potentially serious consequences, and have rational treatment protocols. They stand as prototypes for a host of specific, infectious, dietary, toxic, and surgical diseases of childhood. By analyzing what has and has not been accomplished in their care, we can see in microcosm some of the problems of pediatric health care delivery. If we deal with a disease that can be diagnosed, one for which an efficacious treatment exists, and yet find that the results of care fall short of what we should expect, then we must ask where the system is going awry.

At the outset, it is important to recognize the distinction Starfield draws between efficacy and effectiveness. Efficacy is a measure of the precision of diagnosis and the outcome of treatment as demonstrated by scientific tests of the results under optimum conditions. Effectiveness is a measure of the degree to which good health is attained in patients with the specified disease under current conditions of health care practice.

"Diagnosis" (by which I mean the accurate identification of what is wrong in order to try to right it) occurs in three stages. The first stage is in the domain of lay or popular behavior, the second at the interface between patient and health provider, and the third within the professional domain.

In the first instance, the child's family must recognize a deviation in behavior or appearance and label it as illness (or be oriented toward a regular health checkup; in that case, a condition unrecognized by the family can be identified by the doctor). It may seem like belaboring the obvious to point out that a physician cannot treat a patient who is not seen. Nonetheless, very little research has been devoted to family and popular medical care decisionmaking despite its major impact on health outcomes (Good et al., 1976). There are only scanty data on the relationship between what is and is not considered illness by the family, what actions family members do take to consult either unlicensed or orthodox practitioners, and which of those conditions health practitioners are equipped to treat effectively (Zola, 1972). What is clear is that from 70 to 90 percent of episodes experienced as illness are managed within the lay sector without ever being brought to the physician. Since most illness episodes are self-limited and lack specific medical remedies, this may be a sensible disposition for most of them; but only to the extent that the family makes reasonably sound decisions about when an episode requires more than self-care. Universal health education to prepare an informed public better to make these preliminary judgments and to choose wisely the appropriate source of help is an aspect of health care systematically overlooked in planning for the organization of health services.

The second stage in this sequence is the interface between the patient and the physician, the point at which Starfield stresses the importance of "problem recognition." This requires the physician to recognize both what concerns the patient and what is "wrong" with the patient. The patient may present a symptom as an admission ticket to the doctor's office, but the problem that is bothersome may be quite different. For example, the mother may complain that the child is underweight and not eating well; if the child is within normal limits in the physical examination, the physician may terminate the interview by telling her that the child is fine and that she need not worry; she may leave unsatisfied because what really troubles her is that her husband is ignoring her and the child and *that's* what she wants the doctor to do something about. Or the mother may complain of bed-wetting and mention in a "by the way" that the child is a fire-setter. The doctor may properly conclude that fire-setting is a more ominous symptom than bed-wetting. But unless attention is paid to the presenting complaint, the physician may never succeed in enlisting the mother's cooperation in dealing with the graver problem.

Precisely the same issues arise in connection with physical problems. The complaint may be that the child is underweight; the important problem may be that he is anemic. It is not enough for the doctor to order blood tests routinely; he or she must pay attention to the results when they are reported, know when a low value indicates the need for treatment, and enlist parental cooperation in providing that treatment. A common difficulty in medical practice is the identification of an abnormality which is not a problem from the patient's viewpoint because it is asymptomatic. Hypertension might be an example. Here the patient's family must be persuaded of the importance of treatment designed to prevent symptoms in the future, although the child seems well at the present. On the other hand, the physician may identify a condition that is irrelevant to the patient's health, a functional murmur, for example, which may then induce parental and child anxiety if the physician either overinterprets the findings or lacks skill in communicating the information so as to emphasize that it is a normal variation. The reason for imparting such information is to diminish the chance that it will be misinterpreted in the future.

In customary medical teaching, the concept of diagnosis is focused exclusively on the third stage in the process: thorough history-taking, physical examination, and laboratory procedures. The first two require skill on the part of the provider and cooperation from the patient; the third demands the judgment to order the tests suggested by integrating the history and examination into a provisional diagnosis as well as the discrimination to avoid inappropriate tests lest they yield misleading information.

Medical diagnostic procedures depend on probability; that is, they yield information with certain reliability and validity that is much less than perfect. The patient or his parents may not report a key piece of information (for example, eating paint chips) that would clue the physician to a diagnostic possibility not at all evident from the physical findings. Whether that information is provided is no mere matter of chance or patient idiosyncracy; it is a function of the rapport the physician establishes with the family, the time and care taken in the elicitation of history, and the discernment in choosing the areas to probe (as determined by an assessment of the family's locus in the community. Normal variation between individuals limits the meaning of physical findings. Laboratory tests have appreciable zones of uncertainty. Moreover, an "abnormal" result, even if confirmed on repetition, will, simply by the laws of chance, occur in one in twenty of the normal population. Statistical artifacts contribute an important component to prolonged hospitalization in the effort to track down their significance.

Physicians, no less than patients, are apt to overestimate the accuracy of clinical methods. Whether the task is evaluating physical findings, interpreting diagnostic methods, or integrating the data into a diagnosis, the results of systematic comparison of physician performance "leave little room for complacency" (Koran, 1975); rates of disagreement occur not less than one in ten times and more commonly one in five. Information is no better than the user. Unless the physician is alert to the significance of the information that has been obtained, an abnormal state may be overlooked or misdiagnosed. One of the disturbing findings of the studies reviewed here is the frequency with which abnormal findings, even when recorded, are overlooked, in the sense that they lead to no corrective action. The "right" diagnosis is of no value to the patient and family if it is not communicated effectively in terms that are understood and that result in appropriate treatment.

The point of the diagnostic exercise is the formulation of a treatment program to correct the disorder when it is correctable, or if it is not, to help patient and family to live within the limits it imposes. What matters to the patient is the achievement of the best state of health possible, not the name the doctor gives to what is wrong. There is a disconcerting gap between diagnosis and treatment; that is, the treatment may be wrong (the prescription of the wrong drug or the wrong eyeglasses) or the right treatment may not be followed up (reexamination after ear infection to check hearing). Physician responsibility does not end with writing a prescription for the correct treatment; it is no less essential to assure that treatment recommendations are carried out. It is only in recent years that clinicians have begun to recognize the low level of patient "compliance" with medical recommendations (Charney, 1972). The very term "compliance" may be part of the problem. It evokes the image of orders from the doctor and obedience from the patient. Effective communication of the reasons for the treatment and the benefit it is designed to bring should lead the patient's family, as informed consumers, to elect to do what is in the child's interest. Problems may arise because the physician does not understand the cultural background of the family and may recommend a treatment program that violates family beliefs (Harwood, 1973; Snow, 1974). The health care provider and the family can attain consensus on diagnosis and treatment only when the explanatory models each employs are openly discussed and negotiated (Kleinman, 1976).

The evidence summarized by Starfield and Graef presents a discouraging account of the current performance of medical practitioners in recognizing problems, prescribing appropriate treatment, and providing adequate follow-up. What is perhaps most trouble-some is the lack of an ongoing system to identify errors and feed the information back to the provider as a stimulus to alter behavior. It is a basic assumption of professionalism that practitioners take pride in doing well. However, unless they are systematically informed about deviations from expected outcomes, they have no basis for initiating change in their customary patterns of practice. Some critics of professionals as elites are cynical about internal controls. They argue for external monitoring. Here, again, we confront a major flaw in current reimbursement schemes. There is no coupling between outcome and reimbursement to encourage better performance. Indeed, if anything, existing methods of payment are keyed to procedures rather than to outcomes and to proof that the procedures were carried out rather than to evidence that they were appropriate. There is not only no reward for the physician who takes extra time in a longer office visit to listen to family concerns or to provide personalized instruction and care but actually a negative sanction in the form of set fee per visit; the doctor who spends more time per patient sees fewer patients and earns less income.

It is difficult to visualize a substantial improvement in physician performance in the absence of a link between health maintenance and physician rewards, whether these be income or prestige. Without denying the importance of improving medical education, physician behavior is controlled primarily by the social conditions of medical practice (Freidson, 1970). The results of medical performance must be made as relevant to the practitioner as it is to the patient. To the extent that we rely on the evaluation of process, we require more precise definitions of that process; current methods rely far too heav-ily on peer judgment (that is, what is customary). This may not re-flect the state of the evidence based on comparative trials or may rely entirely on custom because there is no comparative evidence at all. Ultimately, we must devise methods for systematic assessment of the *outcome* of the patient-physician encounter, with due allowance for the characteristics of the patient population served, i.e., age struc-ture, disease prevalence, socioeconomic level, and the like. (Institute of Medicine, 1976b).

VARIATIONS IN HOSPITALIZATION RATES: CONSEQUENCES AND CAUSES

The burgeoning problems of health care costs are dealt with in the third volume of this series. But it is appropriate here, at least briefly, to consider the impact of the physician on those costs. In 1974, hospital care accounted for almost 40 percent of the total health care budget, with physician services costing an additional 18 percent and drugs 10 percent (Chart Book, 1975). The proportion attributed to hospital care has more than doubled in the last forty years, whereas that represented by physician services has shrunk (from 28 to 18 percent). Decisions to utilize the hospital are controlled principally by the physician. Since hospital costs are a large and growing fraction of the medical care budget, one key to cost control is to examine current physician patterns of hospital care utilization to determine whether they are fully rational and, if they are not, whether they can be changed for the better.

Kimm presents a scholarly review of the literature on tonsillectomy and adenoidectomy (T and A). To those unfamiliar with the issue, it will surely appear scandalous that on the order of a million operations are performed each year with nearly four-hundred deaths, a far from trivial number of complications and a cost of nearly $500 million. T and A is the most commonly performed operation in the United States and the most frequent reason for hospitalization of children; yet there is not a *single* fully satisfactory study to evaluate the effectiveness of the procedure. Tradition sanctifies its use; there are no "FDA" requirements for proof of safety and effectiveness for surgical procedures, either innovative or conventional, whereas drugs must meet minimal criteria for introduction onto the market or be certified "generally regarded as safe" to remain on the market. Parents are often more insistent on a T and A for their children to relieve frequent infections or poor appetite than are their pediatricians. Pediatricians are apt to take a more conservative view than ear, nose and throat specialists (with significant exceptions in both categories), but physicians have little more than opinion to guide them in the absence of definitive studies. There are, it should be noted, uncommon disorders (such as sleep apnea) for which T and A may be decisive (Guilleminault et al., 1976).

There is a fundamental question at stake. When a procedure has become customary and yet has never been subjected to an exacting test, does the burden of proof lie with those who argue for discarding it or with those who continue to employ it? I contend that the public as well as the profession must take the position that mere antiquity of a medical or surgical practice is no justification for its preservation (except in the archives). There is an urgent need for the routine surveillance of epidemiologic data to identify procedures in common use which lack an adequate scientific justification. Once such a procedure has been identified, an appropriate public health authority should review the available data and plan for and execute an appropriate controlled clinical trial. In the interim, there would be no ground for denying it reimbursement, although public education on the state of the art might well result in a diminution of its use. The final decision on whether or not reimbursement would be provided (or hospitals prohibited from permitting the procedure to continue) would be based upon the results of an adequate trial. The burden of proof should be placed on the need to demonstrate the utility of the procedure. A dubious or equivocal verdict should lead to a decision not to reimburse. If the value is uncertain and the risks and costs considerable (as with T and A), the procedure should be interdicted.

Wennberg and Kimm demonstrate the uses to which epidemiologic data on hospital utilization rates can be put. They identify twofold differences in age-adjusted admission rates among comparable hospital service areas. When the data are analyzed by specific diagnoses, variations in admission rates by diagnosis are as great as sixfold. There is little to suggest a significant variation in the prevalence rates for those disorders, which could account for the differences in hospitalization. On the other hand, there is a strong association between the number of operating surgeons in practice in an area and the frequency of surgery in the population. Moreover, in accordance with Roemer's "Law," more beds per capita appear to generate more days of hospitalization per capita. Hospital beds are not only costly, but they appear dangerous to health to the extent that they lead to excessive use.

Study of associations does not unequivocally identify causes. Some conclude from this and similar evidence that purely pecuniary self-interest generates medical decisions for surgery. While this may well be true for some practitioners, it is an unwarranted criticism of doctors in general in the absence of direct evidence to support it. A more plausible interpretation emphasizes the extent of diagnostic and therapeutic uncertainty in medical practice. So long as it is far from clear just when the surgical treatment for a particular disorder is essential, it is inevitable that there will be uncertainty among physicians on the decision to employ it. Further, there are conditions, like suspected appendicitis, when too great a reluctance to perform an appendectomy will lead to peritonitis and fatal outcome; in the absence of more precise diagnostic methods, the removal of a substantial proportion of normal appendices is the inescapable cost for minimizing the frequency of ruptured ones. When bed supply is limited, the physicians in a community are more likely to reserve those beds for unavoidable surgery and to defer procedures with elective or uncertain indications.

Though differences of opinion on the proper ratio of hospital beds to population persist, there is a growing consensus that the United States is overbedded (Institute of Medicine, 1976a.) Legislation to enforce a reduction in the total number of beds provides one route for diminishing their unwise use. A second control measure, which has been tried with some success, is the requirement for a second opinion before approval of surgery in nonemergency situations. Three other measures are suggested by Wennberg. Increasing the number of primary care physicians (in relation to specialists) is associated with less use of hospitals. Second, the systematic accumulation of data on hospital bed use in a given health service area and its comparison with corresponding data from similar areas provides important information that can be fed back to practitioners to alter their treatment practices. Finally, differential pricing of insurance premiums in relationship to hospital use in defined geographic areas provides an important incentive for consumers to question those differential costs when they cannot be justified by medical needs.

THE NEW MORBIDITY

"The current major health problems of children, as seen by the community, are those that would have barely been mentioned a generation ago. Learning difficulties and school problems, behavior disturbances, allergies, speech difficulties, visual problems and the problems of adolescents in coping and adjusting are today the most common concerns about children" (Haggerty et al., 1975). This new pattern of morbidity goes well beyond what physicians have been accustomed to dealing with. It has been argued that these are the problems of schools, of welfare services, and of the community rather than of the health care system. Clearly, they are not being adequately managed. The children in question are brought to the physician; whether or not the health care system has remedies more effective than those to be found in other service systems remains to be established. Yet it would seem retrogressive for health practitioners to shun a major problem with broad implications for health on the grounds that ready remedies are not at hand. We do not employ such reasons to exclude care for congenital malformations, malignancy, and chronic disease. It makes far more sense to offer help where we can, particularly because of the strategic position of pediatrics in relationship to child care, and to invest in expanding the base of research knowledge in order to provide better service in the future.

One of those problems, reading failure, can serve as a prototype for the new morbidity. It is highly prevalent, causes substantial anguish, and, when unresolved, constitutes a persisting handicap in occupational and general life adjustment. It is a problem more common in the city than in the suburb, among the poor than the well-to-do, and among ethnic minorities than among majority groups. The ubiquity of academic underachievement is evident from the March 1976 study of the Educational Testing Service (reported in *The Boston Globe*, 27 July 1976). Scholastic Aptitude Test (SAT) scores for fourteen of fifteen large American cities were well below the national mean of 434 on the verbal portion of the test, which measures reading, writing, and vocabulary scores. The six cities where minority children make up more than 50 percent of the school population (Atlanta, Baltimore, Detroit, Newark, Philadelphia and Washington, D.C.) were more than 60 points below the national average. Moreover, fourteen of those cities showed an SAT decline more rapid for the last year than for the previous year.

The pervasiveness and severity of reading disorders are widely acknowledged. But there is no common agreement about causes, other than a growing realization that they are multiple. Reliable identification of subtypes by clinical diagnostic procedures remains a challenge for future research. The results of treatment, whether educational, psychological or medical, are at best uncertain. Claims abound; solid data are hard to find. Yet the unhappy sufferer requires that we support him or her now with the best of what we can offer, even as we search for better methods.

Scholastic underachievement is one component of what is best termed developmental attrition: a sequential and cumulative failure to attain levels of intellectual and emotional development sufficient for personal and social competence (Eisenberg, 1975b). The contributing causes are multifactorial and they interact; malnutrition and an unstimulating environment acting together produce greater distortion in growth and development than the simple sum of each component acting alone. Developmental attrition results from an array of forces: unwanted pregnancy, the complications of pregnancy and parturition, malnutrition, infection, insufficient cognitive stimulation, inadequate emotional support, inferior schooling, lack of an opportunity structure for vocational success, and discrimination by race and class. Correspondingly, efforts at meaningful intervention must be directed simultaneously at each of these impediments to human development.

Are such matters the business of the health care system? I contend, in the words of a colleague, "that a health care system which is properly designed to perform the functions of helping, guiding, supporting and acting as advocate for the people it serves can do so far more effectively than the education, welfare and social service systems; and that so much even of measurable physical illness has significant environmental, social and behavioral components that a health system which is not equipped to deal with these issues will be ineffective even by the narrowest definition of its mission" (Schorr, 1976).

It is not that we are unaware of the shortcomings of the present system (Washington Research Project, 1976), nor that we overlook the limited evidence for the effectiveness of traditional remedies for the new morbidity. Rather, we emphasize the disability and suffering it produces, the lack of available alternative social institutions able to respond to these needs, and the traditional role of pediatrics and public health as advocates for children's needs (Faber and McIntosh, 1966; Richmond, 1977). We need to know much more than we know at present; that is the function of research. In the interim, the children who are ill now deserve the best caring we can offer until curing becomes possible.

PREVENTION: THE PROMISE
AND THE PERIL

There is little to add to Bernick's thorough and sophisticated analyses of the issues in screening for pediatric disease. One additional caveat may warrant explicit acknowledgement.

The prospect of detecting individuals at risk for, or in the early stages of, disease is alluring. We know how difficult and costly (and sometimes impossible) it is to correct disease when it is full blown. In principle at least, early intervention promises to be more effective as well as cheaper. But what is so in principle may not be so in practice; it will depend upon the precision of the methods for the identification, and the effectiveness of the methods for the correction, of specific diseases. Unless the evidence is examined in detail for each proposal, we may be stampeded into a premature diversion of resources away from the provision of care, given the present preoccupation with limiting total health expenditures.

Furthermore, many of the programs for prevention are directed at the individual rather than at the social causes for morbidity and mortality. That focus carries with it two hazards: first, a displacement of the responsibility for ill health from its proper locus, and second, the likelihood that, as a result, the effort will be ineffective. For example, we attempt to educate individuals not to smoke; sensible as this may be, at the same time we permit massive advertising whose purpose is to increase the sale of cigarettes. Is it necessary to comment on the disparity between the pittance committed to the former and the fortune allocated to the latter? Public schools provide a dollop of nutrition education at the same time that food-processing companies saturate children with television advertisements designed to sell poorly constituted snack foods. There can be no argument with the desirability of including health information in public education; it is equally clear (from the poor results we get) that we need to design far more effective curricula. What requires emphasis is the urgency of attending *simultaneously* to the powerful social forces that predictably overwhelm measures directed at the individual alone.

Life style unquestionably affects morbidity and mortality (Belloc, 1973). Patterns of eating, smoking, drinking, exercising, and sleeping have major effects on longevity. Most of this information is no secret to the American public; yet harmful behavior persists. We lack a national health policy to address the social dimensions that influence behavior. The design of cities must attend to the impact of transportation patterns and of siting of recreational facilities on the probability of walking, bicycling, and engaging in physical exercise. Only the control of industrial pollution and other sources of environmental contamination can alter the corresponding population risks; it is beyond the means of the individual to avoid such dangers to his or her health. Screening for lead, though important, will not suffice in the absence of a housing policy that removes the sources of the lead that poisons children. The success of biomedicine in preventing infectious diseases by means of vaccination has created a paradigm for preventive medicine which is inappropriate to the major public health problems of the present. A better metaphor is the sanitation of the water supply; that is, the diminution of the hazard rather than the immunization of the population to increase resistance to the hazard.

Effective prevention of the diseases that now threaten life and function is not likely to come about by magic bullets but rather by broad programs to improve the way we live and the way we work. They will be good for health but they will be costly. The time delays between input and outcome and the complex interactions between the variables are such that it will not be easy to demonstrate the precise impact of environmental interventions. In the meantime, and that meantime is likely to be a long time, the patients who suffer from the diseases that we may one day prevent will need care. It would be a grievous error to trade on the high hopes aroused by the concept of prevention to use it to deny care to those who need it.

REFERENCES

Academy Forum. *Experiments and Research with Humans: Values in Conflict.* Washington, D.C.: National Academy of Sciences, 1975.

Bass, J.W., et al. "Booster vaccination with further live attenuated measles vaccine," *JAMA* 235 (1976): 31–34.

Belloc, N.B. "Relationship of health practices and mortality," *Prev Med* 2 (1973): 67–81.

Bronfenbrenner, U. "The state of American families and children," in *Toward a National Policy for Children and Families.* Washington, D.C.: National Academy of Sciences, 1976.

Charney, E. "Patient-doctor communication: implication for the clinician," *Pediatr Clin North Am* 19 (1972): 263–79.

A Chart Book. See National Center for Health Statistics.

Davis, K. "Health insurance," in *Setting National Priorities: the 1973 Budget.* edited by C.L. Schultze. Washington, D.C.: Brookings Institution, 1972.

Dingle, J.H., et al. *Illness in the Home.* Cleveland, Ohio: Case Western Reserve University Press, 1964.

Editorial. "Vaccination against measles," *Lancet* 2 (1976): 132–34.

Eisenberg, L. "The ethics of intervention: acting amidst ambiguity," *J Child Psychol Psychiat* 16 (1975a): 93–104.

Eisenberg, L. "Primary prevention and early detection in mental illness," *Bull NY Acad Med* 51 (1975b): 118–29.

Eisenberg, L. "Delineation of clinical conditions: conceptual models of physical and mental disorder," in *Research and Medical Practice: Their Interaction.* Amsterdam: Elsivier, Ciba Foundation Symposium 44, 1976, pp. 3–23.

Eisenberg, L. "The search for care," *Daedalus* 106 (1977): 235–46.

Faber, H.K., and McIntosh, R. *History of the American Pediatric Society.* New York: McGraw-Hill, 1966.

Final Report of the Committee on the Costs of Medical Care: Medical Care for the American People. Chicago: University of Chicago Press, 1932.

Friedson, E. *Professional Dominance: The Social Structure of Medical Care* New York: Atherton Press, 1970.

Good, B.J., Eisenberg, L., and Kleinman, A.M. *Report to the Robert Wood Johnson Foundation of the Harvard Research Seminar on Primary Care.* Unpublished, 1976.

Greene, R. *Assuring Quality in Medical Care: The State of the Art.* Cambridge, Mass.: Ballinger Publishing Company, 1977.

Guilleminault, C., et al. "Sleep apnea in eight children," *Pediatrics* 58 (1976): 23–30.

Haggerty, R.J., et al. *Child Health and the Community.* New York: John Wiley and Sons, 1975.

Harwood, A. "The hot-cold theory of disease: implications for treatment of Puerto Rican patients," *JAMA* 216 (1971): 1153–60.

Institute of Medicine. *Controlling the Supply of Hospital Beds.* Washington, D.C.: National Academy of Sciences, 1976(a).

Institute of Medicine. *Assessing Quality in Health Care: An Evaluation.* Washington, D.C.: National Academy of Sciences, 1976 (b).

Kleinman, A.M. "Explanatory models in health care relationships," in *Health of the Family.* Washington, D.C.: National Council for International Health Symposia, 1975.

Koran, L.M. "The reliability of clinical methods, data and judgments," *N Engl J Med* 293 (1975): 642−46, 695−701.

Langmuir, A.D. "Medical importance of measles," *Am J Dis Child* 103 (1962): 224−26.

McDermott, W., et al. "Health care experiment at Many Farms," *Science* 175 (1972): 23−31.

McDermott, W. "General medical care: identification and analysis of alternative approaches," *Johns Hopkins Med J* 135 (1974): 292−321.

McDermott, W. "Evaluating the physician and his technology," *Daedalus* 106 (1977) 135−58.

McKeown, T. *Medicine in Modern Society.* New York: Hafner Publishing Company, 1966.

Mueller, M.S., and Gibson, R.M. *National Health Expenditures: FY 1975.* Research and Statistics Note No. 2. Bulletin of the Social Security Administration, Washington, D.C., 1975.

National Center for Health Statistics. *A Chart Book: Health in the United States.* DHEW Pub. No. (HRA) 76−1233. Washington, D.C.: Government Printing Office, 1975.

Office of Health Economics. *The Cost of the N.H.S.* Information Sheet No. 29. London: 162 Regent Street, 1976.

Richmond, J.B. *Currents in American Medicine.* Cambridge, Mass.: Harvard University Press, 1969.

Richmond, J.B. "The needs of children, *Daedalus* 106 (1977): 247−60.

Snow, L.F. "Folk medical beliefs and their implications for care of patients." *Ann Int Med* 81 (1974): 82−96.

Washington Research Project. *Doctors and Dollars are Not Enough.* Washington, D.C.: Children's Defense Fund, 1976.

White, K.L. "Life and death and medicine," *Sci Am* 229 (1973): 76−89.

Zola, I.K. "The concept of trouble and sources of medical assistance, *Soc Sci Med* 6 (1972): 673−79.

✳ *Chapter 2*

Health Needs of Children

Barbara Starfield, M.D., M.P.H.

Most Americans accept the notion that their health care system fails to be as responsive to their needs as it could be. The tremendous burden of mortality, morbidity, and disability is well publicized and generally considered incommensurate with the technology and civilization that characterize this country.

Data on childhood mortality, morbidity, and disability presented in this chapter are national data and therefore do not depict the particularly acute needs of certain segments of the population, such as the racial minorities and the migrant occupational workers. Juvenile drug-use, teenage pregnancies, and behavior disorders are also under-represented. At least in part this is because of the difficulty of obtaining data on diseases attributable to social and economic forces rather than to defective genes or apolitical microbes. Children under 18 account for 43 percent of those arrested for serious crime, yet these manifestations of ill health are not shown in health statistics because they do not fit the "medical model" of single cause and clear pathogenesis. Illnesses traceable to industrial contamination of the environment, harmful food additives, and high-pressure advertising of noxious products also fail to be identifiable as such in existing health statistics. Disease and health are functions of socioeconomic, environmental, personal, and genetic factors as well as of health services interventions, but existing data systems reflect primarily those health needs that fit the medical model and therefore can be classified into schemes developed by health professionals.

Also conspicuously absent from statistics are those conditions not yet counted as illness but which are precursors of the morbidity and mortality that will become manifest later in life. Little is known of such conditions. But as they are relevant to planning preventive activities in child health care, increasing attention must be devoted to them.

Moreover, even were the health care system to address itself wholeheartedly to reducing mortality and morbidity as currently classified, there would remain an enormous reservoir of disease not thought of now as "health" problems. The costs of attaining health are more than can be borne by the health services sector. Perhaps someday, the values of society may ultimately be measured in terms other than financial return on investment. Future systems for collecting data will reflect these changing societal values, when they occur.

The data presented in this chapter are not new or complete, but they are all that is available on a national level. In their present form they do not point the way to obvious strategies for dealing with the problem of health in childhood. However, analysis of their shortcomings may stimulate new approaches.

CHILDHOOD MORTALITY

As a result of the relatively poor international ranking of the United States in infant mortality, much attention is devoted to it. The development of regionalized perinatal networks and their evaluation should provide much information for policymakers. In view of this effort, we will not address infant mortality and morbidity in this chapter.

Once children have survived their infancy (the first year of life) deaths are relatively rare (Figure 2—1). The death rate in preschool children (age one to four), always a small fraction of that in infancy, was less than 5 percent of the rate under one year of age in the late sixties.

Although significant declines in early childhood mortality rates were evident during the early 1900s, the relative importance of causes of death remained the same. Even in the 1940s, the infectious diseases influenza and pneumonia, gastroenteritis, and tuberculosis were first, third, and fourth in rank respectively and were responsible for about 36 percent of all deaths. Accidents ranked second and congenital malformations, fifth.

By 1950, influenza and pneumonia had dropped to second place, behind accidents, even though the death rate from accidents had declined 25 percent during the interval. Deaths from gastroenteritis fell so sharply that they were no longer among the five leading causes of death in the preschool groups.

Figure 2-1. Five Leading Causes of Death in Children from the Age of One through Four, 1939-41 to 1974 *(rates per 100,000 population)*

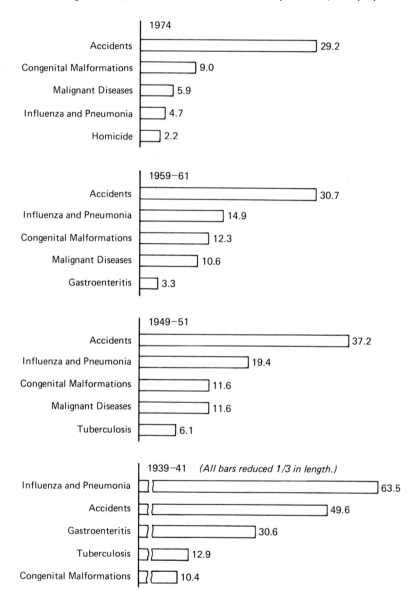

Source for 1974: National Center for Health Statistics. Advance Report, *Final Mortality Statistics 1974* vol. 24, no. 11, Supplement, 3 February 1976.

Source for other years: Shapiro, S.; Schlesinger, E.; Nesbitt, R., Jr., 1968, p. 175.

Note: Alaska and Hawaii included for 1959-61 and 1974.

During the 1950s, death rates from infectious causes showed a further decline, but considerably smaller than in the previous period. Deaths from all infectious diseases still represented nearly 25 percent of the total deaths in this age group by 1959−61. This was due chiefly to the comparatively small decrease in the death rate from influenza and pneumonia. By 1959−61 there were more deaths from these conditions than from all other infectious diseases combined. The death rate for accidents declined only 17 percent during the 1950s; by 1960 they accounted for 29 percent and by 1974 for about 40 percent of all deaths in preschoolers. Homicide, not heretofore one of the top five causes of death, was in fifth place in 1974.

Accidents have been a leading cause of death in school-age children for many years, increasing in relative importance over time (Figure 2−2). The proportion of deaths due to accidents rose from 28 percent in 1939−41 to 48 percent in 1974, although the actual death rate from accidents dropped. In school-age children, influenza and pneumonia, which ranked second as a cause of death in 1939−41, dropped to third place in 1949−51 and to fourth by 1959−61. These were the only infectious diseases remaining among the leading causes of death. Appendicitis, in third place in 1939−41, and tuberculosis, then in fifth place, disappeared as leading causes of death within a decade. By 1974 homicide and suicide had moved into the top five causes of death in school-age children.

The mortality rate for nonwhite children is roughly double that of white children. There is also a vast difference in the cause of death among both groups (Figure 2−3). In fact, the patterns of leading causes of death at ages one through four over the past thirty-five years show that the leading causes of death among nonwhite children tend toward the pattern for white children of ten or more years earlier. Infectious diseases among nonwhite preschool children were responsible for 43 percent of all deaths in 1949−51; this approached the nearly 50 percent of all deaths ascribed to infectious causes among the white group in 1939−41.

The pattern is very much the same among school-age children. Tuberculosis, which did not appear as one of the five leading causes of death among white children even in 1939−41, still ranked fourth as a cause of death among nonwhite children in 1949−51.

CHILDHOOD MORBIDITY

Data on past or current illness may be obtained either by questioning individuals and their families, by professionally conducted examinations, or from records or reports of health practitioners.

Figure 2–2. Five Leading Causes of Death in Children from the Age of Five through Fourteen, 1939–41 to 1974 *(rates per 100,000 population)*

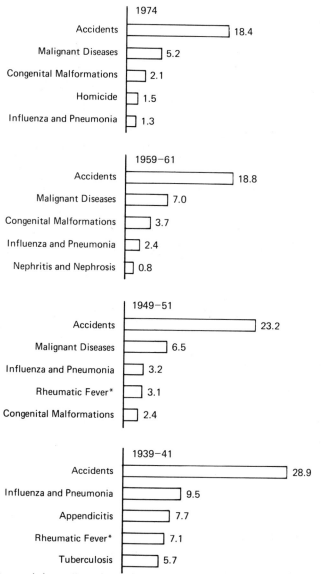

*Includes rheumatic heart disease.

Source for 1974: National Center for Health Statistics. Advance Report, *Final Mortality Statistics 1974*, vol. 24, no. 11, Supplement, 3 February 1976.

Source for other years: Shapiro, S.; Schlesinger, E., and Nesbitt, R., Jr., 1968, p. 177.

Note: Alaska and Hawaii included for 1959–61 and 1974.

Figure 2–3. Five Leading Causes of Death at Ages One to Four Years, by Race *(rates per 100,000 population)*

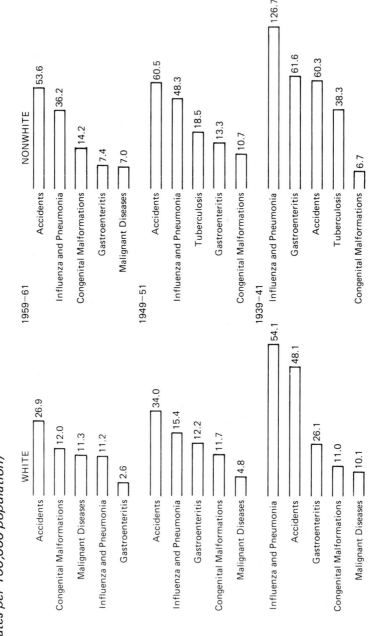

Source: National Center for Health Statistics, 1954a and 1954b; Shapiro et al., 1968.

Household Interview Data

The data on acute conditions in childhood were based upon household interviews during the period July 1973 through June 1974 (USDHEW, 1975).

In obtaining data on acute illness, including injuries, a series of illness-recall questions was used. A condition was considered acute if it lasted less than three months *and* was either medically attended or had restricted usual activity for one day or more. Asthma, hay fever, and rheumatic fever were always classified as chronic, however, even if the onset was less than three months before interview.

In the year ending June 30, 1974, 161,745,000 acute conditions had occurred among children under sixteen, an average of 2.6 per child.

The incidence of acute illness was much higher among children than among adults and higher in preschool children than among those five through fourteen: 303.4 acute conditions per 100 children of ages one through five as compared with 232 per 100 for those of ages six through sixteen.

Injuries, by definition, required medical attention or reduced the child's normal activities by at least one full day. They represented 15 percent of all acute conditions reported, second in incidence after respiratory (54 percent) ailments. A total of 23,633,000 injuries were reported for the year, which is a rate of 37.3 per 100 children, or one injury for every three children.

Respiratory conditions account for more than half of acute conditions among children under fifteen. Their greater frequency in children under four is the major reason why the total incidence of acute illness is higher in this age group than in school-age children. Following respiratory illness and injuries, the major categories of illness are infective and parasitic diseases (14 percent), digestive conditions (4 percent), and all others (12 percent).

Sex seems to have little influence on the incidence of acute illness in children under fifteen years of age except that five through fourteen-year-old boys have an incidence of accidents over one-third higher than girls of the same ages.

Certain differences in residence of children influence the reported incidence of acute conditions. This may be because of lack of awareness of disease, underreporting of disease, or actual differences in their occurrence. Urban children are reported to have more acute illnesses, rural nonfarm children somewhat less, and rural farm children least.

The prevalence of chronic conditions is an important measure of health status because it reflects the burden of illness over long periods of time and because chronic illness may interfere with developmental processes necessary to functioning later in life. Again, a series of illness-recall questions was used, supplemented by a checklist of chronic conditions and a checklist of impairments. A condition was considered chronic if it met the terms of either of these checklists or if it had been first noticed more than three months before the week of the interview and was still present.

In the period July 1959 through June 1961 13,996,000 chronic conditions were reported among children under age seventeen. This means a rate of 226.1 per 1000 population, or almost one condition for each four children. Almost one child in every five had at least one chronic condition. In the period July 1966 through June 1967 over one child in five (23.2 percent) had at least one chronic condition.

The prevalence of some diagnostic conditions was surprisingly high. For hay fever, asthma, and all other allergies the rate was 74.3 per 1000, and for sinusitis, bronchitis, and other respiratory diseases, 34.2 per 1000 for children under seventeen (1959−61 data).

Of the chronic conditions reported, only six out of ten had been discussed with a physicians within the year preceding the date of the interview; 27.9 percent had not received medical attention for more than a year; and, for one out of every ten conditions, no such attention had ever been received.

Family Income.   More chronic conditions were reported for children in higher-income families than for those in lower-income families. This direct relationship between income and prevalence of chronic conditions seems to reflect differing standards of what constitutes illness and differing financial access to medical care. To illustrate, the rate for hay fever, asthma, and other allergies for the income group under $2000 was 43.3 per 1000 children. The rate for these conditions rose with each income group to 104.8 per 1000 children for the group with income $7000 and over, more than two and one half times the rate for the lowest income group. It is unlikely this difference in rate would be substantiated by clinical examination. Reporting of conditions such as "allergies" is undoubtedly heavily related to receipt of medical care, as the health care practitioner is most likely to attach such a diagnosis to a problem and alert the parents to symptoms related to it.

The relative importance of some of the chronic conditions as reported varied among the income groups. Thus, hay fever, asthma, and other allergies accounted for 20.2 percent of the chronic conditions among children in the under $2000 income group; 27.3 percent of conditions in the $2000 to $3000 group; 33.5 percent of conditions in the $4000 to $6999 group; and 40.1 percent (twice that for the lowest group) in the $7000 and over group. On the other hand, paralysis and orthopedic impairments related to observable anatomic or functional derangements rather than to diagnoses expressed in medical terminology accounted for 13.8 percent of chronic conditions reported for the lowest income group, as compared with only 9.7 percent of the conditions reported for the top income group. Similarly, blindness and visual impairments, hearing impairment, and speech defects together accounted for 12.4 percent of the chronic conditions reported for the under $2000 group, contrasted with 6.4 percent for those in the $7000 and over group. Thus, it appears that conditions reportable as symptoms or problems referable to body systems are reported more in lower-income groups, whereas those reflecting a medical diagnosis indicating pathogenesis are reported more by families in upper-income groups. This phenomenon is most likely a result of differences in the extent and nature of medical care received.

Whether or not medical attention was received was dependent to some extent upon income. For all chronic conditions, 56.2 percent had received medical attention within the year preceding the date of the interview if the family income was less than $4000 a year, compared with 64.5 percent if the family income was $4000 or more. In the lower-income families, 15.5 percent of the chronic conditions among children under seventeen had never received medical attention, contrasted with 8 percent of the conditions in families with higher incomes.

Place of Residence. Among children in urban areas, 64.2 percent had received medical attention within one year prior to the interview, as compared with 61.5 percent of children in rural nonfarm areas and 51.9 percent in rural farm areas. In urban areas, 9.1 percent of the conditions never received attention; for children on rural farms the figure was 15.8 percent. How much of this is because of lack of medical resources in rural areas and how much is because of differences in the nature of the illness is unclear.

Data Obtained from Professional Examination

Direct measurement from physical examination and tests is the only way to secure information on unrecognized and undiagnosed physical conditions. Examinations may be done for the specific purpose of assessing health status, or they may be a byproduct of the provision of ordinary health-care services.

Of the specific assessments, the National Health Examination Survey and its sequel, the Health and Nutrition Examination Survey, provide the only data on professionally judged health status representative of the national population.

In 1963—65 the National Center for Health Statistics conducted an examination of a probability sample of six-through-eleven-year-olds. Sociodemographic data for the family and child and current medical care were obtained by interview, as was information on past medical history. A large variety of information on behavior and development was also obtained, along with school records for children in the sample. Physical examination included standardized measurements of general appearance, detailed eye examination, blood pressure, neuromuscular and joint survey, percussion and auscultation of lungs, electrocardiogram, chest X-ray, examination of the ears, the nose and pharynx, audiometry, vision testing and eye examination, dental examination, body measurements, and psychological testing.

On examination, one child in eight was found to have a significant physical abnormality, with higher rates among the black, the poor, and among children in the South (U.S. National Health Survey, Series 11). Four percent of children aged six through eleven were found to be taking medication regularly, over 96 percent on a physician's order. Although selected examination findings (psychological testing, vision and hearing testing, blood pressure, body measurements) have been published, no data on specific physical abnormalities are yet available. As the design of this survey makes it possible to correlate information obtained on interview with that obtained by medical assessment, it could be extremely helpful in selecting appropriate and economical means of assessing health status in the future. For example, it was found that parents both underestimate and overestimate abnormalities in their child's health when compared with medical examination. Although there is a positive correlation between reported present and past abnormality and the finding of one or more defects on physical examination, many children with such histories are found to be normal, whereas many with no history of illness are found to be abnormal on examination.

Data Obtained from Reports of Health Practitioners

The National Disease and Therapeutic Index. The NDTI is a continuing compilation of statistical information about the patterns and treatment of disease encountered in medical practice in the Continental United States. Data are obtained from a panel of office-based physicians who report information on private patients seen over a given period of time. This survey, initiated in 1958, was the first large scale attempt to obtain information on the content of practice within the United States.

In 1974 the bulk of visits to pediatricians was for well-child care and for prophylactic inoculations. The conditions most frequently treated by pediatricians include otitis media, upper respiratory infections, and acute pharyngitis (Table 2—1).

One study (Rosenbloom and Ougley, 1974) indicates that although the pediatrician is the specialist identified with those under sixteen years of age, the pediatrician accounts for only three-eighths of physician-patient contacts for this age group. Half the pediatrician's patients are babies, and he or she does twice as much well-child care as the generalist. Although tabulations for all children seen in the sample practices are potentially available, NDTI publishes its data according to specialty of the physicians. The only comprehensive published data on children comes from an analysis of the practices of pediatricians.

National Ambulatory Medical Care Survey. The National Ambulatory Medical Care Survey obtains statistical information about the provision and use of ambulatory medical care services from data collected from office-based physicians in the United States. (National Ambulatory Medical Care Survey, preliminary data, 1973).

Table 2—2 outlines groups of leading problems, symptoms, or conditions presented to the pediatrician by children of different ages. Table 2—3 outlines the leading diagnoses in these children.

Because of sample sizes and frequencies in both surveys, most of the "problem areas" and diagnostic groupings are too broad to be

Table 2—1. Visits to the Pediatrician, Per Year, by Leading Reasons

	Hospital	*Nonhospital*	*Total*
Well-baby and well-child care	5	1675	1680
Prophylactic innoculation		1260	1260
Otitis media without mastoid	10	675	685
Acute URI multiple sites	10	650	660
Accidents and poisoning	35	440	475
Infective and parasitic diseases	20	445	465
Acute pharyngitis		460	460
General medical examination		390	390
Acute tonsillitis	5	345	350
Gastroenteritis and colitis	40	295	335
Bronchitis	10	315	325
Single birth without mention of immaturity	295	10	305
Medical or surgical aftercare	15	170	185
Asthma	10	160	170

Source: National Disease and Therapeutic Index, 1974.
Reprinted with permission. Copyright by IMS America, Ltd., 1974.

Table 2–2.   Problem Areas Instigating Children's Visits to Office-Based Physicians

2 Years	3–5 Years	6–10 Years	11–14 Years
Nonsymptom	Nonsymptom	Nonsymptom	Nonsymptom
Well baby	Respiratory	Digestive	Musculoskeletal
Respiratory	Digestive	Eyes and ears	Respiratory
General Symptom	General medical exam	Throat soreness	Digestive
Digestive	Eyes and ears	Respiratory	Eyes and ears
Fever/chills	General symptoms	Musculoskeletal	Throat soreness
Cold, flu, croup	Throat soreness	General symptom	Pain in lower extremities
Cough	Fever/chills	Cough	Cough
Eyes and ears	Cough	General medical exam	Pain in upper extremities
Musculoskeletal	Musculoskeletal	Fever/chills	General medical exam

Source: National Center for Health Statistics, 1975.

Table 2–3.   Leading Diagnoses for Children's Visits to Office-Based Physicians

2 Years	3–5 Years	6–10 Years	11–14 Years
Nonillness	Respiratory symptom	Respiratory symptom	Respiratory symptom
Medical specialty examination	Acute respiratory infection	Acute respiratory infection	Nonillness
Respiratory	Nonillness	Nonillness	Accidents
Acute respiratory infection	Nervous system and sense organs	Nervous system and sense organs	Acute respiratory infection
Nervous system and sense organs	Otitis media	Accidents	Nervous system and sense organs
Otitis media	Infective and parasitic	Infective and parasitic	Infective and parasitic
Infective and parasitic	Skin	Medical specialty examination	Medical specialty examination
Ill-defined	Accidents	Skin	Ill-defined
Skin	Ill-defined	Ill-defined	Hay fever
Accidents, poison, etc.		Otitis media	

Source: National Center for Health Statistics, 1975.

useful as indicators of specific health needs in children. The NAMCS sample is being substantially expanded to increase its value in this respect. Moreover, from the cross-sectional nature of the data (only one encounter is obtained per individual episode of illness) it is impossible to assess the extent to which the conditions presented were acute or chronic. Nor can we say how much of a burden they were to the individual patients, although the survey does permit distinction between newly presenting problems and older ones, as does NDTI.

It is difficult to make comparisons between data from the NAMCS and NDTI (National Disease and Therapeutic Index). The NDTI information regarding children (Table 2-1) comes from pediatricians only; data for other practitioners is published but these are not divided by age group so that it is impossible to distinguish the children. The NAMCS survey has a higher response rate of physicians; the extent to which refusals to participate in these types of surveys produce a bias in the findings is unknown, but may be considerable (Tables 2-2 and 2-3). The two studies also use different categories of disease classification; NDTI uses the World Health Organization classification of disease, while NAMCS uses the International Classification of Diseases Adapted (ICDA). NDTI tends to be more specific in its diagnoses than NAMSC.

CHILDHOOD DISABILITY

Disability is the result of a failure of the health care system to adequately counteract disease processes. Because of the social dysfunction that physical or mental disability implies, many professionals other than those in the health field are involved in dealing with it. Therefore, data on its extent and nature cannot be adequately obtained from sources solely within the health system. Thus far, the only comprehensive assessment of disability in the child population of the United States comes from the Health Interview Survey. In this survey separate questions are asked about disability resulting from acute conditions and that resulting from chronic conditions.

Disability from Acute Conditions

The frequent occurrence of acute conditions among children is associated with a large number of days in which children are unable to take part in their usual activities and even may be confined to bed. (For this section, see U.S. National Health Survey, Series 10, 11, 20; National Center for Health Statistics, December 1974); American Academy of Pediatrics, 1971; and Schiffer and Hunt, 1963.)

Perhaps a more significant measure of the effect of acute illness is the rate for restricted-activity days and bed-disability days per 100 children per year. For the year July 1973–June 1974, for children under fifteen there were 1003 days of restricted activity per 100 children due to acute conditions and 461 per 100 children for bed-disability days. This means that on the average, each child under fifteen spent ten days per year prevented from engaging in usual activities and over four of these days in bed as a result of acute illness alone. For children under five, the rate of restricted activity days was slightly higher than for children five through fourteen (1123.6 days per 100 children compared with 951.7). Injuries alone accounted for a loss of 42 days from school, 37 days of bed rest, and 162 days of restricted activity for every 100 school children during the year.

Disability from Chronic Conditions

Chronic conditions among children under age seventeen in 1960–61, the last data available, resulted in 136,660,000 days of restricted activity, or an average of 2.2 days per child, in addition to the number of days for which activity was restricted because of acute conditions.

The conditions classified as hay fever, asthma, and other allergies were the chief cause of the restricted activity. With sinusitis, bronchitis, and other diseases of the respiratory system, they accounted for about one-half of all days of restricted activity due to chronic conditions, and more than half of the days lost from school because of chronic conditions. The single chronic condition causing the highest percentage of days lost from school was asthma.

In addition to data on restriction of normal activities by chronic conditions, the NHS provides information on the extent to which children with chronic conditions are limited in their activities. Nine out of ten children with chronic illness did not appear to be limited in normal activities by their chronic conditions. The remaining 10 percent were limited to some extent (Schiffer and Hunt, 1963). While there may be some lack of comparability due to differences in methods of data collection and processing, it appears that disability has been increasing. In 1967, 1969–70, 1972, and 1974 the percent of children with limitation of activity was 2.1, 2.5, 2.8, and 3.7, and the percent with limitation of major activity was 1.1, 1.3, 1.4 and 1.9.

What Conditions Affect What Activities?

Unfortunately, the published data do not permit assessment of the extent to which different conditions are associated with activity restriction. Most visual impairments, hearing problems, and speech defects are not generally associated with activity restriction. Yet, as they are among the most prevalent problems, their inclusion in the calculations significantly lowers the average disability attributed to chronic conditions.

Looked at from the viewpoint of children with chronic illness, one in twelve such children had limitation of activity due to the illness. About half of these children were restricted in going to school or in their major play activities (if they were preschoolers); the other half were less severely limited. Undoubtedly the total burden of disability is far higher than the general estimates of number of children affected indicate. Moreover, it is important to note that the survey was carried out in the noninstitutionalized population. Thus, the estimates of chronic conditions and disability far underestimate the extent of chronic problems in the child population of the United States. For the noninstitutionalized child population, at least one child in a hundred has a severe disability due to a chronic health problem, and another one per hundred has a less severe limitation of activity.

RECOMMENDATIONS

Existing national health statistics point to areas where major impact for large numbers of individuals might possibly be made. That is, mortality, morbidity, and disability would be decreased. However, the statistics fail to indicate the reasons for the problems or the avenues of approach to their solution.

Accidents and injuries, by far the largest cause of mortality in school-age children and the largest components of morbidity, particularly in preschoolers, might be reducible with better understanding of their causes and commitment to eliminating them. The relative extent to which they result from defective commercial products, familial deprivation, or social irresponsibility is unknown. But it is not unreasonable to postulate that greater attention to design of toys and home devices would increase their safety and that supervised community facilities and day-care centers would provide a safe resource for children whose families are unable to devote sufficient attention to them. More concerted approaches to alcoholism and drug-abuse might also remove much of their impact on child health.

For the other types of morbidity and mortality the approach is not so clear. Perhaps the biggest weakness of existing statistics is their inability to depict relationships among their various components. For example, nomenclature for coding cause of death is different from that designating types of morbidity. The terms used to denote functional disability give no clue to the anatomic, physio-logic, or behavioral factor that caused it. Other means than conven-tional cross-sectional data collection will have to be found if the progression from morbidity to disability or morbidity to mortality is to be understood and dealt with.

The National Center for Health Statistics has pioneered in collect-ing a broad spectrum of data on health needs in the United States. No other nation has yet developed any system to compare with the conceptual and technical sophistication of the phased approach taken in this country. The data already collected and those planned for the future provide an excellent base upon which to build.

The following are a few areas that might be addressed to increase the usefulness of the national system for collecting data.

Much of the existing data has been unexploited. Over ten years have passed since completion of the first Health Examination Survey for School Children. Although much valuable information has been published from this survey, many aspects have not yet been exam-ined. The possibilities for analysis of the data beyond cross-tabulation of variables are many, particularly data dealing with the relationships of findings on medical examination to those elicited by interview. Where the same individuals appeared in two separate phases of the survey (as was the case for the one-third of the young children who were subsequently in the teenage survey) possibilities exist for study-ing the progression of the problems from one time to the next. A coordinated effort to develop hypotheses that could be tested by using the existing data would be worthy of support.

Even data from the Health Interview Survey may be outdated by the time it is published. Much of the data on children available at the time of the writing of this article was fifteen years old. Certainly a means should be found to make the findings available much sooner.

The National Ambulatory Medical Care Survey should be expanded in several directions. At present, it covers only office-based practice. But over 10 percent of medical care, and even more for urban dis-advantaged care-seekers, takes place in institution-based practice (U.S. National Health Survey, Series 10). Studies should be carried out to develop techniques for collecting data from these facilities. At a 1974 biennial meeting of the Public Health Conference on Records and Statistics a suggestion was made to link household surveys with the National Ambulatory Medical Care Survey so that interview data could be continuously matched with data from professional sources on the same individuals. Developmental work in this area could help both to refine the systems for classifying morbidity and disability and provide information on the progression of illness with and without medical care.

A means of classifying disease by severity is urgently needed. In the NAMCS study physicians are asked to rate the "seriousness" of the patient's presenting problem; this is the first large-scale attempt to examine severity of illness in physicians' practices. However, even with this innovation, data from physicians' offices fails to indicate the extent to which reported illness has a poor prognosis or is associated with temporary or permanent disability of varying degrees.

Systems to collect data cross-sectionally should be replaced by those which are longitudinal in nature. Both retrospective and prospective approaches could be profitable.

REFERENCES

American Academy of Pediatrics. *Lengthening Shadows: The Delivery of Health Care to Children.* Evanston, Ill.: author, 1971.

National Center for Health Statistics. *Annual Summary of the United States, 1973.* Monthly Vital Statistics Report. Washington, D.C.: Government Printing Office, July 1974.

National Center for Health Statistics. *News of the Cooperative Health Statistics System.* Washington, D.C.: Government Printing Office, November 1974.

National Center for Health Statistics. *Preliminary Data from the National Ambulatory Medical Care Survey, 1973 Summary.* Washington, D.C.: Government Printing Office, 1975.

National Center for Health Statistics. *Statistical Data Prepared for the Child Health Task Force—Division of Analysis.* Unpublished report, Washington, D.C., December 1974.

National Center for Health Statistics. *Vital and Health Statistics*, Series 10. Data from the National Health Survey. Washington, D.C.: Government Printing Office, July 1963 to present.

National Center for Health Statistics. *Vital and Health Statistics*, Series 11, No. 129. Data from the National Health Survey. Washington, D.C.: Government Printing Office, November 1973.

National Center for Health Statistics. *Vital and Health Statistics*, Series 20. Data from the National Health Survey. Washington, D.C.: Government Printing Office, November 1965 to present.

National Center for Health Statistics. *Vital Statistics of the United States*, Volume 1. Washington, D.C.: Government Printing Office, 1954a.

National Center for Health Statistics. *Vital Statistics of the United States*, Volume 2. Washington, D.C.: Government Printing Office, 1954b.

National Center for Health Statistics. *1972 Life Tables*, vol. 2, series 5. Washington, D.C.: Government Printing Office, 1974.

National Disease and Therapeutic Index Specialty Profile. *Pediatrics.* Ambler, Pa.: IMS America Ltd., 1974.

Rosenbloom, A.L., and Ougley, J.P. "Who provides what services to children in private medical practice," *Am J Dis Child* 127 (1974): 357−61.

Schiffer, C.G., and Hunt, E.P. *Illness Among Children: Data from U.S. National Health Survey.* U.S. Department of Health, Education and Welfare, Welfare Administration, Children's Bureau, Washington, D.C., 1963.

Shapiro, S., Schlesinger, E.R., Nesbitt, R.E.L. *Infant, Perinatal, Maternal and Childhood Mortality in the United States.* Cambridge, Mass.: Harvard University Press, 1968.

U.S. Department of Health, Education and Welfare. *Acute Conditions, Incidence and Associated Disability.* DHEW Pub. No. HRA−76−1529. Washington, D.C., Government Printing Office, 1975.

U.S. National Health Survey. See National Center for Health Statistics, *Vital and Health Statistics.*

✳ *Chapter 3*

Issues in Pediatric Screening

Kathryne Bernick

WHAT IS SCREENING?

Screening procedures are aimed at early recognition and treatment of disease processes at a time when treatment will either reverse the process or slow down its rate of progression (Frankenburg, 1973). Screening tests are not intended to be diagnostic. Rather, screening for a single condition separates from a large group of apparently healthy individuals those who are at increased risk of having that condition and who require more elaborate diagnostic tests (Bailey et al., 1974; Northern and Downs, 1974). Screening tests may be incorporated into routine health maintenance examinations or they may be used in explicit screening programs.

Screening as Part of Health Care Delivery
A number of reasons have been given for including screening in health-care delivery systems. First, screening programs may serve as an entree into ongoing comprehensive care for children who do not have a regular source of medical care. Second, early detection is invaluable for conditions that would hinder a child's later development if left untreated. Vision and hearing screening programs are advocated on this basis. A third rationale is that early treatment may be more economical, less time-consuming, or involve less discomfort than later treatment. It may also be much more effective; treatment after a certain point in the progression of a disease may be of little value.

It is also possible that certain screening tests are performed because they are there. The reasoning goes that if the procedure is available,

41

it should be used. A test for elevated serum cholesterol levels is an example. Some observers have suggested routine inclusion of this test in pediatric screening protocols, speculating that children with elevated levels sustain a high risk of developing coronary artery disease in adulthood.

Finally, screening programs may provide political leverage for child advocacy groups or bureaucrats, in that such programs may point out poor health conditions which indicate a need for improved health services. Similarly, screening may serve to evaluate health services. Their success or failure might be reflected in the results of a screening program.

Legislation for Screening

On the basis of these rationales, screening programs for children have been increasingly advocated in recent years. The federal government has mandated the Early and Periodic Screening, Diagnosis and Treatment program (EPSDT) for all children eligible for Medicaid. California has mandated health screening for school attendance (North, 1974). The inclusion of many screening tests in newborn and preventive pediatric care has been recommended. Some national health insurance proposals suggest financing preventive care for children, including certain screening tests.

Despite increased legislation toward utilizing screening procedures, a number of unanswered questions remain.

Screening as Risk Avoidance

Screening is advocated as a means of avoiding morbidity, mortality, or more expensive treatment in a later stage in the progression of a disease. By permitting early and cheaper treatment in some cases, screening reduces the costs of treating a disease. However, even if the expected future dollar cost of a disease (the probability of getting the disease multiplied by the cost of treatment at a later stage) is less than the cost of the screening test added to the expected cost of immediate treatment if the test is positive, an individual might still be willing to pay for the test. This would be true if pain and suffering were included in the cost-benefit calculations as a real cost. The image of future suffering may be more important than the expected dollar value of a later disease.

Another reason is that screening might reassure by showing the absence of disease. Tests for cancer or anemia may eliminate uncertainty. But these may be of value only when there is a high level of public consciousness about the condition. (Breast cancer is much in the spotlight at time of writing.) Or an individual may be especially in need of reassurance if he or she has good reason to believe that the condition might be present, as in the case of hereditary disease. Such benefits may be outweighed by the dollar cost of the test and the possibility of false positive identification and consequences. Moreover, screening may actually *arouse* anxiety; a parent may not be at all concerned about the chance of his child having a condition before the screening test. A screening program in which a potential defect is singled out for screening is perhaps more likely to have this result than a routine physical examination in which a number of tests are performed.

Screening Prerequisites
Doctors agree that a number of general conditions must be met before screening for a particular disease can be justified.

Serious Consequences. First, the disease should have relatively serious consequences, consequences that might be measured by mortality or by the ability to learn or to earn a living.

Prevalence. Second, the condition should be relatively prevalent. The higher the prevalence the lower the cost of discovering each case.

Controllability. A third characteristic of a disease favorable for screening is that it should be treatable or controllable. If it is not possible to reverse, slow down, or ameliorate the disease or the family's adverse reaction to the disease, there is little value to presymptomatic diagnosis. The exceptions are certain hereditary conditions, such as sickle-cell anemia, whose identification through screening can enable parents to decide whether to run the risk of having more children who might have the disease (Frankenburg, 1974).

Benefits of Early Detection. The prognosis should improve through early detection. The most effective and economical time for treatment must precede the usual time of diagnosis, that is, when symptoms first appear. If treatment is as effective at the same cost at a later stage in the progression of the disease, with no significant effects due to delayed treatment, little is gained by early diagnosis through screening.

What Makes a Good Test?
The availability of a good screening test is yet another criterion. The rest should be reliable, have high validity, cause minimum discomfort and inconvenience, and be low in cost.

Reliability. This refers to the consistency with which a test or observation measures what it is designed to measure. If two persons observing the same phenomenon report the same findings, the test has interobserver reliability. If the same test performed on a given individual on two different occasions gives the same results, there is test-retest reliability (Frankenburg, p. 614).

Validity. The validity of a screening test is the consistency with which positive and negative findings agree with the actual presence or absence of the disease or problem. These are referred to as sensitivity and specificity (Table 3—1). Sensitivity measures the test's usefulness in identifying all the diseased subjects, a/a+c in the first column. That is, the ratio of persons with positive screen test in whom the disease was confirmed to all persons in whom the disease was confirmed. Specificity is the ratio of those with negative screen test confirmed as not having the disease to all persons confirmed as not having the disease (though some were positive to the screen test). In Table 3—1 it is represented by the formula d/d+b.

Low Cost and Discomfort. A screening test should have two other characteristics. It should cause a minimum amount of discomfort and inconvenience and should be low in cost. The direct cost of the

Table 3—1. Relation Between Screening Test Results and Actual Diagnosis

a	b	a + b
screening test positive	screening test positive	all persons with positive test
disease present	disease not present	
c	d	c + d
screening test negative	screening test negative	all persons with positive test
disease present	disease not present	
a + c	b + d	a + b + c + d
all persons with disease present	all persons with disease not present	all persons tested

Sensitivity = a/a + c
Specificity = d/d + b

a = true positive, correct referral
b = false positive, overreferral
c = false negative, underreferral
d = true negative

Source: Frankenburg, 1974, p. 615. Reprinted with permission of *Pediatrics.*

screening component of a screening program includes the cost of instruments and materials used in performing the test, the cost of materials used to obtain specimens, the cost of personnel time spent in obtaining, labeling, and transporting specimens and performing the tests, the costs of training personnel to administer the screening tests, and the cost of time spent in recording results and interpreting them to parents and children.

Analyzing Costs and Payoffs

In order to analyze the costs and payoffs of screening for a particular disease, or to choose a screening procedure from among a range of alternatives for the same condition, the following set of questions might be asked. Chapter 8 gives an example of this approach applied to screening for hearing disorder.

How Prevalent is the Condition? This question should encompass the ages at which people are susceptible and their ethnic and economic background. The answer tells the decisionmaker in what population he is likely to find the greatest yield.

Data on prevalence are also requisite for the development of high-risk criteria for various conditions. Screening children who are at high risk will improve the yield of a screening procedure and hence lower the costs per case found.

How Serious is the Condition? The seriousness of the condition has already been mentioned as a prerequisite for screening. If left untreated or if the treatment is delayed, what happens? This question helps formulate the benefits of the screening program, or the costs of not screening. Does the condition lead to death, or to more serious conditions, to learning disabilities, or to problems in social functioning? For example, it is believed that chronic urinary infections may lead to later renal damage. Hearing loss often inhibits a child's language development.

What is "Lead Time"? Lead time is the interval between the time when the disease process can first be identified using the screening test and the optimal time for treatment. After this point treatment may be of little value or progressively expensive, time-consuming, or uncomfortable. For example, in phenylketonuria (PKU) the screening time starts at a few days of age and lasts about four or five weeks. After approximately six weeks of age, irreversible brain damage generally takes place.

What Personnel are Required to Administer the Tests?   Can parents be trained to test their children at home? Can a paramedic or aide administer the tests or is the expertise of a physician necessary? Some regions may have shortages of certain types of personnel and hence would be unable to initiate programs requiring sophisticated expertise.

What are the Total Costs of the Procedure?   This question and the preceding one will be critical in the development of national health insurance legislation. How often we are willing to reimburse a parent for a procedure and between what ages funding will be available for a certain test are points that must be specified in order to realistically appraise costs. Can the testing procedure be used to screen for other conditions?

What diagnostic procedures and personnel are necessary to confirm the information obtained from the screen? Can treatment be administered at the screening site? Will a few visits be enough or is continuous therapy necessary?

What are the Consequences of False Positive Identification?   These can be costs in money occasioned by a second screening test or diagnostic studies and the cost of unnecessary treatment. More serious are costs in mental anguish of parents and children who are unnecessarily labeled with the disease.

What are the Consequences of False Negative Identification?   These might include: whatever benefits are lost by the failure to make an early diagnosis, false reassurance (which may lead to delay in obtaining medical care even when symptoms occur, and the possibility that symptoms will be given some other explanation (Frankenburg, p. 615; Eisner, pp. 733–34).

Analyses of screening procedures which utilize cost criteria or outcome measures such as estimated cost savings per case detected, or even the yield of new cases, are lacking in the literature on screening. Many so-called evaluations merely describe the program administration or the number of positive findings for various conditions (Allen, 1974; Belleville, 1973; Brown, 1972), although some observers have recently begun to examine screening costs and payoffs in a more analytic way (for example, Frankenburg, 1973; Kunin, 1974; Scriver, 1974). It has yet to be demonstrated that the economic savings or improvement in quality of life rationales are justified for most screening procedures. (PKU and amblyopia detection seem to be exceptions.)

Sensitivity and specificity data, essential for determining the proportion of true cases missed by a screening test, have not been calculated for most procedures. As Northern (1974) points out, most studies fail to rescreen those children deemed normal at the first screening, thus mking it impossible to calculate the validity of the screening test. A systematic accounting of the costs of screening and treatment at different stages in the progression of a disease is also not available for most conditions. Validation of screening findings should be included in program evaluations, if only on a sampling basis, and cost data should be collected.

SCREENING IN PRACTICE

Before initiating programs to ensure screening, it would be useful to know if such a program is needed and, if so, to which children or providers the program should be targeted. Each type of provider will characteristically administer certain screening tests.

In urban areas children are distributed among providers as follows: Solo physicians and hospital outpatient departments (or emergency rooms) each have about 30 percent; public clinics get 16 percent. Fee-for-service associations have 10 percent, and prepaid group practices 6 percent. The other 8 percent is distributed between "no source" and multiple providers (Kessner, 1974).

Which Providers Are Most Likely to Screen?

We might hypothesize at the outset that those providers who usually see patients in crisis or acute-care conditions will be less likely to perform routine screening tests than will providers who see patients for well-child visits. Thus, we would expect a higher probability of screening from a private or prepaid group pediatrician than from an emergency room. It is possible, of course, that children could have more than one source of care, thus altering their chances of being screened.

Evidence on the screening practices of pediatric providers is sparse. A 1970 survey (Morehead, 1971) ranked hospital outpatient departments, OEO neighborhood health centers, group practices, health department well-baby clinics, and Children and Youth projects in terms of whether they provided certain services (Table 3—2). Unfortunately, the scoring system does not permit one to determine the probability of receiving a test in a given setting, but it does allow relative comparisons of providers. Children and Youth programs clearly were most likely to give screening tests. Notably, private group practices scored far below most other providers, including outpatient departments.

Table 3–2. Rankings of Providers for Hemoglobin/Urinalysis and TB Screening of Patients Eight to Twenty-Six Months of Age

Provider	Hemoglobin/Urinalysis Score	Tuberculosis Score
Medical school-affiliated OPD	92	119
OEO neighborhood health centers	94	96
Group practices	62	87
Health department well-baby clinics	56	117
Children and Youth Programs	169	156

Source: Adapted from Morehead et al., 1971.

Table 3–3 displays the results of three surveys of pediatric screening practices. Comparisons between providers are possible for anemia and vision testing. No clear trends are evident in the available data, although record reviews uniformly indicate that much less screening occurs (or is recorded) than providers claim. Neighborhood health centers and prepaid group practices are most likely to claim to routinely perform anemia screening. Public clinics and hospital outpatient departments rank second and third. Private practitioners are least likely, according to two out of three sources, similar to Morehead's ranking in Table 3–2. Vision testing is most likely to be performed (according to provider claims) in prepaid groups. About 45 percent of hospital OPDs and public clinics, and 30 percent of neighborhood health centers say they test vision. Findings for private practitioners vary from 45 to 90 percent.

Because of the limited number of available surveys and the wide discrepancy between self-reported screening behavior and record reviews, applying the figures to the model provides at best a rough estimate of true screening behavior. Table 3–4 attaches probabilities of being screened for anemia to the tree, using Kessner's Washington, D.C. survey (1974). By multiplying the proportion of children seen in a provider organization by the probability of being screened in that setting (according to provider claims) and adding these figures, we see that about 60 percent of all children are likely to routinely receive a screening test for anemia. Since reported screening is much greater than record reviews indicate, the figure may actually be much smaller.

Table 3–5 uses the data for provider distributions among central

Table 3–3. Percent of Providers Surveyed Who Routinely Perform Screening Test

Screening Test	Pediatricians (all claim)				NHC[c]		Hospital OPD/ER[c]		Prepaid Group[c]		Public Clinic[c]
	a	b	Solo[c]	Assoc.[c]	Claim	Record	Claim	Record	Claim	Record	Claim
Anemia	81	25	25	70	100	85	70	25	100	85	85
Urinalysis	90	62	—	—	—	—	—	—	—	—	—
Tuberculosis	—	100	—	—	—	—	—	—	—	—	—
Vision	90	81	45	75	30	9	45	5	90	40	45–50
Hearing	79	62	—	—	—	—	—	—	—	—	—

Sources: [a] Yankauer, National Survey of Pediatricians, 1970, p. 536.
[b] Telephone survey of sixteen private practice pediatricians, San Francisco, 1975.
[c] Kessner, Survey of Washington, D.C. practitioners, 1974, pp. 75–79.

Table 3—4.   Anemia Screening

Setting	Probability of Being Seen in Provider Setting P(A)	Probability of Being Screened in Setting P(B)	Probability of Being Seen in Setting and Being Screened P(A) · P(B)
Solo physician	.30	.25	.075
Association	.10	.70	.070
Prepaid group	.06	1.00	.060
Hospital OPD	.29	.70	.203
Public clinic	.16	.85	.136
No source	.03	0	0
Multiple source	.06	1.00[a]	.060
			.604 probability of being screened

[a]Given benefit doubt—assume will be screened.

Source: Adapted from Kessner, Survey of Washington D.C. practitioners, 1974.

Table 3–5. Anemia Screening

Income	Setting	P (seen in setting)	P (screened in setting)	P (seen and screened)
Low	Private practice	.26	.7 (high) .25 (low)	.182 (high) .065 (low)
	Clinic	.56	.85	.476 .476
	No regular source	.18	0	0 0
				.658 .541
High	Private practice	.77	.7 (high) .25 (low)	.539 (high) .192 (low)
	Clinic	.20	.85	.170 .170
	No regular source	.03		0 0
				.709 .362

Source: Adapted from Kessner, Survey of Washington, D.C. practitioners, 1974, and Weber, 1975.

city SMSA children, separated by high and low income. The results are interesting, in that if we use a high estimate of private practice screening (.7), high-income children are slightly more likely to receive an anemia test (.709 versus .658). If the low estimate (.25) is used, poor children actually are more likely to receive a test (.541 versus .362) because of their lower use of private practitioners.

Table 3—6 uses the same technique to model vision-screening behavior, using Kessner's data (1974). The chances of receiving a vision test are about 53 percent, again a maximum estimate since reported screening is at least twice as high as recorded screening for the three types of providers whose records were reviewed.

Table 3—7 separates the likelihood of vision screening by high and low income. Children of high-income families are more likely to receive a vision screen than are poor children, even when a low private practice estimate is used.

The following tentative interpretations can be made:

1. Having a regular, ongoing source of care provides no guarantee of receiving a screening test. The over-all chances of being screened for anemia or vision problems are 60 percent or less.

2. Private practitioners are not necessarily more likely to screen than public providers of care.

3. Evidence on hospital OPDs is conflicting. According to Morehead (1971), they are not necessarily least likely to screen, yet according to Kessner (1974) record reviews of three provider types showed that OPDs were least likely to screen (or to record screening).

Why Are Screening Rates Low?

Poor Tests. First, it is possible that providers feel a test is inefficacious, has a low yield, or is not indicated in asymptomatic children. For example, sixteen San Francisco pediatricians unanimously reported no use of routine lead poisoning tests, citing few cases seen in the city in recent years. In the same survey, not one physician performed the Denver Development Test, citing it as a poor test. The surprisingly low rate of anemia screening by private practitioners may also result from the possibility that they follow children over a period of time and feel more confident in their ability to note changes without routine screening. Even prepaid groups are apparently not unanimous in their use of the test. Of two Bay Area Kaiser practices, only one routinely performs anemia screening and urinalysis on its preschool patients.[a]

---

[a]Edgar Schoen, Kaiser Permanente/Oakland; and H.R. Shinefield, Kaiser Permanente/San Francisco, personal communications.

Table 3–6.   Vision Screening and Setting

Setting	P (seen in setting)	P (screened in setting)	P (seen in setting and screened)
Solo physician	.3	.45	.135
Association	.1	.75	.075
Prepaid group	.06	.9	.054
Hospital OPD	.29	.45	.130
Public clinic	.16	.5	.08
No source	.03	0	0
Multiple source	.06	1.0	.060
			.534 **P** (being screened)

Source: Adapted from Kessner, Survey of Washington, D.C. practitioners, 1974.

Table 3–7. Vision Screening and Income

Income	Setting	P (seen in setting)	P (screened in setting)	P (seen in setting and screened)	
Low	Private practice	.26	.75 (high) .45 (low)	.195 (high)	.117 (low)
	Clinic	.56	.5	.280	.280
	No regular source	.18	0	0	0
				.475	.397
High	Private practice	.77	.75 (high) .45 (low)	.577 (high)	.346 (low)
	Clinic	.20	.5	.100	.100
	No regular source	.03	0	0	0
				.677	.446

Source: Adapted from Kessner, Survey of Washington, D.C. practitioners, 1974, and Weber, 1975.

Lack of Equipment. Several San Francisco pediatricians mentioned that they did not perform hematocrits and urinalyses because they lacked the requisite facilities. Others admitted they did not have an audiometer in their offices.

Lack of Time. Screening may not be performed because of lack of time. This may certainly be the case in hospital OPDs and emergency rooms. If physicians insist on administering routine screening tests themselves, lack of time will likely be a factor in failure to screen. Even if they are willing to delegate tasks, they may lack sufficient personnel.

Is Someone Else Doing the Testing? Fourth, physicians may think that someone else is providing the screening test. Many practitioners may feel school health programs fill this need, especially vision and hearing tests.

Perhaps More Screening is Done Than is Recorded? Tests may be performed but the results simply not be noted on the patient's record. Or the record may be lost.

Multiphasic Screening

Several different tests or measurements may be applied to the same individual at a single session. This "multiphasic" screening is advantageous in two ways (Allen and Shinefield, 1974). First, it is more efficient to use a single patient contact for several tests and observations and the collection of information. Aside from the convenience to parents and children, recordkeeping costs may be lowered and follow-up costs for two or more conditions may not be much higher than for one. Second, information from one observation can contribute to more accurate interpretation of other observations.

A counterargument is that in multiphasic screening it may become too easy to add superfluous tests. "If 12 chemistry tests cost only a few cents more than a single test because the equipment is automated, the temptation is to do all 12" (Allen and Shinefield, 1974). The interpreter of the results may then be confronted with an excess of distracting information and may tend to overlook significant results. This sort of "technological imperative" also drives up the cost of screening when the "few cents per child" and few minutes of observer time are multiplied by a number of children.

Policy Implications

Several policy implications can be drawn from the evidence. First, merely assuring a regular source of care, through financing or other mechanisms, will not guarantee that a child will receive a screening test. If a screening procedure is considered essential, special incentives or information may have to be offered to providers or parents, or it may be necessary to provide screening and treatment programs outside the regular source of care.

Second, reasons for failure to screen should be examined. If lack of time is the problem, greater use of paramedical personnel might be encouraged, or funds for more of the usual personnel could be provided. If practitioners believe another source of care is providing the test, they should be informed of screening programs in the area.

Third, the practical effect of screening probabilities can only be determined by adding probabilities of receiving diagnosis and treatment to the model. As Kessner (1974) has noted, even if a child receives a screening test, diagnosis and treatment are not assured by having a regular source of care.

REACHING CHILDREN FOR SCREENING

Locating children to be screened is a primary consideration in setting up a screening program. Reaching preschool children is particularly difficult, because children often are not seen in a medical care setting between the time they leave the hospital nursery and the time they enter school. Many of these children also will not be found in a formal day-care setting where screening might occur. Unfortunately, this is also the age group in which certain conditions must be identified and treated, lest irreversible damage occur. For example, the ideal age for identifying hearing disorders is when a child would normally acquire speech. Similarly, the critical age for detecting amblyopia usually occurs before school entry (Belleville, 1972).

Because many children will not have access to regular medical care, it is important to recognize parents' potential role as first contact screeners. Training that would alert parents to signs of developmental progress in their children would help to ensure early detection of conditions, particularly in first children when parents have no prior observational experience. A screening test simple enough for parents to administer would save physician or health associate time. A home vision testing packet, for example, is currently available. Since parents provide continuing care, they could carry medical records. In light of the current mobility of families, such recordkeeping could be valuable.

Choosing a Setting

Where would screening take place? The answer depends on the resources available and the target populations. These questions might be asked:

1. Will the treatment site be separate from the screening site? If so, the probability becomes greater that a child will never reach a treatment setting. This is a common criticism of screening programs. Alternatively, the child may be subject to redundant rescreening, if the initial observations at the screening site are not transmitted to the diagnostic and treatment site.

2. What type of individuals can one expect to pick up at the screening site? A formal day-care setting may reach children who already are in comprehensive medical care settings and would be in less need of a screening program.

3. What is the potential number of children who can be reached through the screening site? Screening in schools may reach all of the children of a given age in a neighborhood. Can the chosen screening site do as well?

4. What incentives are offered? Are transportation, day care, and free medication provided? Can the child or parent be seen in evening or weekend hours? Is there a way to put the initiative on someone other than the person to be screened?

5. What personnel or equipment are potentially built into the system? What has to be brought in new? This obviously affects the cost of operating the program, and also its potential continuity. If an external source of money or help (e.g., government funding) ends, what are the chances that the program will continue on its own? What incentives are offered the operators of the program?

6. What does the program cost? In dollars, in staff, in physical space, or in other resources? What about indirect costs? For example, what is the loss to a true emergency victim if an emergency room nurse is spending five minutes screening another patient?

7. Does the setting affect the proportion of false positives? For example, the noise level or quality of personnel might influence the administration of a test.

8. What is the possibility of prescreening in the setting? A day-care or school teacher might suggest which children should be sent to be screened, if only a limited number of children can be seen.

Screening at a Physician's Office or Neighborhood Health Center. A child could receive screening services as part of regular preventive care. There are several advantages to this approach. First, for most conditions the setting ensures the immediate proximity of treatment. Second, records are centrally located. Third, the public receives more health information from physicians and considers that information to be more reliable than from any other source (Harris, 1973). These considerations ensure a higher probability of compliance than could be had in most other screening settings.

A final advantage of this setting is its low cost. Patient records, trained personnel, and equipment are already present.

The disadvantages are that this setting fails to reach those children who never consult a physician, or who do so only in emergency rooms, and also that children who associate the source of their regular care with injections or other unpleasant events may be anxious or distracted, thus raising the possibility of false positives. The opportunity cost of personnel time for the extra caseload must be considered too.

Hospital Emergency Rooms and Outpatient Clinics. The major advantages of hospital settings over most other screening modes are the preexisting supply of trained personnel, equipment, and physical facilities, and the potential for reaching individuals with no regular source of care. The disadvantages, particularly in emergency rooms, are the possibility of a large number of false positives due to anxiety. If the ailment for which the person is being screened seems unimportant relative to his other problems, care is difficult in a hospital setting.

Mobile Screening. Mobile vans or impermanent setups, such as a table in a partitioned area, may be used in any number of locations where the public is likely to congregate. These have been located in shopping centers, banks, churches, transportation centers (even the Staten Island Ferry), public housing centers, voting polls, and state fairs. Such programs are aimed at detection and only rarely have included follow-up.

This mode of screening may possibly be effective in rural areas, or in reaching those people who do not seek medical attention regularly. It can also, of course, end up as a political tool if the objective is to publicly present high numbers of individuals screened as proof of "services" provided. But mass screening does serve the purpose of informing a lot of people at once about screened conditions and their consequences. These individuals may then ask their doctor about them at some later point.

One disadvantage of mobile screening is that the individual must always be referred out to his personal physician or clinic or to a special treatment center, increasing follow-up costs and lowering the probability of treatment.

A second disadvantage of mobile screening is its uncertain reliability. Do people feel that a shopping center screen, staff, and test results are trustworthy? Would parents be sufficiently impressed to make a follow-up visit to their physician?

Schools or Day Care Centers. Many screening activities could be integrated into existing school health programs or performed in day-care centers or preschools. The audience would be essentially a captive one, and a large number of students could be screened in a short time. Children would be present every day, so follow-up would be easy, and it would be easier to teach screening techniques to classroom groups than to individual children (EPSDT manual).

Cost of such a program would vary, depending on whether it were incorporated into an existing screening program or designed as a new specific intervention.

However, there are several potential disadvantages to this approach. School health programs may fail to transmit information to physicians and parents. Parents may not be available to be counseled about results or to help in screening young children. All diagnosis and treatment, even for the most simple problems, must be obtained through referral, and referral mechanisms are often weak. In addition, there may be legal problems in performing certain of the screening tests on school grounds or by certain personnel in the absence of a physician.

Preschool detection of conditions affecting capacity to learn (such as vision and hearing defects) seems to enjoy nearly unanimous support among otherwise skeptical observers of screening. Yet most school health programs focus their efforts only on children who are already enrolled.

It seems important to persuade administrators of school programs of the probable payoffs of early identification and to encourage them to reallocate some portion of their budgets to preschool children. Since middle ear infections decline after age ten, the resources devoted to screening for hearing loss after this age could be reallocated to screening four- or five-year-olds. Little extra cost would be involved aside from bringing the children to the screening site.

Special Purpose Clinics. Special purpose screening programs exist in many communities to identify visual defects, tuberculosis, lead poisoning, or sickle-cell trait. Such programs may be able to contribute trained personnel, equipment, training, or laboratory analysis to a wide-scale screening program.

The disadvantages are: a child may require visits to several separate sites in order to complete all the tests; recordkeeping is harder when several separate sites are used; and follow-up is often incomplete (EPSDT manual).

State and Local Variations

Special features of the region should also be considered when designing a screening program:

1. To forecast a program's yield, it would be valuable to have data on the proportion of children in the locale to be screened who receive regular comprehensive care, sporadic emergency care, or no care. If a large proportion of children are receiving comprehensive care, screening programs may yield few cases that would not otherwise have been detected.

2. Variations in prevalence of conditions should be noted. For instance, screening for lead paint poisoning in California or other areas of new construction may have a particularly low yield.[b]

3. The available resources (manpower and physical facilities) and the legal constraints should be considered, in order to evaluate the costs and feasibility of screening.

Thus, because of regional variations in resources, prevalence, or proportion of children receiving different types of medical care, blanket national recommendations or mandates for screening may be inappropriate. What is cost-effective in one region may not be in another.

Variations in Personnel. Selection of personnel to administer tests will vary from area to area because of unequal distribution of manpower resources and different legal restrictions. And the choice of personnel will affect the cost of the test or screening program. For these reasons, it is important that health professionals other than physicians be trained to administer various screening procedures and that laws be changed to allow the administration of tests by such personnel in the absence of a physician. Reimbursement mechanisms for the provision of screening services by allied health professionals could be written into national health insurance legislation.

It may be advantageous to have one person administer several tests on a child rather than having the child encounter a different person for each test. Recordkeeping and transfer time will be reduced, and the level of anxiety will be lower, particularly in very young children. Finally, as was pointed out earlier, parents are the ideal first-contact screeners.

APPROPRIATE USE OF SCREENING

Incentives

In addition to the incentives to parents that have been suggested earlier, some observers have recommended offering direct cash incen-

[b]Personal communication from Edgar Schoen, Kaiser Permanente, Oakland, California.

tives to encourage appropriate use. For example, when a mother leaves the hospital with her newborn child, she could be given a certificate or voucher for cash, redeemable when the patient returns at six months of age and at successive times when screening or observation is considered appropriate. The relative effectiveness of these methods has yet to be determined.

Direct personal contact is also effective in reaching parents. It appears to be more successful than notice through posters or news media. However, advertising health services on television during children's programs such as *Sesame Street* or in youth activities such as scouting might help.

Incentives could also be offered to the providers of screening. For example, the Boston City Health Department requires that the results of all Tine tests, free to providers, be reported monthly to the department. If this is not done, the following month's supply is not delivered to the practitioner. Since the physician or clinic then has to purchase the materials, the financial incentive is apparently enough to ensure reporting.[c] Staffs of providers could also be given incentives since they, rather than physicians, are responsible for the actual telephone or mail follow-up. Receptionists, for example, could be given cash bonuses for each case followed through from screen to treatment.

When Not to Screen

It is interesting to consider what incentives could be offered to practitioners in order that they *not* use a screening test. As Lessler (1972) recognizes, any effort to channel or limit the use of screening procedures or programs confronts the fact that early identification of children who may have serious medical problems, through screening, is a very appealing and popular idea. K.D. Rogers' viewpoint is similar:

> The emotional appeal of prevention, the commercial motivation to capitalize on screening processes and equipment, the self-serving use of mass surveys for publicity or program justification by voluntary and official health agencies, and the activism which characterizes modern medicine serve to perpetuate the myth of screening's value and to endorse it unwarrantedly. (1974, p. 174)

Financial disincentives could be utilized. Since most screening procedures performed on an outpatient basis are not currently paid for

[c]Chief of Pediatrics, Harvard Community Health Plan. Personal communication.

by private insurance schemes, discontinuation of payment is not a viable option. However, since some national health insurance schemes propose funding of screening, tests could be selectively included as eligible for reimbursement, based on the criteria mentioned earlier.

Rogers suggests that while elimination of individual screening procedures in the routine physical may be difficult, mass screening such as at school entry should be examined more critically: "Most of these . . . could be eliminated without causing apprehension in parents or physicians, and result in savings of dollars and professional time."

Ethical Dilemmas in Screening

Screening procedures and programs raise a number of ethical questions. For example, in screening a child for elevated serum cholesterol levels, we may on the one hand be offering him the chance of an increased life expectancy if certain dietary measures are taken, while on the other we may be producing an anxious hypochondriac. Similarly, in screening for any disease for which treatment is not available at the present time, many people think we are not performing a service for either child or parent.

False positives raise ethical concerns in that they may cause psychological, if not physical, damage to a child and his parents. Children falsely diagnosed may exist in an "unnecessary limbo where they either perceive themselves or are perceived by others to have a nonexistent disease. Such a person may be as disabled or 'unhealthy' as if he actually has the disease" (Bergman and Stamon, 1967, p. 1008). "Delabeling" children thought to have heart disease or acute rheumatic fever is apparently one of the most frequently performed tasks of pediatric cardiologists. Bergman and Stamon's study indicates that of 93 children initially diagnosed to have heart disease, 81 percent were shown to have been misdiagnosed in a reevaluation two and a half years later. Of these, 40 percent had been restricted in their activity and showed significant physical and psychological damage. The authors conclude that the amount of disability from "cardiac nondisease" in children is actually greater than that due to true heart disease.

Critics of sickle-cell screening programs have argued on the same grounds, pointing out the possibility of misdiagnosis if only electrophoresis analysis is used (a common procedure in mass screening), leading to "grievous diagnostic error inflected upon the innocent patient" (Nalbadian, 1972, p. 501). Even if diagnosis is correct, we should also consider the ethical problems of genetic screening and counseling. As one writer reports: "Persons with sickle cell trait

(HbAS) . . . have been barred from sports by physicians, denied employment, and discharged from jobs; misguided attempts are in progress to defer persons with HbAS from the Armed Forces" (Bowman, 1972, p. 1650).

Inherent labeling problems arise in seeking to screen a particular target population, such as a group distinguishable by race or income. One solution is to screen all members of a group (a school class, for example) regardless of race or economic level, although the yield of the screen will consequently be reduced and the costs per new case elevated.

RECOMMENDATIONS

Several recommendations can be suggested, from which research priorities can be assigned.

Follow-Up

The importance of follow-up in the administration of screening procedures both as part of regular care and in a special program must be emphasized. One value of screening programs is that they introduce children who do not have a regular source of care to ongoing care services. A major criticism of the programs has been that those children with positive test results may never receive diagnosis and treatment because of inadequate referral mechanisms or treatment resources.

Consider Regional Variations

Regional variations in both resources and prevalence of conditions should be considered when planning a screening program or comprehensive health exam protocol. The necessity of training personnel who are unfamiliar with a technique must be included in the costs of a program, as must the provision of new equipment. The capacity of the local diagnosis and treatment organization must be taken into account in selecting the size and setting of a program, in order not to overburden the delivery system.

If the prevalence of a condition is known to be particularly low in an area, screening for that condition may result in wasted resources. In addition, the yield of new conditions must be considered; if many children already receive comprehensive health services, a superimposed screening program will be redundant. Present screening programs should be examined critically for their yield of otherwise undetected cases.

Train Physician Extenders

Most screening tests can be performed by nurse practitioners, nurses, or personnel with less training. To lower the costs of screening and to ensure the possibility of screening in areas with physician shortages, it is important that laws be changed to allow the administration of tests by such personnel in the absence of a physician. Reimbursement mechanisms for the provision of screening services by health professionals other than physicians could be written into national health insurance legislation.

Provide Incentives

If children can be screened for two conditions in a single testing place (co-location), this in itself will be an incentive. The temptation to add superfluous tests must be guarded against, however.

Incentives beyond the provision of physical access may be necessary, too. These might include cash bonuses and media outreach efforts. Providers could also be offered incentives, particularly to ensure follow-up.

Begin with Preschoolers

Preschool detection of certain conditions, particularly those affecting capacity to learn (such as vision and hearing defects), seems to enjoy nearly unanimous support among otherwise skeptical observers of screening. Yet most school health programs focus their efforts only on those children already enrolled in school. It thus seems important to persuade program administrators of the probable payoffs of earlier detection and to encourage them to reallocate some portion of their budgets to preschool children.

Areas for Further Research

Payoffs Against Costs.   Do early detection and treatment of a condition lead to consequences that are greatly different from those of delayed detection and treatment? The type of analysis for hearing impairment outlined in Chapter 8 could be applied to other diseases in an effort to answer this question.

Sensitivity and Specificity.   Data on these are essential for determining the value of performing a screening test, and they are lacking for most screening procedures. As Northern and Downs (1974) point out, studies fail to rescreen those children who are deemed to be normal at the first screening, thus making it impossible to calculate the validity of the screening test. Validation of screening findings should be included in program evaluations, if only on a sampling basis. Such data will be most useful if gathered under actual field conditions, rather than in a perfectly controlled setting, in order to make the figures more congruent with actual testing circumstances.

High-Risk Criteria. These should be developed for various conditions, as has been attempted with hearing disorders. Screening children who are at high risk will improve the yield of a screening procedure and hence lower the costs per case found.

When to Screen? When to Repeat? A critical question for national health insurance legislation will be the ages at which a screening test should be administered, and how often it should be repeated.

Ethical Problems of Screening. These deserve greater attention than they have received from past researchers. Screening for untreatable disease poses a particular dilemma. The consequences of false positive identification also need to be further analyzed. The technological development of prenatal screening procedures should be accompanied by a critical analysis of their ethical implications.

Delivery Modes. These need to be evaluated in terms of their effectiveness as a setting for screening. Criteria might include the referral mechanisms, proximity to a treatment-delivering organization, costs and incentives to operators and parents.

Can Parents Screen? The possibility of educating parents to be screeners should be explored, especially for preschool children. A valid screening test simple enough for parents to administer at home would save health personnel time and reach those young children who do not have regular access to medical care. Training that would make parents alert to signs of developmental progress in their children would also help to ensure early detection of conditions, particularly in first children, when parents have no prior experience.

Know When to Stop

Means of stopping an institutionalized screening procedure, when no longer deemed effective, also merit consideration. As K.D. Rogers points out (1974), screening procedures, particularly when part of primary preventive health examinations, have a certain psychic value to both physician and parent, and may be difficult to eliminate. Removal of mass screening programs may be easier in this respect, but the change may involve political cost.

REFERENCES

Allen, C.M., and Shinefield, H.R. "Automated multiphasic screening," *Pediatrics* 54 (1974): 621–26.

Bailey, E.N., et al. "Screening in pediatric practice," *Pediatr Clin North Am* 21 (1974): 123–65.

Belleville, M., and Green, P. "Preschool multiphasic screening programs in rural Kansas," *Am J Public Health* 62 (1972): 795–98.

Bergman, A.B., and Stamon, S.J. "The morbidity of cardiac nondisease in schoolchildren," *N Engl J Med* 267 (1967): 1008–13.

Bowman, J.E. "Mass screening programs for sickle hemoglobin: A sickle cell crisis," *JAMA* 222 (1972): 1650.

Brown, H.B. "Multiphasic screening for preschool children: I. Methodology and clinical findings in a Spanish-American community," *JAMA* 219 (1972): 1315–19.

Ehrlich, C.H.; Shapiro, E.; Kimball, B.; Huttner, M. "Communication skills in five-year-old children with high risk neonatal histories," *J Speech Hear Res* 16 (1973): 522–29.

Eisner, V. "Early detection and treatment." In *Maternal and Child Health Practices: Problems, Resources, and Methods of Delivery*, edited by H. Wallace, pp. 729–43. Springfield, Ill.: Charles C. Thomas, 1973.

EPSDT Manual. See U.S. Department of Health, Education and Welfare.

Frankenburg, W.K. "Pediatric screening," *Adv Pediatr* 20 (1973): 149–75.

Frankenburg, W.K. "Selection of diseases and tests in pediatric screening," *Pediatrics* 54 (1974): 612–16.

Harris, Louis, and Associates, Inc., *The Public and High Blood Pressure.* Survey conducted for NHLI, Study No. 2313, June 1973.

Holland, W.W. "Screening for disease—taking stock," *The Lancet* (December 21, 1974): 1494–97.

Katz, Jack. *The Handbook of Clinical Audiology*, Baltimore: Williams and Wilkins, 1972.

Kessner, D.M., et al. *Contrasts in Health Status, Vol. 2: A Strategy for Evaluating Health Services.* Washington, D.C.: National Academy of Sciences, 1974.

Kessner, D.M., et al. *Contrasts in Health Status, Vol. 3: Assessment of Medical Care for Children.* Washington, D.C.: National Academy of Sciences, 1974.

Kleinman, J.C., et al. *Emergency Medical Services in the City of Boston.* Cambridge, Mass.: Harvard Center for Community Health and Medical Care, December 1972.

Kunin, C.M. "Current status of screening children for urinary tract infections," *Pediatrics* 54 (1974): 619–21.

Lessler, K. "Health and educational screening of school-age children—definition and objectives," *Am J Public Health* 62 (1972): 191–98.

Lessler, K. "Screening, screening programs and the pediatrician," *Pediatrics* 54 (1974): 608–11.

Lewis, M. *A Policy Decision Analysis for Iron-deficiency Anemia.* Kennedy School of Government, Harvard University, unpublished paper, October 30, 1974.

Morehead, M.A., et al. "Comparisons between OEO neighborhood health centers and other health care providers of ratings of the quality of health care," *Am J Public Health* 61 (1971), pp. 1294–1306.

Moriarty, R.W. "Screening to prevent lead poisoning," *Pediatrics* 54 (1974): 626–28.

Nalbadian, R.M. "Mass screening programs for sickle cell hemoglobin," *JAMA* 221 (1972): 500–02.

North, A.F. "Introduction: screening in child health care," *Pediatrics* 54 (1974): 608.

North, A.F. "Screening in child health care: where are we now and where are we going?" *Pediatrics* 54 (1974): 631–40.

Northern, J.L., and Downs, M.P. *Hearing in Children.* Baltimore: Williams and Wilkins, 1974.

Roberts, J. "Hearing sensitivity and related medical findings among children in the United States," *Trans Am Acad Opthal Otolaryn* 76 (1972): 355–59.

Rogers, K.D. "Screening in pediatric practice—review and commentary." *Pediatr Clin North Am* 21 (1974): 167–74.

Rogers, M.G.H. "The early recognition of handicapping disorders in childhood," *Dev Med Child Neurol* 13 (1971): 88–101.

Scriver, C.R. "PKU and beyond: when do costs exceed benefits?" *Pediatrics* 54 (1974): 616–18.

Silverman, S.R. "Impressions of the studies sponsored by the Committee on Conservation of Hearing," *Trans Am Opthal Otolaryn* 76 (1972): 306–66.

Torrens, P.R., and Yedab, D.G. "Variations among emergency room populations: a comparison of four hospitals in New York City," *Med Care* 8 (1970): 60–75.

Weber, G.I. *Evaluation of an Expanded Public Role in the Financing of Health Care Services for Children: Background Material.* Unpublished draft, 1975.

Zaner, A.R. "Differential diagnosis of hearing impairment in children: developmental approaches to clinical assessment," *J Commun Disord* 7 (1974): 17–30.

Part II

The Cycle of Children's Primary Medical Care

Chapter 4

Efficacy and Effectiveness of Primary Medical Care for Children

Barbara Starfield, M.D., M.P.H.

To assess efficacy and effectiveness we need to examine the interrelationships among the several components of the health care system (Starfield, 1973). The nature of the distinction between efficacy and effectiveness is important. Efficacy denotes the degree to which diagnostic and therapeutic procedures used in practice can be supported by scientific evidence of their usefulness under optimum conditions. Whether or not these procedures are applied adequately in practice, and whether they produce the intended results when so applied are matters of effectiveness. Medical care functions can be thought of as activities performed both by medical providers and the people who need services. To be effective, medical practitioners must recognize problems, translate them into diagnoses, institute appropriate management, and assume responsibility for assuring that the expected effect is achieved. Achievement of the effect also requires that those who need services understand that need, accept it, and agree to take the steps to deal with it.

In the following chapters, five common problems in primary care are analyzed with regard to the available evidence on effectiveness of health care services and efficacy of the procedures most often used to diagnose and treat them. The problems chosen are: iron-deficiency anemia, otitis media, lead poisoning, appendicitis, and streptococcal disease. While these conditions do not represent the entire spectrum of problems in primary care, their management is relatively straightforward and clearly in the province of the physician. (Other types of problems which arise in primary care such as behavior problems and chronic ailments, may require more complex management with the participation of a wider spectrum of professionals.) Moreover the problems which have been selected are relatively common and result in important functional derangements when care is ineffective.

RECOMMENDATIONS

Although the conditions examined in this section cannot be considered representative of problems in primary care, the related defects are sufficiently consistent to indicate important directions for attention. Except for appendicitis, all have chronic sequelae and potential for causing significant disability. Whatever shortcomings are found for these conditions most certainly would be found for conditions with less dramatic, and particularly those with less obvious, somatic manifestations.

The defects elucidated are not likely to be either discovered or addressed by current peer-review efforts. Therefore, it is important that additional attempts be made to develop tools that can be adapted to ongoing efforts in assessing care. Specific recommendations fall into three categories.

Problem Recognition

Inadequate recognition of problems by health practitioners appears to be staggering. There is evidence that practitioners often fail to become aware of common concerns such as visual defects, hearing defects, speech defects, and behavior problems (Starfield and Borkowf, 1969). They also are likely to miss social factors that influence the health of children (Chamberlin, 1971).

In fact, "problem recognition" is not generally accepted as a distinct step in the medical care process, quite separate from the diagnostic process. As the diagnostic process consists of the integration of problems (signs and symptoms) into a coherent clinical entity, the diagnostic process *starts* at the point that a problem or problems are recognized. If problems are not recognized, there can be no diagnostic process or, at best, an inappropriate one. Consider four different scenarios:

1. The patient who does not come for care because there is no perceived need for it. People are often not able to take responsibility for initiating care when it is required. Early tuberculosis is occult; vision and hearing problems may not be evident; the early signs of lead poisoning may be difficult to perceive. Practitioners need to be aware of potential problems in their communities, and to work with

other public health personnel to bring them to care at the earliest possible time.

2. The patient who seeks care for one problem but who is at high risk, albeit asymptomatic, of another one. A child with a history of urinary tract infections may present with a skin problem. The practitioner who does not recognize the previous history, which places the child at high risk of recurrent urinary tract infections, will miss the opportunity to find the recurrence. In our fragmented medical care system, which permits patients to move from one practitioner to another, this is a particularly difficult challenge. It may, however, occur even when the patient remains under the care of one practitioner, as a result of poor recordkeeping or failure to review the records.

3. The patient who comes for care with a set of complaints, but who presents only one of them. Some problems are uncomfortable, and parents may be embarrassed to present them. The child with bed-wetting may be stealing to buy drugs, but the parent will complain only of bed-wetting—a more acceptable symptom. Or consider the child who is treated for his "sore throat" every few weeks but who really is trying to deal with his anxiety about the hepatitis which has just developed in his chronic alcoholic father.

The nature of the communication between practitioners and patients will determine whether the underlying problem is ever elicited. If it is not, neither the presenting problem nor the more basic one are resolvable even if the presenting problem is adequately diagnosed and properly treated. Practitioners usually make the assumption that the patient's main complaint is the one that is present first. Physicians often even call this complaint the "chief complaint." Yet if the process of practitioner-patient communication has not elicited it, patients may express their main concern only late in the interaction, often when they are about to leave the office. Generally, this produces the same effect as when they fail to mention it at all, that is, the physician does not deal with it, assuming that it is "minor" and of little consequence.

4. The patient who does not complain, but has signs indicative of an existing problem. Both the chronic renal problem and the resulting growth retardation are unrecognized because the child looks normal and his age is not taken into consideration in interpreting his physical findings. Another child may have had a laboratory procedure done at a previous visit (or at another facility such as in school) which showed an abnormal result. This result may remain unrecognized because it does not come to the attention of the practitioner or because the

practitioner does not recall its performance and fails to take the initiative to seek it.

None of the quality-assurance mechanisms in existence today address this phase of the medical care process. Yet all of these types of failures to recognize problems are prevalent in practice. How much of the defect is due to patients' lack of access to, and assumption of, initiative in their care and how much to failure of the practitioner is unclear. Undoubtedly, both circumstances are contributory. There is no question that the health care system fails to reach many individuals, particularly those in lower socioeconomic, deprived groups. However, even those who do come in contact with practitioners risk having their problems go unrecognized or inadequately recognized. Koran (1975), in a thorough review of the literature, documents the extraordinary extent of disagreement in the clinical observations of practitioners. Skopek vividly documents the inadequacies in physician-patient communication which result in a failure to recognize problems of major consequence to the patient's health and well-being (Skopek, 1975). Medical education seems unable to address itself to problem recognition, at least not as well as it now does for teaching diagnostic and management skills (Engel and Morgan, 1973). Other means will have to be found to bring problems to the attention of practitioners. Efforts to accomplish this by use of health aides, consumer ombudsmen, or direct assumption of control by patients within health care systems would appear to merit consideration. Training programs to develop and implement curriculae designed to improve recognition of problems should be encouraged, as should efforts to help consumers effectively articulate their needs.

Diagnostic and Therapeutic Efficacy

Despite the resources devoted to compiling criteria for adequate diagnosis and management, there is little evidence that those chosen by the vast majority of peer-review organizations can be justified by available scientific evidence. The Albermarle County Experimental Medical Care Review Organization, under grant from the National Center for Health Services Research, has devoted the past few years to searching for studies that provide scientific evidence for the usefulness of medical care interventions. Among the conditions they considered were hypertension, gastric ulcer, and hip fractures. It is instructive to compare the criteria which they were able to validate by review of the scientific literature with those set by existing peer-review systems. In virtually every area of diagnosis and treatment there are major discrepancies.

Both diagnostic and therapeutic interventions would be served by a concerted effort to obtain validated criteria for the most common pediatric problems. Many unnecessary and costly procedures could be eliminated. The search would also provide information on areas of needed clinical research.

Reassessment

Failure to reassess problems to determine their resolution or non-resolution is an equally important shortcoming in medical care. Physicians tend to assume that their instructions and prescriptions will produce their intended effect; they often do not, even when they are appropriate by all external judgments to the diagnosis. Perhaps the problem was not adequately recognized, or the diagnosis was not accurate, or the patient did not understand the instructions, or there were factors that kept the patient from carrying them out. The best continuing education effort is likely to result when practitioners see their failures. Instead, the patient usually goes to another physician in another attempt to obtain relief. Motives and rewards in our system do not appear to encourage acceptance of responsibility for maintenance of health. And alteration in the nature of professional reward appears remote. Even under proposed new legislation, practitioners will continue to be paid for providing services deemed appropriate by professional peers rather than by demonstrating that they have taken steps to determine if the desired result is achieved. An effective attack on the assumptions on which legislation and quality reviews are based is required if the reward structure of practice is to be changed. For the present, there needs to be a realistic effort to illuminate systematically those facets of care now neglected, the reasons for this neglect, and the effects they have on the health of children. Efforts to make self-assessment an integral part of medical practice should be supported. In addition to its direct benefits on patient care, reassessment is important in providing an understanding of the natural history of illness both with and without interventions. Dealing with this situation will require better categorization of illness and its severity, better recordkeeping, and the development of organizational and financial incentives to facilitate timely reassessment. A means to incorporate information derived from self-assessment into the curriculae of training programs is urgently needed. This is an uncharted area in which pioneers could make important inroads.

REFERENCES

Albemarle County Experimental Medical Care Review Organization. *Otitis Media: Standards for Quality Care.* (1974).

Chamberlin, R.W. "Social data in evaluation of the pediatric patient," *J Pediatr* 78 (1971): 111–16.

Engel, G.L., and Morgan, W.L. Jr. *Interviewing the Patient.* Philadelphia: W.B. Saunders Co., 1973.

Koran, L.M. "The reliability of clinical methods, data and judgments," *N Engl J Med* 293 (1975): 642–46.

Skopek, L. *Sociolinguistic Aspects of the Medical Interview.* Unpublished doctorate dissertation. Georgetown University, 1975.

Starfield, B., Borkowf, S. "Physicians' recognition of complaints made by parents about their children's health," *Pediatrics* 43 (1969): 168–72.

Starfield, B. Health Services Research: A Working Model. *N Engl J Med* 289 (1973): 132–36.

✳ *Chapter 5*

Iron-Deficiency Anemia

Barbara Starfield, M.D., M.P.H.

PREVALENCE

Anemia is the most common hematologic problem in infancy and childhood. Large-scale surveys indicate that approximately 14 percent of all children are anemic (hemoglobins below 10 g/100 ml); the great majority of these have anemia resulting from iron deficiency. Iron deficiency is considered the most widespread nutritional deficiency in the United States (Charlton and Bothwell, 1970; Committee on Iron Deficiency, NAS, 1968; Finch, 1969; Gendel, 1960).

The prevalence of iron-deficiency anemia among the entire child population is unknown. In a study conducted in 1968 in thirty-six "Comprehensive Children and Youth" Health projects, age proved to be related to the frequency of iron deficiency anemia (Maternal and Child Health Services, USDHEW, 1969; Hunter, 1960; Morgan, 1969; Adams and Scott, 1963; Burroughs and Huenemann, 1970; Fomon, 1970; Buest and Brown, 1957; Gutelius, 1969; Haughton, 1963; Lahey, 1957). As Table 5–1 indicates, the highest prevalence rate is found among children six months to two years. These age trends may be the result of using a uniform criterion of hemoglobin (10 g/100 ml or less) to designate anemia. Even if the criterion is raised (11 g/100 ml for the first two years of life, 12 g/100 ml to age six, and 12–13 g/100 ml for adolescents), little decrease in the incidence of iron-deficiency anemia is observed in high-risk populations (Kessner and Kalk, 1973).

The Ten State Nutritional Survey provides probably the most extensive data on the prevalence of anemia in families with low income

Table 5-1. Percentage of Children with Hemoglobin Concentrations 10 g/100 ml or Less *(1968 Children and Youth Survey)*

Age (years)	No. of Children	Percent with Hb concentration 10 g/100 ml or less
0 to 6 months	1722	13.6
6 months to 1 year	1293	22.1
1-2	1813	28.5
2-3	1245	9.2
3-4	1045	3.2
4-5	1107	2.4
5-13	4873	1.9

Source: Maternal and Child Health Service, Children and Youth Survey, 1968.

(Center for Disease Control, 1971). Hemoglobin levels were determined for 32,669 individuals (almost half of them under sixteen from low-income areas in ten states: Washington, California, Texas, Louisiana, South Carolina, Kentucky, West Virginia, Michigan, Massachusetts, and New York. In children under two, between 13 percent and 35 percent showed deficient hemoglobin rates. For those of ages two to five, between 2 and 11 percent had low hemoglobins. (The reason for the wide range will be evident in a later discussion.)

The relationship of iron-deficiency anemia to socioeconomic status is poorly understood. Available data indicate that the prevalence of anemia is inversely related to social class (Fomon, 1967 and 1970; Haughton, 1963; Center for Disease Control, 1971; Danneker, 1966; Hillman and Smith, 1968; Owen et al., 1969; Kripke and Saunders, 1970; Shaw and Robertson, 1964; Pollitt and Leibel, 1976). Nationally among black families there was a noticeable trend toward a higher mean hematocrit level with increasing family income, but this did not pertain in the white population (National Center for Health Statistics, *Mean Blood Hematocrit of Adults*, 1967; Pollitt and Leibel, 1976).

In a study on the nutritional status of preschool children ages one to six in Mississippi, Owen et al. (1969) established a significant relationship between the family's income level and anemia: 24 percent of the children in the lower-income group ($500 annual per capita income) but only 12 percent of children in families with higher incomes had hemoglobin values below 10 g/100 ml.

The Ten State Nutritional Survey employed the Poverty Index

Ratio (Orshansky Index) to separate those above and below the poverty level (Center for Disease Control, 1971). This index is based on income, family size, farm or nonfarm status, and sex and age of head of household. In every surveyed state as well as in New York City, those persons below the poverty level have a higher rate of deficient hemoglobin levels than those above the poverty level.

Hillman and Smith (1968) find low hemoglobin levels to be significantly more common in welfare families than in those not obtaining public assistance. Furthermore, this relationship persists when the data are controlled for ethnicity, as reported by Danneker (1966) in a study on hemoglobin levels for 342 children six months to three years old in Allegheny County, Pennsylvania. Within the black population, the prevalence rates for anemia are highest for those receiving public assistance. Only 19 percent of the total black sample are considered anemic (hemoglobin 10 g/100 ml or less), but 41.2 percent of the blacks receiving public assistance are found to have low hemoglobin concentrations.

Recombining the data according to a crude social class index based on occupation and education of the father, Danneker (1966) showed that the biggest difference is between the two lowest classes: 23.8 percent of black children in the lowest social class and only 7.5 percent of black children in the next lowest social class have low hemoglobins.

FUNCTIONAL IMPACT OF IRON-DEFICIENCY ANEMIA

Justification for the treatment of symptom-free iron-deficiency anemia depends upon evidence that failure to treat it has untoward consequences. Good evidence on this is scant but accumulating (Pollitt and Leibel, 1976). Webb and Oski (1973) showed that scholastic performance in anemic twelve-to-fourteen-year-olds is inferior to that of controls in the same school. Unfortunately, no data on socioeconomic status or nutritional status were reported, and no attempt was made to ascertain responsiveness of the subnormal performance to treatment of the anemia. Joynson and colleagues (1972) reported a defect in cell-mediated immunity in adults with iron deficiency. Unfortunately, the adequacy of the control group in this study is questionable. The complexity of the relationship between the iron-deficient state and resistance to infection is indicated by Weinberg (1974), who argues that low blood iron may provide a host advantage in resisting the invasion of microbes. Macdougall and colleagues

(1975) reported impaired immune responses in iron-deficient children; after treatment with iron, these responses returned to normal.

Although the relationship of deficiencies in immune response and susceptibility to infections was not examined in this study, the findings at least theoretically indicate increased susceptibility of children with untreated iron deficiency. Lanzkowsky's review (1974) indicates that correction of iron deficiency results in improved appetite in children, lessened irritability, and amelioration of pica (craving for unusual food). This last factor is of considerable importance in causing lead poisoning.

EFFICACY OF DIAGNOSTIC PROCEDURES
FOR IRON-DEFICIENCY ANEMIA

Definitions of iron-deficiency anemia have depended upon performance of either a peripheral blood hemoglobin or hematocrit or both. Hemoglobins under 10 grams per 100 milliliters of blood or hematocrits under 33 percent are invariably considered to indicate anemia. The World Health Organization (1968) and the American Academy of Pediatrics (Committee on Nutrition, 1969) recommend the use of a hemoglobin level of 11 or a hematocrit of 33 as an appropriate cut-off. Recent studies have confirmed the usefulness of these latter levels for both screening and diagnostic purposes under circumstances where nutritional iron deficiency is the most common anemia in childhood (as in the United States) (Haddy et al., 1974; Smith and Rios, 1974). Using the percent saturation of transferrin (determined by the ratio serum iron to total iron binding capacity) as the standard, it has been shown that virtually all children with hemoglobins under 11 grams per 100 milliliters or hematocrits under 33 have abnormally low saturation of transferrin. Thus, the specificity of the hemoglobin or hematocrit determinations is excellent.

Unfortunately, the sensitivity of these tests is considerably less. A large number of children with low transferrin saturations have normal hemoglobins and hematocrits, indicating that much subclinical iron deficiency is going undetected. In spite of this shortcoming, the high specificity of these widely used tests makes them valuable: studies using them as a basis for diagnosis are adequate for assessment of clinical efficacy of therapy and follow-up. This is in contrast to the situation with otitis media, where accuracy of current diagnostic techniques is still a major problem.

EFFICACY OF MANAGEMENT FOR
IRON-DEFICIENT STATES[a]

Stages of Deficiency and Indicators

Iron deficiency, if prolonged and of sufficient severity, may result in multiple systemic manifestations involving essentially all cell systems (Ross Conference, 1970). Progressive states of the disease process are characterized by aberrations in iron absorption, transportation, storage, and metabolism which reflect the basic underlying state of negative iron balance. Iron deficiency is relative in degree and kind and is not necessarily revealed by a classical hypochromic anemia (Witts, 1969).

The earliest stage of iron deficiency is characterized by a progressive decrease in the size of the body iron stores and increased iron absorption from the gut. The hemoglobin level may then start to fall and the red cell mass to contract. Plasma iron levels decline and iron-binding capacity rises, so that the percent saturation of transferrin (the principal iron-binding protein in the blood) falls below normal. In frank iron-deficiency anemia, the red cells are undersized and hypochromic (Charlton and Bothwell, 1970; Guest, 1947; Lahey, 1957). Their high level of free protoporphyrin indicates the lack of incorporation of iron into this hemoglobin precursor (Dagg et al., 1967).

The indicators most commonly used to detect iron-deficient states and to follow the response to treatment are: hemoglobin concentration, hematocrit (packed cell volume as a percent of total blood volume), cell appearance as seen by blood smear, and the computation of the three red cell indices: mean volume, mean hemoglobin, and mean hemoglobin concentration. These blood values are usually decreased in anemic states (Lahey, 1957). More sensitive indicators of the condition of body iron stores are: plasma iron and total iron-binding capacity, erythrocyte protoporphyrin, serum ferritin, and histological examination of aspirated bone marrow for stainable iron (Finch, 1969; Dagg et al., 1967; Siimes et al., 1974; Dagg and Goldberg, 1973; Beutler et al., 1958).

The blood picture in iron depletion, especially in early stages, is seen to depend on the degree of anemia, its speed of onset, its duration, and its etiology. Investigators have repeatedly documented that various tissue iron and iron enzyme deficiencies may also occur, sometimes despite apparently normal levels of iron in the circulating blood (Beutler, 1965; Takeda and Hara, 1955; Beutler and Blaisdell,

[a]The author is indebted to Rona Sayetta for her contributions to this section.

1958 and 1960; Dagg et al., 1966; and Jacobs, 1961). Reductions in the heme-containing protein myoglobin and the enzymes cytochrome c, cytochrome oxidase, catalase, peroxidase, isocitric dehydrogenase, succinic dehydrogenase, and the siccinic oxidase system have been demonstrated (Beutler, 1965; Jacobs, 1961, and Dagg et al., 1967; Beutler and Blaisdell III, 1958; and Healy et al, 1955; Mackiewicz et al., 1961). Disturbances in the tricarboxylic acid cycle and the respiratory chain may result, along with marked decreases in the activity of these and other mitochondrial enzyme systems which may incorporate ferrous ions in their structure or require them as cofactors (Beutler and Blaisdell, 1960, and Mackiewicz et al., 1961; Neerhout et al., 1958).

Increasing numbers of studies are being conducted to correlate various indicators of tissue-iron deficits with clinical symptoms or pathologic states other than anemia per se, such as: fatigue, listlessness, loss of appetite, decreased alertness (leading to learning problems in children); pica (which may lead to poisonings such as plumbism with its persistent neurological sequelae); impaired cardiorespiratory function during the performance of muscular work (leading, upon exertion, to palpitations, shortness of breath, and dizziness).[b] Researchers have often been unable to determine whether decreased body-iron levels are a cause or an effect of the conditions with which they are found to be associated.

Methodological difficulties may be involved not only in documenting subjective symptoms as indicators of iron deficiency, but also in performing the more routine blood studies. The hematocrit determination, for instance, may be somewhat unreliable as well as sometimes invalid as an indicator of body-iron stores (England et al., 1972). Similarly, many factors may influence the determination and interpretation of hemoglobin values, such as climatic and barometric conditions, the source of the blood specimens (i.e., capillary or venous); the standardization of the laboratory equipment; the age, race, and sex of the subject; and the onset of puberty. Furthermore, red cell indices may be inaccurate or misleading (Beutler, 1959).

One other measurement problem of particular significance has confounded the findings of nearly all studies devoted to examining plasma or serum iron levels. Most researchers have not taken into

[b]Beutler et al., 1960, and Lahey, 1957; for fatigue, anorexia, and pica. Sulzer, 1971, for learning problems; Blumgart and Altschule, 1948, and Andersen and Barkve, 1970, for impaired cardiorespiratory function during muscular work. Other studies relating iron deficits with states other than anemia are: Herrick, 1927; Pickering and Wayne, 1934; Witts, 1966; Beutler, Fairbanks, and Lahey, 1963; Hutton, 1956; Taymor et al., 1960 and 1964.

account the normal circadian rhythms of each experimental subject, whose wide fluctuations may equal in amplitude at least one-fourth to one-half of the average iron values (Bothwell and Finch, 1962). Plasma iron values appear highest in the morning hours and then decline throughout the day until early evening (Hamilton et al., 1950). The magnitude of the daily fall is directly proportional to the initial level of plasma iron (Paterson et al., 1953). About 8:00 or 9:00 P.M. the values start to rise again slowly toward the next morning's peak. Studies have usually not been controlled for the time of day that blood samples were drawn or the relationship of this hour to the subject's internal biological clock. Moreover, in patients with hematopoietic diseases such as iron-deficiency anemia, the circadian variation in plasma iron values may be reduced or even absent (Neerhout et al, 1958). Consequently, administering iron salts to deficient subjects may stimulate the return of their normal diurnal flux in a rebound effect such that, if plasma iron determinations are made in the mid-morning hours shortly after an oral iron supplement, the experimental group's hematologic response might look unusually good relative to that of the control subjects.

Historical and Experimental Evidence of Iron's Efficacy

Since ancient times, iron has been used in various medicinal preparations on the strength of superstitious and homeopathic beliefs about its restorative powers (Diamond, 1970; Beutler, Fairbanks, and Lahey, 1963; Hebbert, 1950; and Haden, 1938). By the nineteenth century, practitioners such as Dr. Pierre Blaud recognized the clinical value of iron pills for the treatment of chlorosis (the common female iron-deficiency syndrome of that era) (Blaud, 1832). Their observations, however, were not based upon double-blind controlled clinical trials.

Controlled studies dealing with the general clinical efficacy of iron treatment for deficiency states and the prevention of anemia have been conducted in many countries, but deliberate replication of the work of other investigators was seldom carried out because the worldwide dissemination and translation of foreign-language journal articles appears to have been limited. Consequently, duplication of findings was the rule, and few studies contributed new knowledge. The carefully done research studies cited below laid the present firm foundation for oral iron prophylaxis and therapy in pediatric practice.

MacKay (1931). Infants treated with ferric iron and ammonium citrate in their formulas and, later, supplementally had significantly higher average hemoglobin percentages from three months of age onward than did a similar group of untreated infants. Iron treatment not only prevented anemia in the experimental group and cured it in the control group, but also raised treated infants' resistance to infection and considerably improved their rate of growth. It remains unknown whether poor weight gain in iron-deficiency anemia is a direct result of the condition itself or is secondary to the anorexia that frequently accompanies it (Judisch et al., 1966).

Usher, MacDermot, and Lozinski (1935). Infants receiving from 1 1/2 to 3 grains (96 to 190 mg) of metallic iron daily in the form of ferric glycerophosphate showed, at the age of one year, an average hemoglobin value 15 percent higher than that of the control group not receiving supplementation.

Reedy, Schwartz, and Plattner (1952). Premature infants were divided into two experimental groups receiving a commercial iron preparation (a mixture of ferric iron and ammonium citrate, liver concentrate, and copper sulfate amounting to 66 mg of elemental iron per ounce) from the seventh day of life to the ages of three months in one experimental group and to two years in the other. There was also an untreated control group. An unequivocal superiority in hemoglobin concentration and weight gain was demonstrated by all infants receiving iron. The trend in hemoglobin concentration was downward in those whose medication was discontinued after three months, whereas it continued upward in those whose oral iron salt supplementation was maintained.

Sturgeon (1956). Oral iron therapy in the form of ferrous sulfate solution (Fer-in-Sol) was given to infants for six to ten weeks in three doses per day totaling 500 mg (90 mg of elemental iron). At the end of therapy, a significantly greater (0.6 g/100 ml) concentration of hemoglobin was found in the treated group than in the age-matched control group.

Marsh, Long, and Stierwalt (1959). Infants fed supplemental iron in their milk formulas (12 mg ferrous sulfate per quart) had, after three to three and a half months of age, significantly higher values for hemoglobin, hematocrit, and serum iron during the remainder of their first year of life. Of those infants in the control groups who did not receive iron supplementation, those developing anemia responded quickly when changed to the iron-fortified formula.

Gorten and Cross (1964). Premature infants were the sole subjects in both the study group and the control group, which were fed Similac with and without iron, respectively. This study served to replicate and confirm the findings of the Marsh, Long, and Stierwalt study and similar ones.

Andelman and Sered (1966). An iron-containing milk formula (Similac with 2 mg of ferrous sulfate per quart) was fed to a large group of infants for six to nine months, and an unsupplemented formula was fed to a control group. Differences between the two groups in mean hemoglobin concentration, mean hematocrit percentage, mean serum iron, and estimated total body iron were statistically significant in the expected direction at and after the initial nine-to-twelve-week period of life. By one year of age, 76 percent of the control group had developed hematologic evidence of iron-deficiency anemia and were withdrawn from the study, in contrast to 9 percent of the study group. (More than half of the 9 percent did not become anemic until six to twelve months after they had stopped receiving the iron-containing formula.)

Naiman, Oski, Diamond, Vawter, and Schwachman (1964). Fourteen infants and children with nutritional iron-deficiency anemia and an associated high incidence of chronic duodenitis and mucosal atrophy (as determined by duodenal biopsy) were treated with oral ferrous sulfate and ascorbic acid (in an amount equivalent to approximately 50 mg of elemental iron) given three times daily. Milk intake was concomitantly reduced to about one pint daily (Wilson et al., 1964). The expected hematopoietic response to therapy occurred and was measured as mean daily increments of hemoglobin. The untreated control group consisted of eight children with longstanding anemias not due to iron deficiency, in whom no gastrointestinal tract abnormalities were found when biopsied. In most of the iron-deficient patients, gastrointestinal abnormalities were reversed by iron therapy.

Research to elucidate the mechanisms of iron metabolism began early in the twentieth century with the advent of a new quantitative approach (Witts, 1969). Large experimental errors sometimes tended to obscure the findings. Nevertheless, a few meticulous studies of hemoglobin regeneration after repeated phlebotomies and of oral iron intake-excretion balance succeeded in relating hemoglobin formation rates in hypochromic anemic subjects to iron consumption (Whipple and Robscheit-Robbins, 1925; Reimann et al., 1936). By administering an iron salt parenterally rather than orally (to eliminate some of the variables associated with iron absorption and transport), a close linear relationship was established between the amount of iron given and the amount gained in the circulating hemoglobin (Heath et al., 1932). Not until the development of radioactive isotope tracer techniques in the late 1930s was it possible to demonstrate unequivocally that the identical chemical species administered orally as a test dose of an inorganic iron salt was ultimately incorporated into hemoglobin molecules in circulating red blood cells (Diamond, 1970; Hahn et al., 1940; Moore et al., 1944; Pollycove and Mortimer, 1961; and Brise and Hallberg, 1962a). Since most of the experiments conducted prior to World War II relied on hemoglobin as the principal measure of response to iron therapy, and since erythropoiesis is known to be affected by numerous variables (Brise and Hallberg, 1962b), the clear-cut results obtained in some of the early metabolic studies are quite remarkable.

Treatment

Therapies for iron-deficient states involve some methods of iron repletion coupled with measures to prevent any pathological interference with the maintenance of normal hemoglobin levels (Kessner and Kalk, 1973). Loss of hemoglobin iron can be managed by diet and by treatment for the underlying pathology (e.g., intestinal parasites, ulcer, infection with fever, carcinoma, menorrhagia, hereditary hemorrhagic atelangiectasia). Iron intake may be increased through a program of dietary management or by the administration of supplemental iron. In selected severely anemic patients where the time factor is critical, blood transfusions may become the treatment of choice (Jacobs, 1960).

Diet Therapy.   Liver is one of the richest sources of dietary iron.[c] Red meats also contain an abundance, while eggs, vegetables, and certain other food substances contribute to a positive iron balance. Because cow's milk has a relatively low iron content, a limitation of children's milk intake to one pint per day (with adequate total calories) has been recommended. The restriction should begin gradually during infancy along with the introduction of semisolid foods.

   Calculation of the estimated iron needs of rapidly growing infants and children reveals that, even with a good dietary iron intake, there will be times when hematopoiesis will require drawing upon the iron

[c]Specific foods in relation to iron-deficiency anemia are discussed in: (liver and red meats) Heath and Patek, 1937; and (cow's milk) Heath and Patek, 1937; Hallberg et al., 1970; O'Connor, 1967; and Kessner and Kalk, 1973.

revenues of the body (Sturgeon, 1956). If these stores are inadequate for any reason such as poor iron intake during the mother's pregnancy, multiparity, infant prematurity, twinning, clamping of the umbilical cord before pulsations cease (preventing a small but physiologically important transfusion therefrom), or excessive consumption of unfortified milk to the exclusion of a normal mixed diet or blood loss, iron-deficient states may develop. "Available evidence . . . suggests that though physicians should continue to recommend a 'good' diet, they should not depend solely on it for the prevention and cure of iron-deficiency anemia in children."[d]

Gastrointestinal Symptoms. In some infants gastroenteropathy has been described which is induced by whole cow's milk, provokes enteric blood loss, and is not responsive to iron treatment (Hoag et al., 1961). This syndrome causes an iron loss substantially in excess of the amount expected from mucosal cell exfoliation (Conrad et al., 1964). Bovine serum albumin and perhaps other proteins in homogenized milk that has not been heat-treated appear to be responsible for the bleeding (Ross Conference, 1970). An allergic mechanism has been postulated, since these proteins appear to have antigenic properties, antigen-antibody precipitations being demonstrable in the blood (Wilson et al., 1964; Waldman et al., 1967). The integrity of the gastrointestinal tract lining is compromised, permitting foreign protein leakage into the circulation and blood loss from the gut. When affected infants are switched to soy milk formulas, this condition rapidly reverts to normal except for the necessary iron repletion (Ross Conference, 1970).

Iron Supplements During Lactation. The effect on the breast-fed infant or iron supplementation for the mother was examined in a controlled study and found to be "wholly negative" (MacKay, 1931). Similarly, an experiment on lactating animals failed to show augmentation of the mineral content of their milk after ingestion of supplemental iron (Elvehjem et al., 1927). It would seem, then, that iron supplementation for the nursing mother is not an effective way to build up or replenish the baby's iron stores.

Iron-Enriched Baby Foods. These have been marketed in an efort to overcome widespread problems of iron nutrition, and commer-

---

[d]Reasons for inadequate stores of iron in the body are discussed by: Heath and Patek, 1937; Witts, 1969; Usher et al., 1963; O'Connor, 1967; Hallberg et al., 1970; Lahey, 1957. The quote is from Lahey.

cial heat-treated cow's milk formulas and infant cereals have been fortified with iron. Fortified milk formulas have yielded a distinctly superior hemoglobin response relative to control infants receiving unfortified cow's milk. Baby cereals containing iron salts have proved ineffective as a dietary iron supplement. Only about 10 percent of the added iron is absorbed from these two foods, owing perhaps in part to the binding of iron ions with the oxalates, phosphates, and particularly phytates present in significant concentrations either in these foods or in other foods consumed at the same meal. An additional problem is that consumption of milk and cereal may be variable and short term because mothers often change their infants early to whole-milk feeding and family-type cereals as a matter of convenience (Ross Conference, 1970; Hallberg et al., 1970; Schulz and Smith, 1958; Crosby, 1968; Hegsted et al., 1949; Peters et al., 1971; McCance et al., 1943; Sharpe et al., 1950).

Supplementary Iron Therapy: Oral. The preferred route of iron administration is oral rather than parenteral (Smith, R.S., 1965; Witts, 1969; Cope et al., 1956; McCurdy, 1965; Coleman et al., 1955; Lahey, 1957; Wallerstein and Mettier, 1958; Dagg and Goldberg, 1973; Sitarz et al., 1959; Hallberg et al., 1970; Stockman, 1893; Marchasin and Wallerstein, 1964; Goldthorp et al., 1965). Under certain circumstances, it may be desirable to use both routes of administration sequentially, either by initiating or terminating oral therapy with a short course of parenteral iron. Oral and parenteral iron should not be given simultaneously, however, as excessive free iron in the plasma may produce toxic effects. The rectal route of administration and absorption (whose efficacy has been demonstrated experimentally in dogs) has not been pursued in humans, probably because of the general ease and success of oral therapy.

Parenteral iron therapy is indicated:

1. when the patient is completely unable to tolerate any kind of oral iron;
2. when chronic or recurrent blood loss prevents the correction of anemia and replenishment of iron stores by oral iron alone;
3. when a malabsorption problem or syndrome is so great that it prevents the correction of anemia by oral therapy; and
4. when negligence or lack of cooperation is expected to interfere with prolonged oral iron.

Although the first administration of parenteral iron was by subcutaneous injection, the two routes by which it is given today are intramuscular and intravenous (Witts, 1969; Hammond and Murphy, 1960; Dallman et al., 1967; Hallberg et al., 1970; Coleman et al., 1955; Pritchard, 1966; McCurdy, 1965). One drawback of parenteral therapy compared to oral is that its course usually involves repeated injections, although good results from a total-dose-infusion technique (i.e., a single venipuncture) have been reported. Both parenteral routes of administration have also been associated with side effects, severe toxic reactions, and occasional fatalities, the risk of systemic reactions being greater with intravenous injections than with intramuscular.

While the clinical efficacy of iron administration is well established, evidence is scanty regarding the differential efficacy of the various routes of administration. No significant differences in the average hemoglobin response rate to oral versus intramuscular iron therapy have been found. Due to variability in the absorption of oral ferrous sulfate, however, the parenteral preparations do appear to result in a more nearly uniform daily hematologic response, though not necessarily a more rapid one. A comparison of the rate of hemoglobin response between identical twins showed essentially no differences between oral and intravenous iron treatment, although a moderate increase over the rate of response with adequate quantities of oral iron may be brought about by total-dose-infusion. In another clinical study, pregnant patients received either (1) oral ferrous sulfate, (2) intramuscular iron-dextran, or (3) intravenous iron-dextran given in a total-dose infusion. The following results were observed.

	Daily Hb increases *(g/100 ml)*
Oral	0.25
Intramuscular	0.28
Intravenous	0.33

It has been demonstrated repeatedly and unequivocally that human beings absorb bivalent iron salts better than trivalent ones from the stomach and intestinal tract (Vahlquist et al., 1945; Lottrup, 1934; Witts, 1936; Smith, C.H., 1938; Moore et al., 1939; Niccum et al., 1953; Brise and Hallberg, 1962b; Smith, R.S., 1965; Meyers, et al., 1974; Swan and Jowett, 1959). Of the bivalent salts commercially available today, the standard drug used in oral therapy is ferrous sulfate. Ferrous sulfate in tablet form seems to be absorbed at least as well as any other ferrous salt (e.g., the gluconate, fumarate, succinate) and is also the cheapest.

Ferrous sulfate appears to be less well absorbed than ferrous succinate when given in 30 mg solution to the same subjects; however, a statistically significant difference in absorbability of iron from their respective tablet forms was not detected in one study (Table 5-2).

Some published studies have addressed the incidence of side effects and dose intolerance due to oral iron salt therapy (Table 5-3). Only two of the studies included the administration of placebo medication (Kerr and Davidson, 1958; Hallberg et al., 1966b). When the subjects in the former study were informed that they were being given a "control pill," the frequency of side effects was related to whether they were told that the pill was a "known" or an "unknown." The other study concluded that different ferrous compounds have the same incidence and type of side effects when the same amount of elemental iron is administered and that these differ significantly from the effects of placebo administration. The data make it improbable that there are simple iron salts better tolerated than ferrous sulfate.

Efforts to alleviate the incidence of side effects from ferrous salts have taken three approaches: slow-release preparations, the use of iron chelates, and the addition of absorption-enhancing substances. Comparative clinical trials of slow-release versus conventional iron tablets have indicated extremely variable absorption of the former and only minor differences in side effects between the tablets (Crosland-Taylor et al., 1965; Elwood and Williams, 1970; and Ross, J.D.,

Table 5-2. Relative Absorbability of Different 30 mg Ferrous Salt Solutions and Tablets

Ferrous Salt	Absorption Ratio (compound: reference standard)	
	Solution	Tablet
Sulfate (reference standard)	1.00	1.00
Succinate	1.23	0.93
Lactate	1.06	—
Fumarate	1.01	—
Glycine sulfate	1.01	0.97
Glutamate	0.97	—
Gluconate	0.89	0.84
Carbonate[a]	—	0.87
Citrate	0.74	—
Tartate	0.62	—
Pyrophosphate	0.59	—

Sources: Brise and Hallberg, 1962b;   [a] Hallberg, Harwerth, and Vannotti, 1970.

Table 5–3. Tolerance of Oral Iron Tablets in Different Studies by Ferrous Salt and Dosage Tested

Ferrous Salt Tablet Tested	Daily Dosage		Initial no. of subjects	Final no. of respondents	Drug Tolerance	
	No. of tablets per dose × no. of doses per day	Mg of elemental iron per dose × no. of doses per day			Percent respondents with side effects	Percent respondents who discontinued therapy
1. Sulfate						
Kerr and Davidson (1958)	1 × 3	35 × 3	103	93	24.7	0.0
Hallberg, Ryttinger, and Sölvell (1966)	2 × 3	37 × 3	318	286	24.8	8.7
Hallberg, Ryttinger, and Sölvell (1966)	1 × 3	60 × 3	195	170	26.5	8.8
Holmes (1957)	1 × 3	67 × 3	50	50	44.0	0.0
O'Sullivan, Higgins, and Wilkins (1955)	1 × 3	70 × 3	20	20	N.G.	15.0[a]
Beutler and Larsh (1962)	1 × 3	80.44 × 3	37	37	35.1	0.0
Hallberg, Harwerth, and Vannotti (1970)	1 × 2	100 × 2	N.G.	261	31.4	N.G.
2. Gluconate						
Kerr and Davidson (1958)	1 × 3	35 × 3	103	93	21.5	0.0
Berk and Novich (1962)	1 × 3	36 × 3	N.G.	10	40.0	0.0
Hallberg, Ryttinger, and Sölvell (1966)	2 × 3	37 × 3	120	111	31.5	5.4
Gennison (1958)	1 × 3	49 × 3	20	20	10.0	10.0
Hallberg, Ryttinger, and Sölvell (1966)	1 × 3	60 × 3	196	178	27.0	7.3
O'Sullivan, Higgins, and Wilkins (1955)	1 × 3	70 × 3	20	20	N.G.	5.0[a]

(Table 5–3. continued overleaf)

Table 5-3. continued

Ferrous Salt Tablet Tested	Daily Dosage		Initial no. of subjects	Final no. of respondents	Drug Tolerance	
	No. of tablets per dose × no. of doses per day	Mg of elemental iron per dose × no. of doses per day			Percent respondents with side effects	Percent respondents who discontinued therapy
3. *Fumarate*						
Hallberg, Ryttinger, and Sölvell (1966)	2 × 3	37 × 3	118	110	26.4	5.5
Berk and Novich (1962)	1 × 3	40 × 3	N.G.	12	25.0	0.0
Hallberg, Harwerth, and Vannotti (1970)	1 × 2	200 × 2	N.G.	246	29.7	N.G.
Swan and Jowett (1959)	1 × 3	200 × 3	64	64	12.5	1.6
Berenbaum et al. (1960)	1 × 3	200 × 3	22	22	0.0	0.0
4. *Succinate*						
Kerr and Davidson (1958)	1 × 3	35 × 3	103	93	22.6	2.2
O'Sullivan, Higgins, and Wilkins (1955)	1 × 3	70 × 3	20	20	N.G.	5.0[a]
5. *Glycine sulfate*						
Hallberg, Ryttinger, and Sölvell (1966)	1 × 3	60 × 3	200	180	24.4	7.8
Beutler and Larsh (1962)	1 × 3	74.24 × 3	39	39	43.6	5.1
6. *Carbonate*						
Hallberg, Harwerth, and Vannotti (1970)	1 × 2	100 × 2	N.G.	242	31.4	N.G.
7. *Aminoacetosulfate*						
Gennison (1958)	1 × 3	53 × 3	20	20	15.0	0.0

8. *Calcium citrate*					
Holmes (1957)	2 × 3	25 × 3	50	50	0.0	0.0
Kerr and Davidson (1958)	2 × 3	35 × 3	103	93	20.4	5.4
9. *Placebo*					
Kerr and Davidson (1958)					
"unknown" control pill	1 × 3	0 × 3	103	93	21.5	0.0
"known" control pill	1 × 3	0 × 3	103	93	2.2	0.0
Hallberg, Ryttinger, and Sölvell (1966)					
double-blind control	2 × 3	0 × 3	314	284	13.7	2.8
double-blind control	1 × 3	0 × 3	200	177	12.4	1.1
Hallberg, Harwerth, and Vannotti (1970)					
double-blind control	1 × 2	0 × 2	N.G.	241	14.9	N.G.

N.G. = not given.

[a]These subjects were then switched to a different iron compound, which they tolerated.

1963). Likewise, iron chelates may be less well absorbed (perhaps even therapeutically ineffective) and no better tolerated than simple salts (Ross, J.D., 1963). Fat-soluble lipid compounds of iron, ferrocenes, are also characterized by variable absorption and potential toxicity.

Since the absorbability of iron is the main factor determining its therapeutic value, various substances have been combined with ferrous sulfate and tested for their efficacy and side effects (Tables 5–4 and 5–5). Most additives, including the surface-active agents and inorganic salts tested, were found to have no effect on iron absorption. The principal absorption-promoting substances are the carbohydrates mannitol, sorbitol, and xylose, ascorbic acid (vitamin C) and succinic acid or monosodium succinate (Brise and Hallberg, 1962b; Hallberg et al., 1966b; Hallberg and Solvell, 1966; Israels and Cook, 1965).

Assessment of the clinical value of absorption-promoting additives has led to the following conclusions:

1. The administration of carbohydrates in amounts of 4 grams or more markedly increased iron absorption by a mechanism that appears to be related to increased intestinal motility. Consequently, these carbohydrates regularly provoke pronounced side effects of epigastric discomfort, markedly increased bowel movements, and loose stools (Hallberg et al., 1966a).

2. Ascorbic acid seems to function as a reducing agent (i.e., keeping ferrous irons in the reduced state to promote their absorption).

Table 5–4. Effect of Different Additives on Iron Absorption from a 25 ml Solution of Orally Administered Ferrous Sulfate Containing 30 mg of Elemental Iron

Additive	No. of Subjects	Absorption Ratio With/Without the Additive (Mean Value)
1. Surface-active agents[a]		
Polyoxyethylene sorbitan monolaureate (Tween 20)—400 mg	4	1.04
Dioctylosoliumsulfosuccinate (Aerosol–OT)—150 mg	6	1.07
Sodium laurylsulphate—200 mg	4	1.07
Bile acids (cholic acid—146 mg and dehydrocholic acid—37 mg)	4	1.03

Table 5–4. continued

Additive	No. of Subjects	Absorption Ratio With/Without the Additive (Mean Value)
2. Inorganic salts[b]		
Calcium chloride—21.4 mg elemental calcium	4	0.94
Copper sulfate—5 mg elemental copper	4	0.97
Sodium molybdate—0.5 mg elemental molybdenum	4	1.05
3. Carbohydrates[b]		
Mannitol—4 g	4	1.74
Sornitol—4 g	4	1.41
Xylose—4 g	4	1.32
Inositol—4 g	3	1.05
Sucrose—4 g	4	1.02
Fructose—4 g	4	1.03
Lactose—4 g	4	0.85
4. Vitamins		
Ascorbic acid—200 mg[c]	13	1.33
Thiamine hydrochloride—2 mg[b]	5	0.98
Sodium riboflavin–5–phosphate—2.74 mg[b]	5	1.07
5. Amino acids[b]		
1–Cysteine hydrochloride—1 mmole	4	1.15
1–Arginine hydrochloride—1 mmole	4	0.91
6. Other organic acids[d]		
Succinic acid—150 mg	12	1.52
L–Ketoglutaric acid—146 mg	5	1.11
Fumaric acid—116 mg	11	1.08
1–Malic acid—134 mg	3	0.89
d–Malic acid—134 mg	3	0.88
dl–Isocitric acid—192 mg	3	0.87
Oxaloacetic acid—132 mg	5	0.89
Citric acid—192 mg	5	0.62

Sources: [a]Brise, 1962a; [b]Hallberg, Sölvell, and Brise, 1966; [c]Brise and Hallberg, 1962c; [d]Brise and Hallberg, 1962d.

Table 5–5.   Tolerance of Absorption-Promoting Additives to Ferrous Iron Tablets

Iron Compound	Dosage Taken Three Times Per Day		Number of Subjects	Number of Respondents	Tolerance	
	No. of Tablets	Mg of Elemental Iron			Percent Respondents With Side Effects	Percent Respondents Who Discontinued Therapy
Series A[a]						
Ferrous sulfate	2	60	30	30	20.0	0.0
Ferrous sulfate and 200 mg ascorbic acid	2	60	30	30	33.3	0.0
Series B[b]						
Ferrous sulfate	2	74	197	172	27.9	9.3
Ferrous sulfate and 185 mg succinic acid	2	74	200	179	29.6	8.4
Series C[b]						
Ferrous succinate and 185 mg succinic acid	2	74	318	292	21.9	5.1
Ferrous succinate and monosodium succinate corresponding to 185 mg succinic acid	2	74	120	114	28.0	7.9

Sources: [a]Hallberg, Sölvell, and Brise, 1966;   [b]Hallberg and Sölvell, 1966.

Its enhancement of iron absorption, however, appears to be no greater than when succinic acid is used as the sole absorption-promoting additive (Brise, 1962a; Brise and Hallberg, 1962c; Hallberg et al., 1966a). Ascorbic acid also provokes a significant increase in the incidence of side effects. Thirty percent of the subjects who took iron tablets containing ascorbic acid in one controlled clinical trial (a double-blind crossover study) had epigastric pains afterward, but only 3.3 percent experienced this side effect after taking plain ferrous sulfate tablets.

3. The addition of succinic acid to ferrous salts in a 5:1 ratio results in a consistent increase in iron absorption of about 30 percent more than from plain iron tablets. This absorption-promoting effect is obtained regardless of the iron salt used (i.e., the sulfate or the succinate), the iron dosage employed, or whether the form of the additive is succinic acid or monosodium succinate. Its mechanism of action appears to be a direct stimulation of ferrous ion transfer across the mucosal cell barrier. The addition of succinic acid or monosodium succinate causes no increase in the frequency of side effects nor changes their type. Succinic acid has no known toxic properties. Its clinical value, therefore, has been established for shortening the total course of oral therapy necessary to restore body iron (Hallberg and Solvell, 1966; Hallberg et al., 1966a; Israels and Cook, 1965; Brise and Hallberg, 1962c; Hallberg et al., 1971).

Iron in combination with vitamin and mineral elements has not proved superior to iron given alone unless multiple deficiency conditions are known to be present (I. Jacobs, 1960; Witts, 1969; Callender in Jacobs and Worwood, 1974; Lahey, 1957; Wallerstein and Mettier, 1958). It is generally considered inadvisable to administer compound hematinic formulations, except iron combined with folate for women during pregnancy. In some such preparations, moreover, the amount of elemental iron may be inadequate and the mechanism of action of certain other constituents (e.g., cobalt) is not understood and may even represent an effect of metal toxicity. Although copper, in particular, is essential for blood formation, iron supplements usually contain it as an impurity. Pediatric iron preparations in the form of sugar-containing syrups or elixirs rather than plain solutions or tablets should also be avoided because of possible adverse effects of their acids on children's teeth.

Since iron supply is partially a function of iron absorption, the effect of ferrous salt dosage on iron absorption becomes a clinical matter of concern. Experimental evidence indicates that the optimal iron requirement in the human varies between 0.3−0.8 mg per kg of body weight per day.[e] Sufficient iron should be given to ensure the absorption of at least these quantities. Iron absorption is known to vary inversely with the state of body-iron stores and length of treatment, to vary widely between individuals, and to fluctuate within the same person at different times. Assuming an average absorption of 10 to 15 percent of the supplemental iron intake, a minimal effective dose of 4 mg of elemental iron per kg of body weight per day has been suggested and a dosage up to 5 mg per kg per day may be needed to achieve an optimal erythropoietic response.

For prophylaxis in infants and young children, 5 mg per day of concentrated ferrous sulfate solution has been recommended for the period from three to six months of age and 10 mg per day from six months to one year old. For therapy in children up to age three, a dose that furnishes 60 to 70 mg of elemental iron per day is considered satisfactory. The usual therapeutic dose for children ages three to six is 110 mg of elemental iron daily, after which time a full adult dose of 150−200 mg per day may be given. The upper dose for anemic older children and adults treated in clinical practice is considered to be in the range of 200−300 mg of elemental iron daily, although some patients may tolerate 400−500 mg. of iron daily if a more rapid response is desirable.

The usual approach to selection of an iron salt for oral therapy is to try ferrous sulfate first (60 mg of elemental iron per tablet). If bothersome side effects occur, changing salts to the gluconate or succinate (both containing 35 mg of iron per tablet) or ferrous fumarate (65 mg) should be tried. The succinate, although better absorbed, is more expensive. Another approach to improving iron tolerance is to decrease temporarily the number of tablets taken per day or, better yet, to increase initial low doses to full strength gradually over a period ranging from two or three days to as much as two weeks.

The total daily dosage of iron is usually divided into separate doses not only to minimize the incidence of side effects, but also to facilitate absorption (an inverse relationship having been demonstrated between the size of each dose of iron given and the percentage utilized for hemoglobin formation). Although the thrice-daily administration of oral iron is most commonly prescribed, it has been found that a fourth dose taken at bedtime significantly enhances total daily

[e]For dosage, see: Norrby, 1974; Hallberg et al., 1970; Brise and Hallberg, 1962a; Josephs, 1953; Smith, R.S., 1965. For prophylactic dosage in young children, refer to: Callender, in Jacobs and Worwood, 1974; Lahey, 1957; Wallerstein and Mettier, 1958; Hallberg and Solvell, 1966; Witts, 1969; Woodruff, 1969; Hallberg et al., 1970; MacKay, 1931.

iron absorption by an average increase of 60 percent.[f] The effect of administering iron only twice a day, before breakfast and at bedtime (to avoid inhibitory effect of food), has not been studied systematically to determine the feasibility of reducing the customary total dosage and the incidence of side effects with this therapeutic regimen.

Some apparent contradictions in the research literature concern dose scheduling in relation to meals. It has been established that certain foods (e.g., milk, eggs, and bread) tend to inhibit iron absorption through the formation of insoluble iron complexes, whereas orange juice promotes it by helping to keep the iron in a reduced, soluble state. In a controlled clinical study of dose scheduling in relation to food intake, an average of 40 percent less iron was absorbed from a 30 mg dose of ferrous sulfate when given with standardized test meals than when given between them. In another study, subjects who took food just prior to or immediately following the ingestion of iron salts frequently had a smaller rise in serum iron than under fasting conditions. Although much greater absorption of iron tablets occurs if taken in the fasting rather than the postprandial state, the relative difference in absorption of and clinical response to therapeutic doses taken with and without food is not striking in deficient patients who are avid for iron. Taking the tablets immediately after full meals is usually advised to serve as a good reminder to the patient and to reduce the incidence and severity of side effects.

The length of treatment in the absence of continuing blood loss should be at least three months, including a continuation for two months after the hemoglobin concentration has returned to normal levels (Lahey, 1957; Woodruff, 1969; Wallerstein and Mettier, 1958; and Coleman et al., 1955). Once the anemia has been corrected, many additional months of therapy are required to reconstitute tissue iron stores because of a mucosal impediment to iron absorption in excess of the body's current needs. Short-term oral therapy should be regarded, therefore, merely as partial replacement; the patient may still be vulnerable to future anemic episodes.

Supplementary Iron Therapy: Parenteral. The early preparations for parenteral iron administration were chemically unstable colloidal solutions (e.g., saccharated iron oxide) which were injected intravenously. These have been replaced by iron-dextran complex (colloidal ferric hydroxide combined with dextran—Imferon) and iron-sorbitex

[f]The following workers discuss timing of dosage: Schulz and Smith, 1958; Chodos et al., 1957; Callender and Warner, 1968; Steinkamp et al., 1955; Crosby, 1968; Hallberg et al., 1970; Brise, 1962b; Moore et al., 1939; Coleman et al., 1955; Callender in Jacobs and Worwood, 1974; Kerr and Davidson, 1958.

(iron-sorbitol-citric acid complex—Jectofer) for intramuscular use and by iron-dextrin (e.g., Astrafer) and, later, Imferon for the intravenous administration of iron. Imferon given intramuscularly probably still enjoyed the widest use in parenteral iron therapy as of 1970. Another compound that may be suitable for parenteral therapy in children is iron polyisomaltosate, although it has not been investigated thoroughly.

The intramuscular administration and utilization of iron-dextran and iron-sorbitex has been studied (Nissim, 1947; Baird and Podmore, 1954; Scott and Govan, 1954; Lindvall and Andersson, 1961; Fielding, 1961; Wallerstein, 1968; Hallberg et al., 1970; Mereu and Tonz, 1962; McCurdy, 1965). In one comparative study, daily doses of 250—500 mg of iron-dextran and 200 mg of iron-sorbitex were given to ten and nine patients, respectively, until a total dosage of 2500—3000 mg (depending on the initial hematocrit reading) was provided. The daily increase in hematocrit value was slightly greater, on the average, and more nearly constant for the patients receiving iron-sorbitex, but these differences were not statistically significant. Clinical improvement and the incidence of side effects from both preparations were also comparable. Differences have been found, however, in the way Imferon and Jectofer are metabolized in the body. Iron-dextran is absorbed much more slowly and by somewhat different mechanisms from the injection site than is iron-sorbitex. Iron-dextran also has a greater tendency to accumulate in the reticulo-endothelial organs before proceeding to the bone marrow for erythropoiesis, whereas iron-sorbitex is excreted much faster from the body (in the urine and saliva) (Smith, R.S., 1965; Hallberg et al., 1970; Dagg and Goldberg in Callender, 1973).

Differences in the metabolism of intramuscularly injected Imferon and Jectofer are probably largely responsible for observed differences in the nature of their side effects (Dagg and Goldberg in Callender, 1973; Scott, 1963; Hallberg et al., 1970; Bonnar, 1965; Wallerstein, 1968). Because of the possible induction of sarcomas at the site of Imferon injections, this preparation should be avoided in patients with a normal life expectancy. Contraindications to Jectofer include: (1) possible exacerbation of pyelonephritis or other urinary tract infections in patients prone to or unable to withstand such conditions, and (2) probable systemic reactions in folate-deficient pregnant women.

Intravenous administration may be indicated when the patient requires parenteral iron but has a small muscle mass or an abnormality of hemostasis. Intravenous therapy is contraindicated if the patient is prone to developing thrombophlebitis or if there is a special need to keep veins intact for chemotherapy. Iron-dextran and Imferon are both cleared from circulating blood rapidly and are handled initially by the reticulo-endothelial system. Imferon may also be given in a total-dose infusion when repeated injections are undesirable or impractical, unless the patient has an allergic diathesis.

Side effects from all types of parenteral iron therapy given as recommended here are reported to occur in from 1 to 2 percent of the patients receiving it. Their nature and incidence may vary somewhat with dosage, dilution technique, speed of administration, and general physical condition of the patient.

Transfusion Therapy. This type of treatment may be desirable when iron-deficiency anemia (as indicated by a very low hemoglobin level) is associated with the complications of infection or congestive heart failure (Jacobs, I., 1960; Witts, 1969; Meyers et al., 1974; Wallerstein and Mettier, 1958). Additionally, blood transfusion may be considered when emergency surgery is necessary. Contraindications to transfusion include: the risk of circulation overload (causing pulmonary edema and congestive failure), subsequent temporary bone marrow depression or blocking of erythropoiesis, and the discomfort and expense of the procedure. Since it is difficult to cross-match properly the blood of severely anemic patients, there may also be transfusion reactions. Sepsis, homologous serum hepatitis, sensitization reactions, and hemochromatosis may follow multiple transfusions.

EFFECTIVENESS OF MEDICAL CARE FOR IRON-DEFICIENCY ANEMIA

Iron-deficiency anemia proves to be one of the most common hematologic symptoms in childhood. It is the subject of a vast number of studies, as the many references in this chapter attest. However, there is a significant lack of recognition by the medical care system.

Problem Recognition

In a study carried out by Starfield and Scheff, children attending either of two university hospital clinics and having newly discovered low hemoglobin values within a three-month period were identified (Starfield and Scheff, 1972).

Figure 5-1 shows that in twenty-four of fifty-three children (45 percent) laboratory results indicating low hemoglobin were not recognized. Where a hemoglobin check had been ordered because of the presence of a symptom, or because the child had had a history of

Figure 5–1.   Recognition of Low Values in Hemoglobin Determinations Done for Various Reasons

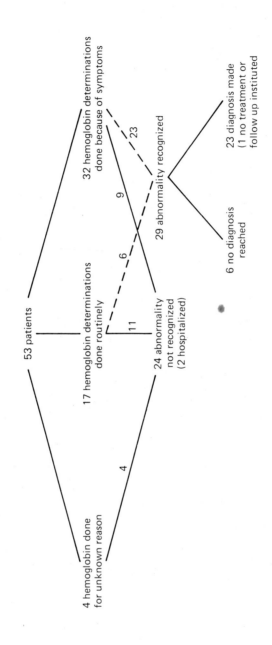

Source: Starfield and Scheff, 1972. Reprinted with permission.

anemia in the past, twenty-three of thirty-two (72 percent) of those with low hemoglobin were recognized. However, where the hemoglobin of the child had been checked in a routine general medical examination, only six of seventeen (35 percent) of the low values were recognized.

Low hemoglobin values were less likely to be recognized in children over two. Although only one-third of the children were over two, almost half of the unrecognized low values were in children in this age group. This phenomenon was not related to the reason for which the hemoglobin had been done; in fact, more of the unrecognized older children had their hemoglobins ordered because of symptoms than was the case for the younger children. When the hemoglobin was done routinely, low values (under 9 g/100 ml of blood) were no more likely to be recognized than higher ones (categorized as 9−9.4 g/100 ml and 9.5 g/100 ml and over).

In a study done by Kessner (1974), two communities in Washington, D.C., were selected, one middle class and one lower class. A random sample of the families (most of whom were black) was chosen. This sample consisted of about 3000 children between the ages of six months to eleven years. The families were interviewed, medical histories were taken, and the children were then examined and tested. The regular source of care for each of the children was identified and contacted; children associated with three types of practice (prepaid group practice, neighborhood health center, and hospital outpatient departments) had their charts reviewed.

The identified physicians were asked whether they routinely screened for anemia. Less than one-fourth of the solo practitioners said they did, while 70 to 100 percent of the physicians associated with all other care organizations stated that they routinely screened for anemia in young children.

The analysis of patient records from the three provider organizations, however, showed a wide variation in the percentage of children who actually had a screening test (hemoglobin or hematocrit) for anemia. Less than one-fourth of the children attending hospital outpatient departments were indeed screened for anemia. However, for both the prepaid group and the neighborhood health center there was evidence from the charts that more than 85 percent of the children had been screened.

As Figure 5−2 indicates, of 169 children six months through three years of age, 28 percent were never screened for anemia. Of those children with a hematocrit or hemoglobin test recorded at any time in their chart, 36 percent had anemia based on the criteria developed for this study. However, there was relatively little information in the

Figure 5—2.   Screening for Anemia of Children Aged Six Months through Three Years in Three Provider Organizations

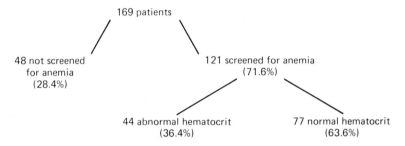

Source: Kessner, 1974. Reprinted with permission.

charts to indicate that the abnormal laboratory values of the children who were screened were actually recognized.

Diagnosis

Recognition of low hematocrit or hemoglobin values is no guarantee that the problem will reach the stage of medical diagnosis. Many investigations utilize screening procedures all of which have inherent lack of sensitivity and specificity. Even more definitive tests which indicate the likelihood of illness generally require either confirmation or, more commonly, the performance of supplementary procedures to produce a definitive diagnosis.

In Starfield and Scheff's study (1972) of twenty-nine children in whom an abnormality was recognized, a tentative or a final diagnosis was reached for only twenty-three. All twenty-three children had a hematocrit determined at the same time as the hemoglobin. Sixteen had at least one other procedure: three a blood cell smear; three a smear and reticulocyte count; four a smear and sickle-cell preparation; three a smear, sickle-cell preparation, and reticulocyte count; two a reticulocyte count only; and one a sickle-cell preparation only. One patient had a stool examination for occult blood loss.

The performance of the additional procedures was related to the reason the hemoglobin had been done. Of the sixteen children with symptoms for whom a diagnosis was made, fifteen had one or more further procedures. In contrast, only one of seven children whose hemoglobin was done routinely had any further procedures to arrive at the diagnosis. The initial diagnosis on all twenty-three patients for whom a diagnosis was recorded was iron-deficiency anemia, but one of these patients was later found to have hereditary elliptocytosis. Two children whose low hemoglobin values were unrecognized subsequently appeared with other types of anemia. One had a sickle-cell crisis requiring hospitalization; another had both a previous and a subsequent hospitalization for a bleeding ulcer.

In Kessner's study (1974), of the forty-four children who had an abnormal hematocrit according to a chart review, there was no diagnosis or treatment recorded for twenty-eight (64 percent) of them.

Thus, in two studies done in the United States, one in a university hospital clinic and one in a community with a variety of types of medical resources, many potential problems that are apparently recognized do not result in a diagnosis.

In a study carried out in England among a population including adults as well as children, it was estimated that less than one-half of the males and less than one-quarter of the females who were anemic would have been diagnosed if one had relied on clinical judgment only and had not actually systematically screened them (Fry, 1966).

In a study done in private practice, 121 cases were assessed: (1) by clinical symptom, (2) by the Talquist test (a color match test), (3) by other laboratory procedure (i.e., hemoglobin, hematocrit) (Hodgkin, 1963). The variations in the clinical and Talquist assessments were large and led to treatment of thirty-seven patients who were not anemic and failure to diagnose ten patients with severe anemia. The laboratory tests were considered more satisfactory. Thus, reliance on clinical acumen to judge the need for care at the time children are seen for the initial visit or test is inadequate. Some mechanisms for adequate communication of information and for assuring that diagnostic procedures will be performed where needed are required.

Management

The generally accepted plan of management consists of:

1. Iron: ferrous sulfate, gluconate, or fumarate to provide 2 mg/kg body weight of elementary iron by mouth three times a day
2. Dietary program: limit milk to one pint per day with adequate total caloric intake
3. Treatment of intestinal parasites and gastrointestinal blood loss (Kessner and Kalk, 1973; and Green and Haggerty, 1968).

Response is usually noted within one week of initiating therapy. Therapy should be continued for one to two months after hematocrit and hemoglobin levels have returned to normal to ensure replenishment of body iron stores. In most cases weekly or biweekly hematocrit and hemoglobin determinations will assist the physician in judging the response to iron therapy. Obtaining a hematocrit and reticulocyte determination one week after initiating therapy will provide early information about the child's ability to absorb ingested iron and his erythropoietic activity. If reticulocyte count and hematocrit have not risen after two to three weeks of adequate therapy, the physician should search further for the cause of anemia. The physician must also be certain that medicine was taken, that the preparation used was an effective one, and that chronic infection was not present. Intramuscular iron as iron-dextran (Imferon) is indicated only in those rare instances in which oral iron may not be tolerated or absorbed or when follow-up is dubious.

Iron in an amount calculated to return hematocrit levels to normal and restore body iron must be given in divided doses. Transfusion therapy with packed red blood cells is indicated only in those children with associated severe infection in whom congestive heart failure is a real possibility, or in surgical emergencies.

In the study of Starfield and Scheff (1972) twenty-two of the twenty-three children with the diagnosis of iron-deficiency anemia were given therapy for it, in all cases oral iron. Thus, if diagnosis was made, it was overwhelmingly likely that specific treatment was instituted. As it is rare to find prescriptive information (dosage, scheduling) in medical records (Zuckerman and Starfield, 1975), it is impossible to determine on retrospective review whether adequate therapy was prescribed, and whether families were, in fact, provided the information and understood it.

Compliance With Therapy

Although compliance is increasingly recognized as a factor in response of conditions to medical interventions, there is only one study of compliance with iron therapy in the pediatric literature. In that study (Starfield and Scheff), seven of twenty-two children given therapy denied received it. Only ten of the iron-deficient children actually received adequate therapy. Despite the low compliance, the degree of deficit in the medical care process was less a result of noncompliance by patients (about 50 percent) than a failure of the system to recognize, diagnose, and institute treatment (about 60 percent).

Follow-up Care

No medical care system can be assumed to have cared adequately for an illness unless it has paid attention to the response to prescribed therapy. In Starfield and Scheff's study (1972) this was addressed by examining plans for follow-up and achieved follow-up in children treated for iron-deficiency anemia.

In this study, only four of the twenty-two patients recorded as having been given therapy had no plans for follow-up; fourteen actually kept that appointment (Figure 5–3). Thus, it appears that for this condition in the two facilities studied, failure of the medical care system is nearly as much to blame as failure of the patient to keep the appointment. Only fourteen of the twenty-two patients treated for iron-deficiency anemia were seen deliberately to ascertain response to the therapy.

John Fry (1966) emphasizes the necessity for follow-up in terms of preventing relapse. In an adult study population, one-third had relapsed at follow-up ten years after initial diagnosis.

Outcome of Medical Care

As the treatment of iron-deficiency anemia is a well-accepted clinical practice, it is appropriate to assess the extent to which medical care succeeds in dealing with it. Because iron deficiency is usually a result of a nutritional deficit, it may well recur even after being successfully treated. Therefore, adequacy of the response to therapy must be judged not only on a short-term basis but also in terms of permanence of the response.

Short-Term Response. Brigety and Pearson et al. (1970) studied hematocrit values in children four to six enrolled in the Head Start Program. As part of this program, there was a summer activity in which two nutritionally balanced meals were served each day. A control group of 108 children received only this diet. An experimental group of 193 children in the program received, in addition to the diet,

Figure 5–3. Follow-Up of Children Treated for Iron-Deficiency Anemia

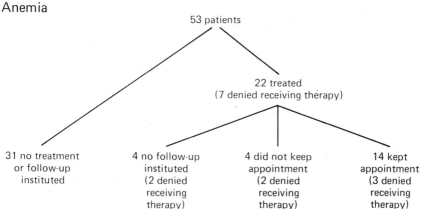

Source: Starfield and Scheff, 1972. Reprinted with permission.

Table 5—6. Short-Term Response in Hematocrit Values to Medicinal Iron as Supplement to Balanced Meals *(Head Start Program Children, Four to Six)*

	Stationary		*Decrease*		*Increase*		
Group	*No.*	*Percent*	*No.*	*Percent*	*No.*	*Percent*	*Total*
Control	72	66	11	10	25	14	108
Experimental	120	62	8	4	65	33	193

Source: Brigety and Pearson, 1970. Reprinted with permission.

a supplement of medicinal iron. Table 5—6 shows the results. Increase was defined as a rise of at least 2 percent. Decrease was a fall of at least 2 percent. Stationary indicates a difference of less than 2 percent between the initial and second hematocrit levels.

Approximately two-thirds of the children showed no change in hematocrit. Presumably they were operating at, or close to, their optimal hematocrit levels. Diet was effective in correcting significant anemia, correction being defined as attaining a hematocrit of 32 percent. No child in either group had a value less than 32 percent at the end of the program. However, significantly greater proportional increases in hematocrit occurred in the experimental group. The mean value of the hematocrit in these children was 1.5 ± 0.1 percent absolute units higher than that of the nonsupplemented group.

A liquid oral preparation containing ferric iron complexed to a low-molecular-weight carbohydrate, requiring only one dose daily, was used in the treatment of fifty-two black children of low to medium-low socioeconomic level (Crawford, 1970). The children lived in a metropolitan area and were treated in private practices for infectious or allergic disorders. All of them had initial hemoglobin levels of 10 g/100 ml or lower. An adequate hematologic response (as judged by hemoglobin, hematocrit, and reticulocyte count) was seen in forty-seven of the fifty-two within three to six weeks of treatment. However, longer-term follow-up was not performed so that outcome other than immediate response was not ascertained.

Long-Term Response. In a study carried out by Fry (1966) in private office-based practice, 222 patients who presented with anemia between 1949—54 were followed (not all were children). In 1959—60, sixty-one (32 percent) out of 189 patients still in the practice were anemic. Of these sixty-one, fifty-five had iron-deficiency anemia. In 1964 the number of patients still in the practice was 175 and of these thirty (17 percent) were still anemic. Twenty-five of these thirty had had primary iron-deficiency anemia.

Fry further estimates that patients with primary iron-deficiency anemia who had relapsed had done so because they had ceased to take their iron supplement.

Figure 5—4 refers again to the Starfield-Scheff study (1972). It combined the results of the hemoglobin determination and interview done in the home six months after the initial clinic visit. The hemoglobin was considered adequate if it attained 10 g/100 ml or higher.

Table 5—7 shows that there is a relationship between actual receipt of therapy and the adequacy of the eventual hemoglobin (Starfield and Scheff, 1972). Although the number of children was small, the findings suggest that if treatment is instituted, the process of follow-up may also be related to good outcome; six of eleven children followed had adequate hemoglobin levels as contrasted with three of eight children not followed.

Table 5—8 shows the relationship between actual ingestion of therapy and outcome and between maternal knowledge of the need for treatment and outcome. Although the taking of therapy is significantly related to a good outcome, an equally good response was obtained if the mother knew about the need for therapy but the child did not take it. The poorest response is in that group of children who did not take therapy and whose mothers did not know of the need for it. Presumably, if a mother knows about the problem it is likely that there are other ways she herself will deal with it besides the medically prescribed regimen.

Table 5—7. Treatment and Outcome of Care in Children with Iron-Deficiency Anemia

	Treatment Instituted		Treatment Not Instituted	
	A Medication Adequately Taken	B Medication Inadequately Taken	C Received Medication Elsewhere[a]	D Received No Medication
Hemoglobin adequate	6	3	3	8
Hemoglobin low	4	6	0	16

The difference between A–C and B–D chi-square test (4.88) is significant with p less than .05.
[a] All three patients took medication adequately.
Source: Starfield and Scheff, 1972.

Figure 5–4.   Therapeutic Outcomes of Patients in Figure 5–3 Six Months after Initial Clinic Visit

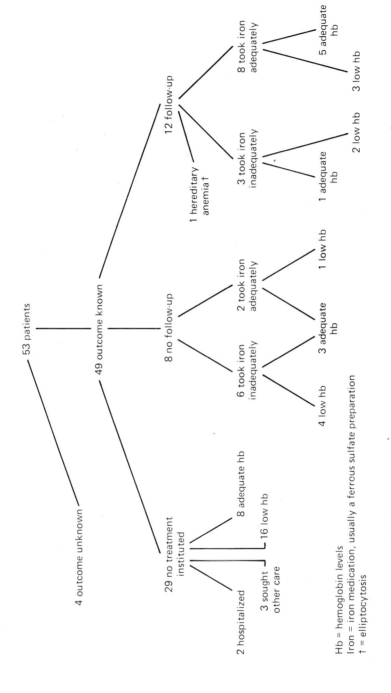

Hb = hemoglobin levels
Iron = iron medication, usually a ferrous sulfate preparation
† = elliptocytosis

Source: Starfield and Scheff, 1972.   Reprinted with permission.

Table 5-8. Relationships between Care and Outcome: Children with Low Hemoglobins

Process	Outcome
	Percent With Adequate Outcome (normal hemoglobin)
Rx given	47
Rx not given	41
Rx taken[a]	69
Rx not taken	33
Of those given medication:	
knew about Rx—took Rx	70 ⎫
knew about Rx—didn't take Rx	67 ⎬ 69%
didn't know about Rx—took Rx	50 ⎫
didn't know about Rx—didn't take Rx	17 ⎬ 25%

[a]Three children received medication in an unrelated facility subsequent to their being seen in the original facility.
Source: Adapted from Starfield, B., and Scheff, D., 1972.

REFERENCES

Adams, M., and Scott, R. "Iron deficiency anemia in Negro infants and children in the metropolitan area of the District of Columbia," *Med Ann DC* 32 (1963): 391.

American Academy of Pediatrics. *Lengthening Shadows: The Delivery of Health Care to Children*. Evanston, Ill.: author, 1971.

Andelman, M.B., and Sered, B.R. "Utilization of dietary iron by term infants," *Am J Dis Child* 111 (1966): 45.

Andersen, H.T., and Barkve, H. "Iron deficiency and muscular work performance: an evaluation of the cardiorespiratory function of iron deficient subjects with and without anemia," *Scand J Clin Lab Invest* 114 (1970): Supplementum.

Baird, I.M., and Podmore, D.A. "Intramuscular iron therapy in iron-deficiency anemia," *Lancet* 2 (1954): 942.

Berenbaum, M.C., et al. "Animal and human studies on ferrous fumarate, an oral hematinic," *Blood* 15 (1960): 540.

Berk, M.S., and Novich, M.A. "Treatment of iron-deficiency anemia with ferrous fumarate," *Am J Obstet Gynecol* 83 (1962): 203.

Beutler, E. "Iron enzymes in iron deficiency. I. Cytochrome c," *Am J Med Sci* 234 (1957): 517.

Beutler, E. "The red cell indices in the diagnosis of iron deficiency anemia," *Ann Intern Med* 50 (1959): 313.

Beutler, E. "Tissue effects of iron deficiency," *Scand J Haematol* 6 (1965): 41 (Series Haematologica).

Beutler, E., and Blaisdell, R.K. "Iron enzymes in iron deficiency. III. Catelase in rat red cells and liver with some further observations on cytochrome c," *J Lab Clin Med* 52 (1958): 694.

Beutler, E., and Blaisdell, R.K. "Iron enzymes in iron deficiency. V. Succinic dehydrogenase in rat liver, kidney and heart," *Blood* 15 (1960): 30.

Beutler, E., and Larsh, S.E. "Relative effectiveness of ferroglycine sulfate and ferrous sulfate," *N Engl J Med* 267 (1962): 538.

Beutler, E., Larsh, S.E., and Gurney, C.W. "Iron therapy in chronically fatigued, non-anemic women: a double blind study," *Ann Intern Med* 52 (1960): 378.

Beutler, E., Robson, M.J., and Buttenwieser, E. "A comparison of the plasma iron, iron-binding capacity, sternal marrow iron and other methods in the chemical evaluation of iron stores," *Ann Intern Med* 48 (1958): 60.

Beutler, E., Fairbanks, V.F., and Lahey, J.L. *Clinical Disorders in Iron Metabolism*. New York and London: Grune and Stratton Co., 1963.

Blaud, P. "On the chlorotic maladies and on a method of specific treatment of these affections," *Rev Med Fr Etrang* 1 (1832): 337.

Blumgart, H.L., and Altschule, M.D. "Clinical significance of cardiac and respiratory adjustments in chronic anemia," *Blood* 3 (1948): 329.

Bonnar, J. "Anaemia in obstetrics; and evaluation of treatment by total dose infusion," *Br Med J* 2 (1965): 1030.

Bothwell, T.H. "The diagnosis of iron deficiency," *N Z Med J* 65 (1966 Suppl): 880.

Bothwell, T.H., and Finch, C.A. *Iron Metabolism*. Boston: Little Brown and Co., 1962.

Brigety, R. and Pearson, H. "Effects of dietary and iron supplementation on hematocrit levels of preschool children," *J Pediatr* 76 (1970): 757.

Brise, H. "Effect of surface—active agents on iron absorption," *Acta Med Scand* (Suppl 376) 171 (1962a): 4.

Brise, H. "Influence of meals on iron absorption in oral iron therapy," *Acta Med Scand* (Suppl 376) 171 (1962b): 39.

Brise, H., and Hallberg, L. "II. A method for comparative studies on iron absorption in man using two radioiron isotopes," *Acta Med Scand* (Suppl 376) 171 (1962a): 7.

Brise, H. and Hallberg, L. "II. Iron absorption studies. Absorbability of different iron compounds," *Acta Med Scand* (Suppl 376) 171 (1962b): 23.

Brise, H., and Hallberg, L. "Effect of ascorbic acid on iron absorption," *Acta Med Scand* (Suppl 376) 171 (1962c): 59.

Brise, H., and Hallberg, L. "Effect of succinic acid on iron absorption," *Acta Med Scand* (Suppl 376) 171 (1962d): 59.

Buest, G.M., and Brown, E.W. "Erythrocytes and hemoglobin of the blood in infancy and childhood. IV. Factors in variability, statistical studies," *Am J Dis Child* 93 (1957): 486.

Burroughs, P.H., and Huenemann, R.L. "Iron deficiency in rural infants and children," *Am Diet Assoc* 57 (1970): 122.

Callender, S.T. "Chapter 14. Treatment of iron deficiency," in A. Jacobs and M. Worwood, eds., *Iron in Biochemistry and Medicine*. London and New York: Academic Press, 1974.

Callender, S.T., and Warner, G.T. "Iron absorption from bread," *Am J Clin Nutr* 21 (1968): 1170.

Center for Disease Control. *Ten State Nutritional Survey in the U.S. 1968–1970: Preliminary Report to Congress.* U.S. Dept. Health, Education, and Welfare, Public Health Service, Health Services and Mental Health Administration, Atlanta, 1971.

Charlton, R., and Bothwell, T. "Iron deficiency anemia," *Semin Hematol* 7 (1970): 67.

Chodos, R.B., et al. "The absorption of radioiron labelled foods and iron salts in normal and iron-deficient subjects and in idiopathic hemochromatosis," *J Clin Invest* 36 (1957): 314.

Coleman, D.H., Stevens, H.R., and Finch, C.A. "Treatment of iron deficiency anemia," *Blood* 10 (1955): 567.

Committee on Iron Deficiency, NAS Council on Food and Nutrition. "Iron deficiency in the U.S.," *JAMA* 203 (1968): 407.

Committee on Nutrition. "Iron balance and requirements in infancy," *Pediatrics* 43 (1969): 134.

Conrad, L.R., et al. "The role of the intestine in iron kinetics," *J Clin Invest* 43 (1964): 963.

Cope, W., Gillhespy, R.O., and Richardson, R.W. "Treatment of iron-deficiency anemia: comparison of methods," *Br Med J* 2 (1956): 638.

Crawford, O.W. "Oral treatment of iron deficiency anaemia," *Ill Med J* 137 (1970): 60.

Crosby, W.H. "Control of iron absorption by intestinal luminal factors," *Am J Clin Nutr* 21 (1968): 1189.

Crosland-Taylor, P., Keeling, D.H., and Cromie, B.W. "A trial of slow-release tablets of ferrous sulphate," *Curr Ther Res* 7 (1965): 244.

Dagg, J.H., Goldberg, A., and Lochhead, A. "Value of erythrocyte protoporphyrin in the diagnosis of latent iron deficiency (sideropenia)," *Br J Haematol* 12 (1966a): 326.

Dagg, J.H., Jackson, J.M., Curry, B., and Goldberg, A. "Cytochrome oxidase in latent iron deficiency (sideropenia)," *Br J Haematol* 12 (1966b): 331.

Dagg, J.H., Morrow, J.J., MacFarlane, B.G., and Goldberg, A. "Sideropenia (latent iron deficiency)," *Q J Med* 36 (1967): 600.

Dagg, J.H., and Goldberg, A. "Chapter 9. Detection and treatment of iron deficiency," in S.T. Callender, ed., "Iron deficiency and iron overload," *Clin Haematol* 2 (1973): 365.

Dallman, P.R., Sunshine, P., and Leonard, Y. "Intestinal cytochrome response with repair of iron deficiency," *Pediatrics* 39 (1967): 863.

Danneker, D. *Anemia in Selected Allegheny County Child Health Conference Populations.* Pittsburgh: Allegheny Health Department, 1966.

Diamond, L.K. "Iron deficiency in history and practice," in *Iron Nutrition in Infancy.* Report of the 62nd Ross Conference on Pediatric Research. Columbus, Ohio: Ross Laboratories, 1970, 16–17.

Dubach, R., Moore, C.V., and Minnich, V. "V. Studies in iron transportation and metabolism: II. The utilization of intravenously injected radioactive iron for hemoglobin synthesis, and an evaluation of the radioactive iron method for studying iron absorption," *J Lab Clin Med* 31 (1946): 1201.

Elvehjem, C.A., Herrin, R.C., and Hart, E.B. "Iron in nutrition. III. The effects of diet on the iron content of milk," *J Biol Chem* 71 (1927): 255.

Elwood, P.C., and Williams, G. "A comparative trial of slow-release and conventional iron preparations," *Practitioner* 204 (1970): 812.

England, J.M., Walford, D.M., and Waters, D.A.W. "Re-assessment of the reliability of the hematocrit," *Br J Haematol* 23 (1972): 247.

Fielding, J. "Intravenous iron-dextrin in iron-deficiency anemia," *Br Med J* 2 (1961): 279.

Finch, C.A. "Iron deficiency anemia," *Am J Clin Nutr* 22 (1969): 513.

Fischbach, R., et al. "Hyposideremia and endogenous depression," *Pharmakopsychiatro Neuropsychopharmakol* 6 (1973): 252.

Fomon, S.J. *Infant Nutrition.* Philadelphia: W.B. Saunders Co., 1967.

Fomon, S.J. *Prevention of Iron Deficiency Anemia in Infants and Children of Pre-school Age.* Washington, D.C.: Government Printing Office, 1970.

Fry, J. *Profiles of Disease: A Study in the Natural History of Common Diseases.* London: E. & S. Livingstone, Ltd., 1966, 98.

Gendel, B.R. "Iron deficiency anemia," *J Miss State Med Assoc* 1 (1960): 39.

Goldthorp, W.O., Spencer, D., and Dawson, D.W. "Reactions to intravenous iron dextran," *Br Med J* 1 (1965): 316.

Gorten, M.K., and Cross, E.R. "Iron metabolism in premature infants. II. Prevention of iron deficiency," *J Pediatr* 64 (1964): 509.

Green, M., and Haggerty, R., eds. *Ambulatory Pediatrics.* Philadelphia: W.B. Saunders Co., 1968, 245−49.

Guest, G.M. *Hypoferric Anemia in Infancy.* Cincinnati, Ohio: Robert Gould Research Foundation, 1947, 144.

Gutelius, M. "The problem of iron deficiency anemia in the pre-school Negro child," *Am J Public Health* 59 (1969): 290.

Haddy, T., Jurkowski, C., Brody, H., Kallen, D., Czajka-Narins, D. "Iron deficiency with and without anemia in infants and children," *Am J Dis Child* 128 (1974): 787.

Haden, R.L. "Historical aspects of iron therapy in anemia," *JAMA* 111 (1938): 1059.

Hahn, P.F., Bale, W.F., Lawrence, E.O., and Whipple, G.H. "Radioactive iron and its metabolism in anemia: its absorption, transportation, and utilization," *J Exp Med* 69 (1939): 739.

Hahn, P.F., Ross, J.F., Bale, W.F., and Whipple, G.H. "The utilization of iron and the rapidity of hemoglobin formation in anemia due to blood loss," *J Exp Med* 71 (1940): 731.

Hallberg, L. "Oral iron therapy—factors affecting the absorption," in Hallberg, Harwerth and Vannotti, 1970.

Hallberg, L., and Solvell, L. "Succinic acid as absorption promoter in iron tablets. Absorption and side-effect studies," *Acta Med Scand* (Suppl 459) 181 (1966): 23.

Hallberg, L., Harwerth, H.G., and Vannotti, A., eds. *Iron Deficiency: Pathogenesis, Clinical Aspects, Therapy.* Proceedings of the clinical symposium, Arosa, Switzerland, March 25−29, 1969. London and New York: Academic Press, 1970.

Hallberg, L., Solvell, L., and Brise, H. "Search for substances promoting the absorption of iron: Studies on absorption and side-effects," *Acta Med Scand* (Suppl 459) 181 (1966a): 11.

Hallberg, L., Ryttinger, L., and Solvell, L. "Side-effects of oral iron therapy: a doubleblind study of different iron compounds in tablet form," *Acta Med Scand* (Suppl 459) 181 (1966b): 3.

Hallberg, L., Norrby, A., and Solvell, L. "Oral iron with succinic acid in the treatment of iron deficiency anaemia," *Scand J Haematol* 8 (1971): 104.

Hamilton, L.D., et al. "Diurnal variation in the plasma iron level of man," *Proc Soc Exp Biol Med* 75 (1950): 65.

Hammond, D., and Murphy, A. "The influence of exogenous iron on formation of hemoglobin in the premature infant," *Pediatrics* 25 (1960): 363.

Haughton, J. "Nutritional anemia of infancy and childhood," *Am J Public Health* 53 (1963): 1121−26.

Healy, W.B., Cheng, S., McElroy, W.D. "Metal toxicity and iron deficiency effects of enzymes in neurospora," *Arch Biochem Biophys* 54 (1955): 206.

Heath, C.W., and Patek, A.J., Jr. "Anemia of iron deficiency," *Medicine* 16 (1937): 267.

Heath, C.W., Strauss, M.B., and Castle, W.B. "Quantitative aspects of iron deficiency in hypochromic anemia (the parenteral administration of iron)," *J Clin Invest* 11 (1932): 1293.

Hebbert, F.J. "Some historical aspects of iron therapy," *Scott Med J* 149 (1950): 385.

Hegsted, D.M., Finch, C.A., and Kinney, T.D. "The influence of diet on iron absorption: II. The interrelation of iron and phosphorus," *J Exp Med* 90 (1949): 147.

Heinrich, H.C. "Iron deficiency without anemia," *Lancet* 2 (1968): 460.

Herrick, J.B. "On the combination of angina pectoris and severe anaemia," *Am Heart J* 2 (1927): 351.

Hillman, R.S., and Henderson, P.A. "Control of marrow production by the level of iron supply," *J Clin Invest* 48 (1969): 454.

Hillman, R.W., and Smith, H.S. "Hemoglobin patterns in low income families," *Public Health Rep* 83 (1968): 61.

Hoag, M., Wallerstein, R., and Pollycove, M. "Occult blood loss in iron-deficiency anemia of infancy," *Pediatrics* 27 (1961): 199.

Hodgkin, K. *Towards Earlier Diagnosis: A Family Doctor's Approach*. London: E. & S. Livingstone, Ltd., 1963, p. 80.

Holmes, J.M. "Ferrous calcium citrate in pregnancy anaemia," *Practitioner* 179 (1957): 295.

Hunter, C.A. "Iron deficiency anemia in pregnancy," *Surg Gynecol Obstet* 110 (1960): 210.

Hutton, C.F. "Plummer Vinson syndrome," *Br J Radiol* 29 (1956): 81.

Israels, M.C.G., and Cook, T.A. "New preparations for oral iron-therapy," *Lancet* 2 (1965): 654.

Jacobs, A. "Iron-containing enzymes in the buccal epithelium," *Lancet* 2 (1961): 1331.

Jacobs, I. "Iron deficiency anemia in infancy and childhood," *Practitioner* 21 (1960): 93.

Josephs, H.W. "Anemia of infancy and early childhood," *Medicine* 15 (1936) 307.

Josephs, H.W. "Iron metabolism and the hypochromic anaemia of infancy," *Medicine* 32 (1953): 125.

Joynson, D., Walker, D., Jacobs, A., and Dolby, A. "Defect of cell-mediated immunity in patients with iron deficiency anemia," *Lancet* 2 (1972): 1058.

Judisch, J.M., Naiman, G.L., and Oski, F.A. "The fallacy of the fat iron-deficient child." *Pediatrics* 37 (1966): 987.

Kerr, D.N.S., and Davidson, S. "Gastrointestinal intolerance to oral iron preparations," *Lancet* 2 (1958): 489.

Kessner, D. *Contrasts in Health Status: Vol. III. Assessment of Medical Care for Children.* Washington, D.C.: Institute of Medicine, National Academy of Sciences, 1974.

Kessner, D., and Kalk, K.E. *Contrasts in Health Status: Vol. II. A Strategy for Evaluating Health Services.* Washington, D.C.: Institute of Medicine, National Academy of Sciences, 1973.

Kripke, S., and Saunders, E. "Prevalence of iron-deficiency anemia among infants and young children seen at rural ambulatory clinics," *Am J Clin Nutr* 23 (1970): 716.

Lahey, M.E. "Iron deficiency anemia," *Pediatr Clin North Am* 93 (1957): 481.

Lanzkowsky, P. "Iron deficiency anemia," *Pediatric Annals* (March 1974): 6.

Lindvall, S., and Andersson, N.S.E. "Studies on a new intramuscular haematinic, iron-sorbitol," *Br J Pharmacol* 17 (1961): 358.

Lottrup, M.C. "Treatment of anemia in children with ferric and ferrous compounds, reduced iron and cupric sulphate," *Am J Dis Child* 47 (1934): 1.

McCance, R.A., Edgecombe, C.N., and Widdowson, E.M. "Phytic acid and iron absorption," *Lancet* 2 (1943): 126.

McCurdy, P.R. "Oral and parenteral iron therapy: a comparison," *JAMA* 191 (1965): 859.

Macdougall, L.G., Anderson, R., McNab, G.M., and Katz, J. "The immune response in iron deficient children: impaired cellular defense mechanisms with altered humoral components," *J Pediatr* 86 (1975): 833.

MacKay, H.M.M. *Nutritional Anemia with Special Reference to Iron Deficiency*, Medical Research Council, Special Report Series No. 157. London: H.M. Stationery Office, 1931.

Mackiewicz, M., Kasprzak, L., Obuchowicz, L., and Michejda, J. "Activity of succinic oxidase enzyme system in experimental anemia," *Acta Physiol Pol* 12 (1961): 255.

Madinaveita, J.L. "Ferrocenes as haematinics," *Br J Pharmacol* 24 (1965): 352.

Marchasin, S., and Wallerstein, R.O. "The treatment of iron-deficiency anemia with intravenous iron dextran," *Blood* 23 (1964): 354.

Marsh, A., Long, H., and Stierwalt, E. "Comparative hematologic response to iron fortification of milk formulation for infants," *Pediatrics* 24 (1959): 404.

Maternal and Child Health Service. *Comments Regarding the March—April*

Children and Youth Survey, 1962. Washington, D.C.: U.S. Department of Health, Education and Welfare, 1969.

Mereu, I., and Tonz, O. "The treatment of iron deficiency anaemia in children with iron polyisomaltosate," *Ger Med Mon* 7 (1962): 82.

Meyers, F.H., Jawetz, E., and Goldfien, A. *Review of Medical Pharmacology.* 4th edition. Los Altos, Calif.: Lange Medical Publications, 1974.

Moore, C.V., Arrowsmith, W.R., Welch, J., and Minnich, V. "Studies in iron transportation and metabolism: Observations on absorption of iron from gastrointestinal tract," *J Clin Invest* 18 (1939): 553.

Moore, C.V., Dubach, R., Minnich, V., and Roberts, H.K. "Absorption of ferrous and ferric radioactive iron by human subjects and by dogs," *J Clin Invest* 23 (1944): 755.

Morgan, A.F. "Nutritional status USA," *Calif Agric Ext Stu Bull* 769 (1969).

Naiman, J.L., Oski, F.A., Diamond, L.K., Vawter, G.F., and Schwachman, H. "The gastrointestinal effects of iron-deficiency anemia," *Pediatrics* 33 (1964): 83.

National Center for Health Statistics. *Mean Blood Hematocrit of Adults, U.S. 1960−62.* Series 11, No. 24. Washington, D.C.: Government Printing Office, 1967.

National Center for Health Statistics. *Hematocrit Values for Youths 12−17.* Series 11, No. 146. Washington, D.C.: Government Printing Office, 1974.

Neerhout, R.C., Armstrong, D.H., Schulz, J., and Smith, N.J. "A quantitative study of the fate of recently absorbed food iron," *Am J Dis Child* 95 (1958): 126.

Niccum, W.L., Jackson, R.L., and Steams, G. "Use of ferric and ferrous iron in the prevention of hypochromic anemia in infants," *Am J Dis Child* 86 (1953): 553.

Nissim, J.A. "Intravenous administration of iron," *Lancet* 2 (1947): 49.

Norrby, A. "Iron absorption studies in iron deficiency," *Scand J Haematol* (Suppl 20), (1974).

O'Connor, P.A. "Nutritional anemia: role of excessive milk intake," *Mich Med* 66 (1967): 432.

Owen, G.M., Garry, P.J., et al. "Nutritional status of Mississippi pre-school children," *Am J Clin Nutr* 22 (1969): 1444.

Parsons, L.G. "The treatment of nutritional anaemia in infants," *Br Med J* 1 (1936): 1009.

Paterson, J.C.S., Marrack, D., and Wiggins, H.S. "The diurnal variations of serum iron level in erythropoietic disorders," *J Clin Pathol* 6 (1953): 105.

Pearson, H.A., Abrams, I., Fernbach, D.J., Gyland, S.P., and Hahn, D.A. "Anemia in preschool children in the United States of America," *Pediatr Res* 1 (1967): 169.

Peters, T., Apt, L., and Ross, J.F. "Effect of phosphates upon iron absorption studied in normal human subjects and in an experimental model using dialysis," *Gastroenterology* 61 (1971): 315.

Pickering, G.W., and Wayne, E.J. "Observations on angina pectoris and intermittent claudication in anemia," *Clin Sci* 1 (1934): 315.

Pollitt, E., and Leibel, R.L. "Iron deficiency and behavior," *J Pediatr* 88 (1976): 372.

Pollycove, M., and Mortimer, R. "The quantitative determination of iron kinetics and hemoglobin synthesis in human subjects," *J Clin Invest* 40 (1961): 753.

Pritchard, J.A. "Hemoglobin regeneration in severe iron-deficiency anemia," *JAMA* 195 (1966): 717.

Reedy, M.E., Schwartz, S.O., and Plattner, E.B. "Anemia of the premature infant: a two-year study of the response to iron medication," *J Pediatr* 41 (1952): 25.

Reimann, F., Fritsch, F., and Schick, K. "Eisenbilanzversuche bei Gesunden und bei Anamischen. II. Unter suchungen über das Wesen der eisenempfindlichen Anamien ("Asiderosen") und der therapeutischen Wirkung des Eisens bei diesen Anamien," *Zeitschrift fur Klinische Medizin* 131 (1936): 1.

Ross, J.D. "Failure of iron-deficient infants to respond to an orally administered iron carbohydrate complex," *N Engl J Med* 269 (1963): 399.

Ross Conference on Pediatric Research. *Iron Nutrition in Infancy.* Ed., N.J. Smith. Columbus, Ohio: Ross Laboratories, 1970.

Schiffer, C.G., and Hunt, E.P. *Illness among children: data from U.S. National Health Survey.* Washington, D.C.: U.S. Department of Health, Education and Welfare, 1963.

Schulz, J., and Smith, N.J. "Quantitative study of the absorption of iron salts in infants and children," *Am J Dis Child* 95 (1958): 120.

Scott, J.M. "Iron-sorbitol-citrate in pregnancy anaemia," *Br Med J* 2 (1963): 354.

Scott, J.M., and Govan, A.D.T. "Anaemia of pregnancy treated with intramuscular iron," *Br Med J* 2 (1954): 1257.

Sharpe, L.M., et al. "The effect of phytate and other food factors on iron absorption," *J Nutr* 41 (1950): 433.

Shaw, R., and Robertson, W.O. "Anemia among hospitalized infants," *Ohio State Med J* 60 (1964): 45.

Siimes, M.A., Addiego, J.E., and Dallman, P.R. "Ferritin in serum: diagnosis of iron deficiency and iron overload in infants and children," *Blood* 43 (1974): 581.

Sitarz, A.L., Wolfe, J.A., and von Hofe, F.H. "Comparative value of intramuscular versus orally administered iron in prevention of late anemia of prematurity," *Am J Dis Child* 98 (1959): 640.

Smith, C.H. "Sedimentation rate in nutritional anemia of infants and children: its response to treatment with iron (ferrous sulphate)," *Am J Dis Child* 56 (1938): 510.

Smith, N.J., ed. *Iron Nutrition in Infancy.* Report of the 62nd Ross Conference on Pediatric Research. Columbus, Ohio: Ross Laboratories, 1970.

Smith, N., and Rios, E. "Iron metabolism and iron deficiency in infancy and childhood," *Adv Pediatr* 21 (1974): 239.

Smith, R.S. "Iron deficiency and iron overload," *Arch Dis Child* 40 (1965): 343.

Starfield, B. "Theory and practice in health services research," *J Pediatr* 83 (1973): 184.

Starfield, B., and Borkowf, S. "Physicians' recognition of complaints made by parents about their children's health," *Pediatrics* 43 (1969): 168.

Starfield, B., and Scheff, D. "Effectiveness of pediatric care: the relationship between processes and outcome," *Pediatrics* 49 (1972): 547.

Steinkamp, R., Dubach, R., and Moore, C.V. "Studies in iron transportation and metabolism. VIII. Absorption of radioiron from iron-enriched bread," *Arch Intern Med* 95 (1955): 181.

Stockman, R. "The treatment of chlorosis by iron and some other drugs," *Br Med J* 1 (1893): 881.

Sturgeon, P. "Studies of iron requirements in infants and children. II. The influence on normal infants of oral iron in therapeutic doses," *Pediatrics* 17 (1956): 341.

Sulzer, J. "Effects of iron deficiency of psychological tests in children," in Committee on Iron Nutritional Deficiencies, Food and Nutrition Board, National Academy of Sciences, National Research Council, *Summary of Proceedings: Workshop on the Extent and Meanings of Iron Deficiency in the U.S.* March 8–9, 1971. Washington, D.C.: National Academy of Sciences, 1971.

Swan, H.T., and Jowett, G.H. "Treatment of iron deficiency with ferrous fumarate: Assessments by a statistically accurate method," *Br Med J* 2 (1959): 782.

Takeda, Y., and Hara, M. "Significance of ferrous iron and ascorbic acid in the operation of the tricarboxylic acid cycle," *J Biol Chem* 214 (1955): 657.

Taymor, M.L., Sturgis, S.H., Goodale, W.T., and Ashbaugh, D. "Menorrhagia due to chronic iron deficiency," *Obstet Gynecol* 16 (1960): 571.

Taymor, M.L., Sturgis, S.H., and Yahia, C. "The etiological role of chronic iron deficiency in production of menorrhagia," *JAMA* 187 (1964): 323.

Usher, R., Shephard, M., and Lind, J. "The blood volume of the newborn infant and placental transfusion," *Acta Paediatr* 52 (1963): 497.

Usher, S.J., MacDermot, P.N., and Lozinski, E. "Prophylaxis of simple anemia in infancy with iron and copper," *Am J Dis Child* 49 (1935): 642.

Vahlquist, B., Neander, G., and Neander, E. "Studies on the absorption of iron. I. Absorption of iron from the stomach," *Acta Paediatr* 32 (1945): 768.

Waldmann, T.A., et al. "Allergic gastroenteropathy: a cause of excessive gastrointestinal protein loss," *N Engl J Med* 276 (1967): 761.

Wallerstein, R.O. "Intravenous iron-dextran complex," *Blood* 32 (1968): 690.

Wallerstein, R.O., and Mettier, S.R. *Iron in Clinical Medicine: Symposium on Iron in Clinical Medicine, University of California School of Medicine, 1957.* Berkeley and Los Angeles: University of California Press, 1958.

Webb, T., and Oski, F. "Iron deficiency anemia and scholastic achievement in young adolescents," *J Pediatr* 82 (1973): 827.

Weinberg, E. "Iron and susceptibility to infectious disease," *Science* 184 (1974): 952.

Whipple, G.H., and Robscheit-Robbins, F.S. "Blood regeneration in severe anemia," *Am J Physiol* 72 (1925): 395.

Wilson, F.J., Heiner, D.C., and Lahey, M.E. "Milk-induced gastrointestinal bleeding in infants with hypochromic microcytic anemia," *JAMA* 189 (1964): 568.

Witts, L.J. "Therapeutic action of iron," *Lancet* 1 (1936): 1.

Witts, L.J. *The Stomach and Anaemia.* London: Athlone Press (University of London), 1966.

Witts, L.J. *Hypochromic Anaemia.* Philadelphia, F.A. Davis Company, 1969.

Woodruff, C. "Nutritional anaemias in early childhood," *Am J Clin Nutr* 22 (1969): 504.

Zuckerman, A.E., Starfield, B., Hochreiter, C., and Kovasznay, B. "Validating the content of pediatric outpatient medical records by means of tape recording doctor-patient encounters," *Pediatrics* 56 (1975): 407.

Chapter 6

Lead Poisoning

John Graef, M.D.

Lead poisoning remains a prominent threat to the health and lives of children today. It is a needless cause of mental retardation, other neurological handicaps, and death. It has medical, social, educational, economic, technical, and political roots (Graef, 1975; Waldron and Stöfen, 1974; Lin-Fu, 1970). Especially important are dilapidated housing; stressed families; lack of awareness about the problem among physicians, health workers, and the public; and inadequate prevention of reexposure.

Primary care for children who have had excessive exposure to lead is of utmost importance, particularly in screening, early recognition, and follow-up. In the absence of adequate prevention it is likely that many children who do not develop acute symptoms will go undiagnosed, with resultant chronic brain disfunction. This may appear as learning disabilities, hyperkinesis, or behavior problems.

Physicians and public health authorities agree that lead intoxication in children is preventable. It is a manmade disease and, as such, is subject to complete control.

If lead uptake is not excessive, it is largely excreted in urine, bile, and sweat. But if lead continues to be absorbed at unusually high rates, tissue levels increase and result in toxic effects on soft tissues, especially bone marrow, kidneys, and brain, and in deposition of large amounts of lead in bone. Blood-lead levels then reflect the equilibrium between absorption and excretion, and between pools in soft tissue and in bone.

At this point some definitions are in order.

Absorption is the process by which a person takes up lead into the body by whatever means.

Metabolic lead poisoning is diagnosed when the absorbed lead produces evident signs or symptoms. Metabolic poisoning may be seen without clinical poisoning but not the converse. *Plumbism, saturnism,* or *lead intoxication* are other terms for clinical lead poisoning.

Subclinical poisoning may be defined as the evidence of morbidity without the classical signs or symptoms of clinical lead poisoning.

Encephalopathy embraces any symptom or sign referable to the central nervous system effects of lead such as projectile vomiting, lethargy, hyperirritability, ataxia, seizures, or coma.

Chelation is the term used to describe the chemical process of removing lead from tissues. The word comes from the Greek *chelos* (crab) and describes the way chelating agents bind heavy metals in a pincerlike configuration. So bound, the metals are effectively neutralized and excreted. Common chelating agents are ethylenediaminetetraacetate (EDTA) and dimercaprol (BAL). These will be discussed under "Therapy."

Increased lead burden is defined by a blood-lead level exceeding $30 \mu gm\%$ or by a 24 hour urinary lead output of more than $1 \mu g$ lead/ mg chelating agent administered. Increased burden is distinct from clinical lead poisoning or intoxication, since under some conditions a child may demonstrate either an elevated blood-lead level, an increased excretion, or both, with little or no evidence of intoxication.

Pica is the term used for the compulsive search for such unnatural "foods" as clay, plaster, paint chips, or laundry starch. It is not to be confused with the normal childhood desire to taste things. Childhood lead poisoning is significantly related to pica. In New York, 70 to 90 percent of children with lead poisoning have been found to have a history of pica (Chisholm and Kaplan, 1968).

SOURCES OF LEAD

Primary sources of lead in the environment are shown in Table 6−1. Lead-based paint remains the major source of exposure in young children. Massachusetts is the only state to have removed from the market exterior as well as interior lead-based paint. Because many homes are painted with not one but several layers of lead-based paint, paint chips from porches, windowsills, hallways, and bannisters are found to contain as much as 40 percent lead. And of course, all of these are readily accessible to a child.

The absorption range has been shown to be approximately 10 per-

Table 6–1. Lead in the Environment

Lead-based paint, interior and exterior
Lead-laden dust and soil
Ceramic glazes, pewter
Lead in foodstuffs—evaporated milk, drinking water
Airborne lead
Industrial lead vapors
Lead in inks, newsprint, and other sources

cent in adults (Kehoe, 1964) and as high as 53 percent in young children (Alexander, 1974). This helps to account for the higher degree of susceptibility to lead poisoning in young children. Certainly, the high absorption figure must be viewed with alarm in calculating acceptable environmental lead concentrations for the younger age group. Under conditions of absorption as high as 50 percent, ingestion of one gram of paint containing 40 percent lead could produce lethal concentrations of blood lead in a typical two-year-old child.

Among other sources of lead exposure in young children, airborne lead and lead in foodstuffs are probably most important. Airborne lead either from automobile exhaust or from smelters apparently contaminates soil and house dust and is ingested, rather than inhaled, during the normal hand-to-mouth activity of small children.

Lead in foodstuffs apparently is derived from faulty canning techniques that expose the contents of the can to lead through the seams. Concentrations well above 100 µg per liter have been observed. In one study, the mean lead level of canned evaporated milk was 202 µg per liter (Mitchell and Aldous, 1974). Such levels could produce an increased lead burden in a growing infant in a matter of weeks.

The presence of lead in ceramic glazes and in paint on toys depends to some extent on the country of origin. In the United States, it is illegal to use lead paint on toys. Ceramics for commercial use must be fired at temperatures greater than 1800°F or lead glazes may not be used. However, such controls do not exist elsewhere, and sporadic cases of poisoning due to these sources are reported. Excessive lead has been reported in the paint coating of wooden pencils. This suggests a widely unrecognized but common source of exposure (Pichirallo, 1971).

Drinking water continues to be reported as a source of lead poisoning in communities with lead-lined pipes or water storage facilities (Goldberg, 1974).

ABSORPTION

In children the generally accepted figure for intestinal absorption of lead in proportion to the amount ingested is as high as one-quarter to one-half (Alexander, 1974). This is considerably higher than in adults (Kehoe, 1964). The mechanism by which lead is transported across the intestinal mucosa is not known, but a number of factors have been shown to influence lead uptake.

In particular, other metals influence uptake, so the amount of calcium and iron in the diet is important (Mahaffey, 1974). Shields and Mitchell (1941) showed the concentration of lead in soft tissues of experimental animals was increased by lowering the amount of calcium and phosphate in the diet, either separately or together, an effect more recently confirmed by Mahaffey and Goyer (1970). Increased lead absorption from the gastrointestinal tract is a reasonable explanation for the increase in body burden of lead resulting from iron-deficient diets. Waxman and Rabinovitz (1966), pointed out that lead inhibited hemoglobin synthesis as a specific antagonist of heme synthesis and as a general heavy metal inhibitor of cell metabolism. Ferrous iron protected both these functions against the action of lead.

It has been postulated that calcium and iron reduce lead absorption from the intestine by competing for binding sites on mucosal cells. An active transport system may be involved, however, perhaps governed in part by the influence of vitamin D. The presence of vitamin D in the diet increases the concentration of lead in the blood (Sobel et al., 1938). This effect has been noticed in children (Rapoport and Rubin, 1941) and might help to explain why outbreaks of lead poisoning among children are greatest in the summer months.

Absorption through the skin is of importance only in the case of organic compounds of lead, particularly the lead alkyls and lead napthalenes. This phenomenon, while of medical importance, does not contribute significantly to lead poisoning in children.

Isotope studies (Rabinovitz et al., 1973) have shown that lead is distributed among three body compartments and is in dynamic equilibrium between them. The largest, bone, contains perhaps 80 percent of the body lead burden in a fairly stable state with a half-life under physiological conditions of approximately two years. Soft tissue lead (half-life 37 days) and blood lead (half-life 29 days) fluctuate readily and are to a large extent interdependent.

Lead in the blood is bound to the red cell or to the plasma proteins, and a small amount is in a free ionized form. Lead bound to red cells is probably in excess of 90 percent of the circulating total (Clarkson and Kench, 1958), but this figure is dose-dependent.

The binding of lead to the red cell membrane is responsible for one of its lesser known toxic effects. The enzyme ATPase is poisoned and potassium "leaks" from the cell, reducing the cell's volume. The resulting rounder shape of the cell makes it less susceptible to osmotic lysis. This reaction, not damaging in itself, provides a useful diagnostic test when blood lead determinations are not available.

Lead is readily transferred from the plasma to the extravascular space but then, Stover (1959) speculates, partially returns as the plasma level declines. It has also been demonstrated that plasma concentrations remain fairly constant despite fluctuations in blood lead (Rosen, 1974). This suggests that there is a dynamic equilibrium between red cell and plasma lead on the one hand and extracellular and intracellular lead on the other. It is the ionic fraction of the plasma lead that can be transferred to other body compartments.

After diffusing into the extravascular space, lead enters the cells. It appears in the cells of the liver and kidney an hour or less after it has been ingested. It appears to be particularly strongly bound to the mitochondria, and this strong affinity is especially relevant to its pathological effects (Waldron and Stöfen, 1974).

Most of the body lead (90 percent or more) is stored in the skeleton and particularly in areas of active bone formation. Bound as a triphosphate, lead is extremely stable in bone under physiologic conditions. However, in altered metabolic states (acute infection or dehydration, marked alterations in vitamin D, serum calcium, or phosphorus) or in the presence of chelating agents, lead may be "mobilized" from its tightly bound form. This accounts in part for the elevations in blood lead often seen during summer months and during acute illness. This point is also important to the primary care physician pondering unexpected changes in blood lead at other times.

The importance of lead in soft tissue calcification may be in its effect as a nucleating agent in addition to its ability to attract calcium to sites of irritation.

EXCRETION

Lead is excreted primarily via the feces and urine. Fecal excretion is far greater and represents ingested lead that has passed unabsorbed through the gut. Urinary excretion of lead occurs both at the glomerulus and the tubules, and the lead is not generally reabsorbed. Excretion is a function of time, not of urine flow, and the physiological factors altering urinary excretion—time of day, diet, and others— have not been well studied. Excess excretion of unbound lead results in toxicity to the renal tubules and a Fanconi-type renal lesion. With the addition of lead-binding chelating agents, primarily EDTA and penicillamine, renal excretion is enhanced as much as ten to fifty-fold in patients with increased lead burden. This fact is of diagnostic value and is used to establish the presence of increased lead burden by means of the lead mobilization test.

PREVALENCE, INCIDENCE AND FUNCTIONAL IMPACT OF LEAD POISONING

The present conditions are reflected in the current estimates of 400,000 cases of childhood lead poisoning. In the U.S. alone there are fifty to two hundred deaths per year related to this cause. In the three-year period 1959—61, lead poisoning was responsible for 79 percent of total deaths from poisoning. (This does not mean that lead poisoning was most frequent but rather that it was most frequently fatal at that time.) Between 1959 and 1963 the fatality rate from increased intracranial pressure remained essentially unchanged at the 25 percent level despite use of chelating agents and various other techniques to lower it. When death occurs, it is usually a result of massive brain inflammation and swelling rather than death of the brain per se. At the Children's Hospital Medical Center, Boston, the last death from lead poisoning occurred in 1960, although there have been a number of cases of encephalopathy since. This undoubtedly reflects increased alertness and earlier diagnosis as well as improved management.

In Cleveland the mortality rate reported for lead poisoning from 1952 to 1958 was 30 percent. Children between one and six are the main victims; those between one and three comprise 85 percent of cases, with the highest incidence at two years. Over 50 percent of all deaths from lead poisoning occur in two-year-olds (Lin-Fu, 1970).

A far greater number of children are permanently damaged. According to some authors (Pearlstein and Attala, 1966; Byers, 1959; Berg and Zappella, 1964), as high as 40 percent of children with symptomatic lead intoxication suffered irreversible neurological sequelae. These include fine and gross motor defects, hyperactivity, dyslexia, memory loss, and developmental defects. Among retarded children lead poisoning has been observed as a consequence of the more pronounced pica seen in such children and the environmental hazard of lead paint coating the walls of older institutions (Gibson et al., 1967).

These sequelae have been seen most frequently following encephalopathy. Byers (1959) in his review of forty-five cases found nine of seventeen children with encephalopathy on diagnosis to have suffered permanent damage. Four died and at least three of the nine suffered new and irreversible loss of mental function. Over all, follow-up was obtained on forty of the forty-five patients, and nineteen of those, including some without gross encephalopathy, suffered persistent psychological irregularities, became overtly and permanently retarded, or died.

These figures are not dissimilar from those of Perlstein and Attala (1966), who reviewed 425 cases of plumbism in Chicago over a ten-year period. Of these cases, ninety-three exhibited mental retardation eighty-five suffered recurrent seizures, nine demonstrated cerebral palsy, and five showed optic atrophy. Since some children suffered more than one sequel, the total found to have permanent damage was 39 percent. With regard to mode of onset, those with encephalopathy on diagnosis had the greatest frequency and severity of sequelae (80 percent). Jenkins and Mellins, (1957), in a study of thirty-two children, nearly all of whom had encephalopathy, found a significantly low mean IQ of 74, with a range from 35 to 115. However, even among those with mild or no presenting symptoms of plumbism the incidence of mental retardation by gross measurement was appreciable (9 percent).

In a large number of children no detectable effect of lead can be measured, yet evidence for damage in asymptomatic lead burden continues to mount. Pueschel (1974), de la Burde and Choate (1972), David (1974), and others have shown neurological irregularities in chronic, low-lead-exposed children without overt symptoms. Silbergeld's studies (Silbergeld and Goldberg, 1974) of lead-associated hyperactivity in mice and the demonstration by others of slow learning in sheep with borderline blood-lead levels are suggestive of animal models with practical application to the human disease.

A seasonal incidence of symptoms has long been observed, with the largest number of cases seen during the summer months. Although not understood, this phenomenon has been generally attributed to alterations mediated by vitamin D in calcium binding and transport and to the association of lead with calcium metabolism (Mahaffey and Goyer, 1970). Many observers suspect, however, that increased incidence in summer may be due to enhanced exposure to soil and exterior paint containing lead as well as to greater family mobility during summer months.

RECOGNITION

Lead poisoning is so often overlooked that some physicians are hardly aware of it at all. Lead poisoning occurs in New York City at the rate of several hundred cases a year; yet one large medical center reported it's staff had not seen a single case in a three-year period. The Poison Control Center in New York used to receive many calls from hospitals referring to "possible lead poisoning" cases. These patients usually not only had clinical symptoms but blood-lead levels considerably above the standard used at that time for positive diagnosis (0.06 mg per 100 ml) (Lin-Fu, 1970).

It should be evident from what has been said that it is especially important to detect the ingestion of lead during the first three to six months that it is happening—before clinical signs appear. Unfortunately, like many other conditions in children, such as anorexia, irritability, lethargy and apathy, abdominal pain, and developmental delay, the clinical signs of lead poisoning are not specific and not easy to interpret. Perhaps the child has an anemia that does not respond to iron therapy; this is one way in which "asymptomatic" lead poisoning shows itself. Perhaps the mother reports aberrant behavior, aggressiveness, or hyperirritability. Chisholm and Kaplan (1968) have observed that the mother may have had a history of pica as well, or other children in the family may have shown it. They list as indications for blood-lead determination the following conditions of family life: a working mother who can't account for her toddler's activities during her absence; arrival of a newborn with subsequent neglect of the older child; and the depressed or alcoholic mother. In sum, they recommend blood-lead testing whenever there is evidence of a toddler not getting much attention and living in a dilapidated pre-World War II house.

Although the clinical face of lead poisoning has been changing, many health workers trained prior to the new concepts still perceive it as an acute, fulminant condition occurring under special circumstances. Lin-Fu (1970) reports the case of a child seen by two physicians. Although the child was known to have pica, one physician thought of paint ingestion as harmless because interior paints manufactured today do not contain lead. The other thought that drinking large amounts of milk would prevent lead poisoning due to paint ingestion.

Interference With Heme Synthesis.   The earliest measurable effect of lead appears to be its capacity to suppress enzyme activity by blocking sulfhydryl groups. This effect is also characteristic of other heavy metals, but in addition lead interferes specifically with heme synthesis (Hernberg et al., 1970). Hence, decreased δ-amino levulinic acid (ALA) dehydratase activity can be measured in the absence of anemia, a fairly late finding in lead poisoning (Gibson et al., 1955). Other steps of the heme synthesis pathway are affected, and the net result is an increase in free erythrocyte protoporphyrin, thereby reflecting an interference in the uptake of iron into the heme molecule. This increase can be measured with a fluorimeter, since erythrocytes with excess protoporphyrin fluoresce and can be quantitated (Piomelli et al., 1973). This test appears to be as accurate as the ALA dehydratase assay and is so simple that a portable device can provide an accurate determination from capillary blood within minutes.

Basophilic Stippling of Red Cells. The precipitation on the red cell surface of ribo-nucleoprotein produces a pattern of basophilic stippling of the erythrocytes (that is, with basic dyes blue dots appear and these are easily seen on a simple smear).

The Hair Lead Test. This test is based on the principle that hair follicles actively excrete lead and that excess intake is reflected in differential patterns of lead concentration along the length of the strands (Kopito et al., 1967). Although the tissue is easily accessible and the test correlates well with increased burden (Pueschel et al., 1972), it is a difficult determination and has not seen wide use.

Measurements of Serum and Urinary ALA. Even though the serum ALA is elevated in intoxication, it is not as sensitive an indicator of lead effect as the FEP (free erythrocyte protoporphyrin) or direct assay of ALA dehydratase activity (Baloh, 1974). Urinary ALA unfortunately does not accurately reflect ALA synthesis unless a twenty-four-hour collection is obtained (Barnes et al., 1972), and this is impractical as a screening test.

Radiography. Although specific for acute or chronic lead ingestion, radiography is expensive, requires interpretation, and is generally reserved for confirmation of suspicious cases.

Blood Lead and FEP. This remains the most reliable of screening procedures, and has been used in the majority of screening programs. But other indirect tests of lead intoxication, such as urinary δ-amino levulinic acid or hair lead, have been tried (Hankin et al., 1970; Kopito et al., 1967). The advent of the free erythrocyte protoporphyrin (FEP) assay shows promise in identifying children with intoxication quickly and simply (Chisholm et al., 1974). Its correlation with asymptomatic increased lead burden has not yet been confirmed. Both blood lead and FEP determinations can be done on capillary blood and require only 10 to 50 ml per determination. Blood lead on such a small volume of blood has the disadvantage of being susceptible to contamination from soil on the skin of the patient unless the skin is carefully cleansed or blood is obtained by venipuncture. The latter procedure, in small children, is difficult enough to have effectively frustrated attempts at mass screening until micromethods and finger-prick became available.

Probably the most accurate way to measure blood-lead level is to use dithizone which, on combination with lead, produces a colorimetric measurement. The advantages of the method are accuracy and relatively low cost of equipment. The disadvantages are that it is a laborious and time-consuming chore and requires a rather large amount of blood. Two more modern methods that are ± 5 percent as accurate are:

1. Atomic absorption spectrophotometry. This is widely used for metal determination and can detect lead with adequate accuracy in as little as 10 μl of blood. The method is now fully automated. It is quick, has low cost per sample, and is simple (when automated). The disadvantages are that the equipment is expensive initially, and when not automated, the method is relatively complex.

2. Anodic stripping uses the ionic charge of the divalent cation and measures the electrical energy required to "electroplate" and remove a particular metal from a known anode. The machine used for this is exquisitely sensitive and highly accurate. (The sensitivity is a drawback, since it measures all contamination as well.) It requires fair skill to prepare the sample; fewer samples can be prepared daily than with atomic absorption. The most frequent use of anodic stripping is as a research tool.

Confirmation of the diagnosis of raised lead burden requires a complete history and physical examination, blood count, and X-rays of the long bones, at least. A useful lead mobilization test is based on the principle that the excretion of lead in urine is enhanced in the presence of the chelating agent ethylenediaminetetraacetate (EDTA) if the body burden of lead is elevated (Tersinger and Srbova, 1959). A positive test is greater than 1 μg lead excreted per mg EDTA injected per twenty-four hours. This test, however, is indicative only of elevated burden, and not necessarily of intoxication. The decision to treat a given child must depend on a weighing of all the known parameters, including his environment.

What Is Normal Level? Lin-Fu (1972) has commented on some of the erroneous concepts regarding "normal" blood-lead levels. One of the points she makes is that most workers, when speaking of normal levels, set them higher than they should because they associate the beginning of abnormal levels with clinical evidence of toxicity. "Symptoms from low-level lead intake may, for example, be overlooked because no one knows what to look for. Thus, children are considered asymptomatic because classic signs and symptoms of lead poisoning are absent." It is true that various studies, cited by her, define levels from 40 μg to 80 μg per 100 ml blood as normal. However, over the last few years the generally accepted idea of the upper limit of normal has been dropping as more sensitive tests of toxicity and associated sequelae have been developed. Most researchers now agree that blood lead above 24.5 μg per 100 ml is potentially dangerous and needs evaluation.

Finally, the development of a technique for analysis of lead in dentine by Needleman et al. (1972) suggests that determination of blood alone is indeed missing many children with elevated lead burden. Mean tooth-lead levels in lead-poisoned children were seven times those of children from suburban Boston, but those of suburban Boston were *two and one-half* times those of Icelandic children (Needleman and Shapiro, 1974). These findings suggest previously undetected increased burden in suburban children.

According to USDHEW (1975), undue lead absorption is present when a child has confirmed blood-lead levels of 30–79 μg per 100 ml or an EP (erythrocyte protoporphyrin) level greater than 60 μg per 100 ml. The exception is where the high EP level is caused by iron-deficiency anemia.

DIAGNOSIS

Evaluation should first include information on the size of the family and the condition of the home or the other places the child frequents —how old the buildings are and their condition. Whether the child has a history of pica is worth asking, but lead poisoning is seen without such a history. The child's appetite, bowel habits, and general behavior are just as important. Often there is a history of lethargy or irritability.

Laboratory Studies

After a complete physical examination, which should include the Denver Developmental Test and other psychometric tests, the following laboratory tests may be helpful.

1. An electroencephalogram. The EEG shows diffuse changes in encephalopathy.

2. Blood-lead values. These can be determined by the methods discussed earlier.

3. A complete blood count, with attention to basophilic stippling of the red cells.

4. The iron-binding capacity of the serum and serum iron levels.

5. Red cell protoporphyrin levels and δ-amino levulinic acid (ALA) levels reflect abnormal hemoglobin synthesis.

6. Assay of hair and teeth for lead. (The latter is presently a research tool.)

7. X-ray film of the skull for widening of sutures (encephalopathy) and X-rays of the metaphyses of the long bones (the wider part of the shaft at the ends) are helpful in that they show increased density when excess lead burden has been present for longer than three months.

8. Lead mobilization test. Urine is collected over twenty-four hours for measurement of the absolute amount of lead excreted. This measurement is done by determining the amount of lead bound by the chelating agent EDTA. The EDTA is given intramuscularly in a single dose of 50 mg per kg body weight, or in three divided doses totaling 75 mg per kg daily. If the twenty-four-hour collected urine yields more than 1 μg lead per mg of EDTA given, the available lead burden of the body is excessive. The concentration of lead in the urine plays no part in this test. The *absolute* amount of lead excreted is what counts. To determine this, the entire twenty-four-hour output of urine is required.

Indications for the lead mobilization test are:

1. Blood lead more than 60 μg per 100 ml whole blood.

2. Blood lead more than 30−60 μg per ml whole blood if at least one of the following is also present: hair lead greater than 100 μg per g in proximal segment, *or* symptoms of lead poisoning, *or* history of pica, *or* positive X-rays, *or* sibling(s) with lead intoxication, *or* unexplained anemia, *or* basophilic stippling of the red cells, *or* positive urinary or serum δ-ALA (δ-amino levulinic acid), *or* decreased erythrocyte δ-ALA dehydratase, *or* aminoaciduria and/or glycosuria, *or* decreased osmotic fragility (Graef and Cone, 1974).

Criteria for Positive Diagnosis

Definitive diagnosis will depend on whatever has seemed important from the evaluation that has been discussed—especially behavioral changes, vomiting, convulsions, or abdominal pain—plus laboratory findings as listed in the preceding section. Table 6—2 sums up the evidence for lead intoxication and also for abnormally high but asymptomatic lead burden.

THERAPY

At all costs, the source of lead must be removed, no matter what the other problems may be. The next step is to start removal from the body of lead already absorbed as quickly and safely as possible.

Ethylenediaminetetraacetate (EDTA) is the most efficient chelating agent for removing lead from soft tissue and from the central nervous system, although it does not remove lead from the red blood cells. It enhances urinary excretion twenty to fifty fold, and can have a toxic effect on the kidneys if given in high doses for a prolonged period. This effect is reversible. EDTA can be given in the form of a salt (Versenate) in standard doses of 50 mg per kg per twenty-four hours for the average patient. If lead poisoning is acute, EDTA is not given by mouth, but intramuscularly or intravenously. When taken by mouth it enhances absorption of lead from the gut.

Dimercaprol (BAL) actually removes more lead from the body per molecule than EDTA because it diffuses into the red blood cells, as EDTA does not, and because it enhances fecal as well as urinary excretion. If the kidneys are impaired (as by EDTA) BAL can still be given, because it is predominantly excreted in bile. Its disadvantages are that it must often be given intramuscularly and has toxic effects even in low doses. The usual dosage is 12 mg per kg daily, up to 24 mg per kg daily in severe cases, in three to six divided doses.

D-penicillamine is a degradation product of penicillin. Presently it is available only on an investigational basis in the United States. It is contraindicated in persons with a history of penicillin sensitivity. The following adverse side effects of penicillamine have been reported: transient eosinophilia, erythematous skin rashes, superficial extravasations of blood, fever, prolonged bleeding time, leukopenia, agranulocytosis and thrombocytopenia, and nephrotic syndrome. Patients receiving this drug must be monitored with weekly urinalyses and blood counts. Adverse side effects of D-penicillamine are apparently dose-related. Serious reactions (i.e., nephrotic syndrome) have been reported in patients receiving 1 to 2 g or more per day. Observations have indicated that dosages not exceeding 30 to 40 mg per kg per day in children have not been associated with serious side effects.

All the chelating agents remove other metals as well as lead. The most important of these is iron. However, zinc, cadmium, magnesium,

Table 6-2.   Clinical and Laboratory Evidence of Lead Intoxication and Asymptomatic Lead Burden

Lead Intoxication	*Asymptomatic Increased Lead Burden*
Clinical	Clinical
Anorexia, constipation, irritability, clumsiness, lethargy, behavior changes, hyperactivity (sequela), abdominal pain, vomiting, fever, hepatosplenomegaly, ataxia, convulsions, coma with increased cerebrospinal fluid pressure	History of pica Environmental lead source Positive family history
Laboratory	Laboratory
Microcytic, hypochromic anemia Basophilic erythrocyte stippling Increased δ-ALA in serum and urine Decreased δ-ALA dehydratase in erythrocytes Increased urinary coproporphyrin Increased erythrocyte protoporphyrin (more than 50 μg per ml whole blood) Decreased osmotic fragility Increased metaphyseal densities on X-ray Aminoaciduria, glucosuria	Blood lead greater than 30 μg per 100 ml Hair lead greater than 100 μg per 100 g in proximal segment 24-hour urinary lead excretion greater than 80-100 mg Lead mobilization test greater than 1 μg per mg EDTA injected per 24 hours Radiocapacity in gastrointestinal tract on X-ray

Source: Graef and Cone, 1974, p. 79.   Reprinted with permission of Little, Brown and Company.

and copper are among other metals excreted during chelation. While less is known about the need for their replacement, the replacement of iron after chelation is an essential part of treatment. This means that long-term iron therapy must be started after chelation.

Safety measures are needed during chelation therapy in the form of monitoring. Serum calcium, urea nitrogen, and routine urinalyses are monitored for evidence of hypocalcemia or renal toxicity. Occasionally symptoms may worsen during therapy, calling for special attention to changes in the central nervous system suggestive of cerebral edema. Such edema calls for special handling as will be outlined in discussing acute intoxication with encephalopathy.

Chelating agents are administered for up to five days at a time. If urinary lead excretion remains higher on the fifth day than 1 µg per mg EDTA injected over twenty-four hours, therapy is discontinued for forty-eight hours, then restarted. Alternatively, if lead excreted on the fifth day is less than 1 µg per mg EDTA, a new lead mobilization test is performed, after a hiatus of at least forty-eight hours.

Acute Lead Intoxication

EDTA should be given intravenously if possible, or intramuscularly if necessary. If the intramuscular route is chosen, the dose can be given twice daily, or even in a single injection—though with somewhat reduced efficiency.

If the lead burden appears high on the basis of blood level of more than 80 µg per 100 ml or markedly increased urinary excretion, both BAL and EDTA are given. BAL is added intramuscularly in three divided doses of 12−24 mg per kg body weight per twenty-four hours. Liver function tests, blood, and urine lead are monitored as well as urinalyses.

Acute Intoxication with Encephalopathy

This is a medical emergency. Maintenance fluids are given. EDTA is begun intravenously, 75 mg per kg body weight daily in three to six divided doses by slow drip. BAL is begun intramuscularly, 24 mg per kg daily in three to six divided doses. Cerebral edema is treated with mannitol and dexamethasone but *chelation therapy is continued* while doing so. The edema will not respond to therapy until the lead burden is reduced.

Seizures are treated with anticonvulsants.

After five days, therapy is discontinued for forty-eight hours, then restarted.

Some of the toxic effects of lead may be intensified if calcium

EDTA is given alone in the presence of very high tissue concentrations of lead. The addition of BAL to CaEDTA minimizes these toxic effects, greatly accelerates urinary lead excretion, and causes a significantly more rapid decrease in blood-lead concentration.

Immediate follow-up of initial parenteral chelation therapy with oral D-penicillamine virtually always obviates the need for repeated courses of parenteral chelation therapy. Close monthly follow-up should be continued so long as the child is at risk.

School officials should be alerted to the child's history. This syndrome produces sequelae (Byers and Lord, 1943).

PREVENTION

Screening

In 1970 the U.S. Congress passed the Lead Poison Prevention Act, which provided funds for screening of children and inspection of housing. The funds were given to individual municipalities to establish laboratory facilities and outreach capability. No provision was made for housing repair, medical costs, or research. Through the use of these and other locally derived funds, a number of cities and smaller communities in the United States have established screening and housing inspection programs.

There is general agreement that with increased screening parents and children become more aware of the dangers associated with lead ingestion. Sachs (1974), for example, reported a decrease in cases of elevated lead levels in an area of Chicago that has been screened annually since 1966. The occurrence of lead encephalopathy also appears to have decreased, although no comparable figures exist.

A concerted effort to screen children at risk for lead poisoning and to treat those with elevated blood lead resulted in marked diminution of incidence over a five-year period in which over 200,000 were tested.

In 1967, a blood-lead level of 50 μg per 100 ml or more was present in 8.5 percent of children tested at a lead clinic (its initial year). In 1968 the number was reduced to 3.8 percent and remained at 2 percent in each of the subsequent years. In all there were 6800 blood level results over 49 μg per 100 ml and three to four times as many between 40 and 49 μg per 100 ml.

Of the 6800 subjects with blood lead of at least 50 μg per 100 ml, there were 77.5 percent in the 50−59 μg range. Close to 10,000 children were admitted to the lead clinic between January 1967 and December 1971.

Four out of five patients had a history of ingestion of peeling paint and broken plaster. In another 10 percent the source of lead was established by disclosure of paint particles in the abdomen on X-ray. Although the screening was directed at a well-child population, 465 of the patients had blood-lead levels between 80 and 275 μg per 100 ml. This incidence, if the disease had been polio, would have been designated an epidemic and a national emergency would have been declared. But no alarm was sounded.

Results of mass screening have been remarkably consistent across the country, with a few notable exceptions. In general, the incidence of children with confirmed blood leads greater than 40 μg percent whole blood is highest in the inner cities, especially among black children (Anderson and Clark, 1974; Needleman and Shapiro, 1974). Table 6–3 shows the results of a survey of thirty communities by the Center for Disease Control (Anderson and Clark, 1974). Some "lead belt" environments produce elevated blood-lead levels in as high as 15 to 25 percent of children under six years of age (Lin-Fu, 1970).

In a house-to-house survey of a run-down neighborhood of Boston, parents of 705 children were interviewed on the children's eating of nonfood materials and on symptoms that might be compatible with lead poisoning. A hair sample was obtained from all the children and examined for lead content. When the concentration of lead was more than 100 μg per g, when there was a difference in concentration between the lead content of the two ends of the hair sample, or when there was some other history of pica, 3 ml of venous blood was obtained for determination of lead content. Ninety-eight of the 705 children were found to have increased lead burden as defined by the criteria of the study (Pueschel, 1972). Surrounding "bedroom" suburbs generally show much lower levels, of 1 to 2 percent of the susceptible population. An exception to this pattern is Pittsburgh, Pennsylvania, where, despite extensive screening, lead poisoning ap-

Table 6–3. Elevated Blood Lead Rates by Age and Black and Nonblack Groupings

	Less than 3 years		*3 years or over*		*Total*	
	No./total	*Percent*	*No./total*	*Percent*	*No./total*	*Percent*
Black	34/373	9.1	50/732	6.8	84/1105	7.6
Nonblack	19/508	3.7	16/656	2.4	35/1164	3.0
Total	53/881	6.0	66/1388	4.8	119/2269	5.2

Source: Anderson and Clark, 1974.

pears to be virtually nonexistent, even in the core city (Moriarty, 1974). This phenomenon has not been explained. Exceptions are also found in modern communities where leaded paint has not been used extensively.

Repair Housing

Insofar as removal of lead paint is part of the therapy, housing must be inspected and repairs initiated immediately. Satisfactory repairs and consequent protection of the child can frequently be accomplished by use of volunteer labor. Wallboard or fiberboard may be used to cover over exposed surfaces. Although there are risks for the workers involved, steaming or sanding lead paint down to the original wood is desirable if the paint is to be removed. Simply painting over lead paint has tragic consequences in children with pica, since, undeterred, they eat through the new layer. However, keeping flat wall surfaces in good repair to prevent flaking and chipping obviously reduces the hazard. Depending on the resources of the community, tax incentives to landlords can help stimulate voluntary compliance with sanitary code statutes, but stiff penalties may be required for noncompliance.

Until the advent of portable X-ray fluorescence, housing inspection required chipping paint from a surface and analyzing the chips in the laboratory by atomic spectrophotometry or other methods. This procedure necessarily reduced the speed and the number of dwellings inspected. Now, a single inspector using a portable X-ray device can inspect as many as fifteen individual units per day without damaging intact surfaces. In large eastern U.S. industrial cities, 50 to 80 percent of dwellings have interior surfaces containing potentially toxic levels of lead. Even in homes where interior paint does not contain lead, exterior paint has been used on windowsills and porches where small children have ready access.

In addition, there is increasing documentation of elevated levels of lead in soil, particularly surrounding highways, near the exterior surfaces of frame housing, and in communities with lead smelters. How much this soil contributes to the elevated burden of a given child is not known, but for many children it appears a likely source.

SUMMARY

In order to eliminate this manmade disease, potentially hazardous sources of lead in the environment should be eliminated. Screening programs have proven effective in identifying such sources, and in identifying children with excessive exposure to lead.

Large sums of money are required on a federal level to provide emergency housing repair, proper inspection, education, and research into newer, more efficient and less costly therapy.

Adequate medical follow-up should be available. Nothing is more frustrating to a community than a screening program that identifies a problem and then provides no follow-up for those found to be in need of medical care.

Finally, adequate provision must be made for the care and rehabilitation of victims of this disease.

REFERENCES

Alexander, F.W. "The uptake of lead by children in differing environments," *Environ Health Perspect* 7 (1974): 155.

Anderson, D.G., and Clark, J.L. "Neighborhood screening in communities throughout the nation for children with elevated blood lead levels," *Environ Health Perspect* 7 (1974): 3.

Baloh, R.W. "Laboratory diagnosis of increased lead absorption," *Arch Environ Health* 28 (1974): 198.

Barnes, J.R., Smith, P.E., and Drummond, C.M. "Urine osmolality and aminolevulinic acid excretion," *Arch Environ Health* 25 (1972): 450.

Berg, J.M., and Zappella, M. "Lead poisoning in childhood with particular reference to pica and mental sequelae," *J Ment Defic Res* 8 (1964): 44.

Byers, R.K. "Lead poisoning: Review of the literature and report on 45 cases," *Pediatrics* 23 (1959): 585.

Byers, R.K., and Lord, E.E. "Late effects of lead poisoning on mental development," *Am J Dis Child* 66 (1943): 471.

Chisholm, J.J. "Chelation therapy in children with subclinical plumbism," *Pediatrics* 53 (1974): 441.

Chisholm, J.J., and Kaplan, E. "Lead poisoning in childhood—comprehensive management and prevention," *J Pediatr* 73 (1968): 942.

Chisholm, J.J., Mellits, E.D., Keil, J.E., et al. "Variation in hematologic responses to increased lead absorption in young children," *Environ Health Perspect* 7 (1974): 7.

Clarkson, T.W., and Kench, J.E. "Uptake of lead by human erythrocytes in vitro," *Biochem J* 69 (1958): 432.

David, O.J. "Association between lower level lead concentrations and hyperactivity in children," *Environ Health Perspect* 7 (1974): 17.

de la Burde, B., and Choate, M.S., Jr. "Does asymptomatic lead exposure in children have latent sequelae?" *J Pediatr* 81 (1972): 1088.

Gibson, S.L.M., Lam, C.N., McCrae, W.M., et al. "Blood lead levels in normal and mentally deficient children," *Arch Dis Child* 42 (1967): 573.

Gibson, K.D., Neuberger, A., and Scott, J.J. "The purification and properties of δ-aminolevulinic acid dehydrase," *J Biochem* 61 (1955): 618.

Goldberg, A. "Drinking water as a source of lead pollution," *Environ Health Perspect* 7 (1974): 103.

Graef, J. "The prevention of lead poisoning," in *The Prevention of Genetic Disease and Mental Retardation*, edited by A. Milunsky. Philadelphia: W.B. Saunders Co., 1975.

Graef, J., and Cone, T.E., eds. *Manual of Pediatric Therapeutics*. Boston: Little, Brown and Company, 1974.

Hankin, L., Hanson, K.R., Kornfeld, J.M., et al. "A dipstick test for the mass screening of children for lead poisoning based on urinary delta-aminolevulinic ̓acid (ALA)," *Bull Conn Agric Exp Station*, New Haven, Conn., 716 (1970).

Hernberg, S., Nikkanen, J., Mellin, G., et al. "ẟ-Aminolevulinic acid dehydrase as a measure of lead exposure," *Arch Environ Health* 21 (1970): 140.

Jenkins, C.D., and Mellins, R.B. "Lead poisoning in children: a study of 46 cases," *Arch Neur Psychiat* 77 (1957): 70−78.

Kehoe, R.A. "Normal metabolism of lead," *Arch Environ Health* 8 (1964): 232.

Kopito, L., Byers, R.K., and Shwachman, H. "Lead in hair of children with chronic lead poisoning," *N Engl J Med* 276 (1967): 949.

Lin-Fu, J.S. "Undue absorption of lead among children—a new look at an old problem," *N Engl J Med* 286 (1972): 702.

Lin-Fu, J.S. "Childhood lead poisoning . . . an eradicable disease," *Children* 17 (1970): 2.

Mahaffey, K.R. "Nutritional factors and susceptibility to lead toxicity," *Environ Health Perspect* 7 (1974): 107.

Mahaffey, K.R., and Goyer, R.A. "Experimental enhancement of lead toxicity by low dietary calcium," *J Lab Clin Med* 76 (1970): 933.

Mitchell, D.G., and Aldous, K.M. "Lead contents of foodstuffs," *Environ Health Perspect* 7 (1974): 59.

Moriarty, R.W. "Screening to prevent lead poisoning," *Pediatrics* 54 (1974): 626−28.

Needleman, H.L., and Shapiro, I.M. "Dentine lead levels in asymptomatic Philadelphia school children: Subclinical exposure in high- and low-risk groups," *Environ Health Perspect* 7 (1974): 27.

Needleman, H.L., Tuncay, O.C., and Shapiro, I.M. "Lead levels in deciduous teeth of urban and suburban American children," *Nature* 235 (1972): 111.

Perlstein, M.A., and Attala, R. "Neurologic sequelae of plumbism in children," *Clin Pediatr* 5 (1966): 292.

Pichirallo, J. "Lead poisoning: Risks for pencil chewers?" *Science* 173 (1971): 509.

Piomelli, S., Davidow, B., Guinee, V.F., et al. "The FEP (free erythrocyte porphyrins) test: A screening micromethod for lead poisoning," *Pediatrics* 51 (1973): 254.

Pueschel, S.M. "Neurological and psychomotor function in children with increased lead burden," *Environ Health Perspect* 7 (1974): 13.

Pueschel, S.M., Kopito, L., and Shwachman, H. "Children with an increased lead burden. A screening and follow-up study," *JAMA* 232 (1972): 462.

Rabinovitz, M., and Waxman, H.S. "Dependence of polyribosome structure in reticulocytes on iron," *Nature* (London) 206 (1965): 897−900.

Rabinovitz, M., Wetherill, G., and Kopple, J. "Lead metabolism in the human: stable isotope studies," *Science* 182 (1973): 725.

Rapoport, M., and Rubin, M. "Lead poisoning: a clinical and experimental study of the factors influencing the seasonal incidence in children," *Am J Dis Child* 61 (1941): 245.

Rosen, J.F. and Trinidad, E.E. "Significance of plasma lead levels in normal and lead-intoxicated children," *Environ Health Perspect* 7 (1974): 139.

Shields, J.B., and Mitchell, H.H. "The effect of calcium and phosphorus on the metabolism of lead," *J Nutr* 21 (1941): 541.

Silbergeld, E.K., and Goldberg, A.M. "Hyperactivity: a lead-induced behavior disorder," *Environ Health Perspect* 7 (1974): 227.

Sobel, A.E., et al. "Influence of vitamin D in experimental lead poisoning," *Proc Soc Exp Biol Med* 38 (1938): 433.

Stover, B.J. "Ph^{212} tracer studies in adult beagle dogs," *Proc Soc Exp Biol Med* 100 (1959): 269.

Tersinger, J., and Srbova, J. "The value of mobilization of lead by calcium ethylene-diamine-tetra-acetate in the diagnosis of lead poisoning," *Br J Ind Med* 16 (1959): 148.

U.S. Department of Health, Education and Welfare. *Increased Lead Absorption and Lead Poisoning in Young Children*. Statement by the Center for Disease Control. Atlanta: Center for Disease Control, March 1975.

Waldron, H.A., and Stöfen, D. *Sub-clinical lead poisoning*. New York: Academic Press, Inc., 1974.

Waxman, H.S., and Rabinovitz, M. "Control of reticulocyte polyribosome content and hemoglobin synthesis by heme," *Biochim Biophys Acta* 129 (1966): 369–79.

Chapter 7

Middle Ear Infection

Barbara Starfield, M.D., M.P.H.

The most common etiologic factors in the development of middle ear infections are acute and chronic infections of the upper respiratory tract. Middle ear infection (otitis media) begins with a blockage of the Eustachian tube resulting from an inflammation. Fluid accumulates in the middle ear and, on appearance, the eardrum appears dull and perhaps reddened. As fluid increases and organisms (bacteria and viruses) multiply, the eardrum changes color and bulges, and the patient experiences pain and hearing loss. With adequate treatment of the infection and inflammation, symptoms subside and the eardrum returns to normal. With inadequate treatment, a potentially destructive process (chronic suppurative otitis) may develop, often accompanied by recurrent purulent discharge and hearing loss.

Chronic otitis, with or without suppuration, may be manifested by an eardrum that is retracted, scarred and thickened, fluid in the middle ear ranging from amber and watery (serous otitis media) to grey and gelatinous, and a chalky white appearance of the malleus and prominence of the short process. The ear may feel full to the patient. Without appropriate treatment (which may have to address allergic, endocrine, or chronic nasopharyngeal conditions), fibrous adhesions and permanently impaired hearing will result. (Kessner, 1973, Green and Haggerty, 1968).

PREVALENCE

Although it is difficult to determine accurately the incidence or prevalence of the disease, the great importance of otitis media in the spectrum of childhood problems is evident. In a review of a three-month period in a private practice group, Breese and his colleagues (1966) found that otitis media was the reason for more than 8 percent of patient visits, about 13 percent of all ill children seen, and 17 percent of all infections.

Similarly, the National Disease and Therapeutic Index (1974) reports otitis media as the third reason for visits to the pediatrician after well baby and child care and prophylactic inoculation. The National Ambulatory Medical Care Survey study lists otitis media as the fifth reason for physician visits for children fifteen and under.

Douglas and Blomfield (1958) in *Children Under Five* noted that 7 percent had "discharge" from their ears at some time or other. The Medical Research Council (1957) in a study of acute otitis media in general practice found that over a period of one year the incidence of acute otitis media in children under ten was 12 percent of the number at risk. In the Miller et al. study, *Growing up in Newcastle-Upon-Tyne* (1960), it was found that almost 20 percent of the 1000 children had had an attack of otitis media by the age of five.

Studies in a variety of practices indicate that most otitis media is seen in young children. Official morbidity statistics from general practice in Great Britain (Logan, 1960) show that when the children are divided into age groups 0—1 year, 1—5 years, and 5—14 years, the youngest group has a 50 percent higher consulting rate than the middle group, and a 30 percent higher rate than the oldest group.

In a study of acute otitis media cases seen in Copenhagen city hospitals (Nielson, 1945), over half the patients were four years old or younger, and the youngest children were particularly susceptible. Similarly, Kessner (1973) indicates that the Johns Hopkins Comprehensive Child Care Program records show that among approximately 1700 cases of otitis media annually, as many as 80 percent per quarter occur in children four and under. Feingold et al. (1966) studied children seen at Boston City Hospital and report that 62 percent of the otitis media cases occur in children two and under.

Surveys carried out in general practice, however, define a somewhat different age range for high risk. In an investigation of a series of cases with serous otitis media treated in general practice, Fernandez and McGovern (1965) found that 68 percent of the children first seen for treatment are between the ages of five and eight. They determined, however, that in 74 percent of the cases, the disease process is established before age four.

Lemon (1961), in a study of four hundred consecutive cases of serous otitis media over a three-year period in a Philadelphia office-based practice, determined that 70 percent of the children experienced onset of symptoms between four and seven, with a sharp peak rate at six. This age pattern is strikingly similar to incidence data from the Medical Research Council's study (1957) on acute otitis media in general practice in Great Britain. This study documents annual incidence for two-year-olds of 14 percent, climbing to a peak of 20 percent at six, and sharply declining among older children. Over-all incidence levels are 12 percent for children ten years and under. Two more recent British studies, based on general practice, produce comparable figures of 10 percent and 15 percent annual incidence in children under ten (Fry et al., 1969; Lowe et al., 1963).

In a ten-year general practice survey, Fry finds the highest annual incidence rates of acute otitis media among four-year-olds, with children four to eight experiencing a high risk of infection. In a Liverpool general practice studied by Lowe et al. (1963) an age distribution with two incidence peaks is observed, the first occurring in the second six months of life and the second in the five-to-six-year age group. In a study of South Carolina children with acute otitis media, Brownlee et al. (1966) document a comparable pattern in the relative frequency of attacks by age.

A study of hearing sensitivity and ear disease in a representative cross-section of the elementary public school population in Pittsburgh, Pennsylvania ($n = 3059$) carried out by Eagles et al. (1967) analyzed the age at which ear disease is most frequently discovered. They concluded that ear disease is most likely discovered for the first time from five to ten.

In a hearing survey conducted in Vancouver, Canada, by Robinson et al. (1967), the highest incidence rates of serous otitis media appeared in children in the first through third grades.

The discrepancies in reports on the age group at highest risk (i.e., preschool vs. school age) point up the fallacy of using data from single types of services for estimates of the epidemiologic distribution of disease. As it is likely that hospital facilities draw relatively more heavily from the younger children than nonhospital sources, it is to be expected that their diagnoses of otitis media will be concentrated in the younger age groups. To date, almost no clinical data have been reported in terms of rates of children at risk. To do this would require that the facility or practitioner know what proportion of children of particular ages are seen in the facility and to what extent each child uses it and for what. Data systems such as those organized by the Johns Hopkins University Health Services Research Center for the Columbia Medical Plan and the East Baltimore Medical Plan can provide such information. Preliminary data from this source (Table 7–1) indicate that just over one of five children enrolled in a plan that

Table 7–1.   Otitis Media in Columbia Medical Plan Enrollees *(percent with at least one episode in specified year)*

	July 1971–June 1972	July 1972–June 1973	July 1973–June 1974
Total enrolled under seventeen	2956	3942	4728
All types of episodes	percent enrollees	percent enrollees	percent enrollees
Total under 17	29.1	27.0	20.9
0–2 years[a]	68.5	54.5	44.1
3–6 years	42.1	41.5	32.1
7–16 years	16.8	16.0	13.3
Purulent episodes			
Total under 17	25.3	22.7	16.6
0–2 years[a]	66.4	53.7	41.9
3–6 years	38.5	35.4	26.9
7–16 years	12.6	11.9	9.1
Serous episodes			
Total under 17	4.3	5.6	5.0
0–2 years[a]	1.7	1.5	2.5
3–6 years	5.0	7.4	6.4
7–16 years	4.3	5.4	4.8
Mixed episodes			
Total under 17	3.4	2.5	2.3
0–2 years[a]	6.4	4.1	4.0
3–6 years	5.9	5.2	4.1
7–16 years	1.8	1.1	1.3

[a] Newborns during fiscal year excluded.
Source: Adapted from Steinwachs and Yaffe, 1974.

covers all health needs has at least one episode of otitis in a year. Over two-thirds of these children have episodes of acute otitis media, and over 10 percent have both acute and serous episodes.

The type of otitis is highly related to age: children under two are much less likely to have a chronic otitis episode than an acute episode (6.5 vs. 46 percent) as are three-to-six-year-olds (10.5 vs. 31 percent), but children aged seven to sixteen are almost equally at risk of serous (chronic) otitis (6.1 percent) as of an acute episode (10.4 percent). These findings appear to indicate that acute episodes are concentrated in the younger age groups, but that by school age chronic otitis media is likely to be a significant problem.

Some studies (Medical Research Council, 1957; Suehs, 1952) have attempted to relate the age distribution to physiological factors or differences of development that might result in greater risk during early childhood. However, it seems that it is the duration, severity, or frequency of otitis media episodes, rather than age, that is connected with the risk of subsequent hearing loss (Fry, 1969; Suehs, 1952; Reed et al., 1967).

Whether the children who are at greatest risk of chronic otitis in the school-age period are those who have had the most problem with acute episodes earlier, or whether ear problems in general are likely to arise for the first time during the school-age period is unclear. Only extensive, large-scale studies will elucidate the natural history of the disease and the way in which medical care influences it.

Although definitive research is lacking, most investigators agree that studies of selected populations indicate that a high rate of middle ear disease is related to low socioeconomic status. Probably this is attributable to a combination of high-risk environmental conditions and poor access to medical care.

In a report on the middle ear disease problem among American Indians and Alaskan natives, Deuschle (1969) concludes that "the most obvious common denominator for high rates of middle ear disease is a poverty-related factor." Kessner (1973) points out that most studies in both Eskimo and American Indian populations have found a relationship between poverty and poor living conditions and middle ear disease.

FUNCTIONAL IMPACT OF OTITIS MEDIA[a]

The Health and Nutrition Examination Survey (U.S. National Health Survey, Series 11, No. 114) provided information both on the relation-

[a]This section relies heavily on the material prepared by Kessner (1973).

ship of age to abnormalities of the ear on otoscopic examination and on the relationships between history of ear problems, otoscopic examination, and hearing testing in children six to eleven. One child in five was reported to have a history of earache, one in eight a history of running ear, and one in twenty-five trouble in hearing. The prevalence of these findings was not higher in older children than in younger ones. Children with a history of ear problems were significantly more likely to have abnormalities of the tympanic membrane (Table 7–2) and lower sensitivity (poor hearing) on audiometric testing than other children. The proportion of children with abnormalities on examination did not change significantly with age within the range covered by the survey.

Unfortunately, this survey provided no information on the relationship between otoscopic or audiometric abnormalities and the receipt of medical care. It does, however, indicate that many children with infectious or allergic disorders have not achieved normality of their ears. The lack of change in prevalence with age, from six to eleven, indicates that much or most of the damage is probably done before the child reaches school age.

Fortunately, with the widespread use of antibiotics, mastoiditis, labyrinthitis, and other serious complications of otitis media have become rare (Medical Research Council, 1957; Fry et al., 1969). Not rare at all, however, is the hearing loss suffered by children with otitis media. The U.S. Health Examination Survey (Series 11, No. 114) findings indicate that about 55 out of 100 children with some history of a hearing problem suffered from either earaches or running ears. Middle ear infections were assumed to be responsible for over 50 percent of all hearing loss in children (Fisher, 1966; Stataloff and Vassalo, 1965; Lowe et al., 1963).

The incidence and prevalence of otitis media in the U.S. is difficult to pinpoint. We do know that in Great Britain about one-half of all children have experienced at least one episode of suppurative otitis media by age eight and, five to ten years after the initial episode as many as 17 percent are suffering loss of hearing (Fry et al, 1969; Lowe et al., 1963). Kessner (1973) points out that the incidence of serous otitis media and its sequelae are difficult to appraise because that form of the disease is often asymptomatic but that is widely viewed as the most frequent cause of hearing loss in children.

There have been several critical reviews (Kessner, 1973; Bluestone and Shurin, 1974; Rowe, 1975) of studies to determine the relationship of middle ear effusions and hearing loss to educational progress. All have concluded that hearing loss is related to poor school achievement, even when the loss is mild. In these studies the degree of loss in speech frequencies is roughly comparable to that occurring in chronic otitis media. The degree of retardation is correlated with the degree of hearing impairment, but even children with slight losses are significantly retarded. Both language acquisition and school learning may be impaired. Rowe (1975) indicates that the effects of secretory otitis media on the social and emotional development of children may be even more important than the effects on language development and academic skills.

EFFICACY OF DIAGNOSTIC PROCEDURES

Acute otitis media is defined as an inflammation of part or all of the mucoperiosteal lining of the middle ear cleft or the tympanic membrane. Predisposing factors include forced nose-blowing, rapid barometric changes, and Eustachian tube aspiration of milk in bottle-fed infants who drink in a recumbent position. Nasopharyngeal secretions due to thumb-sucking and blood-borne viremias may play a part (Lamp, 1973; Hemenway and Smith, 1970a). Obstruction of the Eustachian tube by congenital deformity, traumatic injury, or postoperative complication contributes to the condition by interfering with normal middle ear ventilation and drainage and by causing pressure changes within the middle ear (Armstrong, 1957).

The acute state of otitis media is characterized by fever, redness, and slight swelling or retraction of the eardrum. The inflammation and infection may progress to the point of severe earache, purulent exudate, and perforation of the tympanic membrane. Mastoiditis and meningitis may follow. Particularly in younger children (ages four to eight), episodic recurrence of the disease is common because of the anatomic structure of the Eustachian tube. If the attack is unremitting, it is termed chronic suppurative otitis media.

Until recently, techniques for adequate diagnosis of otitis media have not been available. Paradise (1975) has demonstrated unreliability of otoscopic diagnosis of the middle ear disease. Preliminary data from his studies comparing otoscopic diagnoses with typanometric findings indicate a 15 to 20 percent misclassification with otoscopic examination. The lack of objective and reliable criteria for diagnosis has resulted not only in inability to define epidemiologically the incidence and prevalence of middle ear disease, but has also hampered assessment of the efficacy of various therapeutic approaches. If it is impossible to accurately determine the presence of disease, it is impossible to adequately define population and control groups for study of varied modes of therapy.

The difficulty of diagnosing otitis may be relieved by the technique

Table 7–2.   Ear, Nose, and Throat Findings in Children Six to Eleven with Some History of Ear or Hearing Problems, United States 1963–65

Condition on Examination	Total Prevalence Rate	History of Abnormality							Standard Error for Abnormal Findings
		Hearing Trouble	Ear-aches	Injury to Ear	Drum Opened	Other Ear Operation	Running Ears	Other Ear Trouble	
		Rate per 100 Children							
Total prevalence rate		4.2	26.6	2.4	3.0	0.7	11.8	4.8	
Auditory canal, right									
Normal	84.3	4.0	26.2	2.3	3.2	0.7	11.6	4.7	
Abnormal	15.7	5.4	29.0	2.8	1.9	0.6	12.9	5.4	0.86
Auditory canal, left									
Normal	84.6	3.7	25.7	2.4	3.1	0.7	11.5	4.8	
Abnormal	15.4	6.8	31.5	2.5	2.2	1.1	13.9	5.1	0.85
Drum, right									
Normal	76.5	2.8	24.4	1.9	2.5	0.5	10.6	4.5	
Abnormal	13.5	10.6	37.4	4.7	5.9	2.4	18.0	6.6	
Not visible	10.0	5.9	29.5	3.0	1.8	0.2	12.9	5.3	1.35
Drum, left									
Normal	76.5	3.0	24.2	1.9	2.6	0.6	10.3	4.5	
Abnormal	13.7	10.0	36.2	5.0	5.5	1.8	18.5	6.5	
Not visible	9.8	6.2	32.0	2.4	1.9	0.5	14.7	5.3	1.36

Tonsils								
Removed	13.9	8.6	29.9	5.0	8.2	2.9	16.8	8.6
Tags present	9.6	2.9	25.0	2.1	5.0	1.0	13.4	6.5
Grade I	41.5	3.1	25.8	1.9	1.8	0.4	10.2	3.6
Grade II	33.9	4.0	26.8	2.1	1.7	0.3	11.2	4.1
Grade III	1.2	5.7	29.6	0.0	0.8	0.0	18.1	10.4
Oral pharynx								
Normal	90.0	4.1	26.4	2.4	2.9	0.7	11.7	4.8
Abnormal	10.0	5.5	28.5	2.8	4.0	0.9	13.8	4.7
Nose right								
Normal	80.5	3.8	26.3	2.3	2.9	0.7	11.4	4.7
Abnormal	19.5	5.9	28.0	2.8	3.2	0.8	13.6	5.2
Nose, left								
Normal	80.5	3.7	26.5	2.4	2.8	0.7	11.5	4.7
Abnormal	19.5	6.1	27.4	2.4	3.2	0.8	12.8	5.3
Standard error, total		0.37	0.82	0.16	0.34	*	0.50	0.30

Source: U.S. National Health Survey, 1972.

of tympanometry, particularly in the very young child (Paradise 1976, 1977; Shurin 1977). Tympanometry substitutes the objective measurement of eardrum tension, which reflects the presence of fluid, for the subjective judgment of examination by the human eye. As such it will facilitate studies of diagnostic and therapeutic efficacy and be useful as a teaching device.

Despite the evidence that otitis is one of the most common acute ailments in childhood and that it has far-reaching effects on learning and performance, very little attention has been devoted to its scientific study. Tremendous confusion has resulted from the contradictory nature of published data on epidemiology and treatment, not to speak of the illogical terminology used to denote various stages of illness. In contrast to rare disorders, where scientific study is the rule, the natural history of common conditions has become obscured by the overriding need to deal with them pragmatically. Moreover, the study of esoteric illness is more likely to take place in the scholarly atmosphere of inpatient wards of teaching institutions, in contrast to primary care problems in ambulatory patients. The encouragement of methodologically sound research in primary care problems is of high priority at this time.

EFFICACY OF MANAGEMENT OF OTITIS MEDIA[b]

The treatment of otitis media is important not only because of possible life-threatening complications of the infection, but also because of residual hearing loss. Details of antimicrobial therapy such as drug dosage, contraindications, and toxicities are summarized in three reviews (Hemenway and Smith, 1970b; Glorig and Gerwin, eds., 1962; Armstrong, 1957).

Otitis media is usually a self-limited disease, with spontaneous recovery occurring in the majority of untreated cases. In approximately 75–80 percent of afflicted patients the inflammatory process is rapidly controlled regardless of therapy (Halsted, 1968). In one series, 79 percent of children with earache and red drum had a normal drum in seven to fourteen days without antibiotics and 64 percent of children with aural discharge had their problem resolved in fourteen to twenty-one days without drugs (Fry, 1961).

Two major principles apply to treatment of otitis media: medical control of the infection by chemotherapy, and surgical drainage of pus and other exudates (Fry, 1961). In addition to antibiotics,

[b]The author is indebted to Rona Sayetta for her contribution to this section.

analgesics and narcotics for pain relief and antihistamines and vaso-constrictors for decongestion have been advocated. Incision of the tympanic membrane (myringotomy) may be made more effective by inserting a small piece of plastic tubing for prolonged drainage before the drum heals shut.

Drug Therapies

The literature reveals considerable controversy over antibiotic and decongestant therapies for otitis media. The advent of the antibiotic era has been accompanied by a decline in the perceived virulence of common infecting organisms, but a cause-and-effect relationship is not proved (Harper, 1954). The overutilization of some antibiotics, in fact, has led to resistant mutants either in primary infection or on superinfection. Other dangers inherent in the injudicious use of antibiotic therapy are side effects such as drug fevers, rashes, and itching; allergic sensitization; and the masking of serious secondary symptoms such as mastoiditis and meningitis (Williams, 1966; Hara, 1959). The expense and potential danger of antibiotic therapy, when viewed together with the high rate of spontaneous recovery from otitis media, would seem to dictate a selective approach to the use of such drugs.

Fry in his three-year study (1961) of 283 cases of acute otitis media emphasizes that antibiotic therapy should be started immediately:

1. if the child has serious general illness, including "much distress, high fever, and a raised pulse rate";
2. if the child has had prior severe attacks of otitis media;
3. if severe earache is uncontrolled by analgesics and is accompanied by profuse purulent discharge and mastoid tenderness; and
4. if observation of the patient over a period of twenty-four to forty-eight hours indicates no obvious improvement.

In the Fry series of cases, antibiotics were found necessary by the above criteria in 21 percent of the attacks occurring in patients with earache and a red drum and in 36 percent of those with discharge. Unfortunately, the validity of these assertions was not documented.

Most people agree that diffusely red tympanic membrane without changes in landmarks or light reflex does not require treatment with antibiotics (Halsted et al., 1968).

Ideally, the antibiotics chosen for treatment should be related to the infecting bacteria, and none should be given for viral infections. In actual practice, cultures and sensitivity studies may not be done, the results may fail to identify a responsible pathogen, or it may be necessary to initiate broad-spectrum antibiotic therapy before definitive results become known. Furthermore, it has been demonstrated that the most common culture sites (throat, nasopharynx) are unsuitable for recovering the middle ear pathogen (Hemenway and Smith, 1970a; Blaud, 1972; Nilson et al., 1969).

Past the neonatal period, the overwhelmingly most common bacterial isolates are pneumococcus, hemophilus, and betahemolytic streptococcus. Studies of the effectiveness of particular antibiotics have failed to adequately clarify required therapy. Most are in agreement that the response to particular antibiotics is not well correlated with type of bacterial pathogen and that the response to the most commonly used antibiotics (penicillin, ampicillin, erythromycin) does not differ significantly, even when controlling for type of bacterial pathogen (Strickler, 1973). Therefore, either penicillin or ampicillin is recommended for therapy, but there is no data that bears on appropriate length of treatment (Albemarle County EMCRO Review). Even though many of the studies employ the double-blind technique, most fail either to perform tympanocentesis to isolate bacterial pathogens or to assess compliance with medication. A serious methodologic flaw in all studies is in the assessment of outcome; all use otoscopic examination by single observers as a means of determining whether or not there has been a response to therapy. A review of the literature carried out by the Albemarle County Experimental Medical Review Organization (1974) emphasizes that "the key to the appropriate length of therapy is not the number of days the medication is given but the results of appropriate follow-up." Unfortunately, the nature of that follow-up is not discussed.

Perforation of the tympanic membrane may cause otitis externa. If severe, this may be treated with a topical antibiotic such as colistimethate in the form of eardrops (Graef and Cone, eds., 1974). Generally, however, antibiotic eardrops are of no value in acute suppurative otitis media with a draining ear because they cannot reach the site of infection and may actually increase the rate of complications (Hemenway and Smith, 1970b).

Oral vasoconstrictor decongestants may be employed to provide symptomatic relief, although their clinical efficacy is unproved (Graef and Cone, eds., 1974). One clinical study which involved the use of the sympathomimetic drug pseudoephedrine showed that adding this agent to an antimicrobial regimen of tetracycline, penicillin, or penicillin plus triple sulfonamide had no demonstrable effect on the number of treatment failures, recurrences, or cases of residual fluid in the middle ear when compared to cases treated with tetracycline or penicillin alone (Rubenstein et al., 1965). This study did not include a totally untreated control group.

Regarding the benefit of antihistamines, a chlorpheniramine maleate (Chlor-Trimeton) was added to antimicrobial drugs in another clinical trial of the treatment of acute otitis media (Strickler et al., 1967). For reasons that were not elucidated, treatment failure was observed less frequently when the antihistamine was added to a regimen of penicillin alone or penicillin plus sulfonamides than when it was omitted. Again, no totally untreated control group was included in the study. In another study, Triaminic (a mixture of phenylpropanolamine hydrochloride, pheniramine maleate, and pyrilamine maleate) was helpful (Halsted et al., 1968). Others feel, however, that antihistaminic drugs may prolong respiratory infection by drying the mucosa (Glorig and Gerwin, eds., 1962).

In addition to sympathomimetic nosedrops or systemic drugs and antihistamines, saline or combination nosedrops may be used to keep the nasal passages open (Graef and Cone, eds., 1974). It is doubtful, however, that nosedrops shrink the membranes of the Eustachian tube, and overuse of these irritant solutions may be harmful by causing a rebound effect of the nasal mucosa (Glorig and Gerwin, eds., 1962).

Pain relief may be obtained from glycerine eardrops (Auralgan) applied locally and from aspirin, which also reduces fever (Fry, 1961).

Myringotomy

There is controversy in the research literature regarding the indications for myringotomy in specific cases of suppurative otitis media. Based on case studies, surgical drainage has been advocated to avoid possible complications (Goodale and Montgomery, 1955). The arguments for this procedure are:

1. In the absence of needle aspiration and culture of the middle ear fluid (diagnostic tympanocentesis), the infecting organisms cannot be positively identified. This enhances the risks of antibiotic therapy.

2. Failure to incise the drum to relieve the build-up of fluid pressure behind it may invite rupture, with possible permanent hearing loss as a result.

3. Lack of drainage of purulent exudate from the middle ear may promote possible extension of the disease to the mastoid air cells and beyond. This danger is believed by some to exceed greatly that of possible trauma to the drum by myringotomy (Goodale and Montgomery, 1955).

4. Lack of drainage may prevent an antibiotic from coming into direct contact with the infecting bacteria. Its effectiveness may depend on such contact (Goodale and Montgomery, 1955; Bass et al., 1971).

5. In those patients initially experiencing severe earache, pain may not be relieved by analgesics and narcotics. But it usually is relieved by myringotomy (Roddey et al., 1966).

Prevention of Recurrences

Controlled studies have shown that adenotonsillectomized children have decreased susceptibility to respiratory tract infections, especially throat illness and catarrh, and lower incidence of recurrent otitis media than unoperated controls (Royhouse, 1970; Mawson et al., 1968; McKee, 1963). Although tonsillectomy does not appear to affect the susceptibility of children and adults to infection, adenoidectomy alone does seem to benefit children aged two to eight (Haggerty, 1968; Chamovitz et al., 1960). Tonsillectomy and adenoidectomy, then, should be considered as two separate procedures with different indications for each (Paradise and Bluestone, 1976; Reid and Donaldson, 1970). The indications for adenoidectomy include: recurrent suppurative otitis media and recurrent middle ear effusions or secretory otitis media with resulting conductive hearing loss.

Two well-controlled studies indicate that certain antibiotics may be effective as prophylaxis against recurrent attacks in young children (Maynard et al., 1972; Perrin et al., 1974). The long-term usefulness of this approach in preventing sequelae of otitis media is unknown.

This brief summary of the efficacy of therapy for otitis media points up the need for fresh approaches. Very few of the studies consider the accuracy of the diagnosis itself in allocating children to treatment or control groups. Plans for long-term assessment of response to therapy are lacking. If it is true that 75 percent of instances of otitis media are self-limited, this will have serious implications for the design of studies comparing different modes of therapy. It is no wonder that there are conflicting reports of efficacy of specific antibiotics: the proportion of children at risk of being improved by therapy is actually only 25 percent of study samples. This undoubtedly is much too small a group of children in which to test for significantly different effects produced by various drugs.

EFFECTIVENESS OF MEDICAL CARE
FOR OTITIS MEDIA

Problem Recognition

The data available suggests that failure to adequately recognize ear pathology in children is a major problem, even though otitis media is on of the most common causes of morbidity in infants and young children.

Kessner (1974) reviewed records in practices of physicians identified as the regular source of care for approximately 650 children with a history or examination indicating a possible ear problem. Data bearing on ear disease were found in the medical records of only 213 (32 percent) of these children.

In Pittsburgh, when Eagles et al. (1967) conducted hearing-level determinations and otolaryngological examinations on 5748 supposedly normal elementary school children, he found abnormalities, 94 percent of which were attributable to otitis media, in 746 (13 percent) of them.

Diagnosis

Paradise (1975) showed that physicians missed over 15 percent of effusions in examining the ears of children under age three, even when they were aware they were being tested.

Kessner (1974) also found that appropriate diagnoses are not made in about 25 percent of children, even when physicians recognize that an ear problem is present. In 90 percent of the remaining children, the recorded diagnosis was nonspecific. This study indicated a paucity of recorded diagnostic data in the medical records of these children; fewer than 20 percent mentioned a prior history of otitis, and fewer than 10 percent mentioned complaints of hearing loss. One-fifth of the charts lacked any mention of what the ear looked like on examination.

Management

Criteria for adequate therapy usually include: accepted dosage adjusted to the individual patient, monitoring for contraindications, and monitoring for common side effects according to information detailed in AMA Drug Evaluations, 1971 (Criteria and treatment for acute otitis media from Kessner, 1973).

Treatment of Acute Otitis Media. (1) Antimicrobial drugs. The duration of treatment is seven to ten days. In general, multiple antimicrobials should not be used. Under six years of age, ampicillin is the drug of choice. If the child is six years or older, penicillin G, one of its derivatives, or tetracycline is the drug of choice. If the patient is allergic to penicillin, erythromycin should be substituted. (2) Nasal decongestant. Ephedrine class of compounds should be given orally, no combinations.

Treatment of Nonsuppurative (Serous) Otitis Media. (1) Antimicrobials as described are indicated if there is evidence of concomitant suppurative infection. (2) Antihistamines should be used only if there is evidence of allergy. (3) Nasal decongestant: ephedrine class of compounds by oral route; no combinations.

In Kessner's study assessing medical care (1974), it was noted that 75 percent of the children with recognized otitis media received appropriate antibiotic treatment. Extensive review of the literature and a Medlars search failed to produce any other studies of the extent to which the accepted treatment regimen is prescribed. The National Disease and Therapeutics Index (1974), derived from selected office practices, lists drugs used for the diagnosis of acute otitis media, chronic otitis media, and otitis media nonspecified, but does not indicate the dosage or duration of treatment. At least 57 percent of visits, ranging from 20 percent in chronic otitis media to 67 percent in acute otitis media, were associated with prescription of penicillin or ampicillin, and an additional 16 percent received other antibiotics. Twenty-five percent (range 7−32 percent) received oral cold preparations, 5 percent (range 0−15 percent) nonnarcotic analgesics, 5 percent (range 5−20 percent) corticosteroids with antiinfectives, and 6 percent cold and cough preparations. Only 41 percent of these visits were initial visits, however (49 percent of the visits for acute otitis media), and it is impossible to determine the extent of prescription drugs at the initial visit and the follow-up visits separately in the published material. Further, these visits are to all types of physicians (although 74 percent were to family practitioner or pediatricians) and for all ages (80 percent were under nineteen).

Compliance

Compliance with prescribed medical regimens is uneven but in most places disturbingly inadequate. In a collaborative study of private practices, Charney et al. (1967) showed that only 56 percent of children being treated for otitis media or pharyngitis were taking the penicillin on the ninth day.

Bass and colleagues (1971) in a study at an army base tested urines for the presence of excreted antibiotic at the second and seventh day of therapy, and found compliance rates of 94 percent and 82 percent respectively.

Becker et al. (1972a) drew a random sample of 125 cases from a population of children being treated for otitis media in the Comprehensive Child Care Clinic at the Johns Hopkins Hospital. The children ranged in age from six weeks to ten years. All were placed on a regimen of liquid oral antibiotic. Despite the fact that arrangements were made for a follow-up visit, an hour-long interview conducted in the clinic immediately after the visit with the pediatrician, and medication provided free of charge, a compliance rate of only 49.1 percent on the fifth day of treatment was observed.

Follow-up Care

The functional impact of otitis media, its special importance in causing possible damage to the middle ear and deafness, has been illustrated. It is well known that the disease tends to recur. It is in this context that adequate follow-up must be viewed.

The accepted procedure is to: (1) Reexamine ten to fourteen days after beginning treatment; (2) evaluate hearing if there are repeated infections or evidence of hearing loss; and (3) refer to otolaryngologist if there is persistent infection or effusion not responsive to three courses of treatment; or if there is recurrent infection calling for a decision for tonsillectomy and adenoidectomy.

In Kessner's study (1973) less than 40 percent received a follow-up examination within two weeks after treatment and less than 7 percent were seen within ten to fourteen days.

It was noted previously that one of the most common complications of middle ear infection in young children is conductive hearing loss. Kessner (1973) found that 7 percent of the four-to-eleven-year-olds suffered from hearing loss in the speech frequency range. One of the hardest tasks in the management of deafness after acute otitis media is to identify the affected children; often even the mothers are unaware of the child's disability. Nevertheless, less than 20 percent of the physicians who gave care to the children in his study claimed that they use an audiometer to routinely screen for hearing loss in four-to-eleven-year-olds. Among the charts reviewed, less than 3 percent had records of hearing tests. Even among the 213 children in whom ear pathology was recognized, less than 5 percent had had their hearing tested by their primary provider. (About 10 percent of the children with ear disease had been referred for specialty care at which time hearing may have been assessed, but if it was, there was no record that the specialist notified the primary physician or that the primary physician followed-up with the specialist.)

An additional problem in follow-up is presented when the physician does indeed attempt to follow-up a patient and is unable to do so. Often, as noted above, mothers are unaware of the residual effects of otitis media and, after a week of therapy, believe the child to be "cured."

Fry, in an attempt to follow-up a group of 444 children who had suffered from acute otitis media, was actually able to follow only 400 of them adequately (Fry et al., 1969).

These findings were supported in a compliance study done by Becker et al. (1972b) in which only 40.7 percent of initial follow-up appointments were kept.

There is no information to indicate whether practitioners use prophylactic antibiotics to prevent recurrences.

Outcome

In Kessner's (1973) study, 7 percent of the children with otitis media were known to have suffered hearing loss in the speech frequency. Neil et al. (1966) conducted a survey of 171 cases of otitis media, of whom 121 were followed up with audiometry, and found that only two children suffered permanent hearing loss in both ears and six a permanent loss in one ear. At the first testing, 20 percent of the children had a hearing loss of over 20 db in one or both ears, but in most cases they recovered (the average time between the attack and a normal hearing test being 23 months). A further 15 percent had a minor hearing loss of between 10 and 20 db.

The Medical Research Council report (1957) found 6.5 percent of the children treated for otitis media still had some hearing abnormality six months after treatment.

Olmsted et al. (1961) followed eighty-two children two and a half to twelve years of age following an attack of suppurative otitis media. Fifty (61 percent) had hearing loss (15 db loss in any one frequency) one month after treatment, and 10 (21 percent) had hearing loss that persisted for the six-month period of observation.

A ten-year study of Alaskan Eskimo children (who have an extremely high incidence of otitis media) studied the long-term effects (Kaplan et al., 1973). Histories of ear disease, otoscopic examinations, and audiologic intelligence and achievement tests were obtained from a cohort of 489 children who had been followed through the first ten years of life. Of the 489 children, 78 percent had the first attack during their first two years. Perforations and scars were present in 41 percent. A hearing loss of 26 db or more was present in 16 percent, and an additional 25 percent were in the normal range but had a measurable air-bone gap. Children with a history of otitis media prior to two years of age and a hearing loss of 26 db or greater had a statistically significant loss of verbal ability and were behind in reading, math, and language. Additionally, the children who had an early onset but now had normal hearing with a conductive component were also affected adversely.

Lowe et al. (1963) performed audiometry on sixty-two children in a general practice six months after one episode of otitis media; thirty-four (55 percent) had hearing losses of 30 db or more.

Fry et al. (1969) studied 403 children in general practice in London five to ten years following at least one episode of acute otitis media. Seventeen percent suffered a hearing loss of 20 db or more in at least two frequencies.

Because of the evidence that otitis media may be associated with subsequent hearing loss, it is of concern that practitioners do not routinely assure that treated otitis heals without sequelae. In only about 50 percent of the records in Kessner's (1973b) study was there indication that the ear problem had resolved.

REFERENCES

Albemarle County Experimental Medical Care Review Organization. *Otitis Media: Standards for Quality Care*, mimeo. undated.

Armstrong, B.W. "Chronic secretory otitis media: diagnosis and treatment," *South Med J* 50 (1957): 540.

Bass, J.W., et al. "Erythromycin concentrations in middle ear exudates," *Pediatrics* 48 (1971): 417.

Becker, M.H., Drachman, R.H., and Kirscht, J.P. "Predicting mother's compliance with pediatric medical regimens," *Med Care* 81 (1972a): 343.

Becker, M.H., Drachman, R.H., and Kirscht, J.P. "Motivations as predictors of health behavior," *Health Services Rep* 87 (1972b): 852–61.

Blaud, R.D. "Otitis media in the first six weeks of life: diagnosis, bacteriology, and management," *Pediatrics* 49 (1972): 187.

Bluestone, C., Shurin, P. Middle Ear Disease in Children. *Ped Clin North Am* 21 (1974): 379.

Breese, B.B., Disney, F.A., Talpley, W. "Nature of a small pediatric group practice," *Pediatrics* 38 (1966): 264.

Brownlee, R.G., Delouche, W.R., Cowan, C.C., et al. "Otitis media in children," *Pediatrics* 75 (1966): 636–42.

Chamovitz, R., et al. "Effect of tonsillectomy on the incidence of streptococcal respiratory disease and its complications," *Pediatrics* 256 (1960): 355.

Charney, E., Bynum, R., Eldredge, D., Frank, D., MacWhinney, J.B., McNabb, N., Scheiner, A., Sumpter, E., and Iker, H. "How well do patients take oral penicillin? A collaborative study in private practice," *Pediatrics* 40 (1967): 188.

Deuschle, K.W. "A report on the middle ear disease problem among the American Indian and Alaska natives," (mimeographed report) New York: Mt. Sinai School of Medicine, Department of Community Medicine, March 1969.

Douglas, J.W.B., and Blomfield, J.M. *Children Under Five.* London: Allen and Unwin, 1958.

Eagles, E.L., Wishik, S.M., and Doefler, L.G. "Hearing sensitivity and ear disease in children: a prospective study," *Laryngoscope* (monograph supplement), 1967.

Feingold, M., Klein, J.O., Haslan, G.E., et al. "Acute otitis media in children," *Am J Dis Child* 3 (1966): 361–65.

Fernandez, A.A., McGovern, J.P. "Secretory otitis media in allergic infants and children," *South Med J* 58 (1965): 581–85.

Fisher, B. "The social and emotional adjustment of children with impaired hearing attending ordinary classes," *Br J Educ Psychol* 36 (1966): 319–21.

Frederickson, J.M. "Otitis media and its complications 1967 and 1968," *Arch Otolaryngol* 90 (1969): 387–93.

Fry, J. *The Catarrhal Child.* London: Butterworth, 1961.

Fry, J., Dillane, J.B., Jones, R.F., et al. "The outcome of acute otitis media," *Br J Prev Soc Med* 23 (1969): 205–09.

Glorig, A., Gerwin, K.S., eds. *Otitis Media: Proceedings of the National Conference, Callier Hearing and Speech Center, Dallas, Texas.* Springfield, Ill.: Charles R. Thomas Co., 1962.

Goodale, R.L., Montgomery, W.W. "Dangers inherent in the nonsurgical concept of acute suppurative otitis media," *Ann Otol Rhinol Laryngol* 64 (1955): 181.

Graef, J.W., Cone, I.E. Jr., eds. *Manual of Pediatric Therapeutics.* Boston: Little, Brown and Company, 1974.

Green, M., and Haggerty, R.J. *Ambulatory Pediatrics.* Philadelphia: W.B. Saunders Co., 1968.

Haggerty, R.J. "Diagnosis and treatment: tonsils and adenoids; a problem revisited," *Pediatrics* 41 (1968): 815.

Halsted, C., et al. "Otitis media. Clinical observations, microbiology and evaluations of therapy," *Am J Dis Child* 115 (1968): 542.

Hara, J.H. "Otogenic meningitis in infancy and childhood in the antibiotic era," *Arch Otolaryngol* 70 (1959): 315.

Harper, A.R. "The present trend in the irrelevance of the commoner acute bacterial infections," *Practitioner* 172 (1954): 292.

Hemenway, W.G., and Smith, R.O. "Treating acute otitis media." First of two parts. *Postgrad Med* 47 (1970a): 110.

Hemenway, W.G., and Smith, R.O. "Treating acute otitis media." Second of two parts. *Postgrad Med* 47 (1970b): 135.

Kaplan, G.S., Fleshman, J.K., Bender, T.R., Barum, C., Clark, P.S. "Long term effects of otitis media: a ten year cohort study of Alaskan Eskimo children," *Pediatrics* 52 (1973): 577–85.

Kessner, D.M. *Contrasts in Health Status. Vol II: A Strategy for Evaluating Health Services.* Washington, D.C.: National Academy of Sciences, Institute of Medicine, 1973.

Kessner, D.M. *Contrasts in Health Status, Vol. III: Assessment of Medical Care for Children.* Washington, D.C.: National Academy of Sciences, Institute of Medicine, 1974.

Lamp, C.B. "Chronic secretory otitis media: etiologic factors and pathologic mechanisms," *Laryngoscope* 83 (1973): 276.

Lemon, A.N. "Serous otitis media in children," *Laryngoscope* 72 (1961): 32–44.

Logan, W.P.D. *Morbidity Statistics from General Practice.* London: H.M. Stationary Office, 1960.

Lowe, J.F., Bamforth, J.S., Pracy, R. "Acute otitis media: one year in a general practice," *Lancet* 2 (1963): 1129–32.

McKee, W.J.E. "Controlled study of the effects of tonsillectomy and adenoidectomy in children," *Br J Prev Soc Med* 17 (1963): 49.

Mawson, S.R., et al. "A controlled study evaluation of adenotonsillectomy in children," *J Laryngol Otol* 82 (1968): 963.

Maynard, J.E. "Otitis media in Alaska Eskimo children: an epidemiologic review with observations on control," *Alaska Med* (1969): 93–97.

Maynard, J.E., Fleshman, J.K., Tschapp, C.F. "Otitis media in Alaskan children: Prospective evaluation of chemoprophylaxis." *JAMA* 219 (1972): 597–99.

Medical Research Council. "Acute otitis media in general practice." *Lancet* 2 (1957): 510–14.

Miller, F.J.W., Court, S.D.M., Walton, W.S., Knox, E.G. *Growing up in Newcastle Upon Tyne.* Oxford: Oxford University Press, 1960.

National Disease and Therapuetic Index. Specialty Profile. *Pediatrics.* Ambler, Pa.: IMS American Ltd., 1974.

Neil, J.F., Harrison, S.H., Morbey, R.D., Robinson, G.A., Tate, G.M.T. "Deafness in acute otitis media," *Br Med J* (8 Jan. 1966): 75–77.

Nielson, J.C. *Studies of the Aetiology of Acute Otitis Media.* Copenhagen: Ejuar Munkegasrd, 1945.

Nilson, B.W., et al. "Acute otitis media: treatment results in relation to bacterial etiology." *Pediatrics* 43 (1969): 351.

Otitis Media Planning Committee: *Program plan for otitis media.* Anchorage: Alaska Division of Public Health (mimeographed report), 1966.

Paradise, J.L. *The Pediatrician's View of Middle Ear Infections.* Presented at the International Symposium on Recent Advances in Middle Ear Effusions, Columbus, Ohio, May 29, 1975.

Paradise, J.L., and Bluestone, C. "Toward rational indications for tonsil and adenoid surgery," *Hosp Practice* (Feb. 1976): 79–87.

Paradise, J.L., Smith, C.G., Bluestone, C.D. "Tympanometric detection of middle ear effusion in infants and young children," *Pediatrics* 58 (1976): 198.

Paradise, J.L. "Testing for otitis media: diagnosis *ex machina*," *N Engl J Med* 296 (1977): 445.

Perrin, J.M., Charney, E., MacWhinney, J.B., McInery, T.K., Miller, R.L., Nazarian, L.F. "Sulfisoxazole as chemoprophylaxis for recurrent otitis media," *N Engl J Med* 291 (1974): 664–67.

Reed, D., and Dunn, W. "Epidemiologic studies of otitis media among Eskimo children," *Public Health Rep* 85 (1970): 699–707.

Reed, D., Struve, S., Maynard, J.E. "Otitis media and hearing deficiency among Eskimo children: a cohort study," *Am J Public Health* 57 (1967): 1657–62.

Reid, J.M., and Donaldson, J.A. "The indications for tonsillectomy and adenoidectomy," *Otolaryngol Clin North Am* 3 (June, 1970), 339.

Robinson, G.C., Anderson, D.O., Moghadam, H.K., et al. "A survey of hearing loss in Vancouver school children. I. Methodology and prevalence," *Can Med Assoc J* 97 (1967): 1199−1207.

Roddey, D.F. Jr., Earl, R., Haggerty, R., "Myringotomy in acute otitis media: a controlled study," *JAMA* 197 (1966): 849.

Rowe, D.S., "Actue suppurative otitis media," *Pediatrics* 56 (1975): 285.

Royhouse, N. "A controlled study of adenotonsillectomy," *Arch Otolaryngol* 92 (1970): 611.

Rubenstein, M.M., McBean, J.B., Hedgecock, L.D., Strickler, G.B. "The treatment of otitis media in children. III. A third clinical trial," *Am J Dis Child* 109 (1965): 308.

Sataloff, J., and Vassalo, L. "Hearing loss in children," *Pediatr Clin North Am* 12 (1965): 895−917.

Steinwachs, D.M., and Yaffe, R. *Developing Patterns of Primary Care: Relationship of Patterns, Process Criteria, and Resources.* Paper presented at the Operations Research Society of America, National Meeting, Las Vegas, Nevada, November 1974.

Strickler, G.B. "How many more treatment trials in otitis media?" *Am J Dis Child* 125 (1973): 403.

Strickler, G.B., et al. "Treatment of acute otitis media in children. IV. A fourth clinical trial," *Am J Dis Child* 114 (1967): 123.

Shurin, P., Pelton, S., Finkelstein, J. "Tympanometry in the diagnosis of middle ear effusion," *N Engl J Med* 296 (1977): 412.

Suehs, O.W. "Secretory otitis media," *Laryngoscope* 62 (1952): 998−1027.

U.S National Health Survey, Series 11, No. 114. Public Health Service, U.S. Department of Health, Education and Welfare. Washington, D.C.: Government Printing Office, 1972.

Williams, J.R. "Surgical mastoiditis masked by antibiotics," *N.Y. State J Med* 66 (1966): 1102.

✳ *Chapter 8*

Screening for Hearing Impairments

Kathryne Bernick

Screening for hearing impairment is one of the more established pediatric screening procedures. It has been included in school health programs since 1927 (Northern and Downs, 1974) and supported by funds from the Maternal and Child Health and Crippled Children's services for many years (Kakalik et al., 1974). It represents a major portion of EPSDT (Early and Periodic Screening, Diagnosis and Treatment) examinations. A total of nine screenings are recommended between birth and age six, with screening every two years thereafter (USDHEW, 1974). Even those who are increasingly skeptical of many pediatric screening procedures continue to advocate hearing screening (Holt, 1974; Bailey, 1974; Frankenburg, 1973).

The policymaker who must decide whether to fund hearing screening programs or include hearing evaluation in an early detection protocol is faced with a number of questions. Which children, at what ages, should be screened? What tests should be employed? Perhaps most important, does early identification improve a child's academic performance or quality of life, relative to detection and treatment at a later stage?

The first issue to be faced is whether to screen at all, and if so, whether to screen a high-risk population, which will raise the yield, or to screen all children regardless of risk status. This choice is represented at point *A* in Figure 8–1. The next point, *B*, is the selection of an appropriate screening test. Any test will pass and fail a certain proportion of children, as seen at point *C*, depending upon the prevalence of the condition in the population and upon the reliability

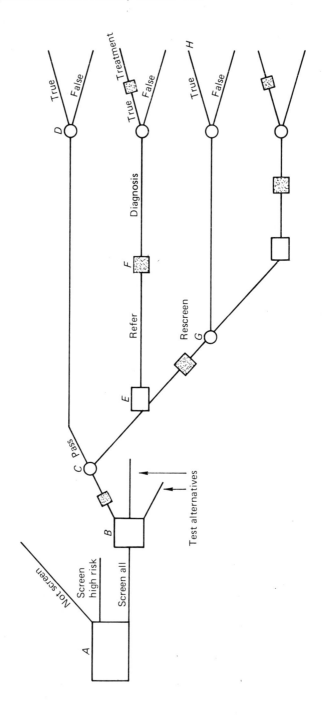

Figure 8–1. Screening Tree

and validity of the test. Of those who pass the test, a number will not be true negative (point D). Similarly, of those who fail, only some will have the condition, as shown by the branches at the end of the tree. These probabilities depend on the sensitivity and specificity of the various tests.

Once the results of the initial screening findings are known, as at point E for example, a decision must be made as to whether to refer children with positive results for diagnosis immediately (to point F) or to rescreen before referral (to point G). Rescreening may be desirable when a test produces a large number of false positives or when the diagnostic tests are relatively expensive. Once again, the sensitivity and specificity of the second screening test and diagnostic tests will determine the number of true positives and the proportion of individuals who will receive treatment.

The consequences of the various paths are shown at the tips of the branches, as at point H. Such outcomes might include the benefits of early recognition and treatment when a true condition is identified and treated, reassurance when no disease is found, or misdiagnosis or labeling when false positive identification occurs.

Then we fold back the tree, moving from right to left, multiplying the outcome measures by the consecutive probabilities of their occurrence, and incorporating the costs of the tests along the way. When we arrive back at point A, we should have some notion of which path we should follow.

Figure 8–2 provides a simple example of the folding back process. There are two action choices, A and B, which cost us 5 and 2 points or dollars respectively. A will result in an outcome of 10 with a probability of .4, or an outcome of 30 with a probability of .6. Similarly,

Figure 8–2. "Folding Back" Tree

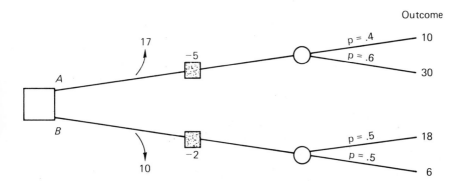

in B we have a 50-50 chance of getting 18 or 6. To determine the strategy with the biggest net payoff, we make these calculations:

Action A: $.4 \times (10) + .6 \times (30) - 5 = 17$

Action B: $.5 \times (18) + .5 \times (6) - 2 = 10$

Thus, we choose action A because it gives us the highest net outcome.

In order to carry out an analysis of this type, detailed information is needed. High-risk criteria, their predictive value, and the initial costs of identifying high-risk children must be specified. Alternative testing procedures must be known, as well as the costs, sensitivity, and specificity associated with each. The probability of second screening findings, given initial screening test results, must be known. Costs of diagnosis and treatment should be specified. The consequences of the probable events must be known. A tree that attempted to determine the optimum time between rescreenings and the best ages at which to screen would be even more complicated. If we assume that everyone will not necessarily reach the diagnostic and treatment stages, we must have information on the proportion who will drop out along the way.

TYPES OF HEARING LOSS

There are two major types of hearing loss, sensorineural and conductive. Sensorineural loss results from lesions of the auditory nerve system: in the inner ear, in the nerves going from the inner ear to the brain, or in the brain itself. The loss may be caused by heredity, a developmental abnormality, maternal infection (for example, by syphilis or first-trimester German measles), or Rh incompatibility. Such causes are hereditary or congenital. Sensorineural loss may also be acquired through acute infectious disease (such as meningitis, mumps, and viral diseases), side effects of certain drugs (such as streptomycin), tumors, and prolonged exposure to high-intensity noise.

Conductive loss is caused by lesions in the external or middle ear which interfere with the conduction of sound to the inner ear. This type of loss results from occlusions of the auditory canal (such as wax), serous or acute otitis media (middle ear infections), and perforations of the eardrum. Conductive loss may fluctuate over time.

A 1964 study estimated that approximately one-half of hearing loss is inherited, 20 percent acquired prenatally or perinatally, including congenital infections and malformations, and the remainder results from postnatally acquired infections of the ears or central nervous system (Fraser, cited in Bailey, 1974, p. 131). More recent studies argue that chronic ear infections are *the* most frequent cause of childhood hearing loss (Valadian and Carroll, unpublished; Holm and Kunze, 1969). One review concluded that "middle ear infections are probably responsible for well over 50 percent of all cases of hearing loss (including sensorineural) in children." (Kessner et al., 1973).

The extent of hearing loss is measured in terms of how loud a sound must be, at any given pitch, before an individual can hear it. Loudness is measured in decibels (db), a decibel being the minimal change of loudness that can be detected by the human ear. Soft speech is measured at 30 db, average conservation at 50 to 60 db, and loud voices at 70 db. Pitch is measured in frequencies or cycles per second (cps). In hearing tests, a loss greater than 15 db at any frequency is considered significant. Because most speech sounds occur within 500 and 2000 cps, any hearing loss between these frequencies causes more functional impairment than losses at other frequencies (Valadian and Carroll, unpublished). Conductive hearing loss may involve a deficit of up to 60 db, while sensorineural loss may be as high as 100 db (Simonton, cited in Glorig, 1965).

INFORMATION AFFECTING POLICY

Prevalence

A number of estimates are available for the prevalence of hearing impairments (Table 8−1). Estimates for conductive loss range between 2 and 10 percent, much less for congenital loss (0.1 to 0.2 percent). Prevalence also varies with economic status of families and is said to be higher among inner city populations. One study estimates that low-income populations have a 10 to 15 percent greater prevalence (Frankenburg, 1973). It may also vary with age, being higher during the first few years of school than during the later years (USDHEW, 1974).

Seriousness

The consequences of hearing impairment are important to know in determining the seriousness and costs of the disorder relative to other conditions, and in measuring the payoffs at the end of our decision tree for hearing screening. They depend on the age of onset, the severity, and the type of impairment. Generally, the earlier and greater the loss the greater the damage to academic and social development (Goetzinger, in Katz and Illmer, 1972). Conductive hearing loss is less deleterious than sensorineural loss, since the ability to under-

Table 8–1.   Prevalence Estimates for Hearing Loss

Source	Type of Loss	Rate
Bailey (p. 131)	"severe loss"	1/1000 (age not specified)
	"persistent bilateral impairment of more than 30 db	8/1000
	"some degree of impairment"	15 to 30/1000
Kakalik (p. 117)	"serious and permanent deficits"	slightly more than 1/2 percent of children 0–21
	"less severe but still significant: 15+ db"	10 percent of all children
Frankenburg, 1973 (p. 170)	all losses	3 to 5 percent among school-age children
USDHEW (EPSDT) (pp. 123–24)	congenital loss	1/1000
	conductive loss	10 percent among 2-to-5-year olds
	conductive loss	2 to 10 percent among school-age children
Northern and Downs (p. 97)	congenital loss	1/2000 at birth
	"mild to moderate loss."	4 percent by age two

stand speech is greater, but even fluctuating conductive loss accompanying otitis media has been shown to adversely affect language skills (Holm, 1969).

The duration of lead time allowing maximum remediation of hearing impairment and developmental delay is not shown (Bailey et al., 1974). It may be several months or years, depending on the severity of the hearing impairment and the nature of the loss. Many conductive hearing losses have short lead times and resolve spontaneously (Frankenburg, 1973). This implies that screening at frequent intervals would be necessary to catch most cases. Data that relate the extent and duration of loss during early childhood to the degree of later dysfunction do not appear to be available.

Symptoms

Symptoms of hearing loss may not be recognized until after the expected period of language development. Symptoms may include failure to develop language patterns typical of chronological age, speech defects, and behavioral or emotional problems. Middle ear infections, which cause variable or sometimes permanent hearing loss, may involve fever and pain for a short period, and drainage from the ear. If a child stops complaining after the initial period, a parent may conclude that nothing is wrong and fail to bring the child in for medical attention, while the infection may nevertheless persist. Education of parents to be prescreeners may be particularly effective in such cases.

High-Risk Registers. These have been advocated as a means for selecting a newborn population at greater risk for further evaluation. Factors include (USDHEW, 1974):

Family history of hereditary childhood hearing loss
Maternal infections (e.g., rubella)
Physical defects of ears, nose, or throat
Birthweight below 1500 grams
Bacterial meningitis
Elevated serum bilirubin levels
Abnormal otoscopic findings (Frankenburg, 1973)
Respiratory distress (Ehrlich et al., 1973)
Premature birth (ibid)

A neonatal high-risk register in which 17,000 children were followed for three years had a sensitivity of 72 percent and a specificity of 93 percent. (Recall that this means the test will be positive in 72 out of every 100 diseased subjects, and will identify 93 out of every 100 normal subjects as normal. Seven percent normal patients will remain suspect.) The prevalence of congenital hearing loss in such a register which covered 7 percent of the population was at least thirty-five times greater than in the general population (Northern and Downs, 1974). Further research is needed to determine the predictive value of high-risk registers of older children.

Participation of Parents. By six months a child begins to localize sound and by two years most children will have begun to use simple words. Parents can perform a simple "localization" screen by making sounds behind and to the side of the child, who should turn to localize the sound. The test is reported to have a predictive value of 10 percent (Bailey et al., 1974).

Electric Audiometers. These can be used after a child reaches three or four. The sweep check method presents tones of varying frequencies at a preset volume level (often 1000, 2000, and 4000 cps at 15 or 25 db). If a child cannot hear the tone at one or two frequencies, he fails the test (Eisner, 1973; USDHEW, 1974). Play-audiometry is used with young children; toys or pictures associated with sounds maintain the child's attention. One such test (VASC) has been shown to have a sensitivity of 70 percent and a specificity of 70 to 92 percent.

In older children, pure tone testing without play conditioning can be used. Individual pure tone screening, when compared with threshold hearing tests for validation, has been found in school-age children tested under ideal testing circumstances to have a sensitivity of 85 percent and a specificity of 98 percent (or overreferrals of 2 percent and underreferrals of 15 percent) (Northern and Downs, 1974). Because of a large number of false positives in screening using puretone audiometry under less ideal conditions, two tests are usually performed before referral. For greater reliability, it is recommended that audiologists perform the screening.

Otoscopy. This checks for abnormalities of the ear, including redness, retraction and perforation of the eardrum, and scarring, which would indicate a past or continuing middle ear infection. Nurses and volunteers may be trained to perform otoscopy (Northern and Downs, 1974) in most states; in others a physician must perform the procedure.

When threshold screening was compared with otoscopic examination (the latter as validation) of school-age children, the audiometric screen had only a 29 percent sensitivity (missing 71 percent of the abnormal by otoscope-testing) but identified 87 percent of the normal by otoscope. As Northern and Downs point out: "Such under-referral completely obviates the usefulness of the test if what we are looking for is past or present ear disease" (1974). Otoscopic exams alone are equally insensitive, especially to sensorineural losses: 68 percent of hearing losses were not identified by this exam, while 86 percent of children with normal hearing were identified (Northern and Downs, p. 103).

Studies like Melnick's (discussed in preceding paragraph and cited in Northern and Downs) are rare in that they submit the entire population studied to both the screening test and the validation test. Most studies have only applied the validation test to the cases that were positive (abnormal on the screening test) leaving the entire negative (presumed normal) population untested. This approach fails to demonstrate the validity of a screening test. In order to carry out the type of analysis described at the beginning of this chapter, such information is essential. It could be collected in a preschool screening program by including some follow-up of both positive and negative results, if only on a sampling basis for the presumed normals.

Cost estimates for hearing screening vary. It should be emphasized that the choice of personnel has a major effect on the cost of a test. Using the salary schedule suggested by the California Medi-Screen Program Cost Analysis (1973), if a health aide performs a five-minute task (for example, localization and otoscopy) the cost is $ .27; if a nurse, $ .50. If a physician administers the procedure, the cost jumps to $1.45. Aggregated over 1000 children, the cost savings could be as much as $1190 if an aide can substitute for a physician.

SCREENING SCHEDULE

There appears to be some but not complete consensus as to how early and at what intervals a child should be screened, as indicated in Table 8-2. A questionnaire for high-risk status at birth is generally agreed upon, as well as screening at school entry, but appropriate intervals during this period and after entering school are not well defined in the literature. Presumably congenital losses will have appeared by the preschool years, but losses caused by recurrent infections may not be apparent until later.

When considering screening in schools, it is worthwhile to note that in one study about 85 percent of all ultimate hearing losses were identified by examinations through eight years of age (USDHEW, p. 124). Since the incidence of middle ear infections declines rapidly

Table 8-2.   Suggested Ages and Frequency of Screening

Source	Test	Ages
California Title 17, Article 3.1	Localization; observation speech + language development	Begin 6-8 months, until age 3-4 (interval not stated)
	Pure tone audiometry	Begin age 3-4; intervals thereafter not stated
Kaiser-Oakland (Schoen)[a]	Otoscopy + questionnaire	All pediatric visits, interval not stated
	Pure tone audiometry	Only on referral, as indicated by questionnaire
USDHEW (EPSDT, 1974)	High-risk questionnaire	Birth; if suspect, test at 2 or 3 months and at intervals thereafter
	Questionnaire	6, 12, 18, and 24 months
	Pure tone audiometry	3, 4, 5, 6, and 8 years and every 2 to 3 years thereafter
Kakalik et al. (1974)	High-risk questionnaire	Birth; if suspect, 1 to 3 times between 0 and 5, less frequent if not suspect
	Pure tone audiometry	School entry
Bailey et al. (1974)	High-risk questionnaire	Birth
	Localization	8 to 12 months
	VASC	3 to 4 years
	Pure tone audiometry	School entry and "regular intervals," and when "indicated for academic or behavioral problems in the school-age child"

[a]Personal communication.

after age ten, otoscopic evaluations may be less indicated after this age. Before this point, it is not clear how often such exams would be needed since middle ear infections can recur frequently. Screening in the peak incidence months could catch the majority of infections.

False Identification

Consequences of False Positives. The extent of the false positive identification problem has not been defined. It will include the costs of further screening and diagnostic tests to determine the absence of a hearing impairment. Nowhere in the literature is there any indication of how often a child with normal hearing is erroneously treated for hearing disorders.

False Negatives. Untreated middle ear infections may lead to a permanent hearing loss. In addition, whatever benefits a child obtains from early rehabilitation are lost by the failure to make an early diagnosis.

Diagnostic Tests

These tests include threshold audiometric testing, where children are presented with different frequencies at gradually decreasing volume levels. At each frequency the lowest volume the child can hear with each ear is measured (Eisner, 1973). Complete audiologic exams are priced between $35 and $80. More sophisticated tests include electrodermal and electroencephalic audiometry, used for very young children or handicapped children who cannot respond to other tests. These can cost up to $250 (Kakalik, 1974, Table 5.8; Topp, personal communication). Allergy testing and physical examination of the ear may also be required. Sometimes wax or other debris must be removed before further testing can proceed.

Treatment

Treatment for hearing disorders varies depending upon the severity and type of impairment. The majority of children with hearing impairment have defects in the better ear which lie within the 15 to 45 db range, a mild loss. Children falling in this range are easily helped by speech reading, use of a hearing aid, language work, tutoring in certain subjects, physical placement in the classroom, soliciting the cooperation of other children in the class and of other parents.

Children with losses in the 45 to 60 db range and over face more complex problems, requiring special classes and techniques effective in reducing academic lag. For children with losses greater than 60 db treatment is less helpful, particularly if the loss occurs prior to language acquisition. One observer pessimistically comments that "despite the widespread use of hearing aids, visual aids, and modern teaching methods, the deaf child's educational lag has not been dramatically reduced in the last half century." (Goetzinger, cited in Katz, 1972, p. 686).

Some conductive loss can be treated medically or surgically. Decongestants and antibiotics are used in treating middle ear infections. Sensorineural loss is not usually helped by medical or surgical therapy. Hearing aids and special training are used instead, although amplification is of little help when the threshold is greater than 85 db (Simonton, cited in Glorig, 1965).

There is no discussion in the literature of the degree of compliance with prescribed therapy. For example, are hearing aids periodically checked for accuracy? Do parents make sure they are turned on when worn? Do parents practice lip reading at home with their children, if home reinforcement is ordered by the therapist?

EVALUATING POLICIES

The technique of decision analysis, introduced in Figure 8–1 and repeated in Figure 8–3, may be applied to the decisionmaker's problem of evaluation. While not enough information is available to determine an ideal strategy, the framework is nonetheless useful in laying out the issues and options and in pointing to research needs.

Figure 8–3. Screening Choices

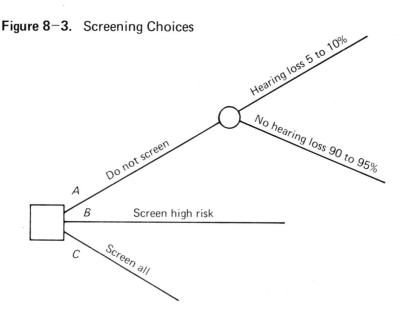

Suppose we are confronted with a captive population of four-year-olds. The tree may simply be extended to incorporate the options of screening sequentially at different ages and the possibility of not reaching all children.

We are faced with three major choices (Figure 8−3): not to screen; to screen only a high-risk group, determined by an initial parent interview or questionnaire; or to screen all of the children.

Option A: No Screening

If we follow option *A* and screen no children, what are the results? This policy in the short run costs us nothing in staff time or dollars, but what are the consequences of the *A* branch for the children involved? The 90 to 95 percent of children with no hearing loss (estimated from prevalence data) are not affected. None of these children will be subject to the possibility of false positive identification, nor will their parents bear any costs or anxiety which might be aroused by the screening test itself. (Neither will the parents have the benefit of knowing the child has no hearing disorder.)

The outcome for the 5 to 10 percent of the children who do have a hearing impairment or middle ear infection is variable. Profoundly deaf children will most likely already have been discovered by this age and treatment will have begun. Children with mild to moderate impairment and sudden hearing loss from infection or hereditary causes may not yet have been detected however.

Thus, if we fail to screen, four undesirable results will ensue:

1. Children who have not yet been suspected by parents or teachers of having abnormal hearing will lose whatever benefits are to be gained through early treatment.

2. Children suffering from undetected middle ear infection may face chronic and permanent hearing loss.

3. When eventually detected, the rehabilitation for the Group 2 children may cost more than if it had been started earlier.

4. In addition, those children who suffer obvious behavior or communication difficulties may be labeled with an emotional or cognitive disorder. As such, they will be subject to greater parental anxiety and misallocated diagnostic tests.

In order to fully evaluate the nonscreen policy we need to know prevalence data. Estimates are available for this, but other requisite information is not. This includes:

the proportion of hearing-impaired children who have not yet been detected at this age;
the consequences of not starting treatment;

the proportion of hearing-impaired children who are mislabeled; and

the proportion of ear infections which result in concomitant or later hearing loss

Option B: High-Risk Screening

If we follow option *B* and screen only high-risk children, the tree is extended as in Figure 8—4. The central problem in pursuing this strategy is the identification of criteria which are accurate predictors of hearing loss. Little data on high-risk attributes in older children exist. Assuming the development of a set of criteria and that we administer the interview or questionnaire at a reasonable cost, what are the consequences?

The consequences for the children who are not deemed to be at risk and will not be screened are similar to those in option *A*. Those children who are free from hearing impairment are slightly affected, if at all. Children who do have a loss lose the benefits of early treatment, or may be mislabeled. They may even be slightly worse off than under policy *A*, for some parents may interpret the identification of a high-risk group as meaning that other children are at no risk (Holt, 1974). The false sense of security may increase the chance of delayed treatment and mislabeling over the chance if parents had been given no information at all.

The consequences for the children who are deemed to be at greater risk and screened will follow the pattern of screening all children, as will be outlined in option *C*. Since greater yield is expected from this group than from a screen of all children, costs per case will be lower. In the group of high-risk children who pass the screening test, there may be less chance of mislabeling, since parents will have been forewarned of the possibility of hearing loss. But anxiety produced by the label "high risk" must also be considered.

Figure 8—4.   Extended Screening Tree

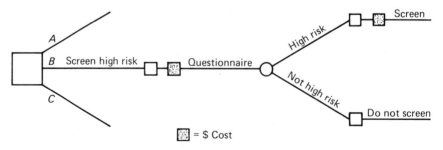

$\boxed{}$ = $ Cost

Option C: Screen All

Analysis of option *C*, screening all children, becomes more complex. The decisionmaker has a choice of tests to be administered alone or in combination. The tests may even be repeated before referral in order to lower the number of referrals. The choices and results are represented in Figure 8—5.

The policymaker must pay for the initial screen, as shown by the cost symbol. He or she has three choices: audiometry alone, audiometry and otoscopy, or otoscopy alone. Each involves different costs and each will pass a different proportion of children, that is, will find them to be normal. Audiometry alone will identify many children who may have a hearing loss, but will fail to identify children with abnormal eardrums who may have had past ear infections and may be subject to recurring infections. But it will not identify every child who cannot hear. Performing both procedures is more expensive but will identify more children who need to be followed up.

When a child fails he can either be referred immediately or rescreened. This choice is represented at decision node 1 of the tree's "fail" branch. If referred, the cost of diagnostic tests must be included: the toll along the "refer" branch. Children who are shown to have true losses upon diagnosis will be treated, gaining whatever benefits are conferred by treatment, again paying a toll. Children who have no loss will be reassured, but only at the expense of diagnostic tests. Depending on the number of false referrals, the local medical community may become antagonistic.

Rescreening will lower the proportion of false positives who are referred, thus lowering the possibility of parental anxiety, physician resentment, and diagnostic costs. The cost of the second screen must of course be considered. A proportion of children will pass the second test, as shown at point 2. Those who fail will be referred for diagnosis, at point 3, and the consequences will be similar to those of the second branch.

Treatment costs and benefits must be included for those children who are referred after the first or second test and who are declared to have a true loss or infection, as at point 4 for example.

To evaluate this strategy, we must consider:

1. the cost of each initial screening option and follow-up costs to ensure rescreening, diagnosis, and treatment;
2. the proportion of children who will pass or fail each type of screen and the proportion of these who actually have hearing disorders;
3. the probability that a child who has failed and is rescreened will pass or fail, and the conditional probabillty of a true loss, given two failures;

Figure 8–5. Screening Tree with Costs

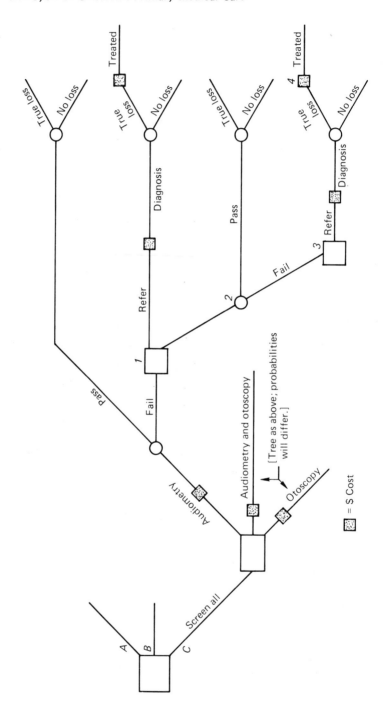

4. cost of diagnosis;
5. costs of over-referring (delayed tests for children who really need them, parental anxiety, professional resentment);
6. costs of delayed treatment for children who pass tests but actually have true hearing impairments; and
7. costs and benefits of treating children who fail tests and receive treatment

CONCLUSIONS

Keeping in mind that the costs and benefits of screening for hearing will have to be considered relative to screening for other conditions when resources are constrained, the following conclusions can be drawn:

1. The prevalence of hearing loss and ear disease is high, when compared to that of other pediatric disorders.
2. Existing evidence indicates that undetected loss leading to delayed treatment has serious consequences, particularly if the loss occurs during the period of language development.
3. Screening can be relatively inexpensive and is not painful.
4. Treatment for hearing loss and ear disease is available, although its effectiveness in severe cases has been questioned.

For these reasons, screening for hearing disorders and ear disease, particularly in preschool children, appears to have high payoffs. Training young parents to be aware of signs of developmental progress and ear disease and to report possible abnormalities would encourage early identification and treatment of such disorders.

5. Test selection depends both on resources and on goals. If the objective is detection of educationally adequate hearing, audiometry alone may be sufficient. If, however, the objectives include searching for past or present ear disease, as a strategy for preventing hearing loss, otoscopy should be performed as well.

For Further Research
Several key areas of uncertainty warrant further research:

1. Information is lacking on measures of academic and social performance by type of impairment (sensorineural vs. conductive) and age of onset. In addition, no attempt has been made by researchers to relate treatment received, such as use of a hearing aid, to academic performance.

2. It is not clear at what preschool ages children should be screened or followed through a high-risk register. Given the greater costs of screening younger children, it seems important to know whether the outcome differs greatly if treatment is initiated at six months or two years or four years of age. This issue will be crucial if national health insurance finances screening tests only for selected age groups.

3. It would be useful to develop high-risk criteria with good predictive value for older children (as well as to sharpen the validity of the current available neonatal risk registers). The use of such pre-screening questionnaires enables the screening of a smaller cohort with an expected greater yield than mass screening, and hence lowers costs per case detected.

4. Sensitivity and specificity data for preschool children need to be collected. In order to do this, follow-up of both positive and negative test results is required, if only on a sampling basis for the presumed normals.

5. Several data bases are available which could be used to explore the validity of tests, high-risk criteria, and possibly the consequences of detection at different ages as well. EPSDT programs, limited to low-income families, are presently screening a large cohort of preschool children. Children enrolled in Kaiser health plans could also be examined, providing a better cross-section of income levels. California's new Child Health and Disability Prevention Program is another potential data source.

REFERENCES

Anderson, C.V. "Screening the hearing of preschool and school age children." In *Handbook of Clinical Audiology*, edited by J. Katz, pp. 520–39. Baltimore: Williams and Wilkins, 1972.

Bailey, E.N., et al. "Screening in pediatric practice," *Pediatr Clin North Am* 21 (1974): 123–65.

Bordley, J.E., and Hardy, J.B. "A hearing survey on preschool children," *Trans Am Acad Opthal Otolaryn* 76 (1972): 349–54. (cited in Kalalik, J.S., et al.)

California, State of. Title 17, Article 3.1. "Child health and disability prevention program regulations," xerox, pp. 1–20.

California Department of Health. "Medi-screen program cost analysis and rate review." Preliminary Report No. 40–73–I, prepared by William J. Cole, Financing Operations Program, xerox, September 1973.

Ehrlich, C.H.; Shapiro, E.; Kimball, B.; Huttner, M. "Communication skills in five-year-old children with high risk neonatal histories," *J Speech Hear Res* 16 (1973): 522–29.

Eisner, V. "Early detection and treatment." In *Maternal and Child Health Practices: Problems, Resources, and Methods of Delivery*, edited by H. Wallace, pp. 729–43. Springfield, Ill.: Charles C. Thomas, 1973.

EPSDT Manual. See U.S. Department of Health, Education and Welfare.

Frankenburg, W.K. "Pediatric screening," *Adv Pediatr* 20 (1973): 149–75.

Fraser, G.R. "Profound childhood deafness," *J Med Genet* 118 (1964): 131 (cited in Bailey).

Glorig, A. "Screening tests." In *Audiometry: Principles and Practices*, edited by Glorig, pp. 17–184. Baltimore: Williams and Wilkins, 1965.

Goetzinger, C.P. "The psychology of hearing impairment," in Katz, 1972, pp. 666–93.

Goldstein, R., and Tait, C. "Critique of neonatal hearing evaluation," *J Speech Hear Disord* 36 (1971): 3–18.

Hardy, W.G. "Evaluation of hearing in infants and young children," in Glorig, 1965, pp. 207–23.

Hodgson, W.R. "Testing infants and young children," in Katz, 1972, pp. 498–519.

Holland, W.W. "Screening for disease—taking stock," *The Lancet* (December 21, 1974): 1494–97.

Holm, V.A., and Kunze, L.H. "Effect of chronic otitis media on language and speech development," *Pediatrics* 43 (1969): 833–39.

Holt, K.S. "Screening for disease—infancy and childhood," *The Lancet* (November 2, 1974): 1057–61.

Kakalik, J.S., et al. "Improving services to handicapped children with emphasis on hearing and vision impairments." Santa Monica, Ca.: Rand Corporation, May 1974.

Katz, J., and Illmer, R. "Auditory perception in children with learning disabilities," in *The Handbook of Clinical Audiology*, edited by Katz. Baltimore: Williams and Wilkins, 1972.

Katz, Jack. *The Handbook of Clinical Audiology*, Baltimore: Williams and Wilkins, 1972.

Kessner, D.M., et al. *Contrasts in Health Status, Vol. 2: A Strategy for Evaluating Health Services.* Washington, D.C.: National Academy of Sciences, 1973.

Kessner, D.M., et al. *Contrasts in Health Status, Vol. 3: Assessment of Medical Care for Children.* Washington, D.C.: National Academy of Sciences, 1974.

Kleinman, J.C., et al. *Emergency Medical Services in the City of Boston.* Cambridge, Ma.: Harvard Center for Community Health and Medical Care, December 1972.

Lessler, K. "Screening, screening programs and the pediatrician," *Pediatrics* 54 (1974): 608–11.

Lewis, M. *A Policy Decision Analysis for Iron-deficiency Anemia.* Kennedy School of Government, Harvard University, unpublished paper, October 30, 1974.

Melnick, W.; Eagles, E.L.; and Levine, H.S. "Evaluation of a recommended program of identification and audiometry with school-age children," *J Hear Disord* 29 (1964): 3–13 (cited in Northern, pp. 102–04).

Moriarty, R.W. "Screening to prevent lead poisoning," *Pediatrics* 54 (1974): 626–28.

North, A.F. "Screening in child health care: where are we now and where are we going?" *Pediatrics* 54 (1974): 631–40.

Northern, J.L., and Downs, M.P. *Hearing in Children.* Baltimore: Williams and Wilkins, 1974.

Roberts, J. "Hearing sensitivity and related medical findings among children in the United States," *Trans Am Acad Opthal Otolaryn* 76 (1972): 355–59.

Rogers, M.G.H. "The early recognition of handicapping disorders in childhood," *Dev Med Child Neurol* 13 (1971): 88–101.

Silverman, S.R. "Impressions of the studies sponsored by the Committee on Conservation of hearing," *Trans Am Opthal Otolaryn* 76 (1972): 306–66.

Simonton, K.M. "Audiometry and diagnosis" (cited in Glorig, 1965, pp. 185–206).

U.S. Department of Health, Education and Welfare. *A Guide to Screening for the Early and Periodic Screening, Diagnosis and Treatment Program (EPSDT) Under Medicaid.* Prepared by the American Academy of Pediatrics. Washington, D.C.: author, (SRS) 74–24516, June 1974.

Valadian, I., and Carroll, L. *Child Growth and Development: A Programmed Text.* School of Public Health, Harvard University, unpublished.

Zaner, A.R. "Differential diagnosis of hearing impairment in children: developmental approaches to clinical assessment," *J Commun Disord* 7 (1974): 17–30.

Chapter 9

Streptococcal Pharyngitis and Rheumatic Fever

John Graef, M.D.

In industrialized nations respiratory infections and inflammation (for example, asthma) far exceed intestinal problems so common in the underdeveloped nations. While the bulk of these infections are viral and generally self-limited, the small proportion attributable to bacteria represent a disproportionate challenge. Undiagnosed, they are potentially serious, and they are almost always treatable. For the primary care physician, the problem is sorting out from the melange of clinical manifestations those signs and symptoms most suggestive of bacterial disease, using appropriate diagnostic tests, correctly interpreting the results, and applying efficacious therapy at low cost, if possible, and at minimal risk to the patient.

Streptococcal pharyngitis is chosen as an example of this problem because: (1) it is fairly common; (2) its natural history and manifestations have been well studied; (3) efficacious therapy is readily available; and (4) untreated, it may lead to serious sequelae.

The most serious of the complications of streptococcal pharyngitis is acute rheumatic fever. This can produce rheumatic heart disease with severe valvular heart damage. Recognition and efficacious intervention in acute rheumatic fever challenges the primary care physician. Its treatment is not really a primary care issue, but its prevention certainly is.

In fact, prevention of rheumatic fever, as a primary-care challenge, is one of the more complex problems. It involves a series of observations and potential interventions which, while efficacious taken separately, have not been entirely effective taken together. A case in point is the cost-effectiveness approach to the problem. It is not surprising to learn that improving the socioeconomic status of American children is as effective or more effective than the best of the commonly available medical approaches.

It is estimated that only about 5 percent of all attacks of acute respiratory infections are bacterial. Nearly all of these follow invasion by streptococcus pyogenes. About 95 percent of the streptococcal infections are caused by group *A* beta-hemolytic streptococci, pharyngitis being the most common (Breese and Disney, 1954; Moffet et al., 1964).

In infants and children streptococcal pharyngitis occurs as a subacute nasopharyngitis with a thin serous exudate. If untreated, the illness may persist for several weeks and can lead to suppurative complications. In young children, infections of the middle ear (otitis media), the mastoid, and the meninges may occur if the organisms spread from the pharynx to other sites.

In older children and adults the disease is more acute. It is characterized by intense nasopharyngitis and tonsillitis with a purulent exudate. The cervical lymph nodes are usually tender and enlarged. There is also edema and intense redness of the mucous membranes. Fever is usually high with regular rises.

Typically, streptococcal pharyngitis is characterized by a sudden onset of fever and sore throat. This occurs within forty-eight to seventy-two hours after initiation of infection. In small children the onset may be insidious and the fever is usually low grade and persistent. In older children and adults as a rule onset is more abrupt and fever is higher. As the disease progresses there may be headache, malaise, and generalized aching. Abdominal pain may be accompanied by nausea and vomiting.

In the absence of treatment, unless suppurative complications (e.g., otitis media) develop, pharyngeal symptoms begin to lessen spontaneously in three to four days. Within seven to ten days these symptoms usually disappear and temperature returns to normal.

During this phase of pharyngitis the organisms may be cultured from a throat swab since they are living and dividing in the tissues of the nasopharynx. It should be remembered that the symptoms may be mild, moderately severe, or even subclinical, in which case the infection is recognized only by a subsequent rise in antibody titer.

Nonsuppurative complications may follow mild or inapparent infections as well as severe ones. Rheumatic fever is an uncommon complication but is the most serious because of its damage to the heart muscle and valves.

Scarlet fever is a complication of streptococcal pharyngitis that is now relatively uncommon in adults. The rash of scarlet fever is caused by the extracellular erythrogenic toxin elaborated by the streptococci. Scarlet fever is most common in children between two and ten. The usual incubation period between infection and appearance of the rash is two to four days with a range of one to seven days. The first signs are those of streptococcal infection.

The exanthem may appear within twelve hours or may be delayed. It consists of diffuse erythema with punctate red spots which blanch on pressure. The extremities are usually the last to be involved. The skin of the face is usually clear of rash but may show marked flushing except around the mouth. An exanthem usually involves the tongue, palate, pharynx, and tonsils. The pharynx may become edematous and reddened. During the course of the disease the appearance of the tongue changes from "strawberry" to "raspberry." In the first two days it is covered by a thick white coat through which reddened papillae project (the strawberry effect) and during the fourth or fifth day the white coating begins to disappear and the surface glistens with raspberry red papillae. Complications similar to those of pharyngitis can develop, which makes recognition of scarlet fever important, not only to reduce its toxicity but to prevent its sequelae.

INCIDENCE AND PREVALENCE OF STREPTOCOCCAL THROAT INFECTIONS

Kaplan et al. (1971) found that there were two peak ages for the occurrence of streptococcal pharyngitis: five to seven and twelve to thirteen. Markowitz (1963) found that about 40 percent of streptococcal infections in a pediatric population occurred between the ages of two and six. Streptococcal infections are rare in children under two, most common in school-age children, decrease in adolescents, and are rare in adults.

Rantz et al. (1948) estimated that about 80 percent of children between the ages of five and fifteen showed evidence of past contact with hemolytic streptococcus capable of stimulating antistreptolysin 0.

Carriers for group A streptococci are defined as those children with streptococci in their throats without illness, who show positive cultures but do not show a rise in antibody titer. The presence of group A streptococcus, therefore, probably has no meaning in the etiology of the underlying pharyngitis except as an epidemiologic observation.

Carrier rates are estimated to range from 10 to 40 percent in children during the school year (Cornfield et al., 1961; Quinn et al., 1975). The over-all average rate is 15 to 20 percent.

RECOGNITION OF STREPTOCOCCAL PHARYNGITIS

As previously discussed, commonly found clinical signs and symptoms of streptococcal pharyngitis are sudden onset of fever (101° to 104° F), severe sore throat, pain on swallowing, tonsillar or pharyngeal exudate, and redness of the pharyngeal soft tissues. The cervical lymph nodes are tender and enlarged, and there may be generalized aching. Abdominal pain, nausea, and vomiting occur more commonly in children than in adults.

Several studies have indicated that the disease is more likely to be streptococcal in origin if two or three of these symptoms occur simultaneously, particularly if adenitis is present (Breese et al., 1965).

When it occurs, scarlet fever is the most reliable clinical sign.

Many cases of group A streptococcal infection go unrecognized because there are several obstacles to the accurate recognition of a group A etiology on clinical parameters alone; Breese and Disney (1954) estimated that on a single visit, based on clinical evidence alone, 30 percent of cases would be missed. (The importance of clearly differentiating acute pharyngitis is emphasized, because only group A streptococcal pharyngitis is known to lead to rheumatic fever.)

One problem is that of the subclinical infections which are never brought to the attention of the physician, perhaps one-third to one-half of true group A infections (Rammelkamp, 1952; Gordis and Markowitz, 1969). Symptoms are so mild that the patient is not prompted to seek medical attention. (Since approximately 50 percent of all attacks of rheumatic fever are preceded by subclinical or asymptomatic infections, the importance of this group cannot be overstressed.) According to Gordis and Markowitz (1969), another third of patients still do not seek attention, although their symptoms are recognizable.

DIAGNOSIS

No single sign is highly diagnostic of group A streptococcal pharyngitis, although pain on swallowing and vomiting occur twice as often in streptococcal as in nonstreptococcal infections. These same signs may be present in nonbacterial pharyngitis or in pharyngitis caused by other groups of beta-hemolytic streptococci. The difficulty is

Table 9-1. Clinical Findings Related to Laboratory Findings in Group A
Streptococcal Infection

Predictions From Clinical Findings	Number of Cases	Confirmation by Culture	Percent Accuracy of Clinical Findings
Positive	495	372	75
Negative	704	540	77

magnified by the fact that very little upper respiratory illness is
caused by streptococci to begin with.

Correlation of Clinical and Laboratory Findings

Several studies have been made to correlate the recovery of organisms from cultures with clinical findings. Breese and Disney (1954),
estimating the correlation between clinical and laboratory findings,
found the results shown in Table 9-1. In other words, clinical diagnosis alone was about 75 percent accurate.

In the study by Siegel et al. (1961) in Chicago, and one by Kaplan
et al. (1971), pharyngeal or tonsillar exudate and adenitis were correlated significantly with recovery of beta-hemolytic organisms. In
fact, adenitis was found to have the best clinical correlation with a
positive culture. Group A streptococci appeared on culture for 49
percent of patients with swollen glands, and only with cervical adenitis was there a significant correlation with an antibody response. Of
those with adenitis and a positive culture, 61 percent showed a rise in
one or both of ASLO or antiDNAse-B antibodies. However, only 42
percent of patients with group A culture plus an antibody rise presented with adenitis. As for blood-phase reactants, in the Chicago
study no correlation was seen between the recovery of beta-hemolytic
organisms and an elevated white count.

These studies point to the fact that there is indeed only fair correlation between clinical findings and bacteriological results (Kaplan
et al., 1971). The predicting value of clinical manifestations in relation to antibody rise is no better than in relation to a positive culture.
Because of this, physicians who attempt to diagnose a group A streptococcal pharyngitis on the basis of only clinical parameters, as often
occurs (Czoniczer et al., 1961; Grossman and Stamler, 1963; Gordis
et al., 1969), *will do so with a wide margin of error.*

In a later study by Breese et al. (1970), attempts were made to
correlate the number of organisms in the culture (degree of positivity)
with clinical and epidemiological data. The following conclusions
were drawn:

1. The severity of the streptococcal infection was proportional to the number of organisms found in the culture.

2. Accuracy of clinical findings in order of decreasing correlation, as related to results of the culture were: abnormal pharynx, abnormal cervical glands, sore throat, headache, bad breath, temperature of 100.5° F or more.

3. The number of cultures with a low degree of positivity (few organisms) was found to be significantly higher in asymptomatic carriers.

4. The higher the degree of positivity ratio (number of positive cultures/number of cultures taken), the higher the proportion of patients with increased ASLO antibody titer.

Breese et al. concluded that

> in those epidemiologic situations the frequency of streptococcal infection increases as also does the proportion of strongly positive cultures. This degree of positivity ratio also increases in groups of ill patients in proportion to the importance of streptococcus in those illnesses. In the individual patient, significant disease due to the streptococcus, and thus requiring antibiotic therapy, is usually associated with a large number of streptococci in the cultures of that individual. (p. 21).

The physician then has the problem of clearly differentiating true streptococcal infection from the carrier of group A or other beta-hemolytic streptococci, whose illness is nonstreptococcal in origin (Kaplan et al., 1971). It is important to differentiate carriers from true infection, but in view of the high carrier rate among school children this is a difficult problem. Often the risk of complications is overestimated because infection rates are not adjusted for the prevalence of streptococcal carriers in the general population (Wannamaker, 1972). Breese et al. (1970) suggest that significant clinical disease is usually associated with large numbers of organisms in the culture. In chronic carriers only a few colonies of beta-hemolytic streptococci are present and these may be non-group A. Normal carriers represent: non-group A infections, insignificant acquisitions, and residual carriers from past illness.

Because the cultures with a few colonies of beta-hemolytic streptococci are often reported as positive even without etiological significance in the underlying infection, Breese suggests that laboratories should routinely report the number of organisms in cultures. It should be noted that although Breese places a lot of importance on the degree of positivity of the cultures, others question the value of such data because of the differences in the prevalence of carriers in different populations at different times (Kaplan et al., 1971; Wannamaker, 1972). Krause et al. (1962) found that the number of colonies as well as the number of typable strains decreased with time in untreated streptococcal infections (Table 9−2).

If true streptococcal infection is defined as that with a positive culture plus a rise in antibody, and if the attack rate of rheumatic fever is related to the magnitude of the antibody rise (Stetson, 1954), then it would seem that it is important in the diagnosis to obtain an antibody titer. However, a rise in antibody titer can be noted only after the initial visit and is therefore useful only retrospectively (Wannamaker, 1972). It is usually done only in special studies.

Fluorescent Antibody Technique. Warfield et al. (1961) and Moody et al. (1963) have demonstrated the use of a fluorescent antibody technique for identification of group *A* streptococci. The advantages over the throat culture technique are that the results can be reported after two to four hours of enrichment in broth cultures inoculated with throat swabs, without isolation of pure cultures, and the cost of the technique is less than the blood agar method. The test differentiates group *A* streptococci that are pathogenic for man from nonpathogenic groups.

In all cases where difficulties arise in diagnosis, final judgment should depend on clinical findings, culture results, an immune response, epidemiological evidence, previous history of infections, and infections in siblings. Of course, all of these data are rarely available to the physician at the time of the initial visit. One approach is that of Breese and Disney (1954), who have suggested that if the symptoms of symptomatic patients do not respond to antibiotics within a few days, the disease is not streptococcal in origin.

TREATMENT STRATEGIES
FOR STREPTOCCAL PHARYNGITIS

Given the poor clinical and bacteriological correlation in diagnosing streptococcal pharyngitis, the problem of initiating therapy is sub-

Table 9−2. Attenuation of Beta-Hemolytic Streptococcus Five and Ten Weeks After Infection

Number of Patients With More Than Ten Colonies in Initial Culture	After Five Weeks	After Ten Weeks
	Percent Patients Positive	*Percent Patients Positive*
	100	80
65	*Percent With Less Than Ten Colonies*	*Percent With Less Than Ten Colonies*
	less than 80	less than 50

stantial. Even following guidelines (Honikman and Massell, 1971) and taking throat cultures in all illnesses with sore throat plus a temperature of 38.3° C (100.9° F) or higher, and in all illnesses with sore throat plus a temperature of 37.3° C (99.1° F) or higher, 12 percent of the potentially dangerous cases are missed (i.e., those with an antibody rise). On the other hand, it is estimated that if all patients with fever or respiratory illness are treated with penicillin without a throat culture, at least 80 percent will receive treatment that is useless, since they will have a viral illness rather than a strep infection. Thus many investigators advocate the throat culture to aid in diagnosis and treatment decisions.

Tompkins (1975) and his associates conducted a cost-effectiveness study on throat culturing and treatment of only positive culture patients versus treatment of all patients. He examined three possibilities: culture all patients and treat those with positive cultures with penicillin; treat all patients with penicillin; neither treat nor culture any patients. Development of rheumatic fever, penicillin allergy, and cure were examined as possible outcomes. The cost of the initial medical evaluation, cost of treatment, and the cost of any adverse outcome, including economic loss due to early death, were included in the estimated cost.

Table 9−3 summarizes the predicted incidence of acute rheumatic fever (ARF) in 100,000 patients and the estimated cost per patient of following the three strategies.

In both the endemic and the epidemic situation, treating all patients would result in three to nine more cases per 100,000 patients of serious *nonfatal* allergic reactions than if only those with positive cultures were treated. They found no deaths would occur from penicillin allergy.

Table 9−3. Cost Effectiveness of Treatment Strategies

Medical Strategy	Predicted Incidence of ARF/1000 Patients		Cost/Patient[a]	
	Epidemic	*Endemic*	*Epidemic*	*Endemic*
Culture and treat all	4.4 cases	330 cases	$76.59	$26.97
			$65.51	$21.42
Treat all	2.5 cases	17 cases	$49.50	$24.90
			$44.44	$19.84
Neither culture nor treat	21.2 cases	175 cases	$238.06	$32.94
			$238.06	$32.94

Source: Tompkins et al., 1975.   [a] benzathine penicillin
oral penicillin

Tompkins concluded that in epidemic and most endemic situations treating all patients who have acute pharyngitis with penicillin is more cost effective than treating only those with positive cultures.

Importance of Treatment

The aim of treatment is to eradicate streptococci from the nasopharynx. It is not enough to treat clinical symptoms alone. Catanzaro et al. (1958), among others, demonstrated that persistence of the organism following inadequate treatment is a major factor in failure to prevent rheumatic fever. Denny et al. (1950) showed that early treatment with penicillin may result in inhibition of antistreptolysin 0. Stollerman (1960) showed that a marked immune response is also important in the development of rheumatic fever, and it has been shown that patients who have complicated (i.e., untreated) streptococcal infections generally show higher antibody titers than those who do not.

Rammelkamp and Stolzer (1961) investigated the effect of penicillin therapy for streptococcal infection on incidence of rheumatic fever according to time of initiation of treatment. They reported that rheumatic fever was potentially preventable as long as four weeks after onset of symptoms of the pharyngitis. The following results were shown:

Time therapy instituted (days)	Percent reduction of acute rheumatic fever
0	98
8	90
14	67
21	42
29	8

Catanzaro et al. (1954) found that penicillin given as late as nine days after onset of the streptococcal infection led to 82 percent reduction in the incidence of rheumatic fever.

Effects of No Treatment

Streptococci may be carried in the nasopharynx for extended periods following an untreated infection. There will be a gradual decline in the number of organisms. As noted earlier, many of these individuals will culture less than ten colonies, and frequently the strain is nontypable and nonpathogenic during the convalescent stage (Krause et al., 1962).

The symptoms of streptococcal infections are self-limiting. However, under epidemic conditions approximately 3 percent of all untreated infections are followed by rheumatic fever and endemically the attack rate is about one-tenth that (0.33 percent). In addition, other complications (acute glomerulonephritis, impetigo, otitis media) may occur or spread among families.

Sulfonamides were the first antimicrobial agents used to prevent streptococcal infections in subjects with rheumatic fever (Coburn and Moore, 1939). But Morris and coworkers (1956) showed that sulfonamides are not maximally effective in eradicating the streptococcus and preventing rheumatic fever once the infection has started. They are effective in preventing recurrence of streptococcal disease in rheumatic subjects.

Penicillin is a potent bactericidal agent and is the drug of choice in reducing the incidence of streptococcal infections and preventing rheumatic fever. Massell and coworkers (1948) were the first to suggest that treatment of streptococcal infections with penicillin might prevent rheumatic fever. Denny et al. (1959) showed that of 798 infections among military recruits treated with penicillin, only two definite cases of rheumatic fever developed in contrast to seventeen among 804 untreated patients.

Current recommendations of the American Heart Association are:

Intramuscular benzathine penicillin G

Children: One intramuscular injection of 600,000 to 900,000 units. The larger dose is preferable in children ten years of age or older.

Adults: One IM injection of 900,000 to 1,000,000 units.

Oral crystalline penicillin G

Children and adults: 200,000 or 250,000 units three or four times daily for ten days.

Erythromycin

Children and adults: 3 to 10 mg/kg/day in three to four doses. (Markowitz and Gordis, p. 262).

Of the available antimicrobial agents, the penicillins are the least toxic. Massive doses, in excess of 100 million units of penicillin G, have been given without major adverse effects (Smith and Young, 1969). Leukopenia has rarely been seen, but nephritis has been reported. Irritative reactions and pain may develop at the site of intramuscular injections. Nausea, vomiting, or diarrhea may follow oral administration. Fever may develop during therapy and may be confused with relapse or superinfection. Occurrence of central nervous system effects is usually confined to patients with impaired renal function given doses of penicillin G in excess of 20 million units per day (Lerner et al., 1967).

Hypersensitivity reactions occur in 5 to 10 percent of patients receiving penicillin therapy. Parenteral administration is more frequently incriminated in this. Breese et al. (1965), compared schedules of therapy, found no greater tendency of intramuscular penicillin to cause sensitivity reactions. Only 0.1 percent of all penicillin reactions are anaphylactic, but 10 to 25 percent of these may be fatal.

Although Brumfitt et al. (1959) demonstrated that therapy does not significantly shorten the duration of symptoms as compared to symptomatic therapy, Breese et al. (1965) showed that fever could be lowered in three days with penicillin treatment versus one week with no treatment. However, no symptomatic therapy was employed. Surprisingly, intramuscular benzathine penicillin was the slowest in reducing the temperature.

Rosenstein et al. (1968) showed that 39 (12 percent) of a group of 331 children with group *A* streptococcal pharyngitis developed bacteriologic relapses after a full ten days treatment with penicillin. It is estimated that, on the average, 10 to 15 percent of patients will show some beta-hemolytic streptococci after completion of treatment, although not all prove not to be group *A*. It is possible that these apparent failures may be accounted for by noncompliance or by reexposure to streptococci via infected siblings (Stillerman and Bernstein, 1964), or the course of therapy may not have been long enough to eradicate the organisms. Breese et al. (1965) suggest that "recurrences after the first month are new infections and not therapeutic failures" since they found no significant differences in the attack rates of streptococcal infection after the first month of treatment with different penicillin schedules. Looking at asymptomatic carriers, Cornfield et al. (1961) and Phibbs et al. (1958) demonstrated that penicillin therapy did not significantly lower the carrier rate in school children. However, Wannamaker et al. (1953) demonstrated that 1,000,000 units twice daily for ten days of benzethacil penicillin was more effective in reducing the carrier rates as well as the streptococcal disease rates, than the same amount for five days or no treatment at all.

PROPHYLAXIS

Several methods of prophylaxis are available. Sulfadiazine or penicillin can be given by mouth. They have been shown to be of approximately equal effectiveness in the prevention of recurrences (Wood et al., 1974; Feinstein et al., 1964). With sulfadiazine there is the need to monitor for toxicity. Programs of sulfonamide prophylaxis established in the military forces were initially effective in controlling streptococcal epidemics (Coburn, 1949). There were some fatal reactions to the drugs, however, and resistant strains appeared which led to eventual return of high disease rates (Commission on Acute Respiratory Disease, 1945). Benzathine penicillin G, given intramuscularly in monthly doses, is much more effective than either sulfadiazine or oral penicillin in reducing streptococcal infections and rheumatic recurrences. Erythromycin can be used if the patient is sensitive to both penicillin and sulfonamides.

Streptococcal Immunization

Lancefield (1962) showed that the M-protein has antiphagocytic activity and that the virulence of the group A streptococci is related to this protein. The M-protein can stimulate type-specific antibodies which can neutralize its antiphagocytic property. It has been demonstrated that the M-protein is antigenetically related to human cardiac tissue and therefore may be important in the pathogenesis of rheumatic fever. Although immunization with M-proteins would theoretically be the ideal method of preventing streptococcal infections, there are several obstacles. First, antibodies against the M-protein protect only against the infecting type, and there are many types (over fifty are known). Second, it has been difficult to develop a vaccine with low toxicity. Fox et al. (1966) suggest immunizing infants, since they have fewer and less severe hypersensitivity reactions than older children. Third, serious cardiac effects could result from injection of streptococcal products (Massell et al., 1969).

RHEUMATIC FEVER

Rheumatic fever remains the most serious complication of streptococcal pharyngitis. The risk of recurrence, although diminishing after puberty, continues throughout life. It is a preventable disease, but much depends on the ability to recognize the streptococcal infection that precedes it. Unfortunately, pharyngitis, even in children at high risk, is often treated without throat culture and thus specific identification is lost. Mortality rates have shown a steady decline over the years.

Definite rheumatic fever is established by use of the Jones criteria as revised by the American Heart Association in 1965 (Table 9—4). The presence of two major criteria or one major and two minor criteria is fairly diagnostic of rheumatic fever. Supporting evidence comes from signs of preceding streptococcal infection.

Table 9—4. Jones Criteria for Rheumatic Fever

Major Manifestations	*Minor Manifestations*
Carditis	Clinical
Polyarthritis	
Chorea	Fever
Erythema marginatum	Arthralgia
Subcutaneous nodules	Previous rheumatic fever or rheumatic heart disease
	Laboratory
	Acute phase reaction
	Elevated erythrocyte sedimentation rate
	C-reactive protein
	Leukocytosis
	Prolonged PR interval on electrocardiogram

(Revised by the American Heart Association).

INCIDENCE AND PREVALENCE OF RHEUMATIC FEVER

Unlike acute streptococcal infections, rheumatic fever's incidence is low in children two to six; it usually occurs between six and fifteen. It is rarely seen in children under two years. Rosenthal et al. (1968) estimated that only 0.5 percent of all children with first rheumatic attacks admitted to the House of the Good Samaritan in Boston between 1939 and 1966 were under three years. Studies conducted at the Warren Air Base by Denny et al. (1950) estimated that under epidemic conditions, 3 percent of untreated streptococcal infections resulted in rheumatic fever.

If untreated, the acute suppurative phase of streptococcal pharyngitis is followed by a latent or quiescent period. Two percent of all rheumatic attacks are associated with short latent periods. The patient may appear well during this phase, although immunologic studies may show a continuing rise in the titer of antibodies to streptolysin O (ASLO), an antigenic product of beta-hemolytic streptococcus.

The length of the latent period is variable. It usually lasts one to three weeks. In a study conducted by Rammelkamp and Stolzer (1961), 24 percent of the patients had latent periods longer than thirty-five days, while 7 percent had less than five days, and 2 percent had two-day periods, as was mentioned. There was no evidence that recurrent attacks were associated with shorter latent periods. In a number of patients, long latent periods were related to reinfection

with a different type of streptococcus without overt clinical symptoms.
Rantz et al. (1945) suggested that the greatest incidence of rheumatic fever in school-age children after six years was as a result of repeated infections. They also suggested that differences in incidence of rheumatic fever were due to the changing pattern of the immune response with age (Rantz et al., 1951). This concept, while still considered valid by most authorities, continues to defy precise scientific explanation.

Rheumatic fever appears to be more prominent in temperate than in warmer climates. Siegel et al. (1961), observed children between the ages of three and sixteen in Chicago, estimated that the attack rate of rheumatic fever was about 0.33 percent. The American Heart Association estimates from national survey data for 1973 that there were 2,750,000 cases of rheumatic heart disease and rheumatic fever, of which children accounted for 1,100,000 and adults 1,650,000. These figures are based on a total population of 209,851,000, of which 38,983,000 were between the ages of five and fourteen. The American Heart Association also estimates that there are 100,000 new cases of rheumatic fever or rheumatic heart disease per year. Most are in children five to nineteen.

Gordis et al. (1972) give attack rates of rheumatic fever in Baltimore, 1960−64, as 13.3 per 100,000 for children five to nineteen, 2.3 per 100,000 for recurrences, and 15.6 per 100,000 for all attacks. An over-all figure, corrected for nonhospitalized cases, is 24 per 100,000.

Mortality statistics show a steady decline over the years. Table 9−5 compares deaths from rheumatic fever and rheumatic heart disease

Table 9−5. Mortality Statistics for Rheumatic Fever

	1968		1973	
	Deaths	*Population*	*Deaths*	*Population*
Total	16,358	199,861,000	13,847*	210,400,000
< 1 year 1−5	9 } 13 }	18,521,000	2 } 15 }	16,714,000
(5−13) 5−14	116	41,149,000	*58*	*34,700,000*
(14−24) 15−24	241	33,129,000	*200*	*43,100,000*
25 and over	15,979	107,060,000	13,572*	115,800,000

*approximated from death rate.

in 1973 and 1968 compiled by the American Heart Association. These are actual counts compiled from the National Health Examination Survey figures.

Examination of earlier mortality statistics indicates that much of the decline in death rates seems to have begun in 1910 before antimicrobial therapy. It is hard to estimate to what extent the decline in death rates is due to the availability of antimicrobial therapy, since the rate of decline does not seem to have accelerated much over the past two decades. Some of the decline may be due to the decrease in severity of the disease.

Recurrence

Before preventive measures became available, 60 to 70 percent of rheumatic subjects had one or more recurrences (Roth et al., 1937). Even with preventive measures, approximately 5 percent of patients on oral prophylaxis (less than 1 percent on parenteral penicillin) still have recurrences (Markowitz and Gordis, 1972). The patient may fail to comply with the regimen, or the prescribed therapy may be inadequate.

PROBLEMS IN THERAPY

Despite the availability of the therapeutic measures that have been discussed, first attacks of rheumatic fever continue to be seen. In two Toronto studies, it was shown that there was essentially no change in the prevalence of rheumatic fever over a period of thirteen years (Gardiner and Keith, 1951; Rose et al., 1964).

Accessibility to Care

Unfortunately, rheumatic fever in the United States is primarily a problem of the poor, who receive medical care mainly where follow-up is a problem. This is true especially in large cities, where there is less of an intimate, continuous relationship between medical personnel and the community than in rural areas. Difficulties in transportation, prolonged waiting times or time lost setting up appointments, inaccessibility of medical services, crises within a family—all constitute obstacles.

Quality of Care

Many first attacks of rheumatic fever may be mishandled because the physician does not suspect an antecedent streptococcal infection and does not take a throat culture (Czoniczer et al., 1961; Grossman and Stamler, 1963; Gordis, 1969). Since children at high risk are mainly treated in outpatient departments, emergency rooms, or neighborhood health centers, medical services may be inconsistent. Frequently in these settings pharyngitis is treated without a throat culture, and even if one is taken, it may be hard to recall the patient. Emergency rooms all too frequently are staffed by the least experienced house staff with little or no supervision or guidance. Nor are private physicians necessarily skillful in their management of streptococcal infections.

A number of studies have tried to determine why efforts to prevent first attacks of rheumatic fever have fallen short of expectations. Czoniczer et al. (1961) studied 105 rheumatic fever patients admitted to the House of the Good Samaritan in Boston. They discovered that *none* of these patients had received adequate treatment for the preceding streptococcal infections. Of a total of 105, 69 had not been seen by a physician. Of these, 16 had subclinical infections when seen by the authors, 38 had mild infections, and 15 had severe infections. Of the 36 who had been seen by a physician, 14 were incorrectly diagnosed, and the other 22 had had inadequate treatment or none at all.

Grossman and Stamler (1963) studied the adequacy of treatment in 110 children in Chicago with acute rheumatic fever. They reported similar results: of 110 patients, only 17 had had throat cultures, and only 10 received adequate therapy. They estimated that 84 percent of these cases could have been prevented.

Finally, Gordis et al. (1969) analyzed the histories of 261 patients with first attacks of rheumatic fever to determine adequacy of management of the antecedent streptococcal infection. One-third had had no history of clinically overt respiratory infection and therefore were not prompted to seek medical attention; one-third had symptoms and received medical attention but still developed rheumatic fever. The authors estimated that two-thirds of these cases could have been prevented.

Patient Compliance

Even when physician care is adequate, the patient may have difficulty carrying out the therapeutic program. Mohler et al. (1955) found that 34 percent of patients under treatment for streptococcal pharyngitis did not take the prescribed course of penicillin. Similar studies show that a large percentage of patients are noncompliers. Bergman and Werner (1963) found that of 59 children on a ten-day course of penicillin prescribed by a clinic, 56 percent stopped taking the medication by the third day, 71 percent by the sixth day, and 82 percent by the ninth day. Charney et al. (1967) assessed compliance with a ten-day schedule in all children in a private practice by testing the urine and found that 81 percent were still taking medication on the fifth day and 56 percent were still taking it on the tenth day. Compliance apparently is not better in private practice than in a clinic.

Lack of compliance in comprehensive pediatric care perhaps results from the lack of continuous relationship between physician and patient. Gordis and Markowitz (1971) tested this hypothesis between two groups of rheumatic fever patients, one in a traditional comprehensive care setting, the other in a continuous program, where each patient was seen by one of two physicians on each visit. They found no essential difference in compliance between the two groups.

One approach to problems in administering medication was suggested by Breese et al. (1956), who proposed that 400,000 units of oral penicillin given twice daily would avoid children taking medication at school during the day, since one dose could be given in the morning and one in the evening. The use of benzathine penicillin given intramuscularly also precludes the need to monitor patient compliance.

Socioeconomic Factors

As early as 1920, Poynton observed that rheumatic fever was rarely seen in private practices but had a higher incidence in hospital practice. Several studies since then (Perry and Roberts, 1937; Clark, 1940; Quinn and Quinn, 1951) have demonstrated the relationship of low socioeconomic status to high incidence of rheumatic fever. One obvious concern is that patients of this status are least likely to seek or receive adequate medical care.

The cost of medical care is a significant factor in preventing patients from seeking medical attention. Even with federal health insurance, parents frequently must sacrifice a whole day's pay in order to have their children examined. This is impractical for low-income families, and therefore some means must be found for easier management of these children, and less waiting time. A survey in Baltimore hospitals (Markowitz and Gordis, 1972) showed that the charge for throat examination, culture, and penicillin in an outpatient setting ranged from $25 to $41. Such costs have certainly increased since then. Comparable services in private pediatric settings ranged from $10 to $15. In many areas cost of culturing is high because of unnecessary identification of nonstreptococcal organisms and antibiotic testing.

Other factors play a role. Large families living in close quarters have greater susceptibility to streptococcal infection and eradication is more difficult. This is especially true where there is overcrowding;

it is estimated that about 50 percent of siblings in a low-income household will acquire streptococci after infection of one member. Not only do families under financial stress seek care less readily, but follow-up is also problematic. Transiency, incorrect addresses, no telephones, and language barriers confound the medical care agency attempting to convey specific services.

Finally, good health and adequate nutrition are interdependent. Protein-deprived, environmentally assaulted children with poor defenses are subject to a variety of infectious agents. Such simple protections as personal hygiene may not be present, giving way to impetigo, primarily a streptococcal disease, and beginning the cycle that inevitably leads to the higher attack rate for rheumatic fever.

RECOMMENDATIONS

Hold Down Family Contacts

Family contacts account for the high rate of spread of streptococci when there is an infection in a household (Breese and Disney, 1956; James et al., 1960). Ideally all members of a family, especially in high-risk areas, should have throat cultures done. When positive cultures are found it is suggested that the full therapeutic course of penicillin is indicated; the others should be treated prophylactically. The potential danger of treating all members of a family, without benefit of a throat culture, is that prophylactic doses of penicillin may suppress overt symptoms without eradicating the organisms. Moreover, obtaining throat cultures from all members of a family presents the problem of getting the family to an emergency room or a neighborhood health center, since many of these families do not have a private physician.

Rosenstein and Markowitz (1969) go one step further and suggest that since large low-income families in overcrowded areas are at greater risk, antibiotic therapy should be considered for all siblings of the child first seen in this setting.

Initiate Community Programs

Community measures must be tailored to suit individual community needs. In ghetto areas treatment can be provided in the schools. Children of these areas do not usually have family physicians. If referred, they may go untreated. Parents are reluctant to battle the long wait at an outpatient clinic and may also delay for other reasons already mentioned.

Some communities have carried out mass culturing of school children in some areas as a method of controlling streptococcal infections (Bunn and Bennett, 1955; Phibbs et al., 1970). In Casper, Wyoming, a program was instituted to culture all symptomatic children, and all asymptomatic children are examined each week for pharyngitis (Phibbs et al., 1970). Children with positive cultures are required by state law to stay out of school until proper treatment is initiated.

In the San Luis Valley this program was modified so that children with positive cultures go to their physician voluntarily. Only a small number of asymptomatic children are cultured each week on a continuous rotation basis (Zimmerman et al., 1971).

Although the prevalence of streptococcal infections seemed to have been favorably affected by these two programs, most investigators feel that mass culturing is not practical for all communities, especially in low-incidence areas.

Several investigators have shown the effectiveness of mass prophylaxis in treating streptococcal infections and reducing the carrier rates during epidemics in the military (Wannamaker et al., 1953; Bernstein et al., 1954; Morris and Rammelkamp, 1957). Such a program of mass prophylaxis could be applied on a limited scale in certain situations in the civilian population. Poskanzer et al. (1956) demonstrated the efficacy of mass prophylaxis in a school population during epidemics.

Educate Parents and Physicians

Many streptococcal infections will not be brought to medical attention because parents may not recognize or attend to the variety of signs their children may show. Few know or understand the relationship of "strep throat" to rheumatic fever. Czoniczer et al. (1961) suggest that parents should take the child's temperature four times a day if he or she seems unwell and should consult a physician if the temperature is 101° F or more (by mouth). While this seems extreme, programs to enhance parental awareness are obviously a necessary part of any adequate primary care approach to prevention.

Physician education is needed too. Unawareness of adequate preventive measures is one of the major obstacles to primary prevention. Physicians should recognize the role of adequate throat cultures, especially if clinical symptoms are not diagnostically clear and in high-risk areas. Czoniczer et al. (1971) recommend that a throat culture should be taken unless the cause of fever is obvious. There is also a continuing need to acquaint physicians with the importance of *appropriate* and *adequate* therapy after the diagnosis is made. Tetracycline, for example, is more frequently prescribed for children than it should be.

Improve Comprehensive Care Programs

These programs were established to provide better care to low-income groups than could be obtained in traditional clinic settings. In 1971 Gordis and Markowitz did a study on a small group of patients to determine if there were any differences in management of infants in a comprehensive care setting versus a traditional care setting. No differences were found in utilization of services, morbidity, or mortality. In 1973 a statistically more accurate study was done (Markowitz, 1973) on a larger population combining children aged five to fourteen from different Baltimore programs. The incidence of hospitalized attacks of rheumatic fever was used as the morbidity index.

Using this study as a model for evaluating programs, it was found that comprehensive care resulted in a significant reduction in the rate of rheumatic fever when compared to the ineligible population. From 1960–64 to the two-year period 1968–70, there was a 60 percent decrease in the comprehensive care group, but the rates remained relatively unchanged in the rest of the city.

The declining incidence resulted from a reduction in preventable cases, in other words, those preceded by clinically overt respiratory infections. The incidence in cases without prior history of clinically apparent respiratory infection was not changed.

Early and accurate recognition and treatment of group *A* beta-hemolytic streptococcal pharyngitis is an important part of adequate primary care for children. This is true especially because of its serious sequela of rheumatic fever.

Taken separately, the various parts of the recognition process—throat culture, fluorescent antibody tests, community culturing, penicillin or sulfonamide prophylaxis and therapy—are highly efficacious when done correctly. Yet data for Toronto show essentially no change in the prevalence of rheumatic fever over the thirteen-year period from 1951 to 1964. While mortality has been dropping steadily, this almost certainly represents improvement in over-all management of heart disease rather than improvement in prevention of rheumatic heart disease per se. The drop was evident even before antibiotics, for example.

Still there is hope. Data by Gordis (1973) on the impact of comprehensive care and programs in selected communities have shown that a concerted effort can reduce the attack rate of rheumatic fever and the prevalence of streptococcal infection in general. This means that careful and well-planned measures can be effective.

We are struck by one inescapable fact. While it is encouraging to note that primary care workers applying well-established medical techniques can have an impact on a target problem, that impact is a drop in the bucket compared to the awesome difference in streptococcal-related disease incidence between upper and lower socioeconomic groups. The inevitable conclusion is that effective reduction in prevalence and attack rate of rheumatic fever lies not primarily in throat cultures but either in treating everyone with pharyngitis as Tompkins (1975) suggests, or in improving the nutritional and environmental status of the poor. This means improving sanitation, ventilation, and nutrition, as well as getting patients to play a part. Ultimately it will call for provision of adequate access to care and health supervision at a cost within the means of the ordinary family. If we remember the current cost of treating patients with valvular heart disease, for example, it seems foolish to focus only on the medical components of the problem. This would seem to miss the forest for the trees.

REFERENCES

Bergman, A.B., and Werner, R.J. "Failure of children to receive penicillin by mouth," *N Engl J Med* 268 (1963): 1334.

Bernstein, S.H., et al. "Mass oral penicillin prophylaxis in control of streptococcal disease," *Arch Int Med* 93 (1954): 894.

Breese, B.B., and Disney, F.A. "Factors influencing spread of beta hemolytic streptococcal infections within family group," *Pediatrics* 17 (1956): 834.

Breese, B.B., and Disney, F.A. "Accuracy of diagnosis of beta streptoccal infection on clinical grounds," *J Pediatr* 44 (1954): 670.

Breese, B.B., et al. "The clinical and epidemiologic importance of the number of organisms found in cultures," *Am J Dis Child* 119 (1970): 18.

Brumfitt, W., O'Grady, F., and Slater, J.D. "Benign streptococcal sore throat," *Lancet* 2 (1959): 419.

Bunn, W.H., and Bennet, H.N. "Community control of rheumatic fever," *JAMA* 157 (1955): 986.

Catanzaro, F.J., et al. "Prevention of rheumatic fever by treatment of streptococcal infection. II. Factors responsible for failure," *N Engl J Med* 259 (1958): 51.

Catanzaro, F.J. "The role of streptococcus in the pathogenesis of rheumatic fever," *Am J Med* 17 (1954): 749.

Charney, E., et al. "How well do patients take oral penicillin? A collaborative study in private practice," *Pediatrics* 40 (1967): 188.

Clarke, P.J. "Clinical and public health aspects of juvenile rheumatism in Dublin," *Irish J Med Sci* (Mar. 1940): 97–118.

Coburn, A.F., and Young, D.C. *The Epidemiology of Hemolytic Streptococcus during World War II in the United States Navy.* Baltimore, Md.: Williams and Wilkins Co., 1949.

Coburn, A.F., and Moore, L.V. "The prophylactic use of sulfamilimide in streptococcal respiratory infections with especial reference to rheumatic fever," *J Clin Invest* 18 (1939): 147.

Commission on Acute Respiratory Disease. "Fort Bragg, N.C.: A study of a food-borne epidemic of tonsillitis and pharyngitis to B-hemolytic streptococcus type V," *Bull Johns Hopkins Hosp* 77 (1945): 143.

Committee on Rheumatic Fever, Council on Rheumatic Fever and Congenital Heart Disease. *House Officers' Knowledge of Group A Streptococcal Pharyngitis and Its Management.* Reprinted from the *Am J Dis Child* 124 (1972): 47–50, by the American Heart Association, 1972.

Cornfield, D., et al. "Streptococcal infection in a school population: preliminary report," *Ann Int Med* 49 (1958): 1305.

Czoniczer, G., Lees, M., and Massell, B.F. "Streptococcal infection: The need for improved recognition and treatment for the prevention of rheumatic fever," *N Engl J Med* 265 (1958): 951.

Denny, F.W., et al. "Prevention of rheumatic fever: treatment of the preceding streptococcic infection," *JAMA* 143 (1950): 151.

Feinstein, A.R., et al. "Oral prophylaxis of recurrent rheumatic fever. Sulfadiazine vs. a doubly daily of penicillin," *JAMA* 188 (1964): 489.

Fox, E.N., et al. "Antigenicity of the M-proteins of group A hemolytic streptocci," *J Exp Med* 124 (1966): 1135.

Gardiner, J.H., and Keith, J.D. "Prevalence of heart disease in Toronto children," *Pediatrics* 7 (1951): 713.

Gordis, L., and Markowitz, M. "Environmental determinants in rheumatic fever prevention," in *Streptocci and Streptococcal Diseases: Recognition, Understanding and Management*, edited by L.W. Wannamaker and J.M. Matson. New York: Academic Press, 1972.

Gordis, L. and Markowitz, M. "Evaluation of effectiveness of comprehensive and continuous pediatric care," *Pediatrics* 48 (1971): 766–76.

Gordis, L., et al. "Studies in the epidemiology and preventability of rheumatic fever: III. Evaluation of the Maryland rheumatic fever registry," *Public Health Rep* 84 (1969): 333.

Grossman, B.J., and Stamler, J. "Potential preventability in just attacks of acute rheumatic fever in children," *JAMA* 183 (1963): 985.

Honikman, L. H., et al. "Treatment of group A streptococcal infections," *Am J Dis Child* 117 (1969): 451.

James, W.E., et al. "A study of illness in a group of Cleveland families. XIX. The epidemiology of the acquisition of group A streptococci and of associated illnesses," *N Engl J Med* 262 (1960): 687.

Kaplan, E.L., et al. "Diagnosis of streptococcal pharyngitis: Differentiation of active infection from the carrier state in the symptomatic child," *J Infect Dis* 123 (1971): 490.

Krause, R.M., and Rammelkamp, C.H., Jr. "Studies of the carrier state following infection with group A streptococci. II. Infectivity of streptococci isolated during acute pharyngitis and during the carrier state," *J Clin Invest* 41 (1962): 575.

Lancefield, R.C. "Current knowledge of type specific M antigens of group A streptococci," *J Immunol* 89 (1962): 307.

Lerner, P.I., and Weinstein, L. "Infective endocarditis in the antibiotic era," *N Engl J Med* 274 (1966): 199.

Markowitz, M. "Eradication of rheumatic fever: An unfulfilled hope," *Circulation* 41 (1970): 1077.

Markowitz, M. "Cultures of the respiratory tract in pediatric practice," *Am J Dis Child* 105 (1963): 12.

Markowitz, M., and Gordis, L. *Rheumatic Fever.* Philadelphia, W.B. Saunders Co., 1972.

Massell, B.F., et al. "Rheumatic fever following streptococcal vaccination, Report of three cases," *JAMA* 207 (1969): 1115.

Massell, B.F., et al. "Orally administered penicillin in patients with rheumatic fever," *JAMA* 138 (1948): 1030.

Moffet, H.L., Cramblett, H.G., and Smith, A. "Group A streptococcal infections in a children's home. II. Clinical and epidemiologic patterns of illness," *Pediatrics* 33 (1964): 11.

Mohler, D.N., et al. "Studies in home treatment of streptococcal disease. I. Failure of patients to take penicillin by mouth as prescribed," *N Engl J Med* 252 (1955): 116.

Moody, M.D., et al. "Flourescent antibody identification of group A streptococci from throat swabs," *Am J Public Health* 53 (1963): 1083.

Morris, A.J., and Rammelkamp, C.H., Jr. "Benzathine penicillin G in the prevention of streptococci infections," *JAMA* 165 (1957): 664.

Morris, A.J., et al. "Prevention of rheumatic fever by treatment of previous streptococci infections. Effect of sulfadiazine," *JAMA* 160 (1956): 114.

Perry, C.B., and Robert, J.A. "Study on the variability in the incidence of rheumatic heart disease within the city of Bristol," *Br Med J* (suppl.) 2 (1937): 154.

Phibbs, B., et al. "A community wide streptococcal control program," *JAMA* 214 (1970): 2018.

Poskanzer, D.C., et al. "Epidemiology of civilian streptococcal outbreaks before and after penicillin prophylaxis," *Am J Public Health* 46 (1956): 1513.

Poynton, F.J. "Acute rheumatism in children," *Br Med J* 2 (1920): 858.

Quinn, R.W. "Carrier rates for hemolytic streptococci in school children," *Am J Epidemiol* 82 (1965): 1.

Quinn, R.W., and Quinn, J.P. "Mortality due to rheumatic heart disease in the socioeconomic districts of New Haven, Conn.," *Yale J Biol Med* 24 (1951): 15.

Rammelkamp, C.H., and Stolzer, B.L. "The latent period before the onset of acute rheumatic fever," *Yale J Biol Med* 34 (1961): 386–98.

Rammelkamp, C.H., et al. "Studies on epidemiology of rheumatic fever in the armed services," in *Rheumatic Fever. A Symposium*, edited by L. Thomas. Minneapolis: University of Minnesota Press, 1952.

Rantz, L.A., et al. "Antistreptolysin O response following hemolytic streptococcal infection in early childhood," *Arch Int Med* 87 (1951): 360.

Rantz, L.A., et al. "Antistreptolysin 'O'. A study of this antibody in health and in hemolytic streptococcus respiratory disease in man," *Am J Med* 5 (1948): 3.

Rantz, L.A., et al. "Etiology and pathogenesis of rheumatic fever," *Arch Int Med* 76 (1945): 131.

Rose, V., et al. "Incidence of heart disease in children in the city of Toronto," *Can Med Assoc J* 91 (1964): 95.

Rosenthal, A., et al. "Rheumatic fever under 3 years of age," *Pediatrics* 41 (1968): 612.

Rosenstein, B.J., and Markowitz, M. "Unpublished observations cited by Gordis, L., and Markowitz, M.: Environmental determinants in rheumatic fever prevention," in *Streptococci and Streptococcal Diseases: Recognition, Understanding and Management*, edited by L.W. Wannamaker and J.M. Matson. New York: Academic Press, 1972.

Rosenstein, B.J., et al. "Factors involved in treatment failures following oral penicillin therapy of streptococcal pharyngitis," *Pediatrics* 73 (1968): 513.

Roth, I.R., et al. "Heart disease in children. A rheumatic group. I. Certain aspects of the age at onset and of recurrences in 488 cases of juvenile rheumatism ushered in by major clinical manifestations," *Am Heart J* 13 (1937): 36.

Stetson, C.A., Jr. *The Relation of Antibody Response to Rheumatic Fever in Streptococcal Infections*. New York: Columbia University Press, 1954.

Stillerman, M., and Bernstein, S.H. "Streptococcal pharyngitis therapy," *Am J Dis Child* 107 (1964): 35.

Stollerman, G.H. "Factors determining the attack rate of rheumatic fever," *JAMA* 177 (1961): 823.

Tompkins, R., et al. "An analysis of the cost-effectiveness of pharyngitis management and acute rheumatic fever prevention," *Health Serv Res* (1976).

Wannamaker, L.W. "Perplexity and precision in the diagnosis of streptococcal pharyngitis," *Am J Dis Child* 124 (1972): 352–58.

Wannamaker, L.W., et al. "The effect of penicillin prophylaxis on streptococcal disease rates and the carrier state," *N Engl J Med* 249 (1953): 1.

Warfield, M.A., et al. "Immunofluorescence in diagnostic bacteriology. II. Identification of group A streptococci in throat smears," *Am J Dis Child* 101 (1961): 160.

Wood, H.F., et al. "Rheumatic fever in children and adolescents. III. Comparative effectiveness of three prophylaxis regimens in preventing streptococcal infections and rheumatic recurrences," *Ann Int Med* 60 Suppl. 5 (1964): 31.

Zimmerman, R.A., et al. "An effective program for reducing group A streptococcal prevalence," *Pediatrics* 48 (1971): 566.

✳ *Chapter 10*

Appendicitis
John Graef, M.D.

It may strike the reader as odd that although the removal of the inflamed appendix is widely accepted as efficacious treatment at the tertiary care level, there remains an incidence of morbidity and mortality associated with appendicitis, particularly in children under two years of age.

While this condition is not so prevalent as to represent a significant threat to the health of children at large, it warrants closer examination. Given the known efficacy of surgery, why is the incidence of perforation as high as it is? What accounts for the difference in morbidity and mortality between age groups? What is known about the evaluation of possible appendicitis at either the primary or the tertiary care level? Why do surgeons claim that as high as 30 percent normal appendices should be present at surgery to guarantee removal of all abnormal ones?

Within the pediatric age group, appendicitis is the most frequently occurring abdominal disorder requiring emergency surgical management. The persistently high perforation rate, particularly in infants, with its consequent increased morbidity and mortality (several times higher than that in the adult population), remains a challenge to the primary health care system in recognizing an essentially curable disease (Fields and Cole, 1967).

The material presented here is intended to emphasize the need for careful study of what is efficacious intervention at the primary care level in the effective treatment of appendicitis in small children.

INCIDENCE AND PREVALENCE

According to Gross (1957), appendicitis is rare (0.4 percent of surgical cases) during the first year of life, uncommon during the second year (3.9 percent of cases), but then is seen with somewhat increasing frequency. The majority of cases occur during the first three decades. Males are affected slightly more than females. It is the most common disorder of childhood requiring emergency abdominal surgery.

During 1971, an estimated 4,029,000 children less than fifteen years of age (excluding newborns) were discharged from the nation's nonfederal short-stay hospitals (*Surgical Operations*, 1971), approximately 14 percent of all discharges. Within this group there were 2,340,000 surgical operations of which 99,000 (4 percent) were appendectomies. This is 31 percent of appendectomies for all age groups. Looking at it another way, in 1971 one out of 100,000 American children underwent an appendectomy.

MORTALITY AND MORBIDITY

Due to generally improved methods of treatment, preoperative and postoperative care, anesthesia, and the use of antibiotics, the mortality associated with appendicitis has progressively declined during the past few decades. To the extent that mortality and morbidity do occur, they are almost without exception associated with perforation of the appendix or postoperative complications.

During the period 1953−63, a study of 6915 cases of appendicitis affecting people of all ages at the Los Angeles County Hospital confirmed that the mortality rate is higher among children than adults. Among thirty cases of primary acute appendicitis in infants thirty-six months of age or younger, two deaths were noted (6.7 percent). Gryboski (1975) quotes a mortality rate in infants (primarily due to perforation) of 9.5 percent, although it is not clear how that figure is derived. Schaupp et al. (1960) discuss nineteen cases of appendicitis in the first month of life and point out that in this age group fatalities resulted in all cases of perforation.

Rupture of the inflamed appendix is very much more frequent in young children, between 83 and 90 percent of cases in children less than two years (Figure 10−1). As to over-all frequency of rupture, Lansden's (1963) figures from Children's Hospital in Akron, Ohio (Figure 10−2) are somewhat at odds with Longino et al. (1958). However, three reports dealing exclusively with appendicitis in the infant or toddler group confirm the general impression that although

Figure 10–1. Frequency of Rupture, by Age

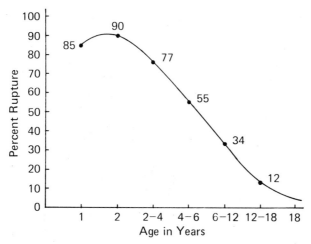

Source: Adapted from Gross, 1957 and Longino et al., 1958.

the frequency of the disease is low in this age group, the incidence of perforation and subsequent morbidity is extremely high. Rowe (1966) combined the statistics of four large series involving 566 children under four and found the incidence of perforation to be 77 percent. Fields et al. (1967) confirmed this incidence almost exactly, and Bartlett et al. (1970), reviewing 40 cases in the age group under two, found ruptured appendices in thirty-three cases (82 percent).

It is interesting to note that in all the series discussed there is no significant difference in morbidity over a fifteen-year-period 1950–65 (Lansden, 1963). This might be due in large measure to a failure of problem recognition at the primary care level, since perforation is usually a result of delay in definitive diagnosis.

PROBLEM RECOGNITION

The signs and symptoms suggestive of appendicitis vary with age. It has been suggested that the triad of abdominal pain, fever, and vomiting should be considered indicative of appendicitis until proved otherwise. However, Longino, Holder and Gross point out the importance of age differences:

> In older children, symptoms follow the more classical course of periumbilical pain followed by nausea, vomiting, low-grade fever and, in a few hours, shift of the pain to the right lower quadrant. In smaller children, vomiting is apt to occur before the parents are aware of any abdominal discomfort (1958, p. 238).

Figure 10–2.   Acute Appendicitis in Children, Perforation versus Age

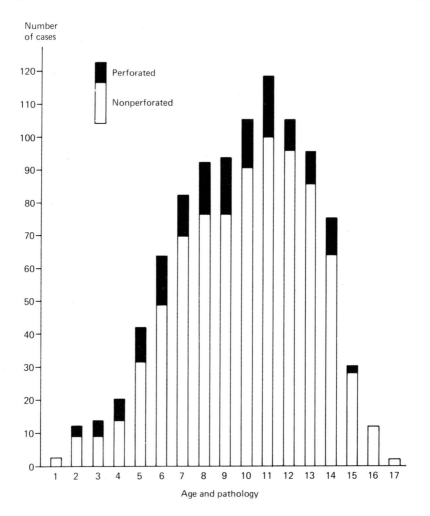

Source: Lansden, 1963. Reprinted with permission.

The problem for the primary care physician is that such symptoms in the infant may only represent gastroenteritis, usually of the viral type.

It is often suggested that the delay in diagnosis (particularly common among the poor) may be due to a failure of parents to seek help early. While this may be true in older children, in whom the symptoms may be less severe initially, it is not borne out in the group below the age of two.

Indeed, as Gryboski (1975) points out: "The delay in making the diagnosis is usually due to failure to consider this disease in the infant." Such failure is reflected in the observation of Bartlett et al. (1970) that of the forty infants with acute appendicitis seen at Children's Hospital Medical Center in Boston, the majority were seen by a physician prior to admission and had been treated for a diagnosis other than acute appendicitis.

The correlation between delay in diagnosis and incidence of rupture is confirmed by Lansden (1963) in his series from Children's Hospital of Akron, Ohio (Table 10—1).

Unfortunately, there are no studies that account for the differences in time of admission. Figure 10—3 demonstrates the frequency of symptoms found in the infants from Bartlett's series (Bartlett et al., 1970). While one can argue that such symptoms can represent benign conditions, the classic triad pointing to appendicitis— vomiting, fever, and pain—is most frequent even in infants. This is followed closely by lethargy, and these symptoms generally represent serious enough conditions to warrant close examination *whatever the diagnosis.* On the other hand, in half or fewer of these patients, nausea, feeding problems, and diarrhea were present, and these are vague enough to be less than helpful. In the infant, fretfulness, crying, disturbed sleep, and resistance to handling are early signs of trouble (Rowe, 1966). Again, this observation is important whatever the ultimate cause.

Fields et al. (1957) summarize some of the difficulties in diagnosis:

1. Failure to consider the increased morbidity in the younger age groups.
2. Difficulty in interpreting the history. The story of onset of abdominal pain in the infant or small child is usually unreliable, frequently missed, or ascribed to coexisting disease.

Table 10—1. Duration of Symptoms Related to Pathologic Conditions

Condition	*Duration of Symptoms Prior to Hospital Admission*
Acute appendicitis without complications	30.2 hours
Pathologic condition other than appendicitis	45.3 hours
Perforation or abscess formation	71.4 hours

Source: Adapted from Lansden, 1963.

Figure 10–3. Incidence of Observed Symptoms and the Physical Signs in Forty Infants with Acute Appendicitis

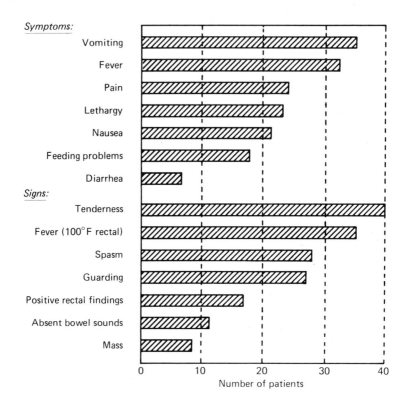

Source: Bartlett et al., 1970. Reprinted by permission of *Surgery, Gynecology & Obstetrics.*

3. The frequency with which vomiting occurs in extra-abdominal conditions in infants.

4. The inappropriate use of antibiotics, which may alter and conceal but not necessarily prevent the natural course of the disease.

5. More rapid and fulminant progression of the disease in young children and infants than adults, resulting in earlier perforations.

It is misleading to apply to children observations pertinent to diagnosis and management of adults. For example, vomiting is more likely to be evident to parents than abdominal discomfort, thereby masking the frequency with which other more subtle abdominal symptoms may occur. In Bartlett's series (Figure 10–3) vomiting was reported in thirty-six of forty infants and pain in twenty-five of forty. Finally, it is important to point out that pain in infants may be manifest only indirectly. The child may be irritable, may draw up his legs, and may have little appetite. All these symptoms may be present even without crying and still represent abdominal discomfort.

DIAGNOSIS

While in some cases there may be helpful laboratory and radiological signs, most authorities state that the diagnosis of appendicitis in infants or in adults is primarily a clinical decision based on a high index of suspicion and the previously mentioned triad of abdominal pain, mild fever, and localized tenderness.

There is no characteristic history or sine qua non in the diagnosis of appendicitis. In the infant, loss of appetite and irritability may be the only evidence, and these complaints are present in many other conditions. Because of the fulminant nature of the condition, these initial symptoms may quickly give way to vomiting and lethargy as perforation with generalized abdominal inflammation occurs (Gryboski, 1975).

Gross (1957) suggests that vomiting is present in almost all cases and is supported in this observation by Bartlett et al. (1970) and Lansden (1963). Again, the difference in age groups alters the frequency of historical observation significantly, but it is safe to say that a history either of abdominal pain or nausea and vomiting, or both, can be found in almost all cases of acute appendicitis in children. It is up to the practitioner to distinguish the severity of these symptoms from those seen with otitis media, pneumonia, simple gastroenteritis, and other less threatening conditions.

When the predominant symptom is abdominal pain, the age of the child determines its value in the diagnosis. In older children the more characteristic type of periumbilical pain occurs, which typically shifts after a few hours to the right lower quadrant, accompanied by additional symptoms and signs. While this picture can be present in other conditions, the shift of the pain with time is particularly indicative when combined with repeated physical examinations.

Of other associated symptoms shown in Figure 10−3, constipation is more frequent than diarrhea except when perforation occurs. Then the reverse is true. Lansden (1963) noted antecedent upper respiratory infection in one-third of his patients. Low-grade fever is the rule except in the event of peritonitis, when temperatures above 103° are more frequent. Urinary complaints are infrequent unless abscess of the appendix and pelvic inflammation are present.

Gross (1957) points out that only a small percentage of children have a history of previous attacks of abdominal pain. When the child has such history, it may be related to the current diagnosis and appendofecaliths (calcified blood vessels) are more apt to be found on X-ray. In Lansden's series, 25 percent of these patients had "normal" appendices.

It should be noted that data vary widely from hospital to hospital regarding the rates at which the removed appendix is found to be histologically normal. Neutra points out that one variable in this disparity is the data base of the patient's history.[a] Reports from the Johns Hopkins Hospital (*Medical World News*, 10 March 1975) maintain that, given the "clinical value of this diagnosis, careful monitoring of the evolution of signs and symptoms has led to a reduction in false positive appendectomies to below 5 percent." (The usual figure is 15 to 30 percent.) Rowe suggests that to avoid perforation, "one must willingly accept to remove one normal appendix in five" (1966). (This is a higher proportion of normal appendices than is sometimes allowed for, and it is obviously important that there should be no concomitant rise in over-all morbidity or mortality either from false positive *or* false negative assessments.) The important point made by Neutra is that the clinical decision is made on at best vague and varied symptoms of undetermined duration and that careful observation adds the dimensions of evolution and objectivity to available historical information about the patient. Applied to children without obviously severe symptoms and excluding infants, there is reason to believe that improved histories would yield significant improvement in diagnostic accuracy. Unfortunately, objective data are not available for infants.

Finally, a number of reports allude to the frequency of coexisting disease, particularly in infants. Eufrate and Gordon (1964) noted that 22 percent of a series of 135 patients had concomitant disease, usually in the upper respiratory tract. There are no controls in this series, however, and Gross (1957) points out that respiratory diseases are common in this age group anyway. Fields et al. (1957) found fourteen of thirty-eight infants with appendicitis to have coexisting disease including measles, chickenpox, typhoid fever, acute tonsillitis, nasopharyngitis, and acute gastroenteritis. In eight of the fourteen, acute appendicitis was not suspected at time of admission, and significant delays in diagnosis occurred. While the accuracy of the various diagnoses other than appendicitis might be open to question, it is reasonable to conclude that in some cases acute appendicitis,

[a]Raymond Neutra, unpublished.

accompanied by other obvious conditions, may go unrecognized for considerable time.

Physical Examination

Once again, caution must be used to distinguish age groups. Examination of infants is frequently difficult and objective signs hard to evaluate. Nevertheless, patient, gentle examination is possible, and even if the specific diagnosis is only guessed at, the infant at risk may be identified.

Rowe (1966), Gross (1957), and Lansden (1963) agree that the most constant finding is abdominal tenderness usually localized to the right lower quadrant. While this can readily be demonstrated in older children, younger children (under four) and infants pose a problem, particularly infants. Little improvement can be made on the following dissertation by Longino, Holder, and Gross (1958) on the proper abdominal examination of a child with suspected appendicitis:

> Time spent in gaining the cooperation of the child is well worthwhile. The examination of the abdomen of a crying, kicking child is not only impractical but the findings are utterly worthless. While one is trying to gain the child's confidence, much information can be obtained by observation. The extent of dryness of the skin, the position of the legs, the type of respiration, the luster of the eyes or the extent to which they are sunken, and the reaction to those about him may give one a good idea as to just how sick the patient is and may give a hint of the site of the pathologic process.
>
> If the child is resting quietly in the parent's arms, it is a good practice to palpate the abdomen gently before moving him. Merely leaving the parent's arms is frequently enough to upset a child for some time. The abdomen should be palpated gently with warm hands, starting on the portion of the abdomen which is least likely to be tender, then progressing to the area which is most likely to be tender. Tenderness is the most constant single finding in appendicitis and is almost inevitably present. The tenderness is usually maximum in the right lower quadrant, but may be most intense in the right upper quadrant or left lower quadrant. The appendix in the child is longer in relation to the size of the abdominal cavity than in adults and hence may present maximum tenderness over a comparatively larger area. Muscle spasm is the second most common finding. This is best detected by simply resting one's hand on the abdomen and noting after a few moments whether there is relaxation of the abdominal musculature during inspiration. In simple appendicitis, the findings are usually localized, while in ruptured appendicitis the findings are more diffuse. Bowel sounds are, as a rule, hypo-active but in the case of a spreading peritonitis may be hyperactive. When an appendiceal abscess is present, it may be palpated abdominally but is more often detected on rectal examination.

There are a small number of sick children who, in spite of almost infinite patience on the part of the examiner, are too irritable to be adequately examined. In this group of children, usually the 2 to 4 year olds, it is most helpful to administer a barbiturate rectally. We prefer pentobarbital using a dosage of 5.5 mg per kg of body weight dissolved in 10 ml of isotonic saline and given via a small rectal catheter. This dosage is safe and usually produces sound sleep in 30 to 45 minutes. The child can then be examined without difficulty. The parents are also much happier since the child is sleeping quietly and is in no obvious discomfort. The physical findings are not masked by this medication. Muscle spasm persists but voluntary guarding is absent. When a tender area is palpated, the child will arouse momentarily from sleep and then drop back into slumber after the examining hand is removed. Under these conditions, the findings are much more valid than in an irritable, crying child. (An opiate is, of course, never used for this purpose.) (p. 239).

All authors agree that after the abdominal examination, a complete physical examination must be performed both to discover other possible causes of abdominal pain such as pneumonia or streptococcal pharyngitis and to discover coexisting conditions. This must include a rectal examination irrespective of the age of the child. Longino et al. (1958) suggest that positive findings (localized tenderness, a firm tender mass or "boggy" tenderness) are present in three-fourths of cases. Lansden (1963), noting that the rectal examination was helpful in at least 50 percent of his cases, also commented on the frequency with which this important part of the physical is omitted by house officers. (If that observation is true in a hospital examining room, how much more frequently is the rectal exam omitted in a primary care setting!) On a dissenting note, Schaupp et al. (1960), discussing only the first month of life, commented that abdominal distention and vomiting were the two most common findings and that "localized signs, rectal examination and leukocyte count have been of *no* assistance."

On this last point the distinction must be drawn between rectal findings in uncomplicated appendicitis and those in perforation or abscess. It requires a skilled observer to uncover them, but the findings of the latter are usually there. Given the increased frequency of perforation or abscess in the very young, it certainly seems worth the examiner's effort to learn this skill.

Laboratory Findings

Generally, laboratory findings are not specific enough to be of help. There is no laboratory test which is positive only in appendicitis. However, roentgenographic findings are often helpful and may be quite specific, particularly in the presence of complications.

Lansden (1963) reported "significant" leukocytosis in 84 percent of patients, with an increase in polymorphonuclear leukocytes and a "shift to the left" (relative increase in young polymorphs) in 88 percent. He comments that since more than half of patients with normal appendices had neither of these findings, it would be wise to ask for a period of observation for patients with other symptoms suggesting appendicitis but without these specific signs.

Bartlett et al. (1970) found a range of from 10,000 to 25,000 white cells per cu. mm. Most of their patients had above 15,000 white cells per cubic millimeter and a marked shift to the left. However, virtually all of these had perforations.

Gryboski (1975) suggests that while the range of white cells may be between 12,000 and 15,000, it is low or normal in 40 percent of babies less than two years. (This is not documented, however.) She agrees that a WBC count over 20,000 is suggestive of perforation.

Clearly then, the white blood count, while at least moderately elevated in many cases, can actually be misleading in the absence of controlled studies indicating its significance in this and other conditions. Marked increase in both immature and mature polymorphonuclear leukocytes is suggestive of bacterial invasion and is by no means diagnostic of single conditions. As a generalization, white blood counts (even with low-grade fever) greater than 20,000 per cu. mm. warrant careful evaluation, blood cultures, and roentgenograms to rule out focal bacterial infection.

Like white blood cell count, urinalysis is of relatively little help except as a negative finding to rule out other conditions causing abdominal pain. The following points are worth note:

1. In the presence of appendiceal or pelvic abscess in proximity to the ureter, a small number of red or white cells may be present.
2. A concentrated urine is compatible with dehydration in cases of prolonged vomiting or diarrhea.
3. Organisms in the urine do not necessarily mean that some other infection in the urinary tract is at fault rather than appendicitis. This is particularly true if the process has extended into the peritoneum.

Despite the high frequency of perforation in infants, it is interesting to note that in Bartlett et al.'s (1970) series only three infants had abnormal urinalyses and two of these showed partial obstruction of the right ureter on the pyelogram. This suggests that urinary abnormalities should be carefully and completely evaluated when they do occur, particularly in infants.

Roentgenograms have been shown to be of considerable value in establishing the diagnosis and deserve particular consideration. Bartlett, Eraklis and Wilkinson (1970) examined the cases of forty-one infants under two years of age undergoing appendectomy for acute appendicitis. Of twenty-four infants who had preoperative roentgenograms, twenty-one had at least two abnormalities indicating acute appendicitis.

Most important was that of the twenty-one X-rayed patients who had perforated appendices at surgery, all were diagnosed preoperatively by the presence of free intraperitoneal fluid. The authors comment that free intraperitoneal gas which is thought by Longino et al. (1958) to be helpful was present in only one infant. Calcified fecaliths (impacted material at the site of inflammation) were present in nine patients, six of whom had perforation. This abnormality can be readily recognized by a nonradiologist.

In contrast to this work, Lansden (1963), looking at the entire pediatric age group, agreed that X-rays are helpful in diagnosis of rupture or abscess formation, but he does not recommend "routine films," although it is not clear why. Rowe (1966) also comments that X-rays are not helpful in the nonperforated cases but may be in complicated or advanced cases. Neither cite data or controls for these comments.

Based on existing data, and in view of the high rate of perforation in infants, it can be surely stated that abdominal X-rays are helpful in this age group. Their value in older children remains to be seen.

SUMMARY

Although the prevalence of acute appendicitis is not very high compared to other conditions in the primary care setting, it is still the most common abdominal condition in childhood requiring surgery. This places the primary care physician in the role of having to identify children with this condition in the context of other similar conditions, many of which are less threatening than appendicitis but indistinguishable from it in signs and symptoms. This underscores the problem, particularly when the high mortality from appendicitis (10 percent in infants and almost 100 percent in neonates) is considered. The fact that this mortality is almost uniformly associated with perforation whenever it occurs makes early recognition, careful observation, and diagnosis most important in preventing perforation.

Problem recognition is compounded by the vagueness of signs and symptoms, particularly in infants. Older children can express complaints suggestive of the diagnosis, but younger children and infants in particular must be assessed by skilled observers. It is apparent from Bartlett et al.'s study (1970) that even when parents of infants seek care for their children promptly, the underlying condition is often misdiagnosed. No data are currently available to explain this observation but some circumstantial inferences can be drawn with caution. Two reasons in particular may account for missed diagnosis.

1. The level of pediatric assessment skills varies widely among providers in primary care settings. It is not clear whether or not surgeons, pediatricians, general practitioners, or nurses are "best" at recognizing or at least suspecting appendicitis in small children. Experience may also vary widely. Some primary care providers may have had little if any acute care experience even in pediatric training programs, while others may have spent half or more of their training and subsequent experience on the "front lines."

2. Use of diagnostic tools also may vary widely from setting to setting. In fact, it is apparent that there is considerable disagreement even among "experts" over the value of various procedures. Even the use of X-ray is most helpful *after* perforation has occurred in identifying signs of peritonitis.

This raises an interesting question. To what extent might the availability of diagnostic procedures alter the pattern of misdiagnosis? While no data are available on this point, it is not a foregone conclusion that the presence of an X-ray machine in a neighborhood health center would automatically increase the percentage of correct early diagnoses. For one thing, interpretation of X-rays is a science in itself. The training in diagnostic radiology available to most primary care providers is at best highly variable. Furthermore, there is no evidence that current X-ray techniques, blood counts, or other lab tests can really be useful in early diagnosis, because so few infants are evaluated at that early stage. Retrospective studies suggest that X-ray at least is worth a try, but it remains the clinicians' index of suspicion that tips the balance in favor of diagnostic tests in the first place.

There are many other arguments for increasing the availability to the primary care provider of commonly used, potentially valuable laboratory tools. However, such providers often show gaps in their understanding of even the changes in the blood count early in the development of potentially serious disease.

One point appears clear, however. Given the difficulty of diagnosis of acute appendicitis, a period of intense observation appears to enhance the likelihood of accuracy. That such observation is difficult to achieve goes without saying. It is rare that a primary care facility has either the space or the inclination to observe children over a period of time, particularly when dealing with large numbers of children. Frequently the secondary or tertiary care center is asked to undertake this task. Without the perspective of the primary care provider, the end result is Rowe's comment previously cited: "We must tolerate 20−30 percent normal appendices at operation" (Rowe, 1966). Given the potential for improved diagnostic accuracy, this rate is clearly unacceptable.

Has the relative availability of secondary and tertiary care to the affluent resulted in a greater accuracy of diagnosis? We doubt it. While a child with abdominal pain may indeed see a surgeon more quickly in the suburbs, we are unaware that fewer normal appendices are removed. In fact the availability of surgical intervention may have just the opposite effect and produce a greater frequency of unnecessary procedures.

It is clear that while ultimate therapy for appendicitis is efficacious and the prevalence of the condition not alarming, this condition continues to plague primary care providers, particularly when it appears in infants. It is a model for problems in early recognition of disease in conditions where early recognition appears to be the key to reducing morbidity and mortality, such as meningitis, osteomyelitis, and other severe infections. Because appendicitis mimics so many other conditions in its early behavior, the primary care provider must have either a high index of suspicion or improve his recognition of diagnostic clues to identify this condition before its hazards are apparent.

Despite the frequency of the problem, few data are available suggesting progress in finding early specific signs. And unfortunately, primary care practices are monitored only sporadically, or after disaster strikes. One would certainly welcome closer scrutiny.

REFERENCES

Bartlett, R.H., Eraklis, A.J., and Wilkinson, R.H. "Appendicitis in infancy," *Surg Gynecol Obstet* 130 (1970): 99−104.

Cantrell, J.R., and Stafford, E.S. "The diminishing mortality from appendicitis," *Ann Surg* 141 (1955): 749.

Eufrate, S.A., and Gordon, D.L. "Acute appendicitis in children," *N Y Med J* 64 (1964): 2981.

Fields, I.A., and Cole, N.M. "Acute appendicitis in infants thirty-six months of age or younger," *Am J Surg* 113 (1967): 269.

Gross, R. *Surgery of Infancy and Childhood*. Philadelphia: W.B. Saunders Co., 1957.

Gryboski, J. *Gastrointestinal Problems in the Infant.* Philadelphia: W.B. Saunders Co., 1975.

Lansden, F.T. "Acute appendicitis in children," *Am J Surg* 106 (1963): 938–42.

Longino, L.A., Holder, T.M., and Gross, R.E. "Appendicitis in childhood," *Pediatrics* 22 (1958): 238–46.

Medical World News, 10 March 1975.

Nelson, W.E. *Textbook of Pediatrics.* Philadelphia: W.B. Saunders Co., 1975.

Rowe, M.I. "Diagnosis and treatment: appendicitis in childhood," *Pediatrics* 38 (1966): 1057–59.

Schaupp, W., Clausen, E.G., and Ferrier, P.K. "Appendicitis during the first month of life," *Surgery* 48 (1960): 805.

U.S. Department of Health, Education and Welfare. *Surgical Operations in Short Stay Hospitals.* NCHS Series 13, No. 18. Washington, D.C.: Government Printing Office, 1971.

Wilkinson, R.H., Bartlett, R.H., Eraklis, A.J. "Diagnosis of appendicitis in infancy: the value of abdominal radiographs," *Am J Dis Child* 118 (1969): 687–90.

Chapter 11

Reading Disability

Cynthia Longfellow
Elsie Freeman, M.D.

The child reaching the age of four or five is entering one of the healthiest periods of his life. He has survived the risks of the neonatal and infancy periods, and has passed through a period of relatively high morbidity during his early childhood years. With the onset of schooling, a new set of problems confronts those entrusted with the well-being of the child—problems of education and social-emotional development. In this chapter, we will focus on the learning-disabled child, in particular, the child with reading problems.

There are several reasons for the inclusion of reading disability in a book documenting children's health needs.

1. The impact of the problem is extensive. It has been estimated that as many as 15 to 20 percent of school-age children have reading problems.

2. Learning problems and psychosocial problems have been labeled the "new morbidity" of the 1970s (Haggerty et al., 1975). More and more parents are bringing their children to the family doctor citing this problem as their primary complaint. Certainly reading disability represents a serious threat to the child's cognitive and emotional development.

3. Despite the extensive research literature, the proliferation of learning disability clinics in pediatric hospitals, and the large numbers of learning disability programs in the schools, there remains substantial disagreement about the definition of learning disability and how its potential causes may be averted by primary preventive measures.

Experts disagree on appropriate diagnostic measures and little convincing research has been done to validate the effectiveness of various treatments.

TERMINOLOGY

"Dyslexia," "minimal cerebral dysfunction," and "developmental dyslexia" are examples of some thirty terms that have emerged from the research over the years in an attempt to classify reading disabled children. The proliferation of so many classificatory terms, should alert one to the difficulty researchers have had in developing a satisfactory understanding of the general problem.

The terminology often tends to be misleading, because it implies that the syndrome can be attributed to some physiologic abnormality. The label "minimal cerebral dysfunction" exemplifies this problem. Certainly some children with evidence of minor neurologic abnormalities might justifiably be described as having minimal cerebral dysfunction, but children with neurologic difficulties comprise only a small proportion of all children with reading difficulties. Conversely, not all children with a cerebral dysfunction have difficulty reading. All too often researchers investigating brain-damaged children who could not read have ignored children with similar brain damage who could read, and thus incorrectly concluded that the brain damage caused the reading disability.

In addition, certain terms give the erroneous impression that there are specific syndromes, such as "hyperkinesis," "dyslexia," "minimal brain damage," or "specific learning disability." However, the terms are often used interchangeably, and there are ample data that a sample of children classified as hyperkinetic or dyslexic in fact contains a highly heterogeneous group of children (Rutter et al., 1970a; Stroufe and Stewart, 1973; Conners, 1971).

We prefer that children who have reading problems should be described by their symptoms, that is, as reading disabled, a term that has no implications as to etiology. We also suggest that no children be excluded from consideration, such as those who have received an inferior education, or are culturally different, or emotionally disturbed. While limiting one's focus may be appropriate for the researcher, the clinician or educator, faced with the child who cannot read, must consider a wide variety of possible causes and make remedial plans accordingly.

WHEN IS A CHILD READING DISABLED?

At what point does one decide a child's reading skills are poor enough to warrant the label of reading disability? When is a child really behind? Some authors define "behind" as one or two standard deviations or years behind some norm. It can also be argued that "behind" depends on the age of the child, in other words, that being one year behind at the end of grade one is different from being one year behind at the end of grade six. There is also some difference of opinion as to the appropriate norm. Some define what is expected in terms of the reading level typical for children of the same age or grade level. Others argue that the expected achievement should be that predicted by a child's intellectual potential. The advantage of comparing achievement to potential is that this method picks up the child of above average potential who is functioning only at grade level. The disadvantage is that this method misses the child who scores unreliably on standard IQ tests—often the child who cannot read the instructions, or who is from a cultural group other than the norming population, or who is too emotionally disturbed to concentrate.

Table 11–1 gives some common definitions of reading disability from which one sees that children excluded by one definition can be included by another. The more complex norms which arrive at an expected grade level by a combination of age, experience, and IQ are theoretical formulations and do not really correct the disadvantages of using only an age norm or only an IQ norm. In the absence of any longitudinal studies that compare adult achievement to early school achievement, it is difficult to know how much behind at what age represents a significant educational handicap.

We suggest that as an initial screening device the clinician and planner accept the simplest device, which begs the fewest questions about native ability: reading disabled children should be those who are significantly behind the reading achievement norm for their age. This means six months to one year behind in grades one through three, and two years behind thereafter.

PREVALENCE OF READING DISABILITY

Given the widely different definitions and measures of reading disability, it is not surprising to discover that estimates of prevalence vary widely. Table 11–2 lists research-based prevalence estimates which range from 3 to 50 percent.

The increased frequency of reading disability in certain populations has been observed repeatedly. For example, reading ability is

Table 11–1. Classifications of Reading Disability

Category[a]	Type	Disadvantages
1. 2 years behind grade level expected by chronologic age.	Norm for age	Misses child who is very bright and ought to be ahead of grade level.
		In absence of longitudinal studies 2 years is an arbitrary choice. In the lower grades 6 months may be more appropriate; in high school 3–4 years may make more sense.
2. 2 years behind grade level expected by mental age	Norm for IQ	Misses child who does poorly on IQ tests although truly of normal potential. Particularly misses children therefore of lower social classes and minority groups, resulting in a social class bias.
		Again, choice of 2 years is arbitrary.
3. 28 months behind reading level predicted by age and WISC IQ score (Rutter et al., 1970a).	Combined norm for age and IQ	Not clear that this remedies disadvantages named in 2, including arbitrary choice of time "behind."
4. A learning quotient that incorporates achievement versus an average of chronologic age, mental age, and current grade level.	Norm involving chronologic age, achievement, and experience	Quotient of 89 is arbitrary.
		Not clear that this remedies social class bias as found in 2.

Learning quotient is
Achievement Age
divided by Expectancy
Age where EA = (mental
age + chronologic age +
grade age) divided by 3.
A learning quotient of
89 or less is taken as a
cutoff for learning dis-
ability (Myklebust,
1967).

Mathematically, it is proper to average mental age,
chronologic age, and grade age only if they are of
equal weight. But the appropriate relative weights
are not surely known here. In data collection it
makes more sense to keep these variables separate.
Children of the same learning quotient are not
necessarily comparable. Better to analyze age, IQ,
and experience categories separately.

---

[a] Sometimes Category 1 and Category 2 are expressed as 2 standard deviations behind norm for age or norm for IQ. This means
a child does worse than 95 percent of children of that age or IQ. Again, there are no data that a 95 percent cut-off is wise. 75
percent might be better. At present, the choice is arbitrary.

Table 11–2.   Estimates of Reading Disability Prevalence

Prevalence Percent	Method of Estimation	Source
5.7	28 months behind level predicted by IQ (9–10 year olds)	Rutter et al., 1970, p. 41 Isle of Wight
7.5	Learning quotient less than 89, excluding children of IQ below 90, or with deficits in visual or auditory acuity, or defined as emotionally maladjusted by the Cattell Children's Personality Questionnaire	Myklebust, 1971, p. 217 U.S. public school children
8.6	28 months behind level predicted by age (9–10 year olds)	Rutter et al., 1970a, p. 41 Isle of Wight
12	Sixth-graders, 2 years behind grade level	Eisenberg, 1966 suburban, white
11.1	Black females	More and Welcher, 1971 Baltimore
12.9	White males	
14.3	White females	
15.8	Black males	
	7 year olds, 1 year behind grade level expected by age	Collaborative perinatal project, from middle and upper levels of socioeconomic classes
15	Learning quotient less than 89	Myklebust, 1971, p. 217 U.S. public school children
20.8	Reading ability one standard deviation below level predicted by IQ (6–10 year olds)	Malmquist, 1958 Sweden
25	Six-graders scoring 2 grades behind in reading as measured by the Metropolitan Achievement Test	Boston public school children As reported in the *Boston Globe*, 21 March 1975

28	Sixth-graders, 2 years behind grade level in reading	Eisenberg, 1966 Urban school excluding those in classes for retarded
36	Sixth-graders, 2 years behind grade level	Eisenberg, 1966 Rural black poor
50	Ninth-graders scoring 1.8 grades behind national norms in reading as measured by the Metropolitan Achievement Test	Boston public school children Reported in *Boston Globe*, 21 March 1975
50	Sixth-graders who are black, Mexican-American, Puerto Rican, or Indian are 1 standard deviation behind mean in reading for white urban children. Sixteen percent of white urban children are 1 standard deviation behind the same norm	Approximate extrapolation from Coleman's data, 1966

seen to decrease with decreasing taxable income, decreasing socio-economic status, where the father's occupation is unskilled or manual, or where the father is often out of work (Malmquist, 1958; Morris, 1966; Rutter et al., 1970a). It also decreases with level of education of either parent at any given income level (U.S. Census, 1960; Coleman, 1966; Malmquist, 1958).

It has also been shown that geographic location is of importance. In general, children from metropolitan areas do better than those from rural areas. Even within metropolitan or nonmetropolitan areas reading achievement is higher in the Northeast, Midwest, or Western U.S.A. than in the Southeast or Southwest (Coleman, 1966). Inner city children are more likely to read poorly than suburban children: Eisenberg (1966) reported reading levels at two years behind expected grade level for 28 percent of inner city children and 15 percent of suburban children.

Studies have shown that on average white children do better than black children, who generally do better than Mexican-Americans, Indians or Puerto Ricans (Coleman, 1966; U.S. Census Bureau, 1970). Orientals seem to constitute the only nonwhite, non-Anglo group that performs on a level with the white population (Coleman, 1966). Children of foreign-born parents tend to be behind grade level, although children of mixed parentage are not (Coleman, 1966).

It is clear that reading difficulties are one of the most prevalent of children's disorders, and that the magnitude of the problem is greater, for whatever reason, among some child populations than among others. The prevalence of reading disability ranks highest when compared to the rates of other children's disorders such as serious psychiatric disturbances (7 percent), physical handicaps (6 percent), and intellectual retardation (3 percent) (Rutter et al., 1970a).

CORRELATES OF READING DISABILITY

It has been widely assumed that certain correlates of reading disability are actually its cause, at least in some children. But it is not widely appreciated that causality is very difficult to prove. Some factors highly correlated with reading disability may turn out to be end products, cosymptoms along with academic difficulties, rather than causes. Thus, if an unknown factor causes motor clumsiness and reading disability simultaneously, treating motor clumsiness will have little effect on reading skill. To emphasize our lack of sure knowledge we will speak of correlates rather than causes of reading disability.

The correlates of reading disability fall into three major categories:

constitutional factors, emotional factors, and social or environmental factors. Clearly, these categories are not as separable in reality as we make them for purposes of discussion.

Constitutional Factors: Intelligence

It is generally accepted that a child who is mentally retarded will not achieve academically. In practice, a diffusely poor performance on several individually administered IQ tests is taken as evidence of generalized intellectual retardation. Usually an IQ score two standard deviations below the norm (70 on the WISC) is seen as sufficient explanation for a reading disability.

Before making a diagnosis of intellectual retardation it must be understood that IQ tests, although the only practical measure of intelligence, are far from perfect and share with other test procedures problems of validity and reliability. For these reasons, to properly assess intellectual ability in the reading-disabled child, one should test on several occasions, using individually administered tests that do not depend on a child's being able to read, tests that take cultural differences into account, and tests that tap a variety of intellectual functions, not simply verbal skills.

Even if we had a perfect IQ test, it is not clear that a low intelligence is a fixed biologic defect in all children. Indeed, there is evidence to suggest that intelligence may be related to psychiatric difficulties (Staver, 1953) and to certain background factors, including social class, income, institutionalization, family size, family attitudes, and family communication style (Deutsch, 1968; Dennis, 1960; Anastasi, 1956; Wachs et al., 1971; John, 1963; Walberg and Marjoribanks, 1973). Others suggest that the ability to think can be taught; thus, intelligence can increase (Whimby, 1975). For these reasons, one must be cautious in ascribing a child's reading disability to an intellectual handicap, and then assuming the problem is irremediable.

Constitutional Factors: Neurologic Damage

Where there is evidence of severe neurologic damage along with academic difficulties (e.g., paralysis, severe incoordination, seizures), it is often inferred that the cerebral damage explains reading difficulty. Signs of localizable brain damage indeed may be sufficient at times to account for reading difficulties in some children. But some children, even with severe brain damage or abnormal EEG, can read adequately (Hartlage and Green, 1973). Given this variability, more research needs to be done to define precisely which sorts of cerebral lesions predict specific learning disabilities.

Much more confusing and arguable is the current vogue for explaining reading difficulties on the basis of minimal brain damage. This concept remains diffuse for the following reasons.

Uncertain Definition. In practice, minimal neurologic dysfunction is diagnosed when abnormalities (often called "soft signs") are found on what is called the extended neurologic examination. But the component parts of this extended neurologic exam vary tremendously from author to author and from clinic to clinic.

Uncertain Validity. Operationally, many items on the extended neurologic exam have been developed through testing children who present in clinics with behavioral and educational difficulties. Only a few authors have tried their test battery on normal children. It is clear that many academically and behaviorly normal children perform abnormally on at least some of the items (Rutter et al., 1970a; Peters et al., 1975). How many items a child can fail and still be academically normal is not yet clear, but some children do have signs consistent with what some call minimal brain damage, and yet they are academically normal. Only a few authors have tried their test battery on children known to be brain damaged who are nevertheless academically normal. These authors note that they have frequently had to discard what appeared to be promising leads because a defect appearing in reading-retarded children also appeared in controls who were capable readers though brain damaged (Mattis et al., 1975). Thus, not all signs of neurologic dysfunction lead inevitably to learning difficulties.

Uncertain Reliability. Generally there is also little available data on reliability which takes into account the child's motivation or experience.

Some of the available data on findings from neurological exams are summarized in Table 11–3.

With the exception of a study by Rutter et al. (1970a), there are no population-based studies in which all children were assessed by extended neurologic examination. Rutter et al. found some "soft sign" abnormalities in 18.6 percent of children with reading retardation and in 13 percent of control children. The data further suggest that minimal cerebral dysfunction refers to a heterogeneous group of children with highly variable neurologic signs. The investigators found no subpopulations of children with specific clusters of abnormalities when they examined a whole population. Only Mattis et al. (1975) can describe any homogeneous subpopulations, and it appears that these subgroups account for a small proportion of all children with school difficulties. What one can say from the data is that, as a group, children who are known to be learning disabled (but not retarded and not grossly brain damaged) perform statistically less well on some of the items of the extended neurologic exam than children who are not learning disabled. But since not all learning-disabled children do poorly on the extended neurologic examination, it is difficult to predict reading disability on that basis (Black, 1973).

Constitutional Factors: Higher Cortical Functioning

Deficits in higher cortical functioning (sometimes called cognitive deficits) have come increasingly to be cited as explaining learning difficulties. The term "higher cortical functions" is not precisely or consistently defined and covers whatever functions might theoretically be essential to thinking, e.g., perception, memory, attention, symbolic thinking, language. Some authors test for certain of these functions, e.g., memory and language, in the extended neurologic examination, and include abnormalities under the rubric "minimal neurologic dysfunction." Our decision not to lump deficits in cognitive processes with defects on the extended neurologic exam is arbitrary, not based on any theoretical or empirical notions, and done purely for purposes of discussion.

The difficulty in the study of higher cortical function defects and reading disability is that what is studied depends on one's theory of which functions are essential to reading. There are a great many theories, often conflicting or not substantiated.

One theory might be: A child is asked to read aloud. He must maintain his attention to the task (focal attention) and be able to screen out all stimuli that might distract him, such as, another child's talk or a memory of an earlier conversation (nondistractibility). The child must know when looking at the printed page that *b* is different from *d* (visual discrimination). If a child can recognize *c-a-t* he must be able to associate each letter with a particular sound (letter-sound association). To do this he must have learned at some point that some sounds are different from other sounds (auditory discrimination) and that sounds can be represented by letters (symbolic thinking). He must also remember from this previous experience what sound to associate with each of the letters of *c-a-t*. He must be able to mobilize the motor apparatus to say each sound and to blend the sounds (articulation and sound-blending skills). Finally, having said "cat" he must on a higher level have some comprehension of the meaning of this word (receptive language skills). At each stage his

Table 11–3.   Findings on the Extended Neurologic Exam, and Note on Genetic Data

Author	Significant Positive Correlations With Learning Problems	No Correlation With Learning Problems	Comments
Rutter et al., 1970a 9–12-year-old boys and girls	1. Poor coordination 2. Motor impersistence—inability to hold still in a specific stance 3. Confusion of right and left	1. Poor constructional ability 2. Choreiform movements 3. Strabismus 4. Left hand, foot, eye dominance or mixed laterality	1. Only epidemiologic study where all children are examined so there is no selection bias. 2. Found no specific syndromes, rather marked heterogeneity. 3. Some abnormalities in 18.6 percent of reading retarded as compared to 13 percent of reading normal children. Unfortunately, no control group feasible for grossly brain damaged but reading normals. It appears a child can have an abnormal exam but read normally.
Peters et al., 1975 10–11-year-old boys	1. Items of fine motor coordination 2. Presence of associated movements 3. Mixed laterality (conflicts with Rutter's data) 4. Finger agnosia 5. Dysgraphesthesia 6. Strabismus, or can't converge eyes	1. Motor impersistance (conflicts with Rutter's data) 2. Right-left confusion (conflicts with Rutter's data) 3. Choreiform movements	1. The methodology of the extended neurological exam is described in helpful detail. 2. Not purely a study of learning problems. Some children referred for behavioral problems. 3. Children with learning disabilities score abnormally on about half the items until after age 10, when they score significantly abnormally on only 14 percent of the items.

Source	Findings	Comments
Peters, 1975 (continued)	7. Many more items correlated with learning disabilities in younger children, including right-left confusion, choreiform movements and some items measuring motor impersistence.	4. The special neurological exam is said to be useful clinically, but it is not clear how many or which failures specifically predict the presence of a learning disability. No data to suggest that the special neurologic exam can be used predictively. Seems more in the nature of a danger signal, or circumstantial evidence. Note that results conflict with Rutter's data.
Prechtl, 1962	1. Of selected children known to have choreiform movements, 90 percent had trouble reading.	1. May be a special syndrome which leads to learning disabilities, especially where the eye muscles are affected.
Wolff and Hurwitz; 1966, 1973	1. 33 percent of children with learning difficulties exhibited choreiform movements as opposed to 11.4 percent of presumably normal population.	1. The 11 percent of controls with choreiform movements, although equal in IQ and achievement to other controls, had more unfavorable teacher ratings as regards work habits, maturity, and attention.
Summarized by O'Malley and Eisenberg, 1973; Stroufe and Stewart, 1973	1. Hyperkinesis, short attention span, distractability.	1. Hyperkinetic syndrome is not synonymous with learning disability or minimal brain damage. 2. Group of children is not homogeneous. Some children with hyperkinesis have intellectual retardation, some have gross brain damage, some are primarily emotionally disturbed.

(Table 11–3. continued overleaf . . .)

Table 11–3. continued

Author	Significant Positive Correlations With Learning Problems	No Correlation With Learning Problems	Comments
Mattis et al., 1975; Butler et al., 1973	1. Problems of speech articulation in combination with poor motor coordination as defined by substandard performance on a test of sound-blending and on a test of copying geometric figures.		1. Present in poor readers but not in brain damaged controls who could read.
Hallgren, 1950 Rutter et al., 1970a	1. Family history of reading disability. 2. Reading disability highly correlated in monozygotic as opposed to dizygotic twins.	1. DeAjurea-guerra et al., 1968, question of genetic mode of transmission.	1. Hallgren's view is that developmental dyslexia follows an autosomal dominant pattern of inheritance. This finding is not supported by other research. 2. Rutter also finds an increase in reading difficulties in families, but points out this may be not genetic inheritance but social, with parents' attitudes and habits shaping the child's approach to reading. 3. IQ not controlled in twin study.
Various authors	1. Reading disability is associated with non-right-handedness or abnormal cerebral dominance. Cited by Zangwill, 1960; Galifret-Granjon and deAjuriaguerra, 1951.	1. Several epidemiologic studies fail to confirm these observations (Rutter et al., 1970; Morris, 1966; Malmquist, 1968).	1. In fully right-handed individuals, language functions are mostly lateralized to the left hemisphere of the brain. There is increased incidence of retarded speech development in non-right-handed children (Zangwill, 1962). From this arose the hypothesis that non-right-handed children had a failure of normal cerebral lateralization

Table 11–3. continued

Author	Significant Positive Correlations With Learning Problems	No Correlation With Learning Problems	Comments
			and that this "incomplete cerebral dominance" might be a cause of dyslexia.
2. Although this may be true for a small subcategory, it certainly is not true for all reading-disabled children.
	2. Right-handed children, with left-sided cerebral lesions demonstrated by EEG and neurologic exam, have more difficulties with reading and spelling than right-handed children with right-sided cerebral lesions (Black, 1973).		
Geschwind, 1962; 1967	1. The hypothesis that there is a specific anatomic lesion to be found in reading disabled children.		1. Never demonstrated by autopsy material in children with reading disability. Data depends on lesions found in adults who could read, then sustained an injury and subsequently lost the ability to read.

short-term memory must be intact so that by the time he reaches t he has not forgotten c and a.

With this model in mind, one would test for deficiencies in attention, distractibility, visual discrimination, letter-sound association, auditory discrimination, short-term memory, articulation, sound-blending, long-term memory, intersensory integration, and receptive language skills. These factors might be weighted differently according to the theoretical model the researcher posits, and of course with a somewhat different model one might conceptualize altogether different functions. In fact, the steps by which a child learns to read are not known with certainty.

As we have already suggested, it is also incorrect to assume that whenever a specific function is found to be abnormal in poor readers and normal in average readers, the function is essential to the reading process. Mattis et al. (1975) found several deficits, for instance in visual memory, in reading disabled children, and also in brain-damaged children who were largely poor readers. This might have tempted the researchers to conclude that visual memory is essential to reading and that defects in visual memory go along with brain damage, hence that a visual memory deficit as a manifestation of brain damage is a probable cause of reading disability. But the authors looked at brain-damaged good readers and found that they too had defects in visual memory.

Even if we knew the essential cognitive functions and how they related to each other, testing for them is another matter. Authors disagree on what particular tests really measure; for instance, does the Bender (a design-copying test) measure visual perception, memory, or motor coordination? Making a test that measures one cognitive function only is very difficult. Moreover, performance on tests is often altered by age, IQ, experience, brain damage, motivation, or various environmental factors. Let us review several lines of research with particular attention to the limitations of the data.

Visual Perception

Interest in visual perception arose because it was noticed that reading disabled children have a tendency to reverse and confuse letters. As early as 1917, Bronner described a single case of reading disability in terms of faulty "visualization," the evidence being the boy's faulty performance on the Binet Memory for Designs test and his testimony of inability to visualize figures. Feldes in 1921 in a study of intellectually subnormal children found that nonreaders had difficulties in perception of differences between visually presented figures.

In more recent work with brain-damaged children, Frostig et al.

(1962) observed selected areas of perceptual impairment in children with learning disabilities and inferred from this that the learning problems are caused by the perceptual defects. It should be noted that Frostig did not control for IQ or brain damage, both of which are highly correlated with visual perceptual abilities. This type of work has given rise to the popular association of visual perceptual difficulties and learning difficulties.

The validity of many perceptual tests is questionable. For example, it has been shown that hyperactive children's scores on the Frostig test can improve with amphetamines. This raises the question of whether the children have a visual perception problem or a problem of poor impulse control and distractibility (Conrad et al., 1971).

Performance on tests of perception, which purport to measure a universal cognitive process, can also be influenced by noncognitive factors. As an example, there is evidence that emotional attitudes can affect visual perception (Pettigrew et al., 1966; McGinnies, 1966). Some tests used to assess perception (e.g., Bender, Ravens and ITPA) have been shown to be sensitive to social class variables (Koppitz et al., 1959; Sperrazzo and Wilkins, 1959). Lower-class black children do worse than middle-class blacks, and Mexican-American and Indian children also score below the norm on several ITPA subtests (Kirk and Kirk, 1971). This does not mean that Mexican-American children or Indian children have an abnormal cerebral organization.

Given this catalogue of validity problems, it is not surprising to find that studies contradict each other even when researchers control for brain damage and IQ (Table 11–4). Although visual perceptual difficulties may be important in a small subsample of children with reading difficulties, the emphasis on them as a common cause of reading disabilities needs to be reevaluated (Larsen and Hammill, 1975; Myers and Hammill, 1969).

Auditory Perception

Deficiencies in auditory perception have also been cited as reasons why children cannot read. Auditory perception includes the ability to distinguish same versus different words or sounds (phonemic or nonphonemic auditory discrimination), the ability to remember sounds, numbers, or words (auditory memory), and the ability to blend isolated sounds into words (sound blending). As with studies on visual perception and reading, many studies fail to control for brain damage, age, IQ, or emotional and social factors and must be questioned. Performance on the Wepman Test of Auditory Discrimination varies with social class (Deutsch, 1968). Where IQ has been controlled, a significant association has been found between reading

Table 11—4. Abnormalities, Visual Perception, and Reading Disability

Correlation with Reading Disability	*No Correlation with Reading Disability*
8–10-year-olds of average IQ who read badly do worse on reproducing the designs on the Bender. This is not true for the 11–12-year-old poor readers who perform normally (Lachman, 1960).	9–10-year-olds, poor readers, with IQ controlled do no worse than controls on tests of reproducing designs, or making shapes with matches. This is the only study to look at all children with reading defects in a community, not a selected population (Rutter et al., 1970a).
10–12-year-olds, IQ-matched poor readers do worse than good readers on the Ravens, which requires the subject to choose which visual pattern best completes an incomplete larger visual pattern (Goetzinger et al., 1960).	10–12-year-olds, IQ-matched poor readers do same as controls on ability to distinguish figure from ground (Goetzinger et al., 1960).
There seems to be a small group of 8–18-year-old poor readers who have a WISC performance IQ at least 10 points below the WISC verbal IQ and a Raven score less than the equivalent performance IQ. This is the only study in which the defect was found to distinguish poor readers from children who are definitely brain damaged but can read (Mattis et al., 1975).	48 subjects divided into poor, average, good readers, controlled for IQ, showed no difference in visual discrimination (find the same or different form) or visual memory (Hammill et al., 1974).
First-graders, of normal IQ, who read badly do worse on various tests: recognition of similarities in pictures, ability to duplicate designs from a model (Goins, 1958).	50 subjects of same age, IQ, and degree of reading retardation. Performance on Frostig Test correlated with the presence of gross neurologic dysfunction (Black, 1973). This raises question of how much the correlation of poor performance on certain perceptual tests with reading may have to do with brain damage.
Performance on the Children's Embedded Figures Test and on a test of visual perceptual closure correlates significantly with reading, with IQ held constant. The correlations are modest (Bruininks, 1969).	

competency and sound-blending abilities, and also with word discrimination abilities (Bruininks, 1969; Chall et al., 1963; Harrington and Durrell, 1955; Goetzinger et al., 1960). The correlation with word discrimination skills tends to disappear as the child gets older (Wepman, 1960). Wedell (1973) and also Hurwitz and Wolff (1975) discuss evidence that poor readers do not perceive or tap out rhythms as well as normal readers.

The modest correlations found in these studies remind us, however, that many individual good readers score poorly and many poor readers score well. Thus, auditory perceptual difficulties, when present, do not necessarily predict poor reading, nor does it seem that auditory perceptual difficulties are even a common cause of reading disability (Hammill and Larsen, 1974).

Intersensory Integration

Birch and Belmont (1964) have proposed an intersensory integrational defect model to explain reading disability. These authors devised a procedure in which children were asked to listen to a sequence of taps and to identify which visual pattern of dots best corresponded to these taps. Because the task requires the translation of auditory material into visual patterns, it has been thought of as an example of visual-auditory integration or intersensory integration. Birch and Belmont studied nine-to-ten-year-old poor readers randomly chosen from among all poor readers in a whole city. Control good readers were matched for age, sex, and social class. Even when the study was limited to boys of IQ greater than 100 the auditory to visual score was significantly worse for poor as compared to good readers. A study by Kahn and Birch (1967) further supports a correlation between poor reading and difficulty with audiovisual integration, while other studies fail to find any significant association when IQ is partialled out (Ford, 1967; Bruininks, 1969; Vandevoort and Senf, 1973).

Using a different measure of intersensory integration, Blank and Bridger (1966) tested the ability to translate visual flashes into printed dot patterns and found that when IQ is controlled, poor readers do worse than good readers. They further discovered that poor readers were worse at verbally describing the number of flashes and the pattern of pauses. From these data they conclude that a sensory stimulus needs to be conceptualized by verbal labeling before it can be translated into another sensory modality. The same data could be interpreted differently, however, to reflect a memory or attention problem. These experiments, though quite elegant, should demonstrate to the reader how the concept of intersensory integration, along with many of the models of higher cortical functions, belongs to the realm of experimental psychology.

Constitutional Factors: Language

It can be said that reading is a kind of language skill. Wepman (1962) argues that because children with defective auditory discrimination develop poor ideas of words they hear and then learn poor speech from such beginnings, they are ill prepared to deal with reading. Some theorize that sophistication in language must occur before there can be sophistication in thought processes and problem-solving (Nisbet, 1953; Hess and Shipman, 1965). In this latter case a failure of language development might be seen to dampen cognitive development and thereby to limit the ability to solve the problem of learning how to read. Some social and ethnic groups have a fully differentiated language system, but one that is essentially foreign to mainstream English as used in the schools. This difference has been used to explain the greater prevalence of reading disability in certain subgroups. Certain language and communication patterns within the family have been thought to relate to psychiatric disturbance (Jacob, 1975). It might be theorized that certain communication styles may be conducive to better mental health and thus indirectly to academic achievement. It can be seen that the exact nature of the relationship of language and reading is not yet clear.

The available data suggest that there is an association between reading problems and delayed acquisition of speech (Rutter et al., 1970a; Ingram, 1963). Of 250 children referred to a child psychiatric clinic and found to have "educational maladjustment," Ingram and Reed (1956) found that 31 percent had evidence of expressive aphasia (using the wrong word, inability to give the names of people or objects, or to use the correct syntax even though one "knows" the correct answer). He also found evidence of articulatory disturbance (distortion of speech sounds, substitutions of one sound for another, irregularities of rhythm, disturbances of intonation and stutter). Rutter et al. (1970a) find a significant correlation of reading retardation with poor complexity of language and inadequacy of description. Mattis et al. (1975) find in their highly selected population of reading-retarded children that 39 percent of the poor readers have a syndrome of dysnomia (inability to give name of object), difficulty imitating speech, and a disorder of auditory discrimination. These disabilities were not present in controls who were brain damaged but could read. Vogel (1974) finds that poor readers are deficient in oral syntax.

In all these studies the mean IQ of the educationally retarded children is within the normal range and does not differ significantly from the mean for controls. However, no statistical adjustment is made for variations in subject IQ within groups (Ingram and Reed, 1956; Rutter et al., 1970a; and Mattis et al., 1975). Myklebust (1973) describes difficulties in finding opposites and in defining words in a group of reading disabled children who are three to four years behind the controls in expressive language skills. But on nonverbal measures of intelligence the reading disabled in his study are distinctly behind the controls.

To date there have been no studies on a whole population of language-disturbed children to determine what proportion have reading difficulties. More studies are necessary which partial out the effect of IQ, brain damage, and cultural experience. It is not clear how language pathology affects reading ability. It would seem useful, however, to consider the possibility of undiagnosed language pathology in the study of children with reading disability.

Conclusions

From our examination of the data on reading disabilities and deficits in higher cortical functioning, we conclude:

1. With respect to any defect in higher cortical functioning, be it of language, perception, or central processing, research findings remain inconclusive and sometimes contradictory. These findings are nonetheless often worthy of further research. Researchers and educators should not ignore apparent cognitive defects in a child, but any presumption of cause in cases of reading disability must be tentative.

2. Even if some reading-disabled children have a specific cognitive defect, it does not follow that this defect is shared by all reading disabled children. Findings that are true for a limited subsample should not automatically be construed as pertaining to the population of all reading disabled children.

Emotional Correlates of Reading Disability

Generally, children who are psychotic or severely neurotic are not examined further for specific learning disabilities. As with mental retardation, the psychosis is quickly blamed for scholastic failure. The fact remains, however, that there are many severely disturbed children whose academic achievement is normal. Why some psychotic children can learn and others not is as yet unexplored.

In regard to milder degrees of emotional disturbance, it is unclear whether the emotional disturbance causes the learning disability, whether emotional disturbance is secondary to repeated failures, or whether both emotional disturbance and reading retardation are end products of the same process. Despite the heat of the controversy, little data exist to shed light on the problem.

To begin with, how should we define mental illness? The presence of "emotional disturbance" depends on the criteria for disturbance, and in the case of behavioral problems, these criteria are highly variable, often unstandardized, and at times subjective. Moreover, emotional disorders are themselves extremely variable, and it is difficult to design a questionnaire or standard interview that is all-inclusive. Another difficulty is that the populations studied often are not stratified by IQ, degree of reading disability, or age. Given these qualifications, one may examine the scant evidence documenting an association between emotional illness and learning disability.

In the Isle of Wight study, Rutter et al. (1970a) determined maladjustment in the sample of reading retarded children on the basis of the thirty-minute psychiatric interview with the child. He found that the 8.1 percent of children twenty-eight months behind the reading level predicted by IQ showed "definite marked disorder" compared to 1.4 percent of the control group. A study by Clark (1970) reports "indications" of emotional problems for 58 percent of a group of eight-year-olds who have been reading far below age level for at least two years. A comparison group of children who had initially been identified as reading backward but who were making improvements revealed only 38 percent of the group as having emotional problems. Morris (1966) studied seven-to-eleven-year-old school children in England and found a statistically significant difference between "good" and "poor" readers by teacher assessment of nervousness, alertness, lethargy or depression, and lack of concentration. Poor readers also showed a significantly greater anxiety for adult attention, and greater hostility as well. Malmquist (1958) found significant differences between good and poor readers in teacher ratings of "nervousness," but no differences by parent report of specific nervous symptoms (thumb-sucking or nail-biting, for example). These and other epidemiologic studies at least suggest that some children with reading disability have more "emotional disturbance" than the normal reading population.

Study of individual cases selected from psychiatric clinic populations may also give some insight into the nature of emotional problems as they relate to reading, at least for some children. Such studies have described children with a neurotic inhibition of curiosity, boys who identify scholastic achievement as too feminine, children who lack appropriate role models, those who view learning as too competitive and have a conflict over the expression of aggression or independence, depressed children, and finally some children who see failing as a solution to the problem of sibling rivalry (Sylvester and Kunst, 1943; Pearson, 1952; Blanchard, 1935, 1936, 1946; Weinberg et al., 1973). The difficulty with such studies is that there is no control population of children with similar psychiatric conflicts but without reading disability. Lacking such comparative studies and lacking detailed analyses of the progress of psychotherapy, it is difficult to understand the etiology of the reading disability or the essential elements which must be changed for improvement to occur.

Emotional disturbance and reading disability are also linked in work on juvenile delinquency and academic difficulties. Various studies estimate that 60 to 84 percent of delinquents are two or more years behind in reading (Critchley, 1968). This kind of correlation has led some authors to propose that delinquency is a consequence of the frustration of repeated school failure (Connolly, 1971). Critchley even suggests that dyslexia should be used as a defense in legal proceedings and reviews the work of a Danish judge who "pleaded for the medico-legal recognition of the handicap of word blindness."

The coincidence of delinquency and reading retardation is indeed noticeable, but it remains unclear which is cause and which effect or whether both conditions are discrete consequences of broader familial and social forces. While 88 percent of New York street gang members are two or more years retarded in reading, the figure for nongang members in the same neighborhood is a remarkable 56 percent (Labov, 1970). In an environment where so many youngsters read poorly, the question remains whether the association between reading retardation and delinquency would persist after partialling out the effect of socioeconomic class, intellectual retardation, psychosis, or marked family pathology.

Effect of the Family. The question of emotional disturbance has also been explored as it relates to parent-child interaction in the families of reading-disabled children. In families of reading-disabled children communication seems to be characterized by more silence, more irrelevant comments and less explicit information than in families of normal children (Peck and Stackhouse, 1973).

Milner (1951) studies the relation between reading readiness and patterns of parent-child interaction in first grade black children. High-scorers on the California Test of Mental Maturity had mothers who took them places or read to them. Their mothers tended to have more education and to have more expectations of the child. They reported that they hugged the child and encouraged his or her conversation at mealtimes. The converse seems to be true of low-scorers and their mothers. Low-scorers in addition had real difficulty thinking of three wishes, could not think when they had been "real" happy, had no storybooks, and spoke a great deal of physical punishment. Della Piana et al. (1966), in scoring taped conversations between six-grade girls and their mothers found that mothers of highly verbal girls compared to mothers of less verbal girls expressed more positive affect and more total warmth.

Individual case studies, unfortunately uncontrolled, also suggest a relationship between academic problems and family dysfunction. Parents of poor readers have been described as overwhelmed by fears of sexuality, menses, death, illness, separation and the revelation of secrets (Hellman, 1954; Pearson, 1952; Staver, 1953; Miller and Westman, 1964). There is repeated reference to parental discord, disunity in child rearing practices, threatened disruption of the home, using the child as ally or scapegoat in the battle with the other parent, or using the child's handicap as a diversion from the parents' struggles (Hellman, 1954; Pearson, 1952; Stewart, 1950; Miller and Westman, 1964). Discipline is most often described as erratic, with excessive punitiveness seesawing into overindulgence (Weiss et al., 1971; Missildine, 1946; Sylvester and Kunst, 1943).

In summary, it appears that children with reading retardation have a higher incidence of individual psychopathology, of delinquency, and of family and parental disturbance. For some children these psychological disturbances may exacerbate another problem, e.g., neurologic dysfunction. For others the emotional pathology may be a consequence of the frustrations of repeated failure. Even when the emotional problem appears to be secondary to the scholastic difficulties, it is not of lesser importance, and for some, reading remediation may not succeed until the emotional attitudes can be changed.

Environmental Factors: School
and Teacher Variables

Poor teaching or teaching inadequate to a child's needs is a correlate of reading failure with which few would argue. In practice, however, there is considerable dispute about the adequacy of the schools and about what school factors specifically correlate with educational achievement.

From his data on educational achievement, Coleman concludes that "differences in school facilities . . . are so little related to differences in achievement levels . . . that, with a few exceptions, their effects fail to appear, even in a survey of this magnitude" (Coleman, 1966, p. 316). He found that over-all only 10 to 20 percent of the variability in verbal abilities among children could be accounted for by differences between schools. These differences between schools are subdivided into three types: differences in the students themselves, differences in the community or background of the students, and differences in school facilities per se.

As much as 32 percent of the variability between schools can be accounted for by differences in background factors (material items in home, size of family, parents' education, stability of marriage, parents' interest in education, and educational aspirations for child). People of similar backgrounds tend to live in similar neighborhoods and send their children to the same school. This finding implies that part of the superiority of the suburban high school is out of the hands of the school department and depends on the home environment, unless of course nonparents can in some ways supplement an impoverished background.

The second class of between-school differences includes differences in the students themselves. The question is whether an individual's exposure to a group of peers of better educational background and higher educational aspirations improves that individual's achievement. Coleman finds that such peer effects do account for an increase in achievement, especially for minority groups. As the percentage of white students increases, achievement is also found to increase. He suggests that the impact of integration may depend on white peers' having better motivation, higher aspirations, and a more sophisticated background.

Finally, the Coleman report examines what are called intrinsic school factors. These are found to account for less school-to-school variance than do student background or peer effects. Facilities (school size, laboratories, expenditure per pupil, number of library volumes), curriculum factors (such as an accelerated program and tracking), teacher attitudes and the teacher's background, experience, family educational level, and vocabulary score make very little difference for whites, but do have a somewhat more significant impact on minority group achievement. Of the school factors, teacher characteristics are by far the most important, especially for minority groups.

Given this data and given that teachers and composition of students body are part of the school, it becomes difficult to accept the notion that schools make no difference.

Summers and Wolfe (1975) have demonstrated that one difficulty with the Coleman study is that it measures change in the *average* student performance in a whole school as it relates to average teacher or school characteristics. This approach obscures within-school effects and does not tell us whether certain types of students will benefit most from certain types of teachers. Yet it is at the level of interaction between individual students and teachers that we might hypothesize the largest effects occur.

Summers and Wolfe analyzed data on achievement for each individual in relation to family income, school resources, and teacher qualities. They found that few attributes are effective for all students. Many school resources affect students differently—some even in opposite directions. On the other hand, certain school values seemed to make no difference to achievement scores: physical facilities (playground, science labs, age of building, physical condition of building), whether teachers got degrees beyond the B.A. or scored higher on the National Teacher's Exam. From this kind of data the authors question the common practice of salary increments for added education credits or degrees in school personnel, or the concern in school committees for upgrading physical plants. It was also found that for low-income, low-achieving students, the presence of counselors or remedial education programs does not increase achievement. Thus, these researchers agree with Coleman that some school inputs on which large sums of money are expended seem irrelevant to reading achievement.

Other inputs do seem to matter. Achievement is affected by class size, school size, teacher experience, and the quality of the college attended by the teacher. The effect varies, depending on race, income, and achievement level. For example, low-achievers fare much better if class size is less than twenty-eight, if the school is small, if the teacher is new, or if there are more high-achievers in the class. On the other hand, high-achievers can tolerate larger classes, larger schools, and do better with experienced teachers.

Other studies support the conclusion that certain school inputs can be manipulated to improve achievement, especially for minority groups and low-achievers. Achievement, participation, and satisfaction are higher in small schools (Barker and Gump, 1964). High teacher expectations can improve performance (Rosenthal, 1968). Reading performance can be improved by the teacher with a systematic plan for correcting errors and building skills, by the teacher whose methods are flexible, imaginative and individualized, and by the teacher with good relationships with the pupils (Morris, 1966).

In summary, certain school inputs seem to be correlated with higher academic achievement, especially for minority groups and low-achievers. These include small class size, small school size, racially mixed school, classes of mixed ability, teacher's experience, teacher's expectations, teacher's graduation from a better college, teacher's having sound but flexible teaching methods.

Systematic evaluation is needed now to determine which school or teacher inputs maximize academic achievement. How much can school programs reverse the effect of depriving environments? Can clinicians develop a systematic, validated method by which to assess the adequacy of the school? It seems fair to say that an assessment of the child with learning problems should include a check on the quality of his schooling.

SUMMARY

Children with reading disabilities are a heterogeneous group. Some may have intellectual deficits, others have neurological problems, still others have emotional difficulties or have had schooling experiences which have been inadequate. Any one of these correlates accounts for only a portion of all children with academic difficulties.

There is as yet no comprehensive longitudinal study in which the frequency of constitutional, emotional, environmental, and teaching factors is tabulated for each learning disabled or control child. Which of these factors are relatively rare? How do mild degrees of deficiency interact to produce a reading disability? We cannot now say that constitutional factors are more important than family pathology, social milieu, or teacher's style. Nor are we able to predict reading ability from performance on an examination of neurologic or perceptual function, or from an assessment of mental health. This ambiguity suggests that in investigating a child with a learning disability, there is no scientific basis for failing to investigate any potential cause, e.g., the school or the family. Nor is there any basis for supposing an organic cause simply because medical technology and training dictate an extended neurologic examination.

The available data suggest that for the individual, as opposed to the whole group of children with reading disabilities, one or more of the following may correlate with academic failure:

1. a general deficit of intellectual ability;
2. certain severe neurologic deficits as indicated by abnormalities on EEG or general neurologic exam;
3. some symptoms which have heretofore been lumped under the term "minimal cerebral dysfunction" but might better be approached individually. These include hyperkinesis, choreiform movements, and problems with motor coordination (Table 11-3);
4. certain difficulties in auditory and visual perception that may be of importance in some younger children;
5. language pathology;
6. individual or family pathology; and
7. certain experiential factors, including school experiences.

We must emphasize again that a correlate is not necessarily a cause, and that remediation of any of the above may have no effect on the reading disability.

SCREENING FOR READING PROBLEMS

At what age should children be screened? The argument is frequently advanced that if we could identify children with potential reading problems at a prereading age, we could prevent the extensive rate of reading failure in our schools. The main advantage is to identify children with any serious learning handicap. For example, the child might have a hearing or language problem that would prejudice reading ability.

A second reason the planner may wish to screen children at the prereading stage is to identify those children who are at risk, who appear to be headed for academic difficulty on the basis of their performance on certain readiness tests. While serious cases can be referred for immediate diagnosis and treatment, most children identified as having potential reading problems can simply be monitored carefully in their classroom performance.

Such a screening program may assist the teacher in planning curricula individually to accommodate the particular needs of children identified as at risk. In addition, a rough estimate of the extent of potential reading problems in an entering kindergarten class enables planning for the appropriate type and number of supportive services to ensure that all children learn to read. There is some evidence to suggest that remediation for older disabled readers (eight years and over) is not as effective as it is with younger disabled readers (Cashdan and Pumfrey, 1969; Muehl and Forell, 1973−74). This evidence strengthens the rationale for early screening.

Developmental screening is an example of early screening that has been increasingly recommended. Developmental screening evaluates the child's rate of development against age norms for the emergence of various behaviors in four main areas of functioning: gross-motor coordination, communication skills, fine-motor coordination, and social and emotional behavior (Thorpe and Werner, 1974). A significant deviation from developmental norms may indicate a problem. While developmental screening is not concerned specifically with reading disabilities, it does identify problems in areas of functioning that presumably can directly affect learning and reading once the child enters school.

Developmental questionnaires can be filled out by a pediatrician or by a trained aide simply by observing the child who is asked to perform a number of different acts such as reaching for objects, waving goodby, walking alone, saying a two-word sentence, and building a tower of blocks. (These items are taken from the Rapid Developmental Screening Checklist, Committee on Children with Handicaps,

1972.) Information may also be obtained by asking the parent. Developmental screening has been recommended for all children as early as nine months (Guide to Screening for the EPSDT Program under Medicaid, 1974), around two years of age, again at three years when speech should be well developed, and at the onset of schooling at five years (Campbell and Camp, 1975).

While the argument for early screening is appealing, it is not altogether practical. Specifically, developmental screening has a number of limitations. Validity is questionable because the examiner has to distinguish between a child's refusal to perform a task and his or her inability to do the task. Astute observations are required, and judgment must be made concerning the adequacy of the child's performance. Testers must use the same criteria in making their judgments in order for the instrument to be reliable (Thorpe and Werner, 1974). Furthermore, few studies on the predictive validity of these tests have been carried out. Presently it is felt that developmental screening is not a reliable or valid device for identifying young children at risk for later educational disability (Kearsley, 1975).

One of the difficulties associated with early screening is that psychological measures are less reliable for younger children. The young child may not have understood what was expected, may be frightened by the strange situation, or may not feel like playing the "games" that the tester has introduced. The confidence placed in a single test score of a young child must be qualified, and the decisions based on these measures should be made with caution.

Another problem with early screening is that children at this age are developing at different rates. Four- and five-year-olds—kindergarteners and first-graders—may be at very different developmental levels. The concept of school readiness is based on the idea that there is a developmental level appropriate for school learning, a level when all aspects of functioning (perceptual, motor, emotional, physical) are well integrated (Ilg and Ames, 1965).

On the basis of a number of different developmental test ratings, Ilg and Ames found that grade placements were considered "questionable" for about one-third of the children in each grade; ratings of "unready" were given to about 10 percent of the kindergarteners and first-graders, and over 20 percent of the second-graders. Thus, what appears as a potential reading problem may actually just be a slower rate of development, and the child will be ready to read within a year or two.

A third problem is that of predictive validity—predicting later school achievement from early behavioral characteristics. A review of the literature on predicting adult outcomes from child characteristics suggests that there is relatively little stability in measures of IQ or achievement prior to the age of eight to ten (White et al., 1973). In addition, we do not know which prereading behaviors—such as visual discrimination, fine motor control, or left-right discrimination—signify readiness for reading or are predictive of future reading ability. Although some of the correlations between these behaviors and reading achievement are very high, this information cannot be interpreted causally to mean, for example, that good auditory discrimination will improve future reading ability.

Despite the desirability of early screening, the limitations associated with it seem sufficient to advise that screening take place after the child has begun to be instructed in reading rather than before. A reasonable time for screening would be after a year of reading or reading readiness instruction. In most schools this means at the end of kindergarten or first grade. At this point, reading and other psychological tests can be used with greater confidence in their reliability. The teacher's observations, too, can become an effective screening procedure.

Meanwhile, research efforts should focus in parallel on two questions to determine the practicality of prereading screening:

1. Is it possible to establish reliable criteria for identifying children "at risk" for reading problems and other learning disabilities?
2. Are there effective preventive measures that can be applied to an at risk population?

Screening Methods: Single Tests

The simplest approach to identifying children with reading problems is to administer a single reading or reading readiness test. While many such tests are published, the planner who wishes to use one should be aware of certain factors critical to a test's efficacy as a screening device.

Validity. Of particular concern in screening is content validity, the ability of the test to measure reading ability; and predictive validity, the ability of a test to predict accurately future reading performance for the prereader or beginning reader. The validity of a screening test is usually described in terms of its sensitivity and specificity. (Sensitivity refers to the percentage of children with reading problems who are correctly identified by the screening test; specificity refers to the percentage of children without reading problems who are correctly screened.)

Unfortunately, very little work has been done on the predictive validity of screening instruments, whether they be single tests or batteries of tests. Many studies conducted among school-age children calculate a correlation coefficient relating the screening test score to some other criterion of reading ability (i.e., concurrent validity). While this statistic tells us something about the degree of association between screening test results and reading performance for the entire child population being studied, it does not tell us how well the test predicts for individuals (Goodman and Wiederholt, 1973). Moreover, in some validation studies only the group identified as having reading difficulties is followed up, yielding information on the number of true positives and false positives but telling us nothing about the children who were initially identified as having no problems.

There is no absolute standard of sensitivity and specificity on which to base the selection of a screening test for reading problems. The decision depends on the purpose of the screening program, prior estimates of percentage of children with reading disabilities, and potential costs and benefits of correct or incorrect case finding. Is it intended to refer positively identified children for a complete diagnostic work-up? Or will positively identified children be rescreened with a second test? Or will remedial measures of some kind be given immediately to those children positively identified? In each case, the planner must determine whether it is more important that readers or nonreaders be correctly identified, and for which group errors in identification can more readily be tolerated.

Probability of Correct Identification and Expected Value. For a screening test to be efficient it must give a better chance of correctly identifying children with reading problems than if we had used no screening test at all (Stringer, 1974). To put it another way, if we randomly select a child for a diagnostic evaluation to determine whether or not he or she has a reading problem, the chance that the child really does have a problem is p, the prevalence rate of reading problems for that particular age-grade group. If we select for a diagnostic evaluation a child who has already been screened, we can calculate a new probability for the chance that the child does indeed have a reading problem. The question we are asking then, is what is the probability that a child has a reading problem given that she or he is screened as positive? This probability is calculated from Bayes' theorem of inverse probability.[a]

[a]
$$P(B/A) = \frac{P(B) \times P(A/B)}{P(B) \times P(A/B) + P(B') \times P(A/B')},$$

where

$P(B/A)$ = P of having a reading problem, given that the child is screened positive; *(continued overleaf)*

Table 11—5 presents the probability of correct identification for three screening instruments. As an example, if we use the Jansky-DeHirsch Screening Index to screen a population for whom the estimated prevalence of reading disability is .10, the chance that a child screened as positive actually has a reading problem is .26. While this figure is not very high, it does increase our chances of identifying a child with reading problems than if we had used no test at all. On the other hand, it means that 74 percent of the children screened as positive would not have reading problems!

The probability of correct identification also varies according to the prevalence estimate used. Thus, if the estimated rate of reading difficulties were .20, the Screening Index's predictive accuracy increases to .44.

Finally, the probability of correct identification varies according to the sensitivity and specificity rates. Although the Meeting Street School Screening Test has a lower sensitivity than the Screening Index, its higher specificity improves its accuracy in correctly identifying non-readers.

Reliability. Reliability refers to the stability or consistency of an individual test score. The reliability coefficient of a test tells us how much the obtained score can be expected to vary from the true score (Lyman, 1963). It is essential that the test be interesting and appropriately designed in order to maintain the full attention, understanding, cooperation, and motivation of the child. Discouragement, fatigue, and anxiety can contribute a large amount of error variance to the child's score.

For purposes of psychological research, a reliability coefficient of .80 or higher is usually considered acceptable on tests (Frankenburg, 1975). In one review only about one-third of a group of reading tests had reliability coefficients at this level on any of three measures of reliability, test-retest reliability, internal consistency, or alternate-form reliability (Hoepfner, 1970). In light of this limitation, some of the problems of validity discussed above may be artifacts of low reli-

---

$P(B)$ = P of having a reading problem;

$P(A/B)$ = P of being screened positive, given that the child has a reading problem (sensitivity);

$P(B')$ = P of not having a reading problem;

and $P(A/B')$ = P of being screened positive, given that the child does not have a reading problem (false positives, or 1 – Specificity)

Table 11-5. Probability of Correct Identification

	Probability of a Child's Having a Reading Disability, Given that He Screens Positive (p B/A), Based on an Estimated Overall Prevalence of 0.10	Probability of Having a Reading Disability on Screening Positive, Based on a Prevalence of 0.20
The Screening Index (Jansky and deHirsch, 1972) Sensitivity .79 Specificity .75	0.26	0.44
Meeting Street School Screening Test (Hainsworth and Siqueland, 1969) Sensitivity .51 Specificity .86	0.29	0.48
Isle of Wight Screening Battery (Rutter et al., 1970) Sensitivity .98 Specificity .95	0.68	0.83

ability. Low reliability of reading screening tests, to the extent it is a fact of life among young children, may set an upper bound on the efficiency we can expect.

Norming Data. Norming procedures are also critical to the interpretation of a child's test score. The meaning of an individual child's test score is based on how he has done relative to the group of children on whom the test was standardized. A review of some eighty to ninety elementary school reading tests indicates that only about a dozen of these instruments were normed on a sample that is representative of the U.S. population in geographic areas, ages, races, ethnicity, and types of schools and school districts (Hoepfner et al., 1970).

Cost Factors. There is a wide variation in the cost involved in administering and scoring tests, including the cost of employing specialized personnel and the time cost of administering the test.

A sampling of screening tests is presented in Table 11-6, including information on content, reliability, validity, and norming procedures. Only three tests were identified that had data available on sensitivity and specificity rates. All three have been included in the table. Other tests include reading and reading readiness tests which could be used for initial screening.

Multiple Tests

Does the use of multiple tests improve the predictive validity of a screening program? The practical issue is how much is gained in accurate identification of reading failure with the addition of each test or item, and at what costs are these gains made in terms of time and money, and false positives.

In the Rutter et al. study, only about two-thirds of all backward and retarded readers were identified by a group reading achievement test. By using scores from the group reading test and from two group intelligence tests, the investigators were able to identify over 90 percent of all children nine and ten years old with reading difficulties (Rutter et al., 1970a).[b] (See Table 11-7.) Thus, the addition of the two intelligence tests added 85 minutes of testing time and improved the sensitivity rate by 23 percent. By using the entire screening battery, the investigators were able to improve their identification accuracy to 98 percent of all backward readers, although then the entire

---

[b]Remember that some children who are reading at grade and age level on a reading test may be considered reading-retarded because their IQ scores predict a much higher level of reading achievement.

Table 11–6. Screening Tests

Test	Content	Reliability Coefficients	Validity	Norming Data	Comments
The Screening Index (Jansky and deHirsch, 1972) Individually administered at end of K	letter-naming picture-naming word-matching copying figures sentence repetition	.89 .86 .52 .23 .40	sensitivity: .79 specificity: .75 correlation with second-grade reading achievement: .66	The Index was standardized on approximately 400 New York City public school children. 53 percent of sample was white, 42 percent black, and 5 percent Puerto Rican.	In the validation study the criterion measure for reading failure was a grade level score of 2.2 or lower on a silent paragraph reading test, given at the end of second grade. Thus, 34 percent of the children were designated as having reading problems. If one were to vary the criterion for defining a reading problem, the sensitivity rate would also vary.
Metropolitan Readiness Test (Hildreth and Griffiths, 1949) Group test for end of K, beginning of grade one	vocabulary comprehension information matching numbers (human figure drawing—supplementary)	.89	correlation with reading achievement: .4–.53	Standardized in 56 communities in 26 different states. A total of 15,081 white children were included.	The norming sample is not representative of the American population. Sensitivity and specificity rates cannot be determined because the data reported are not complete.

(Table 11–6. continued overleaf . . .)

Table 11-6. continued

Test	Content	Reliability Coefficients	Validity	Norming Data	Comments
Meeting Street School Screening Test (Hainsworth and Siqueland, 1969) Individual test for ages 5–7 1/2	motor-patterning and coordination copying forms repeating words and sentences memory counting telling a story language-sequencing	.85	sensitivity: .51 specificity: .86	Standardized on 500 kindergarten and first-grade children from East Providence, R.I. Children were selected to represent the population socioeconomically according to 1966 U.S. Census data.	The sensitivity and specificity rates in this study were determined by using, as the criterion measure for a learning disability, a composite achievement test score below the 50th percentile, one year following screening. Note, in contrast, that a reading score 1 standard deviation below the mean would fall in the lower 16th percentile. The low sensitivity rate (.51) means that 49 percent of the children with learning disabilities (according to the authors' definition) were missed by this test.
Isle of Wight Screening Battery (Rutter et al., 1970) Group administered test for 9–11-year-olds	verbal intelligence test nonverbal intelligence test mechanical arithmetic test reading test copying figures	.90–.97 for all tests	sensitivity: .98 specificity: .95	The reference group for the study was the entire 9–11 population of the Isle of Wight, all of whom were screened. Thus, all children were compared with their peers on the Isle of Wight.	This battery uses several tests. The criterion measure for reading failure in this study was a reading-accuracy comprehension test score of 28 months or more below the child's chronological age. The high sensitivity rate (.98) means

Test	Subtests	Reliability	Validity	Standardization	Comments
	teacher's rating of child's schoolwork				that only 2 percent of children with reading problems were incorrectly identified by the test battery.
Wide Range Achievement Test (Jastak & Jastak, 1965) Individual test for K and primary grades	arithmetic spelling: copying marks, printing own name, spelling to dictation reading: recognizing and naming letters, pronouncing words	.92–.98 for reading and spelling	correlation of reading subtest with other reading tests: .74–.89	The 1963 revision of the WRAT was standardized on over 5000 children selected from seven states. Apparently no attempt was made to obtain a representative sample.	This test has extremely high reliability. The norming sample may not be representative. There is no data available on the test's predictive accuracy as a screening test.
Gates-MacGinitie Reading Tests (Gates and MacGinitie, 1965) Group test for grades K–12	picture vocabulary comprehension of sentences and paragraphs	.81–.87	correlation with other reading tests: .79 and .84[a]	Test was standardized on 40,000 children in 38 communities, representative of the nation by size, geographical location, average educational level, and average family income.	Unfortunately, there are no data available on sensitivity and specificity.

[a]Davis, 1968.

Table 11-7.   A Multiple-Test Screening Battery

	Testing Time in Minutes	Cumulative Testing Time in Minutes	Cumulative Sensitivity	False Positives
Group reading test	20-25	20-25	.67	.01
Group verbal IQ test	40-45			
Group nonverbal IQ test	40	100-110	.90	*
Form copying test	5-10			
Arithmetic test	30	150		
Teaching rating of backwardness	a	a	.98	.05

[a] Figures not available.
Source: Adapted from Rutter et al., 1970a.

test time totaled about two and a half hours. Taking this much time, the rate of false positives was only 4 to 5 percent, very low compared to the other screening tests we have examined.

Other work correlating screening test scores and reading achievement scores also supports the use of multiple indices (Jansky and de-Hirsch, 1972).

Currently there is a growing trend toward more comprehensive screening. The Council on Child Health (1973) recommends that screening for learning disabilities should include information on the child's physical, mental, emotional, and social development plus "formal sampling"—i.e., testing—of the child's cognitive, perceptual, language, and motor skills. The general rationale for recommending a more comprehensive battery is that the nature of the problem is so diffuse and so complex that at present no single test can adequately tap all the factors that might indicate a reading disability.

There are a number of practical advantages in using a multiple-test approach to screening. Accuracy in identification increases as the screening battery becomes more diagnostic. Also, because the nature of the problem is complex and not well understood, and because young children's test scores tend to be unreliable, redundancy of information can be very important in determining whether or not a child has a reading or learning problem, even at an initial stage of identification.

There are also potential economies of case finding, because a comprehensive battery can represent a number of different disciplines, such as psychology, education, and speech and language pathology. It can be used to screen for all problems that might affect the child's educational development, not just reading problems. The Isle of Wight population study showed that over one-quarter of all handicapped children (physical, psychiatric, intellectual, and educational handicaps) had multiple handicaps. Specifically, of the nine- and ten-year-old children who had reading difficulties (educational handicaps), 43 percent had additional handicaps (Rutter et al., 1970a).

The extensive overlap of problems suggests that it may be difficult to isolate a single problem, especially at the screening stage. In fact, it may be far more valuable to screen children for all problems at one time and in one place, rather than trying to differentiate among problems at an early stage.

The main disadvantage of a multiple-test screening battery is that because it is semidiagnostic in nature, it is more costly and time-consuming, involves more specialists, and sacrifices the special feature of simplicity usually associated with screening programs. In order to determine whether or not a referral for diagnosis is indicated, the clinician or group of specialists must evaluate the information from the multiple sources: the tests, the interviews, the medical history, the developmental history, and the observations of the child made by the various personnel. Criteria for selection may be highly variable.

Teacher Observations as a Screening Method

If a screening test or battery can offer no improvement in prediction over a teacher's best estimate, then it may make little sense to invest in a screening test. The teacher, through daily observations of the child, may be the best screening device a school can offer.

Teachers' judgments are an essential source of information in the identification process. In many cases teachers' recommendations alone, or teachers' recommendations in conjunction with test results, may be used in making the decision to refer children for further testing (Schneider, 1974). Teachers may assess students informally on the basis of observations and impressions, or they may use a more formal instrument such as a pupil behavior-rating scale.

A few studies have compared teachers' assessments of their students to the results obtained on tests. Myklebust and Boshes (1969) tested the usefulness of their Pupil Behavior Rating Scale in distinguishing children with learning disabilities from those without problems. This rating scale covers areas that are traditionally covered by tests (receptive and expressive language, gross and fine motor development, and concept formation) in addition to observations of other behaviors appropriate for learning. The authors found that not only did all of the items on the Pupil Behavior Rating Scale discriminate between learning-disabled children and the normal controls at a significant level, but also that in a discriminant analysis of forty-nine variables used in the diagnostic battery, the Pupil Behavior Rating Scale was ranked second in order of statistical significance, preceded only by a test of syllabication. Teachers' ratings of their students were even sensitive to differences between children with no problems and those with minor problems. While this instrument looks promising, information is needed concerning its predictive validity before it can be recommended.

Other studies report that teachers' rankings of student abilities and their identification of students who are "at risk" are highly correlated with achievement test results (Morgan, 1960; Ferinden and Jacobsen, 1970).

Not all studies confirm the perspicacity of teachers. Most notably, the Rutter et al. study (1970a) used a teacher rating of "markedly backward" in school work as part of their screening program: only about one-fifth of children found to have reading problems were so rated by their teachers. In this study teachers gave their over-all impression of their students and did not use a formal rating instrument.

A pupil rating scale or behavior checklist often can be a valuable screening device. First, it provides a more structured format for utilizing the teacher's observations. Because students are all ranked on the same behavioral categories, one can make meaningful comparisons among the observational data. Second, it enables the clinician to include areas for assessment that are not usually testable, such as cooperation and social acceptance (Bryan and McGrady, 1972). Third, this screening procedure is not stressful to the child in any way; he does not have to take a test or be "put on the spot" to perform. Furthermore, the problem of reliability of young children's test results is eliminated, although it is replaced with the problem of the reliability of the raters. Finally, it is an economical procedure; no specialized personnel are required. Teachers, even paraprofessionals, can be trained in a short amount of time to use the observational instrument. It takes only a few minutes per pupil to rank each child on twenty or thirty items.

One of the main disadvantages of an observational instrument is that the behavioral categories may not be clearly defined in operational terms; thus, all teachers may not be referring to the same behavior when they rate the child as uncooperative or inattentive. A second problem is that teacher's ratings are inevitably subjective, and thus the behavioral checklist may be a less accurate instrument over time than a standardized test. Some pupil-rating scales have obtained interrater reliabilities as high as .90, although most report interjudge agreement in the .70s (Spivak and Swift, 1973).

Parents as Screeners

Usually as part of a comprehensive screening examination, information on children's background is obtained from their parents in an interview or on a questionnaire. The information is then considered in conjunction with other information from the testing battery. It remains to be established if parents alone can accurately identify the presence or absence of learning difficulties in their children.

One study suggests that mothers are very attuned to problems in the development of their infants (Knobloch et al., 1973, as reported in Hobbs, 1975). The investigators found that mothers' responses to a questionnaire identified over 90 percent of the infants (twenty to thirty-two weeks old) who had developmental difficulties as confirmed by a subsequent medical evaluation. If parents can recognize problems during the early months of life, they could probably do the same when the child comes of school age. The problem remains, however, that what parents mean by a "reading problem" often can turn out to be something quite different from what the teacher, psychologist, or other professional would identify as such.

Questionnaires have been developed for parental identification of learning problems. McLeod's *Dyslexia Schedule* (1968) represents one such effort. Parents are asked for information on the child's prenatal and perinatal development, history of developmental milestones, language functioning, handedness, nervous habits, and other personality characteristics, as well as for information concerning the reading problems of other family members. This particular questionnaire has been criticized, however, for the extremely small sample on which it was initially tested and for its dubious validity as a screening device (Buros, 1972). In general, a screening program based on parent questionnaires is likely to have the following advantages and disadvantages:

Parent-based screening is relatively easy to implement. For example, parents can fill out a questionnaire when they register their children for school. Like any screening test that uses observational reports, the process is completely unobtrusive to the child.

The main drawback to the use of parental reports is that data based on recollection is notably unreliable (Yarrow et al., 1970). Also it is difficult to obtain objective and comparable reports when parents interpret their own child's behavior.

In sum, very few cross-validation studies have been conducted for reading screening tests, developmental screening tests, or for any of the other screening procedures. Without this information it is impossible to judge the screening ability of the procedure in question. Furthermore, meaningful comparisons among different screening methods cannot be made. Unless tests are cross-validated using a criterion for reading disability that is applicable to a large population, their usefulness is severely limited. However, identification of poor readers should continue. It is hoped that a systematic approach to such identification will ensure that any child with a reading problem is picked up, whatever his or her grade of reading. Presently, the best method appears to be a combination of several reading and aptitude tests along with the teacher's observations and ratings of the child.

DIAGNOSTIC TESTING

Diagnosis differs from screening in that it is more detailed and usually conducted at a second stage only on those children identified by screening as likely to have reading problems. There is a growing trend toward multidisciplinary approaches to diagnosis, assessing different areas of cognitive functioning, physical and emotional health, and environmental variables (Council on Child Health, 1973; Waugh and Bush, 1971; Lerner, 1971; Myers and Hammill, 1969; Bannatyne, 1971; Roswell and Natchez, 1964). This trend is a result of the complex picture of reading failure that has emerged from the research literature. Table 11-8 illustrates the type of examination that would have to be conducted if one were to test for all of the variables that have been correlated (or hypothesized to be causally related) to reading failure.

Other authors suggest that in most cases of reading failure a comprehensive evaluation involving a number of different professionals is not indicated. Rather, the reading teacher or classroom teacher should conduct the evaluation by formal and informal techniques, personal observations of the child in a variety of classroom situations, and information obtained from other school personnel who have contact with the child. These authors sometimes recommend diagnostic teaching—determining the best method of teaching the individual child through the use of trial lessons (Rosewall and Natchez, 1964). The trial lesson technique presents the child with a reading lesson based on a particular approach and then requires that the teacher observe how the child responds to the lesson, his level of interest and attention, his ability to learn and retain what is presented, and his style of response. This method actually combines diagnostic and treatment steps.

Validity of Diagnosis
Diagnostic tests relating to perceptual and cognitive functions have been developed from highly theoretical models of information processing (e.g., Illinois Test of Psycholinguistic Abilities [Kirk, 1968],

Table 11–8.   Multidisciplinary Approach to Diagnosis

Purpose of Procedure	Kind of Procedure	Test or Reference	Comments
I. Establish general state of health	Obtain complete medical history, do complete physical exam. Also establish auditory and visual acuity	Standard Pediatric Exam	
II. Establish integrity of neurological system	Examine cranial nerves, sensory and motor and cerebellar functions, reflexes	Standard Neurologic Exam Abnormalities called "hard signs"	Should include obtaining a history of head trauma, unconsciousness, seizures, meningitis, complications of pregnancy and delivery, cyanosis, delayed acquisition of milestones.
	Examine coordination, ability to persist in a motor stance, right-left orientation, presence of associated or abnormal movements, eye tracking, ability to identify numbers drawn in hand (graphesthesia), ability to identify number of fingers touched (finger localization), etc.	An extended or special neurologic exam, sometimes used to diagnose minimal cerebral dysfunction, sometimes "suspect" neurological damage. Abnormalities called "soft signs." Peters et al., 1975 Towen and Prechtl, 1970 Clements and Peters, 1962 Page-El and Grossman, 1973 Rutter et al., 1970b.	Still a new area, not standardized. Some of these functions can be "abnormal" at one age, will be found to be "normal" later in same child. Role of experience not studied. No clear implications for treatment of learning disabled child. May serve only as "danger signal" of something else wrong, perhaps with higher intellectual functions.
III. Establish some idea of intellectual potential	Group-administered paper and pencil tests	IQ Tests: Otis-Lennon (1970) Lorge-Thorndike (1966), among others.	Group tests are screening devices only. A child who appears below normal must be further evaluated. Tests require a child to be able to read. No way to assess anxiety, boredom, illness, etc., since there is no individual evaluation. Norms questionable.

(Table 11–8. cont'd. overleaf . . .)

Table 11-8. continued

Purpose of Procedure	Kind of Procedure	Test or Reference	Comments
	Individually administered tests	WISC (Wechsler, 1949)	Probably best IQ test. Has nonverbal and verbal scales. A child's IQ score tells how that child performs in relation to other children his own age. Subtests allow for assessment of various areas. No consistent subtest patterns have been found for all learning disabled children.
		Stanford-Binet (Terman and Merrill, 1964)	Primarily verbal. Better for dull child than WISC. Gives mental age which gives no idea of ability in relation to other children of same age and erroneously gives impression child actually has the development of a child of that mental age. Has no underlying theory of intelligence: always regarded itself solely as predictor of academic success. All verbal tasks penalize disadvantaged children.
		Leiter International Scale (Arthur, 1952)	Probably best nonverbal test, useful for language disturbed, foreign speaking, or disadvantaged children.
		Ravens Progressive Matrices (Raven, 1962)	Nonverbal, but in some studies does not correlate with other measures of intelligence. May be better used not as IQ, but as measure of spatial ability.
		Peabody Picture Vocabulary (Dunn, 1970)	Child's response is nonverbal, but child must be able to comprehend completely verbal utterances of examiner. Intelligence is equated with verbal discrimination.

	Ability	Tests	Comments
IV. Assess higher intellectual functions		Harris-Goodenough Draw-a-Person	Although used, not generally agreed to be a measure of intelligence. Also requires dexterity, body perception. For intelligence not better than group IQ.
		Some of these tests are included in "extended neurologic" exam of some authors.	Standardization often poor. Abnormalities may correlate with brain damage, experience, social class, and not with just reading disability. Abnormality may also be consequence of whatever is causing reading disability, not a cause of reader disability. Treatment of these abnormalities premature.
1. Visual perception	Ability to perceive same vs. different	Visual discrimination using subtests from Frostig, Positions in Space (Frostig, 1966).	
	Ability to organize spatial relations: copy figures, run pencil through mazes, reconstruct designs	Visual-motor integration, and Visual and spatial integration. Bender (1951); Spatial Relations and Eye Hand Subtest of Frostig; Block design, Object assembly, Picture completion from WISC; Beery-Buktenica Visual Motor Integration Test (1967).	WISC subtests do not require motor dexterity, but others do. Child may be misdiagnosed as having a visual perceptual problem when problem is with fine motor coordination. Occasionally Bender figures are shown briefly, then taken away, which then adds a memory requirement. Beery-Buktenica has norms from ages 2–15 and provides samples in the manual to which a clinician can match a child's production.
	Ability to distinguish figure from ground, forms hidden inside other forms	Figure-ground discrimination, embedded figures, visual discrimination Figure-ground subtest from Frostig; Children's Embedded Figures Test, (Karp and Konstadt, 1963).	

(*Table 11–8. cont'd. overleaf . . .*)

Table 11-8. continued

Purpose of Procedure	Kind of Procedure	Test or Reference	Comments
	Ability to remember a visual stimulus	A visual memory test Visual Sequential Memory Test from ITPA (Kirk et al., 1968); Memory for designs (Graham and Kendall, 1960); Test of Visual Retention (Benton, 1963).	Graham-Kendall standardized only to 8 years, and has drawing component, so fine motor discoordination must be ruled out.
	Ability to complete an incomplete picture	Picture completion test Subtest from WISC	Probably not a separate category, but associated with ability to organize spatial relations.
2. Auditory perceptions	Ability to perceive same vs. different sounds or words	Auditory discrimination: phonemic (words); nonphonemic (sounds) Wepman Test of Auditory Discrimination (phonemic) (Wepman, 1960).	
	Ability to complete incomplete words	Subtest from ITPA, auditory closure	
	Ability to blend sounds into whole words	Tests sound-blending, phonetic skills Subtest from ITPA, Roswell-Chall Test of Auditory Blending (Chall, 1963).	Apparently Roswell-Chall is only test which, with IQ controlled, can predict reading ability (Hammill, 1975).
	Ability to remember sounds	An auditory memory test Digit span subtest from WISC or ITPA	This is a short-term memory task.
	Ability to remember and reproduce rhythm sequences	Other tests may be sequencing and also involve motor expression. Rhythm task from Seashore Test	The Seashore is published as a music aptitude test, but various of its subtests may be useful in assessing auditory perceptual

			skills: auditory figure-ground, tone discrimination, duration discrimination.
		of Musical Ability (Seashore et al., 1957).	
3. Audio-visual integration	Ability to find that visual pattern which correlates best with auditory sequence of dots	Intersensory integration tests Birch and Belmont, 1964; Blank and Bridger, 1966.	Birch and Belmont task relates auditory dots to visual dots. Blank and Bridger relates visual flashes (temporal) to visual dots (spatial).
4. Language	Obtain a history of first words, phrases	Generally agreed that words after 24 months, sentences after 36 months is severely delayed (Schwartz and Murphy, 1975).	Language evaluation is in its infancy. Few pediatricians, psychiatrists or reading specialists assess developmental aphasia or are familiar with methods of diagnosis. Few standardized tests exist, and most tests, being informal, depend on the clinician's familiarity with normal language. For examples of the normal, see Menyeek (1969). For a discussion of cues to language disorder, see Schwartz and Murphy (1975): a language disabled child has a decreased vocabulary, impoverishment of abstract vocabulary (e.g., feelings), difficulties with plurals, possessives, proper use of past tenses, difficulty with articulation.
	Ability to pronounce syllables, words without slurring, omissions, substitutions	Jehna Developmental Articulation Test	Jehna test only goes to 9 years. In normal children, over-all intelligibility of speech is not seriously impaired, even when, as part of normal development, they make certain errors in articulation. Some consider articulation problems, when present alone, to be evidence of a motor uncoordination problem (Mattis et al., 1975). However, articulation problems are also found together with more severe problems of language expression and comprehension.

(Table 11–8. cont'd. overleaf . . . .)

Table 11–8. continued

Purpose of Procedure	Kind of Procedure	Test or Reference	Comments
	Ability to name objects, describe objects, use grammar correctly, use abstractions, use proper rhythm and intonations	Tests for expressive aphasia Requiring child to name pictures, objects (Oldfield-Wingfield, cards). How many words can you say in one minute? (Binet) Tell me everything you can about this object (Verbal expression subtest, ITPA). Tell me a word that rhymes with ____. (Binet) Definitions (Binet; Vocabulary subtest of WISC). Tell me in what ways these things are alike (Binet).	Strictly speaking, a child who is only reading disabled should have normal spoken language. But at older ages lack of experience through reading may hamper development of abstractions and more complex language tasks.
	Ability to name objects, describe objects, use grammar correctly, use abstractions, use proper rhythm and intonations	Sentence Memory as a test of grammar, ability to categorize. (Binet and Spencer Sentence Memory) Use of syntax (grammatic closure, ITPA).	Sentence memory is a test of language ability rather than memory because a child will not incorporate and repeat unfamiliar grammatical structures. Sentences must not merely get longer, but grammatically more complex.

Ability to comprehend vocabulary, grammar, meaning	Tests for receptive aphasia. Ask child to point to the picture corresponding to the name said by the examiner (Peabody Picture Vocabulary). Ask child to follow a series of directions as in the token test (Mattis et al., 1975).	This is the child whose mother says, "I have to repeat things three times," or, "He never seems to understand what I ask." There are few good standardized items, but the child with receptive aphasia will inevitably be found to have expressive difficulties, and be picked up by these tests.
V. Establish child's own emotional health	Individual psychiatric interview	Must include some report of behavior from parent or school. All too often, does not follow a standard form, with an attempt to touch on certain standard topics, but follows a hit-or-miss pattern, and therefore depends heavily on the skill of the interviewer.
	Questionnaires or standard psychological tests	Gets around problem of variability in that all children are given same test, but may not be best way to assess mental health. For any particular type of questionnaire, one should review standardization data.
VI. Establish family's emotional health, also family's resources, income, interest in learning, etc.	Usually done by interview with mother, or by home visit. Interview with whole family might be more suitable. Direct observation may be more accurate, but of course, expensive.	With this and following categories, no clear norms or methods established, but clinician must be aware that problems in these areas may be contributory to child's individual problems. What is needed theoretically is a developmental scheme for family life.

(Table 11–8. cont'd. overleaf . . . .)

Table 11–8. continued

Purpose of Procedure	Kind of Procedure	Test or Reference	Comments
VII. Establish climate of community, peer group, etc. to learning			Same as above (VI). Some estimate might be obtained by asking children themselves how much academic achievement is debunked by peers, what the drug and alcohol problem is like, even at the seventh and sixth grades, how noisy the classrooms are, etc.
VIII. Establish adequacy of school, teachers, methods	Some level can be estimated by achievement of school in relation to national norms, by number of dropouts, and by percent of grade that go on to college. Direct observation of child's classroom would be preferable but expensive.		Same as above (VI). Certainly one estimate of adequacy for a child with special needs might be how long it took the school to refer the child, and how hard they have tried to remedy the problem.

Frostig [1964] tests of visual perception). A child who performs poorly on some part of the test is diagnosed as having a particular problem, such as an auditory sequencing problem or a visual memory problem. Differences in diagnoses give the impression of extreme precision in differentiating distinct clinical entities. However, different diagnoses may be a reflection of different theoretical approaches, or they may merely depend on which test is used. Moreover, failure at a diagnostic item is often mistakenly interpreted as a cause of the reading difficulty. Instead, it may be a co-end product, along with reading disability, of some other disturbance.

Use of Information. Tests may provide a wealth of knowledge about the child's functioning, but this information can be obscured in technical jargon. Unless psychometric findings can easily be translated into operational terms so that the educator can proceed confidently with remedial planning, nothing is gained. For example, it may serve little purpose to tell an educator that a child with a reading problem has an "auditory sequencing dysfunction." If instead he is told that the child has difficulties in analyzing a word into its component sounds and then recombining those sounds to form the whole word, he will find it easier to formulate concrete educational objectives from the assessment. Similarly, the label "psycho-neurotic reaction" is of little use, but a detailed statement by the psychiatrist describing the child's coping styles and areas of conflict and how they relate to academic behavior might be very useful.

Several studies have been conducted to determine how teachers perceive the usefulness of diagnostic work-ups done by outside reading clinics. Waugh (1970) found that only 38 percent of the teachers who responded thought that the report had been useful. Pope and Hacklay (1974) report that 88 percent of their sample of teachers and guidance counselors considered the diagnostic information useful. However, 74 percent of their sample also indicated that they would have liked to have a conference with the clinic, so presumably the lines of communication could have been opened still further.

Nichol (1974) conducted a five-year follow-up study on a sample of children who had been referred to psychiatrists for evaluation for academic difficulties. In only 20 percent of all cases referred were the psychiatric evaluations found to be helpful to the school. Children were referred to psychiatrists in a number of different settings, only one of which was found to be satisfactory. The psychiatric consultation service that was contracted to the school was considered most satisfactory in its communication with the schools, compared to psychiatric services in hospital inpatient and outpatient units, in community mental health centers, or in private practice.

Is Diagnosis Necessary?

In general, there is little evidence that we know how to use differential diagnosis of neurological, cognitive or perceptual difficulties in designing learning experiences for children, or that differential diagnosis is necessary for effective treatment (Bateman, 1971; Black, 1973). Much of the research on matching type of treatment to the child's diagnosed style of learning (for example, auditory or visual) suggests that there is no relationship between the two in terms of effectiveness of treatment (Bateman, 1971; Robinson, 1972). Furthermore, there is little agreement about whether treatment should build on the assessed strengths of the child, or whether it should concentrate on the areas of weakness (Stodolsky and Lesser, 1967).

This does not mean, however, that in the future we will never be able to make a convincing case for detailed diagnosis. While the classification of disabled readers into categories such as "auditory" and "visual" has not proved useful, there is some evidence that other categories may have implications for follow-up procedures. As an example, Mattis et al. (1975) operationally defined three mutually exclusive dyslexic syndromes on the basis of results from an extensive (four to eight hours) battery of tests. Mattis notes that while the reading and spelling errors of these nonreaders would not differentiate these groups, the extensive battery did identify three distinct types of deficiencies. He implies that treatment for the three groups of children thus differentiated would have to proceed along very different lines. As an example, the group identified as having a language disorder certainly will require concurrent speech and language therapy. These children might learn best through a sound-blending approach. They might have to initially bypass the learning of letter names and sight words because of their specific anomia.

Certainly the classification of readers can be of prognostic value. Yule (1973) found that the reading backward children (reading below age level) had progressed more in reading and spelling than had the reading retarded children (reading below potential).[c]

Finally, the presence of a reading disability can be used as a predictor to other disturbances. Children with reading disabilities may

[c]Reading backward is defined as "an attainment in reading accuracy or comprehension on the Neale test which was 2 years 4 months or more below the child's chronological age." Reading-retarded is defined as "the attainment on either reading accuracy or reading comprehension which was 2 years 4 months or more below the level predicted on the basis of the child's age and Short WISC IQ" (Yule, 1973, p. 245).

have problems that need special attention in and of themselves, such as deafness, language problems, psychiatric disturbance, even if treating these problems has little effect on reading *per se.*

Summary

There are certain limitations to present diagnostic procedures:

1. The validity of many of the tests used in diagnosis is in question;

2. Some areas of functioning traditionally included in an assessment have little relevance to reading skills;

3. Translating information from tests and other noneducational professions into instructional objectives presents a problem;

4. Differential diagnosis may not be of consequence for effective follow-up treatment of reading problems. The assumption that a diagnostic evaluation will lead to the "right," i.e., efficacious, course of treatment is at present unwarranted;

5. It is not clear that diagnostic information is deemed useful by those responsible for remedial planning, or that it even reaches those persons for whom it is intended.

One might ask then: Why are diagnostic procedures generally recommended and included in a program servicing children with reading problems? There are a number of reasons:

1. Parents may be reassured by the fact that there is a name and possibly a cause for their child's reading problems. They can become more supportive of their child and can reinforce any effects of remedial treatment (Bateman, 1971). But giving a name to the condition may have a negative effect if it results in lowering the parents' expectations for the child.

2. The participation of educators in the diagnostic process serves to heighten their awareness of other disciplines and thus contributes to interdisciplinary communication (Bateman, 1971).

3. Diagnosis provides valuable information for basic research and for research on the efficacy of treatment. Only by having a clear record of the specific characteristics of each child can we begin to accumulate evidence for which treatment, given how often, works for whom. We also may discover subcategories of children for whom no treatment works.

4. Individual diagnosis can identify other troubles such as hearing or vision problems, gross neurological problems, serious perceptual and language problems, individual or family emotional disturbance.

It also gives an over-all notion of the adequacy of the child's schooling to date.

5. Finally, some argue in favor of extensive evaluations from a concern for equity (Children's Defense Fund, 1974). Too often children, especially the poor and nonwhite, are discriminated against by being diagnosed, labeled, and then cast aside on the basis of a single test score or teacher's recommendation. Equity advocates argue that it is a child's right to receive a thorough assessment of his behavior and functioning by a variety of personnel, using a variety of procedures, in a variety of settings. They emphasize that evaluation should be focused on prevention rather than on intervention, and that tests to measure behavior should be replaced by observations of the child's behavior in various situations.

There is a problem here too, however, in that diagnosis will not necessarily become more accurate by increasing the number of professional assessments. It could as easily be argued that the probability of stigmatizing or labeling the child is directly related to the number of professions represented by the examiners. Certainly most middle-class children are spared such an ordeal unless their parents seek it out.

In conclusion, it would appear that more information is necessary before detailed data from the extended neurologic exam or from the tests of perceptual and cognitive function can be reliably integrated into remedial planning. From present information it is difficult to make recommendations for the minimal diagnostic process. Having some data in the following areas would seem to be of importance: the presence of debilitating illness, visual and auditory acuity, general intelligence, gross neurologic disease, language pathology, individual and family mental health, and adequacy of education.

From the studies on follow-up it appears that if diagnostic services are to be truly effective, there is a need for better coordination between diagnostic and treatment services. Ideally, if assessment is to be conducted, then assessment services should be available within the school itself. The presence of both diagnosticians and remedial planners at the same site may reduce the gaps in communication between the two, ensure continuity of assessment and follow-up, and reduce the number of children who get "lost" at each stage of the process. Where diagnosis must involve a professional who practices outside the school, either the school should contract to a limited number of professionals with whom they can have ongoing contact, or someone should act as a coordinator between the evaluating clinician and the remedial planner, ensuring that diagnostic information will be communicated and understood.

TREATMENT OF READING PROBLEMS

Effectiveness of treatment can be measured in a number of ways: by statistically significant differences in the reading test scores of control and experimental groups; by a minimum gain in reading achievement score in a given time period; by bringing the child's reading ability to the level that is expected of someone of his or her age and grade; or by maintaining the child's improved reading ability over a given number of years after the intervention. Successful treatment may also be evidenced by the acquisition of specific reading skills and improvement in general school behavior.

We have selected a number of different treatment types for review, although in fact there is as much variation of treatment within types as there is between types. Remedial treatments can be classified into three basic categories: (1) treatments that teach nonreading skills which are assumed to transfer to reading skills, (2) treatments that modify behaviors or improve the child's psychological status in order to enable him to learn to read, and (3) treatments which directly teach reading skills, building up the child's sight vocabulary and developing his phonics and word attack skills.

Of course, no study that sets out to evaluate a program for disabled readers is able to isolate the remedial curriculum as a single variable. It is always contaminated by others: the physical setting of the treatment, the particular teacher involved, and the number and nature of the children.

We have been somewhat arbitrary in our selection of the types of treatment to be considered and in the inclusion of the particular studies for discussion. Our aim was to include representative examples of the research which were of sufficiently sound experimental design so that at least some inferences could be drawn.

Perceptual Motor Training

Perceptual motor training has been among the most popular and frequently advocated remedial programs. This treatment is derived from various theories that assume a relationship between perceptual motor skills and reading achievement. Some advocate perceptual motor training in the belief that certain deficiencies cause reading difficulties and must be corrected. Others hypothesize that the learning that occurs in perceptual motor training is transferred to other skill areas, e.g., reading, although the evidence for such transfer is limited (Hurwitz and Wolff, 1975).

Programs are usually identified with the names of prominent researchers. Frostig has developed a program in visual-perceptual motor training which includes training in eye-motor coordination, figure-ground discrimination, form constancy, orientation in space, and spatial relations (Frostig, 1964). Kephart's program emphasizes the importance of motor and kinesthetic development and includes activities such as walking along a balance beam, drawing large circles and lines on a chalkboard, and visually tracking objects (Kephart, 1960). Doman and Delacato have developed a motor patterning program designed to remediate presumed brain damage. The training program includes manipulation of the child's limbs, sensory stimulation, and practice in using a single hand in order to establish hemispheric dominance (Delacato, 1959).

Anderson and Stern (1972) selected children between the ages of six and nine with "visual perceptual deficiencies" and randomly assigned them to one of three groups: a visual perceptual training program on the lines of the Frostig curriculum, a corrective reading program, or a placebo play group which served to control for the effects of the special attention that children usually receive in experimental programs. After sixteen weeks of daily training (or attention), the authors found no significant differences among the three treatment groups in reading level or in visual perceptual abilities. The study suggests that special attention from a teacher in and of itself may be a sufficient factor in effecting advances in reading achievement.

A study by O'Bryan and Silverman (1972) divided boys with perceptual handicaps into three groups. One group received a perceptual motor training program adapted from Kephart, Frostig and Getman. A second placebo control group received a play activity program. A third group received no special treatment. At twelve months no differences were found among the three groups in their scores on achievement tests or on perceptual motor tests. At eighteen months the experimental group made a significant gain on the perceptual motor tests, but again the three groups showed no significant differences in educational achievement. At two years the experimental group continued to show better perceptual motor performance. Both the experimental group and the play activity group made significantly greater progress in reading than the nontreatment group, but the experimental group was definitely not better than the play activity group.

Other studies show that when compared to remedial reading, perceptual motor training does no better in improving reading test scores (Belmont et al., 1973; Sullivan, 1972) although both do better when compared to a no-treatment control group (Halliwell and Solan, 1972). Hamill (1972) strengthens this impression. In reviewing a number of studies that evaluated the effects of visual perceptual motor training programs on reading achievement, he found that a full four-fifths of the studies conclude that this type of training cannot be said to result in improved reading scores.

Apparently, perceptual motor training also can exert incidental effects, some bad, some good. The Doman-Delacato method has been repeatedly cited for the lack of experimental data supporting it as a treatment for reading problems (Hallahan and Cruickshank, 1973; Balow, 1971; Silver, 1975). A statement issued by members of various medical, psychological, and educational organizations sharply criticizes the method, not only for having both unsubstantiated theoretical and empirical basis, but also for the psychological stress it causes parents and for the inappropriate activities it advocates for children (Committee on the Handicapped Child, 1968). On the other hand, Balow (1971) suggests that perceptual motor training, although it does not directly improve reading skills, does improve behaviors that enable the child to learn to read. Motor activities are engaging and motivating to the primary-schooler and allow him or her more opportunities to experience success in school than do traditional academic activities. Thus, self-confidence can be increased.

Whatever its indirect effects, this particular remedial method appears no better for specific reading training than any to which it has been compared, such as corrective reading instruction, or special play groups. In summary, where positive effects of perceptual motor training have been reported, some tentative alternative explanations must be considered: one alternative is that any type of intervention that is structured to include small group instruction with individualized attention seems to have positive benefits for reading achievement, no matter what the content of the intervention. Another hypothesis is that perceptual motor training may improve certain behaviors and skills that enable learning in general, attention, motivation, increased self-confidence, and appropriate classroom behavior. Whether this justifies the expense of implementing a perceptual training program over some other procedure, such as a small activity group, is another matter.

Token Reinforcement Programs

Token economy programs have become increasingly popular as a way of improving reading skills and modifying impulsive behavior or acting out behavior that might interfere with learning to read. Token reinforcement has been used with many different types of children— learning disabled, mentally retarded, emotionally disturbed, and hyperactive. This type of program employs operant conditioning techniques. A behavior to be reinforced is specified; each time the behavior occurs, the child is rewarded with tokens or points that can be exchanged for toys, money, or other desirable commodities or activities. As the behavior is reinforced it should increase in frequency.

Strang and Wolf (1971) used an automated teaching unit to present reading material and to award points for correct responses. The subjects were nine pairs of sixth-graders who were matched on reading achievement and IQ and randomly assigned to the experimental or control group. Both groups were tested once a week after school. Incentives were included in the testing phase for all students. The automated tutoring with reinforcement occurred during school time so that extra hours of academic work cannot be admitted as an alternative explanation.

The authors found that after four months in the program, the tutored students gained an average of seven months in reading grade level, whereas the controls gained an average of four months only. The difference between groups was significant at the .05 level. It is somewhat discouraging to note that the experimental children gained in all areas in which they had been tutored (vocabulary, following directions, and comprehension skills), but showed no improvement in another area in which they had received no instruction. Thus, transfer of learning, or generalization to other areas of learning, had not taken place. The main drawback to making generalizations from this study is that while the experimental group as a whole made significant gains, only one-half to two-thirds of the group (i.e., four to six students) accounted for these improvements. The remaining children did no better than their matched controls.

Evidence from other studies, while reporting dramatic success in improving children's academic performance, is characterized by serious methodological flaws. Samples are often extremely small, containing as few as three or four children (e.g., Ryback and Staats, 1970; Koven and LeBow, 1973). There is no attempt to randomly select students; rather, the sample often represents a hand-picked group of particularly problematic pupils. In many studies there is no control group. No studies have included a placebo praise group, a control group that received *random* praise or tokens or special adult attention. Some studies have used parents (mothers) as the reinforcers, again introducing the confounding factor that it may have been the approval of the mother that motivated the child and not the tokens alone. In one case where a control group was included, the experimental treatment occurred after school, on weekends, and during the summer, thus making it difficult to determine if the rate of reading gains made by the children wasn't merely a factor of the additional time they were spending in academic activities compared to the control group (Wolf, Giles and Hall, 1968).

Token reward systems may well have a dramatic positive effect in changing a child's behavior and improving his or her reading level. While these observations await verification under good experimental design, the repeated reports of reading improvement using this technique deserve further exploration. Under a token economy, the student receives prompt feedback on the responses he or she makes. In this way greater attention to the task can be maintained and the time lags involved in correcting papers or checking workbooks are avoided (Axelrod, 1971). Constant supervision of the student and repeated testing of skills provide the kind of in-depth evaluation and ongoing surveillance that is usually recommended in any careful program for remediation of a reading problem.

The disadvantages of a token reinforcement program are primarily implementation problems (Fine et al., 1974). The use of reinforcements is a very demanding classroom management technique because it requires extensive planning and supervision at all times by the teacher or reinforcer. Adequately monitoring students' behavior so that reinforcements are correctly applied is best done one-to-one, although teachers may be able to work with small groups of four or five children at one time. The audiovisual teaching machine described by Strang and Wolf (1971) may be a reasonable alternative to the use of a parent or teacher, placing fewer physical and psychological demands on the teacher.

Finally, there is the unanswered question of the effect of removing the reinforcement at the end of the program. Is the behavior extinguished, as would be predicted by the operant conditioning paradigm? Or do the reading gains persist? It is argued that if the administration of tokens is accompanied by a few words of praise and encouragement by the teacher or reinforcing person, eventually the praise itself will become a conditioned reinforcement that can be used alone. But long-term studies need to be carried out to show that positive gains will persist when token reinforcement is phased out.

Drug Therapy

The use of stimulant drugs has been recommended in the treatment of hyperactive children who are characterized by "chronic, sustained, severe hyperactivity, marked distractibility to extraneous stimuli, very short attention span, irritability, and hyperexcitability ... emotional lability, low frustration tolerance, learning difficulties, visual-perceptual problems with consequent poor performance in reading and arithmetic . . ." (Solomons, 1971, p. 472). It is estimated that about 3 percent of grade-school children suffer from this syndrome (Freedman, 1971). Reading disabilities may be associated with hyperactivity.

Stimulant drugs have been widely used for many years, despite the fact that until recently many of the efficacy studies have been methodologically unsound and their conclusions debatable (Sulzbacher, 1973; deLong, 1972). Drugs, moreover, at best produce favorable results in no more than three-quarters of cases (Bradley, 1950; Mendelson et al., 1971; Office of Child Development, 1971), yet medication is often prescribed without adequate diagnosis or follow-up. From well-designed drug studies it appears that stimulant drugs are useful in improving motor hyperactivity, disruptiveness, and inattentiveness (Conrad et al., 1971; Comly, 1971; Denhoff et al., 1971; Sprague et al., 1970; Knights and Hinton, 1969). These drugs also appear to improve performance on laboratory tasks of learning, for example in attention and planning on the Porteus maze, and in correct response and quicker reaction time in two-choice discrimination learning (Conners et al., 1969; Conners, Eisenberg and Barcai, 1967; Lasagua and Epstein, 1970; Sprague et al., 1970; Cohen et al., 1971). On the other hand, studies measuring the effect of these drugs on IQ scores seem to contradict one another, some showing no effect, others showing modest improvements (Knights and Hinton, 1969; Conners et al., 1969; Conners, 1971; Conrad et al., 1971). Moreover, there are many studies which show no improvement in general academic functioning, although the duration of follow-up may be too short (Denhoff et al., 1971; Conners et al., 1967; Conrad et al., 1971).

Drugs appear to have a certain usefulness, as described above, but one must keep in mind certain problems in the research on effectiveness.

Diagnosis of Hyperactivity.   Of primary concern is the lack of evidence for a single diagnostic entity of hyperactivity. Hyperactivity, like poor reading, is often a behavior symptom characteristic of many other disorders, including psychological or environmental stress, schizophrenia, retardation, or depression (report of the Conference, 1971). All too often an aggressive, acting-out child in the classroom is "diagnosed" as hyperactive and is put on drugs. A group of hyperactive children may in fact be a highly heterogeneous sample (Stroufe and Stewart, 1973; Conners, 1972). Studies also vary widely on the criteria necessary for a diagnosis of hyperactivity, ranging from objective measures like amount of wiggling on a cushion, to more general impressions like behavior ratings on teacher questionnaires.

Intervening Variables. The effectiveness of stimulant drugs may depend on variables other than hyperactivity alone. Conners (1972) reports that he was able to subdivide a group of hyperactive patients into seven more homogeneous subgroups on the basis of psychological test results. He found that the homogeneous subgroups responded differentially to the drug treatment. Measured intelligence has been mentioned as an important variable affecting the response of a child to drug therapy (Conners et al., 1969). Brain-damaged children may respond better to the stimulant drugs (Lasagna and Epstein, 1970; Satterfield et al., 1973). Not studied yet, but perhaps also of importance, may be such variables as individual or parental psychopathology and the quality of the parent-child interaction. Until the intervening variables and the many behaviors lumped under the term hyperactivity are analyzed into more homogeneous subgroups, it will continue to be difficult to predict who will benefit from drug therapy alone or from drug therapy in combination with other treatments.

Problems of Dosage. One problem that complicates the interpretation of results from many drug studies is that dosages are often varied according to the individual's tolerance to the drug. In order to make dosages comparable for all subjects, it is suggested that a formula be used that calculates the correct dosage according to the child's body weight and is validated according to the child's blood level of the drug. There ought also to be some effort to determine whether the drug was taken, since not taking the medication may considerably alter the interpretation of apparent success or failure.

Deleterious Effects. Some adverse effects have been noted to occur with the use of stimulants including "anorexia, insomnia, gastrointestinal distress, dizziness, fine tremor and coldness of the extremities and pallor of the skin" (Grinspoon and Singer, 1973, p. 537). Although these symptoms are usually mild and may subside as treatment continues, in isolated cases the child's reaction is strong enough to warrant discontinuation.

There is also some evidence to suggest that the therapy may adversely affect physical growth. Significant decreases in the rate of growth (in weight, and in some cases in height) were noted for children who were receiving daily dosages of stimulant drugs over a two- or three-year period (Safer, Allen, and Barr, 1972; Safer and Allen, 1973). There may be an alteration in growth hormone metabolism (Rees et al., 1970). Some authors have also questioned the possibility of deleterious drug effects on the cardiovascular system (Cole, 1975).

The question of drug-abuse also persists. Although Laufer (1971) reported no drug-abuse in adolescents who had taken stimulant drugs for hyperactivity, his data are based on a questionnaire given to parents, who may be quite ill-informed as to their teenagers' habits. While children may not become physiologically addicted to amphetamines, for some children a reliance on drugs may influence later attitudes to drugs and willingness to experiment with psychoactive agents (Stroufe and Stewart, 1973).

It is generally assumed that stimulant drugs either improve the child's behavior or leave it unchanged. On the contrary, some studies report that 10 to 20 percent of children are worse (Bradley, 1950; Comly, 1971). Most authors have looked for positive effects in learning experiments, but some report that beyond a certain dosage, while reaction time may be quicker, accuracy declines (Sprague et al., 1970).

Placebo Effect.   The expectations and the attitudes of those prescribing, administering, or taking the drug (or placebo) can exert a powerful influence on the outcome of the treatment. The placebo effect is likely to influence behavior in about one-third of the adult and child population (Freed, 1962, cited in Freeman, 1966). Similarly, parents or pediatricians who prescribe the drug may convey attitudes of skepticism or disbelief concerning the ability of a drug to improve behavior, with the result that the drug appears to be ineffective (Freeman, 1966). One must be cautious in ascribing true positive (or negative) results as a function of the efficacy of the drug alone.

Long-Term Effects.   It is often said that hyperactive children grow out of their difficulties, but follow-up studies suggest the contrary, that the hyperactive child may have a sort of chronic disease (Weiss et al., 1971; Mendelson et al., 1971). These two-to-five-year follow-up studies suggest that while the motor hyperactivity improves, there remains a degree of distractibility. Moreover, these adolescents are chronic and severe academic underachievers. They have a high incidence of antisocial behavior (contacts with police, breaking of rules). They are beset with low self-esteem, emotional immaturity, hopelessness, and lack of goals. Ninety-two to 100 percent of children in these two samples had been treated with stimulant drugs or chlorpromazine at some time, but their drug therapy histories varied widely. Thus, these data on unsuccessful outcome are contaminated by results from initial drug nonresponders, and by results from those who may not have stuck to drug therapy.

In a one-to-two-year follow-up limited to drug responders, Sleator et al. (1974) report maintenance of improved behavior (as rated by their teachers) over the duration of follow-up. These authors note that for 26 percent of children teachers could not detect the placebo month. This is cited as evidence of remission in the child but might also represent a placebo effect operating on parents or teachers. With our particular interest in drugs and reading disability, we found only one study that cited improvement in reading and spelling, and that for only a specific homogeneous subgroup (Conners, 1971). There is as yet no convincing body of data linking drug treatment with improved reading.

Until it is known which variables predict responsiveness to drugs, it remains uncertain for whom and under what circumstances it may be harmful to administer these stimulants. We conclude that there is a need for studies that control for additional independent variables that may affect treatment outcome. Differential diagnosis may be critical to the efficacy of treatment. Further research is also important to determine in what way drug treatment affects academic outcomes, and what are the long-term effects of the prolonged use of stimulant drugs. In light of this uncertainty, physicians who prescribe the drug should carefully monitor the child's behavior, academic progress, height and growth curves. Drug-free periods are essential. In addition, attention must be paid to remedial education and even to family counseling, where it may be useful. We do not advocate that these drugs be dismissed, but that they be used with appropriate caution and as adjuncts to other therapies.

Psychosocial Treatment

Psychotherapy has been advocated as the preferred treatment for those children in whom the learning disability is felt to be the expression of emotional disturbance (Rabinovitch, 1962). It also has been suggested that before response to remedial teaching can be expected, psychotherapy is necessary in children who have low self-esteem, poor motivation, anxiety, depression, or other disturbances as a consequence of their reading disability (Eisenberg, 1966). Many individual case reports suggest that individual psychotherapy is useful for some children with reading disability who, prior to therapy, failed to make any gains in their reading even with remedial tutoring (Blanchard, 1936; Griffin in Myklebust, 1967; Sylvester and Kunst, 1943; Arthur, 1940). During a six-week period of individual and group non-directive play therapy, and during the post-treatment follow-up, reading retarded subjects have been shown to advance more than they did during the six week pre-treatment observation period (Bells, 1950).

In one six-month study, individual counseling—which "probably could have been carried out by any sympathetic intelligent layman" —was found to be more effective than remedial reading for poor readers who were not considered by their teachers to be emotionally disturbed (Lawrence, 1971). It has also been suggested that group therapy may be effective (Lipton and Feiner, 1956).

A study by Schiffman (1962) examined four different treatment combinations: psychotherapy only, psychotherapy and remedial reading, remedial reading only, and no treatment. The author found an inconsistent effect of psychotherapy but a positive effect of remedial reading. Margolin (1955) also found remedial reading alone more effective than psychotherapy alone, but the best results were obtained by children who received both.

In many individual case reports on psychotherapy or on the history of children with learning disabilities, there is strong evidence of stress between child and parent or indications of parental psychopathology. In recent years, in the field of child psychiatry, there has been an increasing emphasis on treating the child's disturbed family environment as a way of treating the child (Ackerman and Lakas, 1965; Minuchin, 1974), but the effect on reading ability of involving the child's family in psychotherapy has not yet been investigated.

Involvement of parents has also been suggested as an alternative method for treating hyperactive children (Sroufe and Stewart, 1973). Other programs have focused on developing the role of parents as educators of their children and have had considerable success. In these programs, parents teach or tutor their own children in reading and language skills (Ryback and Staats, 1970; Koven and LeBow, 1973; Slater, 1973; Levenstein, 1970; Karnes, 1969; Bronfenbrenner, 1974).

Another form of treatment is aimed at improving the mental health of the community as a whole. Theoretical support for this idea comes from the field of social psychiatry, where it has been shown that members of "disintegrated" communities have significantly higher incidence of psychiatric disturbance (Leighton, 1965). Leighton also maintains that the prevalence of psychiatric disorder declines as a disintegrated community improves its lot, although improved economic opportunities alone are not sufficient to bring about changes in attitude from defeatism, negativism, and suspicion. A program is required that identifies and supports community leaders and helps them teach the community that they, as a group, can achieve shared goals. The assumption is that a person acquires the motivation to learn or to work for future goals in part from the attitudes and experiences of his associates. This assumption finds some support in the data relating school achievement to the aspirations and background of the peer group (Coleman, 1966).

One experiment that reflected such a community orientation was conducted in the Banneker Schools in St. Louis, a twenty-two-school group in a primarily black, low-income area with several housing projects. The project tried to increase the motivation of parents and their children to achieve academically. The director of education urged teachers to teach children the importance of education. Teachers visited homes, and parent meetings were held to show parents that their children were far behind national norms. The parents were urged to get the children to school and to provide appropriate study settings. The program was cited as the reason for the decrease in percent of children in the lowest achievement track from 47.1 percent to 23.3 percent (Shepard, 1959).

In this experiment, reading achievement tests showed a general improvement in all schools, regardless of whether a specific program of propaganda had been instituted. While there is no firm evidence of the utility, in terms of reading achievement, of programs designed specifically to change motivation at the community level, other data from social psychiatry suggest that this approach may be a viable alternative to individual or family therapies (Leighton, 1965; McLelland, 1965).

At least equally important to the solution of subsequent school problems are community health programs aimed at improved maternal and infant health. These may reduce the prevalence of organic problems in the children, as should programs aimed at chronic lead poisoning or child abuse, leading to improved school performance for those children whose family background or living circumstance place them at risk.

Remedial Reading

The majority of children identified as having reading problems are offered a program of remedial reading. Remedial reading is a catchall phrase that includes an immense range of programs, from those that simply mark time to others that are well organized and well implemented. The only similarity among these programs is their direct approach to the teaching of specific reading skills (sight word recognition, phonics skills, word attack skills, familiar word endings, comprehension). Poor readers may be placed in a special classroom where they not only get special reading instruction but an entire curriculum (academic and nonacademic) shaped around the children's special needs. Alternatively, the failing reader may leave the regular classroom for an hour or so each day to be instructed by a special remedial reading teacher. Some disabled readers may be enrolled in summer school reading classes to help them maintain the progress they have made during the year. On a much broader scale, total educational programs have been designed for groups of children who have traditionally been at risk for academic failure.

Remedial Reading vs. Other Methods or No Treatment. In the studies reviewed thus far, "traditional," "corrective," and "remedial" reading programs have usually served as a baseline against which to compare a new technique. In looking back over those studies in an attempt to summarize trends we conclude:

1. Descriptions of the traditional remedial reading programs in these studies are extremely sketchy.

2. Neither remedial reading nor perceptual motor training has been shown to be more effective than the other, and it is not clear whether either has been effective (Halliwell and Solan, 1972; Anderson and Stern, 1972; Belmont et al., 1973).

3. Remedial reading programs may be necessary components of programs which modify behavior, but for certain subgroups of children they do not replace the use of amphetamines or psychotherapy (Lawrence, 1971; Schiffman, 1962; Margolin et al., 1955; Conrad et al., 1971).

4. The results from studies comparing remedial reading to no treatment at all tend to be contradictory, with both positive and negative results reported (Weinberg et al., 1971, Cashdan and Pumfrey, 1969; Buerger, 1968; Shearer, 1967; Lovell et al., 1962).

5. When remedial reading has been compared to a "no-treatment" control group that has received an equal amount of nonspecific attention, there have been no differences between the two groups in their reading achievement scores (Anderson and Stern, 1972). This suggests that the attention received in an experimental program is more important than the reading curriculum itself.

Short-Term vs. Long-Term Effects. Few follow-up studies have been conducted on remedial reading programs. One such study, which suffers from possible bias in sample selection and assignment to treatment and control groups, found that children who received remedial reading instruction for one hour, two to three times a week for, on average, over a year, made significant gains on the Gates Reading Test when compared to a control group that did not receive any special help (Buerger, 1968). But long-term follow-up of the sample from .3 to 5.6 years following termination of remedial reading instruction found no significant differences between the two groups in general mental aptitude and in vocabulary and reading comprehension skills. It was some consolation that a significant number of students who had received remedial reading felt that the special instruction had been beneficial.

Other studies tend to confirm the pattern of immediate short-term gains with a lack of long-term impact (Shearer, 1967; Lovell et al., 1962). This criticism is especially prevalent in the evaluation literature on Head Start, Follow Through, and Title I programs, where immediate positive gains in achievement and IQ scores tend not to be maintained even one or two years following termination of the program.

Matching Teaching Technique to Child's Learning Style. One cherished notion in the literature on remedial reading curriculum is that the teaching method can be matched to the learning style of the individual child. Children are often diagnosed as "visual," "auditory," or "kinesthetic," indicating that they seem to respond best to teaching that depends on sight, sound, or touch.

As an example, the phonics approach or the linguistic approach focuses on the decoding aspect of reading, teaching the child the symbol-to-sound relationships that are necessary for sounding out words. Auditory analysis and synthesis are required to break down a written word into its component sounds and then to recombine the sounds to say the word. The phonics method is considered most suitable for the "auditory" child. Likewise, the "visual" child is considered to profit more from an approach that emphasizes the building up of a sight-word vocabulary, learning words as whole visual configurations.

Smith (1971) used "culturally disadvantaged primary-grade children" to test the hypothesis of teaching according to learning styles. The children were diagnosed as "visual," "auditory," or "control" (neither style dominant) on the basis of their ITPA profiles. Subjects were randomly assigned to one of three teaching methods. Two of the methods were phonics oriented (auditory) and one was more visually oriented. After two years of instruction Smith found no significant differences in reading achievement among the three groups, auditory, visual, and control.

Sabatino and Streissguth (1972) performed another study to test the assumption of learning styles. They classified learning disabled children as auditory or visual learners and randomly assigned them to experimental or control groups. A visual perceptual teaching method was used, and therefore it was hypothesized that the visual children in the experimental treatment would make significant gains in reading. The control group was provided with a program of games and individualized work to offset the possible effects of the increased attention. After twelve weeks of training, the authors found no differences among the groups on reading tests, although both experimental groups (auditory and visual children) made significant gains on a test of visual-motor coordination, a test that explicitly assessed the material taught in the experimental program.

The Sabatino and Streissguth (1972) study reiterates a couple of important points: that both experimental and control groups made significant gains on tests of reading achievement (between their pretest and post-test scores) suggests either that the experimental training had no effect at all, and the gains were due to maturation effects alone, or that the games and individual attention were equally as effective in stimulating growth in reading skills of these learning disabled children as was the experimental program, in which case one might wonder why bother with the experimental treatment at all.

Both of these studies lead us to question the over-all effectiveness of diagnostic and treatment procedures that are aimed at differentiating visual or auditory strengths among groups of disabled readers. Either the diagnostic instruments are not identifying groups of children along dimensions critical for differentially effective treatments, or else the treatments themselves are not sensitive enough to the particular characteristics of the different groups of readers identified by the diagnostic tests.

Setting and Structure of the Remedial Situation. The individualized, one-to-one, or small group situation in which most remedial work is carried on may in itself have highly beneficial effects on the child's academic success. Most school systems simply cannot afford the professional personnel required in an individually based program. Small groups, however, may be a feasible alternative.

An experiment comparing reading instruction in small groups (fifteen children) to reading instruction in large groups (thirty children) showed a significant difference for boys between the two groups, favoring the smaller group, after one year of reading instruction (Balow, 1969).[d] A number of other studies have looked at the effects of classroom size and staff/pupil ratios on academic achievement, and their findings are conflicting (Lovell et al., 1962; White et al., 1973; Coleman, 1966). Summers and Wolfe (1975) suggest that small groups may be relevant to academic achievement for low-achievers, but not for high-achievers.

A study by Sabatino (1971) examined the reading gains in relation to the intensity of the remedial effort: resource room five hours per week, resource room one hour per week, and self-contained special classroom for the whole year. A small control group was included consisting of learning-disabled children who were placed in a regular classroom with no outside remedial work.

The author found that the learning-disabled children in both the resource room settings and in the self-contained classroom made significant pre- to post-test gains in word recognition and reading comprehension as compared to control subjects. The children who spent an hour a day in the resource room made greater gains than did the children who frequented the setting only twice a week for half an hour, and the children in the self-contained special classroom made the greatest gains in reading comprehension.

Another approach has been the use of nonprofessional tutors working in a one-to-one situation with reading-disabled children. One program involving the training and supervision of volunteer reading tutors of all ages has reported positive results in tutee attainment of specific criterion objectives (Ryle and Robbin, 1974).

A study by Cloward (1967) examined the effects on both tutors and tutees of a tutorial program using tenth and twelfth graders to tutor fourth and fifth graders with reading problems. The investigator compared the reading gains of the younger children under three conditions: no tutoring, tutoring twice a week for a total of four hours, and tutoring once a week for a total of two hours. After five months of treatment, Cloward found a significant difference in achievement between four hours of tutoring per week and no tutoring at all. Two hours of tutoring was not reported to produce a significant difference.

One dramatic and unanticipated finding of this study was the result obtained for the tutors. After seven months of instructing elementary disabled readers, the high-school tutors gained twice as many achievement points in reading as did the controls (students who had also

[d]Other studies have suggested that the effects of remedial training are different for boys than for girls. The effects are usually more pronounced for boys (Cloward, 1967; Halliwell and Solan, 1972).

volunteered to tutor). Both experimental and control tutors had been reading below average, so that the experience of tutoring represents a type of effective remedial program for these adolescents as well.

The use of nonprofessional or cross-age tutors does not imply the abolishment of remedial specialists. Rather, it allows for a better distribution of specialized services. The reading specialist can work with children whose problems are most severe, or whose problems require specialized help such as speech therapy, while the nonprofessional tutors can work with children whose reading problems are less serious. One of the potential benefits of using cross-age tutors is that the younger child has a role model, an older child who, through his or her tutoring, gives an example of appropriate school behavior for the child. And the older child's self-esteem is enhanced through his or her role as tutor.

The data on small group settings and individualized tutoring suggest that they may lead to greater gains in reading achievement. Furthermore, too few hours of tutoring may be of no benefit.

Compensatory Education Programs

Concern for the persisting problems of the poor and the minorities has given rise to programs mounted on a broad scale whose goals go far beyond the remedying of a specific problem (e.g., reading failure). The goals of compensatory education include the upgrading of all areas of academic performance as well as improving attitudes of the children toward themselves and their schools.

White et al. (1973) conducted an extensive review of the evaluations of federally funded programs for children and found that in early elementary educational programs there were limited and isolated instances of success:

1. Programs that are characterized by an "amplification of traditional classroom services" resulted in little or no success in improving academic achievement in specific content areas (usually reading and math). Most of the projects funded under Title I of the Elementary and Secondary Education Act (ESEA) fall into this category of educational programs. Teachers' ratings on reading proficiency for a representative sample of participants and nonparticipants in Title I programs indicated a somewhat greater improvement for participants than for nonparticipants. But Wargo et al. (1972) found that both participants and controls in Title I programs in general fell further behind the national norms in the area of reading, although the sample on which they report is not representative.

2. Programs that fall into the category "reorganization of class-

room processes" tend to be more successful in the short term than those that merely extend traditional services. The programs reviewed in this category include instructional television, computer-assisted instruction, behavior modification programs, implementation of new curricula in specific content areas, and over-all classroom reorganization (White et al., 1973). The Follow Through model programs can also be included in this category. The authors found that these programs are often characterized by a high degree of structure and clearly specified behavioral objectives.

In her analysis of the Planned Variation programs in Head Start and Follow Through, Bissell (1973, p. 105) also noted that the programs that had "specific objectives and well-formulated strategies to achieve these objectives" were the most successful in improving achievement in the targeted skill areas. Similarly, the literature on preschool program evaluations shows that the more highly structured and more teacher-directed approaches seem to result in greater (and in some cases, more long-lasting) gains in achievement than the approaches lacking these characteristics (Bissell, 1970; Bereiter and Engelman, 1966; Karnes, 1968).

3. Programs that fall along the dimension of "organizational change" show mixed results. These programs are characterized by "changes in the configuration of traditional schooling which occur outside the classroom" (White et al., 1973, p.57), and include community involvement in planning and administration, parent involvement in the educational process outside the school, performance contracting, and busing. Most noteworthy for positive effects are programs that train parents to teach specific skills to their children. The benefits of directly engaging parents in the education of their children has also been noted in a review of early intervention programs (Bronfenbrenner, 1974).

DISCUSSION AND RECOMMENDATIONS

In reviewing the literature on various treatment programs, we can come up with no treatment that is broadly effective. There is no panacea. It is also not possible to say one treatment is always better than another. Academic performance is improved for certain children after some kind of treatment, but inadequate description of the salient characteristics of both child and therapy make it difficult to understand scientifically what has happened and why.

This does not suggest that we should abandon all efforts to treat reading-disabled children. Given the number of reports of real improvement, it is clear that in many cases reading disability can be cured and efforts to cure should continue. But if we are ever to gain systematic knowledge of the treatment of reading disabilities, we believe the following points must be kept in mind:

1. Inadequate research methodology is the single greatest short-coming in the field of reading failure, rendering results from many studies uninterpretable. Certain requirements should be established by those granting funds and those publishing research:

Definition of Terms. The term "reading disabled" has been applied to a widely heterogeneous population. Populations must be clearly defined in terms of their reading problems. Tests and methods used to identify the samples must be clearly delineated. Ideally, a uniform terminology should be developed so that similarities and differences from one sample to the next become readily apparent. Generalizations from the results must be limited to the appropriate population instead of being broadly (and incorrectly) applied to all children with reading problems.

Control for Confounding Variables. Greater attention must be paid to the many possible confounding variables such as IQ, age, race, neurologic abnormalities, and other background factors like cultural subgroup and family attitudes. Selection of samples should control for as many of these variables as possible.

Description of Treatment. Reading programs used for all experimental groups, both treatment and control, should be explicitly described in terms of their goals and methods so that successful programs can be duplicated elsewhere and comparisons among studies facilitated.

Inclusion of "Placebo" Controls. In addition to no-treatment controls there should also be a placebo control group which receives special attention equal to the experimental group, but of nonspecific content.

Data Analysis. Instead of treating each variable in isolation, multivariate analyses of the data may be more useful. It appears likely that certain constitutional variables in interaction with certain environmental difficulties are more apt to explain the symptoms of reading difficulties. Similarly, the success or failure of certain treatments may depend on the interaction of the treatment with certain individual characteristics.

Follow-up. Follow-up assessments should be conducted in order to determine the long-term as well as the short-term effects of the treatment.

2. Further search for a cure-all effective for all children does not seem a fruitful course to follow. It must be recognized that there are

different subgroups for whom different treatments are likely to be effective. Some treatments which look useless may only have been applied to the wrong children.

3. Some therapeutic programs may fail because they have not been applied intensively enough, or for a long enough period of time. Children who receive too few hours of tutoring per week appear to show no improvement. Programs that run for six months or a year do not seem to have any long-lasting effects, even where significant improvements are noted at first. Children may continue to need help until after they have maintained their achievement for a longer period. How much treatment for how long needs to be determined. There is little point in treating many children if this means that none get enough time to benefit.

4. There is a great deal of data suggesting that multidisciplinary interventions may be necessary: drugs and family counseling, psychotherapy and remedial reading, for example. Some treatments may have failed because they addressed only part of the problem, or because they have interpreted the problem using the conceptual apparatus of only one profession.

5. The significance of the child's home environment is commonly ignored. It has been hypothesized that only by changing aspects of the enduring environment, i.e., the child's family and the community, can significant changes occur in specific behaviors such as educational achievement (Bronfenbrenner, 1974). Inclusion of parents in the remedial process has been successful in a number of cases. When parents are actively involved in their children's education, they also become more committed to certain educational values and thus help to motivate their children. Research is needed to identify the ways in which a family or even a community can support the children's reading achievement.

6. The special, often individualized, attention that characterizes most remedial approaches may be a necessary though not sufficient component of a successful intervention. This attention may not need to be specialized or given by a specially trained professional. The implications for planning are significant: nonprofessional personnel, even other students, may be able to provide at least in part some of the focused attention that the disabled reader needs, whether it be for improving his reading skills, bolstering his self-image, or stimulating his interest and motivation.

7. In a regular classroom setting, where the teacher must instruct a large group of students in many subject areas, it is difficult to attain the degree of specificity of goals and methods commonly found in experimental programs. A clear, explicit statement of program goals

and methods and a focused approach may not only be necessary for good research design, but also for successful classroom outcomes. Ongoing supervision and assessment should take place to ensure that the program is being implemented properly and that the child is attaining the goals as set forth in the program. The child may require an ombudsman to see that what is supposed to happen is really happening and to be sure there are no glaring omissions.

8. Innovative programs should be allowed to run long enough to receive a fair trial. It has been shown that the most successful reading programs become so only after two or three years (Weber, 1971). An extended trial does not preclude evaluative research while the program is ongoing. The results can be used not to decree success or failure of the program, but rather to provide feedback with which to introduce useful modifications.

9. There is a need for a prospective long-term project to study what happens in adult life to children of varying social classes with various levels of childhood reading achievement. Is it the case, for instance, that after acquiring a reading skill at the sixth-grade level, further gains do not predict significantly to outcomes in adulthood? What is the role of reading instruction in breaking or perpetuating socioeconomic inequalities in adulthood, or inequalities in access to knowledge?

10. Effectiveness evaluation should be part of any program, not just part of formal research projects. It makes little sense for parents, communities, or school systems to spend large sums of money on treatment and on professional services without assessment of whether these services are effective.

11. The majority of children who continue to fail in reading are from poor and nonwhite minority families. With these children, reading failure is more likely to be the symptom of a problem than the problem itself. We feel that the difficulties facing these children must be countered on every front—primary health care, community mental health, housing, and education. Those school-related changes should be implemented which have shown promise in improving the academic achievement, such as the inclusion of parents, a carefully planned and structured curriculum, and the use of one-to-one tutoring. But larger socioeconomic adversity should not be dismissed as the core issue needing to be addressed.

REFERENCES

Ackerman, N., and Lakas, N. "The treatment of a child and family," in *Emotional Disturbance and School Learning: A Book of Readings*, edited by D. Clark and G. Lesser. Chicago: Science Research Associates, 1965.

Anastasi, A. "Intelligence and family size," *Psychol Bull* 53 (1956): 187.

Anderson, W.F., and Stern, D. "The relative effects of the Frostig program, corrective reading instruction, and attention upon the reading skills of corrective readers with perceptual deficiencies," *J School Psychol* 10 (1972): 387–95.

Arthur, G. "Therapy with retarded readers," *J Consult Psychol* 4 (1940): 173–76.

Arthur, G. *Leiter International Performance Scale.* Chicago: C.H. Stoelting, 1952.

Axelrod, S. "Token reinforcement programs in special classes," *Except Child* 37 (1971): 371–79.

Balow, B. "Perceptual-motor activities in the treatment of severe reading disability," *Reading Teacher* 24 (1971): 513–25.

Balow, I.H. "A longitudinal evaluation of reading achievement in small classes," *Elementary English* 46 (1969): 184–87.

Bannatyne, A. *Language, Reading and Learning Disabilities.* Springfield, Ill.: Charles C. Thomas, 1971.

Barker, R.G., and Gump, P.V. *Big School, Small School.* Stanford, Calif.: Stanford University Press, 1964.

Bateman, B. "The role of individual diagnosis in remedial planning for reading disorders," in *Reading Forum*, edited by E.O. Calkins. Bethesda, Md.: National Institute of Health and National Institute of Neurological Diseases and Stroke, 1971.

Beery, K., and Buktenica, N. *Developmental Test of Visual-Motor Integration.* Chicago: Follett Publishing Company, 1967.

Bells, R.E. "Nondirective play therapy with retarded readers," *J Consult Psychol* 14 (1950): 140–49.

Belmont, I., Flegenheimer, H., and Birch, H. "Comparison of perceptual training and remedial instruction for poor beginning readers," *J Learn Disabil* 6 (1973): 230–35.

Bender, L. *Bender-Gestalt Test.* New York: Grune and Stratton, Inc., 1951.

Benton, A.L. *The Revised Visual Retention Test, 3rd Edition.* New York: Psychological Corporation, 1963.

Bereiter, C., and Engelmann, S. *The Effectiveness of Direct Verbal Instruction on IQ Performance and Achievement in Reading and Arithmetic.* Champaign, Ill.: Academic Preschool, 1966.

Birch, H.G., and Belmont, L. "Audio-visual integration in normal and retarded readers," *Am J Orthopsychiatry* 34 (1964): 852–61.

Bissell, J.S. *The Cognitive Effects of Pre-school Programs for Disadvantaged Children.* Unpublished thesis. Cambridge, Mass.: Harvard Graduate School of Education, 1970.

Bissell, J.S. "Planned variation in Head Start and Follow Through," in *Education for Children Ages Two to Eight: Recent Studies of Educational Intervention*, edited by J.C. Stanley. Baltimore, Md.: Johns Hopkins University Press, 1973.

Black, F. "Neurological dysfunction and reading disorders," *J Learn Disabil* 6 (1973): 313–16.

Blanchard, P. "Psychogenic factors in some cases of reading disability," *Am J Orthopsychiatry* 5 (1935): 361–74.

Blanchard, P. "Reading disabilities in relation to difficulties of personality and emotional development," *Mental Hygiene* 20 (1936): 384–413.

Blanchard, P. "Psychoanalytic contributions to the problems of learning disabilities," *Psychoanal Study Child* 2 (1946): 163.

Blank, M., and Bridger, W.H. "Deficiencies in verbal labelling in retarded readers," *Am J Orthopsychiatry* 36 (1966): 840–47.

Boston Globe, March 21, 1975.

Bradley, C. "The behavior of children receiving Benzedrine," *Am J Psychiatry* 94 (1937): 577–85.

Bradley, C. "Benzedrine and Dexedrine in the treatment of children's behavior disorders," *Pediatrics* 5 (1950): 24–37.

Bronfenbrenner, U. *A Report on Longitudinal Evaluations of Preschool Programs: Is Early Intervention Effective?* Vol. 2. Washington, D.C.: U.S. Department of Health, Education and Welfare, 1974.

Bronner, A.F. *The Psychology of Special Abilities and Disabilities.* Boston: Little, Brown and Company, 1917.

Bruininks, R. "Auditory and visual perceptual skills related to the reading performance of disadvantaged boys," *Percept Mot Skills* 29 (1969): 179–86.

Bryan, T., and McGrady, H. "Use of a teacher rating scale," *J Learn Disabil* 5 (1972): 199–206.

Buerger, T.A. "A follow-up of remedial reading instruction," *Reading Teacher* 21 (1968): 329–34.

Buros, O.K., ed. *The Seventh Mental Measurements Yearbook.* Vol. II. Highland Park, N.J.: The Gryphon Press, 1972.

Butler, N., Peckham, C., and Sheridan, M. "Speech defects in children aged 7 years: a national study," *Br Med J* 1 (1973): 253–57.

Campbell, W.D., and Camp, B.W. "Developmental screening," in *Pediatric Screening Tests*, edited by W.K. Frankenburg and B.W. Camp. Springfield, Ill.: Charles C. Thomas, 1975.

Cashdan, A., and Pumfrey, P.D. "Some effects of the remedial teaching on reading," *Educ Res* 11 (1969): 138–42.

Chall, J., Roswell, F., and Blumenthal, S.H. "Auditory blending ability: a factor in success in beginning reading," *Reading Teacher* 17 (1963): 113–18.

Children's Defense Fund. *Children Out of School in America.* Washington, D.C.: Children's Defense Fund of the Washington Research Project, Inc., 1974.

Clark, M.M. *Reading Difficulties in Schools: A Community Study of Specific Reading Difficulties.* Harmondsworth, England: Penguin Books, 1970.

Clements, S.D., and Peters, J.E. "Minimal brain dysfunctions in the school age child," *Arch Gen Psychiatry* 6 (1962): 185.

Cloward, R. "Studies in tutoring," *J Experimental Educ* 36 (1967): 14–25.

Cohen, N., Douglas, V., and Morgenstern, G. "The effect of methylphenidate on attentive behavior and autonomic activity in hyperactive children," *Psychopharmacologia* 22 (1971): 282–94.

Cole, S.D. "Hyperkinetic children: the use of stimulant drugs evaluated," *Am J Orthopsychiatry* 45 (1975): 28–37.

Coleman, J.S. *Equality of Educational Opportunity.* Report OE–38001, U.S. Office of Education. Washington, D.C.: National Center for Education Statistics, 1966.

Comly, H. "Cerebral stimulants for children with learning disorders," *J Learn Disabil* 4 (1971): 484-90.

Committee on Children with Handicaps. *Rapid Developmental Screening Check List.* Evanston, Ill.: American Academy of Pediatrics, 1972.

Committee on Drugs. "Use of d-amphetamine and related central nervous system stimulants in children," *Pediatrics* 51 (1973): 302-05.

Committee on the Handicapped Child. "Doman-Delacato treatment of neurologically handicapped children," Statement of the Committee. Newsletter Supplement, June 1, 1968.

Conners, C.K. "Recent drug studies with hyperkinetic children," *J Learn Disabil* 4 (1971): 476.

Conners, C.K. "Stimulant drugs and cortical-evoked responses in learning and behavior disorders in children," in *Drugs, Development, and Cerebral Function*, edited by W.L. Smith. Springfield, Ill.: Charles C. Thomas, 1972.

Conners, C.K., Eisenberg, L., and Barcai, A. "Effect of dextroamphetamine in children," *Arch Gen Psychiatry* 17 (1967): 478-85.

Conners, C.K., Eisenberg, L., and Sharpe, L. "Effects of methylphenidate (ritalin) on paired-associate learning and Porteus maze performance in emotionally-disturbed children," *J Consult Clin Psychol* 28 (1964): 14-22.

Conners, C.K., Eisenberg, L., and Sharpe, L. "Dextroamphetamine sulfate in children with learning disorders: effects on perception, learning and achievement," *Arch Gen Psychiatry* 21 (1969): 182-90.

Connolly, C. "Social and emotional factors in learning disabilities," in *Progress in Learning Disabilities*, Vol. 2, edited by H. Myklebust. New York: Grune and Stratton, 1971.

Conrad, W.G., Dworkin, E.S., Shai, A., and Tobiessen, J.E. "Effects of amphetamine therapy and prescriptive tutoring on the behavior and achievement of lower class hyperactive children," *J Learn Disabil* 4 (1971): 509-17.

Council on Child Health. *Early Identification of Children with Learning Disabilities: The Preschool Child.* Statement of the American Academy of Pediatrics. Evanston, Ill.: American Academy of Pediatrics, 1973.

Critchley, E.M.R. "Reading retardation, dyslexia and delinquency," *Br J Psychiatry* 115 (1968): 1537-47.

Davis, W.Q. *A Study of Test Score Comparability Among Five Widely Used Reading Survey Tests.* Unpublished doctoral dissertation. Carbondale, Ill.: Southern Illinois University, 1968.

Delacato, C.H. *The Treatment and Prevention of Reading Problems: The Neuropsychological Approach.* Springfield, Ill.: Charles C. Thomas, 1959.

Della-Piana, G., Stahmann, R.F., and Allen, J.E. *Influence of Parental Attitudes and Child-Parent Interaction upon Remedial Reading Programs.* Co-op research project S-266. Washington, D.C.: U.S. Department of Health, Education and Welfare, 1966.

DeLong, A. "What have we learned from psychiatric drug research on hyperactives?" *Am J Dis Child* 123 (1972): 177-80.

Denhoff, E., Davids, A., and Hawkins, R. "Effects of dextroamphetamine on hyperkinetic children: a controlled double blind study," *J Learn Disabil* 4 (1971): 491-98.

Dennis, W. "Causes of retardation among institutional children: Iran," *J Genet Psychol* 96 (1960): 47−59.

Deutsch, M. "Role of social class in language development and cognition," *Percept Mot Skills* 27 (1968): 459−68.

Deutsch, M., and Brown, B. "Social influences in Negro-white intelligence differences," *J Social Issues* 20 (1964): 24−35.

Doll, E. *Vineland Social Maturity Scale.* Circle Pines, Minn.: American Guidance Service, 1965.

Dunn, L. *Peabody Picture Vocabulary Test.* Circle Pines, Minn.: American Guidance Service, 1970.

Eisenberg, L. "Reading retardation: I. Psychiatric and sociologic aspects," *Pediatrics* 37 (1966): 352−65.

Feldes, L.G. "A psychological inquiry into the condition known as congenital world-blindness," *Brain* 44 (1921): 286−307.

Ferinden, W.E., and Jacobson, S. "Early identification of learning disabilities," *J Learn Disabil* 3 (1970): 589−93.

Fine, M., Nesbitt, J., and Tyler, M. "Analysis of a failing attempt at behavior modification," *J Learn Disabil* 7 (1974): 70−75.

Fisher, H., and Logmann, J. *Fisher Logmann Test of Articultory Competance.* Boston: Houghton-Mifflin, 1971.

Frankenburg, W.K. "Criteria in screening test selection," in *Pediatric Screening Tests*, edited by W.K. Frankenburg and B.W. Camp. Springfield, Ill.: Charles C. Thomas, 1975.

Frankenburg, W.K., and Dodds, J.B. "The Denver developmental screening test," *Pediatrics* 71 (1967): 181.

Freed, H. *The Chemistry and Therapy of Behavior Disorders of Children.* Springfield, Ill.: Charles C. Thomas, 1962.

Freedman, D.X., chairman. "Report of the conference on the use of stimulant drugs in the treatment of behaviorally disturbed young school children," *J Learn Disabil* 4 (1971): 523.

Freeman, R.D. "Drug effects on learning in children: a selective review of the last thirty years," *J Special Educ* 1 (1966): 17−44.

Frostig, M. *Developmental Test of Visual Perception.* Palo Alto, Calif.: Consulting Psychologists Press, 1964.

Frostig, M., and Horne, D. *The Frostig Program for the Development of Visual Perception: Teacher's Guide.* Chicago: Follett, 1964.

Frostig, M., Lefever, D.W., and Whittlesey, J. "A developmental test of visual perception for evaluating normal and neurologically handicapped children," *Percept Mot Skills* 12 (1962): 383−94.

Galefret-Granjon, N., and deAjuriaguerra, J. "Trouble de l'apprentissage de la lecture et dominance latérale," *Encéphale* 3 (1951): 385−98.

Gates, A.J., and MacGinitie, W.H. *Gates-MacGinitie Reading Tests.* New York: Teachers College Press, 1965.

Geschwind, N. "The anatomy of acquired disorders of reading," in *Reading Disability*, edited by J. Money. Baltimore: Johns Hopkins University Press, 1962.

Geschwind, N. "Neurological foundations of language," in *Progress in Learning Disabilities*, Vol. 1, edited by H. Myklebust. New York: Grune and Stratton, 1967.

Goetzinger, C.P., Derks, D.D., and Baer, C.J. "Auditory discrimination and visual perception in good and poor readers," *Ann Otol Rhinol Laryngol* 69 (1960): 121–36.

Goins, J.T. *Visual Perceptual Abilities and Early Reading Progress*, Supplementary Educational Monograph No. 87. Chicago: University of Chicago Press, 1958.

Goodenough, F.L. *Measurement of Intelligence by Drawings*. Yonkers-on-Hudson, N.Y.: World Book Company, 1926.

Goodman, L., and Wiederholt, J. "Predicting reading achievement in disadvantaged children," *Psychol in Schools* 10 (1973): 181–85.

Graham, F., and Kendall, B. *Memory for Designs Test*. Missoula, Mont.: Psychological Test Specialists, 1960.

Griffin, M. "The role of child psychiatry in learning disabilities," in *Progress in Learning Disabilities*, Vol. 1, edited by H. Myklebust. New York: Grune and Stratton, 1967.

Grinspoon, L., and Singer, S.B. "Amphetamines in the treatment of hyperkinetic children," *Harv Educ Rev* 4 (1973): 515–55.

A Guide to Screening for the Early and Periodic Screening, Diagnosis and Treatment Program (EPSDT) under Medicaid. Prepared by the American Academy of Pediatrics. Washington, D.C.: U.S. Department of Health, Education and Welfare, 1974.

Haggerty, R., et al. *Child Health in the Community*. New York: John Wiley and Sons, 1975.

Hainsworth, P., and Siqueland, M. *Early Identification of Children with Learning Disabilities: The Meeting Street School Screening Test*. Providence, R.I.: Crippled Children and Adults of Rhode Island, 1969.

Hallahan, D.P., and Cruickshank, W.M. *Psychoeducational Foundations of Learning Disabilities*. Englewood Cliffs, N.J.: Prentice-Hall, Inc., 1973.

Halliwell, J.W., and Solan, H.A. "The effects of a supplemental perceptual training program on reading achievement," *Except Child* 38 (1972): 613–21.

Hallgren, B. "Specific dyslexia," *Acta Psychiat Neurol Suppl* 65 (1950): 1–287.

Hammill, D. "Training visual perceptual processes," *J Learn Disabil* 5 (1972): 552–59.

Hammill, D., and Larsen, S. "The relationship of selected auditory perceptual skills and reading disability," *J Learn Disabil* 7 (1974): 429–35.

Hammill, D., Larsen, S., Parker, R., Bagley, M.T., and Sanford, H.G. *Perceptual and Conceptual Correlates of Reading*. Unpublished manuscript. Austin, Texas, 1974.

Harmon, L. "High school backgrounds of science doctorates," *Science* 133 (1961): 679–88.

Harrington, M., and Durrell, D. "Mental maturity versus perception abilities in primary reading," *J Educ Psychol* 46 (1955): 375–80.

Harris, D.B. *Children's Drawings as Measures of Intellectual Maturity.* New York: Harcourt, Brace and World, 1963.

Hartlage, L., and Green, J. "The EEG as a predictor of intellective and academic performance," *J Learn Disabil* 6 (1973): 239–42.

Hellman, I. "Some observations on mothers of children with intellectual inhibitions," *Psychoanal Study Child* 9 (1954): 259.

Hess, R., and Shipman, V. "Early experience and the socialization of cognition modes in children," *Child Dev* 36 (1965): 869–86.

Hildreth, G.H., and Griffiths, N.L. *Metropolitan Readiness Tests.* New York: World Book Company, 1949.

Hobbs, N. *The Futures of Children.* San Francisco: Jossey Bass Publishers, 1975.

Hoepfner, R., et al., eds. *CSE Elementary School Test Evaluations.* Los Angeles: Center for the Study of Evaluation, UCLA Graduate School of Education, 1970.

Hurwitz, I., Wolff, P., Bortnick, B., and Kokas, K. "Nonmusical effects of the Kodaly music curriculum in primary grade children," *J Learn Disabil* 8 (1975): 167–74.

Ilg, F.L., and Ames, L.B. *School Readiness.* New York: Harper and Row, 1965.

Ingram, T. "The association of speech retardation and educational difficulties," *Proc R Soc Med* 56 (1963): 199–203.

Ingram, T., and Reed, J.F. "Developmental aphasia observed in a department of child psychiatry," *Arch Dis Child* 31 (1956): 161–72.

Jacob, T. "Family interaction in disturbed and normal families: a review," *Psychol Bull* 82 (1975): 33–65.

Jansky, J., and deHirsch, K. *Preventing Reading Failure.* New York: Harper and Row, 1972.

Jastak, J.F., and Jastak, S.R. *The Wide Range Achievement Test,* revised edition. Wilmington, Del.: Guidance Associates of Delaware, 1965.

John, V. "The intellectual development of slum children: some preliminary findings," *Am J Orthopsychiatry* 33 (1963): 813–22.

Kahn, D., and Birch, H. "Development of auditory-visual integration and reading achievement," *Percept Mot Skills* 27 (1968): 459–68.

Kaplan, E., et al. *Boston Picture Naming Test,* unpublished, Boston Veterans Administration Hospital, Boston, Mass., 1976.

Karnes, M.B. *A Longitudinal Study of Disadvantaged Children who Participated in Three Different Preschool Programs.* Urbana, Ill.: Institute for Research on Exceptional Children, 1968.

Karnes, M. *Research and Development Program on Preschool Disadvantaged Children: Final Report.* Washington, D.C.: U.S. Office of Education, 1969.

Karp, S., and Konstadt, N. *Children's Embedded Figures Test.* Palo Alto, Calif.: Consulting Psychologists Press, Inc., 1963.

Kearsley, R.B., in *Yearbook of Pediatrics,* edited by S. Gelles. Chicago, Ill.: Yearbook Medical Publishers, 1975.

Kephart, N.C. *The Slow Learner in the Classroom.* Columbus, Ohio: Charles E. Merrill, 1960.

Kirk, S., and Kirk, W. *Psycholinguistic Learning Disabilities, Diagnosis and Remediation.* Urbana, Ill.: University of Illinois Press, 1971.

Kirk, S.A., et al. *The Illinois Test of Psycholinguistic Abilities*, revised edition. Urbana, Ill.: Illinois University Press, 1968.

Knights, R., and Hinton, G. "The effects of methylphenidate on the motor skills and behavior of children with learning problems," *J Nerv Ment Dis* 148 (1969): 643−53.

Knobloch, H., et al. "Do mothers' answers to a questionnaire adequately evaluate the development of infants?" mimeographed paper, 1973, cited in *The Futures of Children*, by N. Hobbs. San Francisco: Jossey-Bass Publishers, 1975.

Koppitz, E.M., Sullivan, J., Blyth, D.D., and Shelton, J. "Prediction of first-grade school achievement with the Bender Gestalt test and human figure drawing," *J Clin Psychol* 15 (1959): 164−68.

Koven, J.T., and LeBow, M.D. "Teaching parents to remediate the academic problems of their children," *J Experimental Educ* 41 (1973): 64−73.

Labov, W. "Language characteristics, blacks," in *Reading for Disadvantaged*, edited by T.D. Horn. New York: Harcourt, Brace and World, 1970.

Lachman, F.M. "Perceptual-motor development in children retarded in reading ability," *J Consult Psychology* 24 (1960): 427−31.

Larsen, S., and Hamill, D. "The relationship of selected visual perceptual abilities to school learning," *J Spec Educ* 9 (1975): 281−91.

Lasagna, L., and Epstein, L. "The use of amphetamines in the treatment of hyperkinetic children," in *Amphetamines and Related Compounds*, edited by E. Costa and S. Garattini. New York: Raven Press, 1970.

Laufer, M.W. "Long-term management and some follow-up findings on the use of drugs with minimal cerebral syndromes," *J Learn Disabil* 4 (1971): 518−22.

Lawrence, D. "The effects of counselling on retarded readers," *Educ Res* 13 (1971): 119−24.

Leighton, A. "Poverty and social change," *Sci Am* 212 (1965): 21−27.

Lerner, J. *Children with Learning Disabilities.* Boston: Houghton Mifflin Company, 1971.

Levenstein, P. "Cognitive growth in preschoolers through verbal interaction with mothers," *Am J Orthopsychiatry* 40 (1970): 426−32.

Lipton, A., and Feiner, A.H. "Group therapy and remedial reading," *J Educ Psychol* 47 (1956): 330−34.

Lorge, I., et al. *Lorge-Thorndike Intelligence Tests.* Boston, Mass.: Houghton-Mifflin, 1966.

Lovell, K., Johnson, E., and Platts, D. "A summary of the reading ages of children who have been given remedial teaching," *Br J Educ Psychol* 32 (1962): 66−71.

Lyman, H.B. *Test Scores and What They Mean.* Englewood Cliffs, N.J.: Prentice-Hall, Inc., 1963.

McClelland, D.C. "Achievement motivation can be developed," *Harv. Bus Rev.* 43 (1965): 6.

McGinnies, E. "Emotionality and perceptual defense," in *Experiments in*

Visual Perception: Selected Readings, edited by M. Vernon. Baltimore, Md.: Penguin, 1966, pp. 376–85.

McLaulin, J.C., and Schiffman, G.B. "A study of the relationship between the California Test of Mental Maturity and the WISC test for retarded readers," cited in *Reading Disability*, edited by J. Money. Baltimore: Johns Hopkins University Press, 1962, p. 50.

McLeod, J. *Dyslexia Schedule.* Cambridge, Mass.: Educators Publishing Service, 1968.

Malmquist, E. *Factors Related to Reading Disabilities in the First Grade of the Elementary School.* Stockholm: Almquist and Wiksell, 1958.

Margolin, J.B., Roman, H., and Harari, C. "Reading disability in the delinquent child: a microcosm of psycho-social pathology," *Am J Orthopsychiatry* 25 (1955): 25–35.

Mattis, S., French, J.H., and Rapin, I. "Dyslexia in children and young adults: three independent neuropsychological syndromes," *Devel Med Child Neurol* 17 (1975): 150–63.

Mendelson, W., Johnson, N., and Stewart, M.A. "Hyperactive children as teenagers: a follow-up study," *J Nerv Mental Dis* 153 (1971): 273–79.

Miller, D., and Westman, J. "Reading disability as a condition of family stability," *Fam Process* 3 (1964): 66–76.

Minuchin, S. *Families and Family Therapy.* Cambridge, Mass.: Harvard University Press, 1974.

Missildine, W.H. "The emotional background of thirty children with reading disabilities with emphasis on its coercive elements," *Nerv Child* 5 (1946): 263–72.

Milner, E. "A study of the relationship between reading readiness in grade one school children and patterns of parent-child interaction," *Child Devel* 22 (1951): 95–112.

Moore, M., and Welcher, D.W. "A descriptive analysis of the seven-year psychological data," *Johns Hopkins Med J* 128 (1971): 332.

Morgan, E.F. "Efficacy of two tests differentiating potentially low from average and high first grade readers," *J Educ Res* 53 (1960): 300–04.

Morris, J.M. *Standards and Progress in Reading.* London: National Foundation for Educational Research in England and Wales, 1966.

Muehl, S., and Forell, E.R. "A follow-up study of disabled readers: variables related to high school reading performance," *Reading Res Q* 9 (1973–74): 110.

Myers, P., and Hammill, D. *Methods for Learning Disorders.* New York: John Wiley and Sons, 1969.

Myklebust, H. *Development and Disorders of Written Language*, Vol. 2. New York: Grune and Stratton, 1973.

Myklebust, H., ed. *Progress in Learning Disabilities*, Vol. 1. New York: Grune and Stratton, 1967.

Myklebust, H., ed. *Progress in Learning Disabilities*, Vol. 2. New York: Grune and Stratton, 1971.

Myklebust, H., and Boshes, B. *Minimal Brain Damage in Children: Final Report.* U.S. Public Health Contract 108–65–142. Evanston, Ill.: Northwestern University Press, 1969.

Nichol, H. "Children with learning disabilities referred to psychiatrists: a follow-up study," *J Learn Disabil* 7 (1974): 118—22.

Nisbet, J. "Family environment and intelligence," *Eugenics Review* 45 (1953): 31—40.

O'Bryan, K., and Silverman, H. "Learning disabilities—directions for research," paper presented at the First Annual International Symposium on Learning Problems, Toronto, 1972. Cited in Wedell, K., *Learning and Perceptive-Motor Disabilities in Children*. London: John Wiley and Sons, 1973.

Oldfield, R., and Wingfield, A. *A Series of Pictures for Use in Object Naming.* Medical Research Council, Psycholinguistics Research Unit, Oxford University Institute of Experimental Psychology, undated.

O'Malley, J.E., and Eisenberg, L. "The hyperkinetic syndrome," in *Minimal Cerebral Dysfunction in Children*, edited by S. Walzer and P.H. Wolff. New York: Grune and Stratton, 1973.

Otis, A., and Lennon, R. *Otis-Lennon Mental Ability Test.* New York: Harcourt, Brace, Jovanovich, 1970.

Page-El, E., and Grossman, H.J. "Neurological appraisal in learning disorders," *Ped Clin North Am* 20 (1973): 599—605.

Pearson, G. "A survey of learning difficulties in children," *Psychoanal Study Child* 7 (1952): 322—86.

Peck, B., and Stackhouse, T. "Reading problems and family dynamics," *J Learn Disabil* 6 (1973): 506—10.

Peters, J.E., Romine, J.S., and Dykman, R.A. "A special neurological examination of children with learning disabilities," *Devel Med Child Neurol* 17 (1975): 63—78.

Pettigrew, T., et al. "Binocular resolution and perception of race in South Africa," in *Experiments in Visual Perception, Selected Readings* edited by M. Vernon. Baltimore, Md.: Penguin, 1966, pp. 347—67.

Pope, L., and Hacklay, A. "A follow-up study of psychoeducational evaluations sent to schools," *J Learn Disabil* 7 (1974): 239—44.

Prechtl, H.F.R., and Stemmer, C.J. "The choreiform syndrome in children," *Devel Med Child Neurol* 4 (1962): 119—27.

Rabinovitch, R. "Dyslexia: psychiatric considerations," in *Reading Disability: Progress and Research Needs in Dyslexia*, edited by J. Money. Baltimore, Md.: Johns Hopkins University Press, 1962.

Raven, J.C. *Coloured Progressive Matrices.* New York: Psychological Corporation, 1962.

Rees, L., et al. "Adrenergic blockade and the cortico-steroid and growth hormone responses to methylamphetamine," *Nature* 228 (1970): 565—66.

Robinson, H.M. "Visual and auditory modalities related to methods for beginning reading," *Reading Rep Quart* 8 (1972): 7—39.

Rosenthal, R. *Pygmalion in the Classroom.* New York: Holt, Rinehart and Winston, 1968.

Roswell, F., and Natchez, G. *Reading Disability: Diagnosis and Treatment.* New York: Basic Books, 1964.

Rutter, M., et al. *Education, Health and Behavior.* New York: John Wiley and Sons, 1970a.

Rutter, M., et al. *A Neuropsychiatric Study in Childhood.* London: Spastics International Medical Publications, 1970b.

Ryback, D., and Staats, A.W. "Parents as behavior therapy technicians," cited in "Treating reading deficits (dyslexia)," *J Behav Ther Exper Psychiatry* 1 (1970): 109–19.

Ryle, A., and Robbin, R. *Evaluation Report of the EdCo Reading and Learning Center 1973–1974.* Cambridge, Mass.: EdCo Reading and Learning Center, 1974.

Sabatino, D.A. "An evaluation of resource rooms for children with learning disabilities," *J Learn Disabil* 4 (1971): 84–93.

Sabatino, D.A., and Streissguth, W.O. "Word form configuration training of visual perceptual strengths with learning disabled children," *J Learn Disabil* 5 (1972): 62–68.

Safer, D., Allen, R., and Barr, E. "Depression of growth in hyperactive children on stimulant drugs," *N Engl J Med* 287 (1972): 217–20.

Safer, D.J., and Allen, R.P. "Factors influencing the suppressant effects of two stimulant drugs on the growth of hyperactive children," *Pediatrics* 51 (1973): 660–67.

Satterfield, J., et al. "Response to stimulant drug treatment in hyperactive children: prediction from EEG and neurological findings," *J Autis Childhood Schiz* 3 (1973): 36–48.

Schiffman, G. "Dyslexia as an educational phenomenon: its recognition and treatment," in *Reading Disability*, edited by J. Money. Baltimore: Johns Hopkins University Press, 1962.

Schneider, A. *Identification, Diagnostic and Remediation Procedures in Selected New Jersey Elementary Schools.* ERIC document, January 1974.

Schwartz, A.H., and Murphy, M.W. "Cues for screening language disorders in preschool children," *Pediatrics* 55 (1975): 717–22.

Seashore, C., et al. *Seashore Measures of Musical Talents.* New York: Psychological Corporation, 1957.

Shearer, E. "Long-term effects of remedial education," *Ed Res* 9 (1967): 219–22.

Silver, L.B. "Acceptable and controversial approaches to treating the child with learning disabilities," *Pediatrics* 55 (1975): 406.

Slater, B.R. "Achievement in grade 3 by children who participated in perceptual training during kindergarten," *Percept Mot Skills* 36 (1973): 763–66.

Sleator, E., von Neumann, A., and Sprague, R.L. "Hyperactive children: a continuous long term placebo controlled follow-up," *JAMA* 229 (1974): 316–17.

Smith, C.M. "The relationship of reading method and reading achievement to ITPA sensory modalities," *J Spec Educ* 5 (1971): 143–49.

Solomons, G. "Guidelines on the use and medical effects of psycho-stimulant drugs in therapy," *J Learn Disabil* 4 (1971): 470–75.

Southern School News. "St. Louis raises levels; central stadium closed," January 1959, p. 12.

Spencer, E. *Spencer Sentence Memory.* Unpublished, Northeastern University, Boston, Mass., 1976.

Sperrazzo, G., and Wilkins, W. "Racial differences on progressive matrices," *J Consult Psychol* 23 (1959): 273–74.

Spivak, G., and Swift, M. "The classroom behavior of children: a critical review of teacher-administered rating scales," *J Spec Educ* 7 (1973): 55–89.

Sprague, R.L., Barnes, K.R., and Werry, J.S. "Methylphenidate and theoredazine: learning, reaction time, activity and classroom behavior in disturbed children," *Am J Orthopsychiatry* 40 (1970): 615–28.

Staver, N. "The child's learning difficulty as related to the emotional problem of the mother," *Am J Orthopsychiatry* 23 (1953): 131–41.

Stewart, R. "Personal maladjustment and reading achievement," *Am J Orthopsychiatry* 20 (1950): 410–17.

Stodolsky, S.S., and Lesser, G. "Learning patterns of the disadvantaged," *Harv Educ Rev* 37 (1967): 546.

Stringer, L.A. "About screening," in *Health Care Screening and Developmental Assessment*, edited by S.P. Hersh and S. Rojcewicz. Washington, D.C.: Government Printing Office, 1974.

Strang, H.R., and Wolf, M.W. "Automated reading instruction in the ghetto," *Child Study J* 1 (1971): 187–201.

Sroufe, L., and Stewart, M. "Treating problem children with stimulant drugs," *N Engl J Med* 289 (1973): 407–13.

Sullivan, J. "The effects of Kephart's percep-motor training on a reading clinic sample," *J Learn Disabil* 5 (1972): 545–51.

Sulzbacher, S.I. "Psychotropic medication with children: evaluation of procedural biases in results of reported studies," *Pediatrics* 51 (1973): 513–17.

Summers, A., and Wolfe, B.L. *Equality of Educational Opportunity Quantified: A Production Function Approach.* Philadelphia: Department of Research Federal Reserve Bank of Philadelphia, 1975.

Sylvester, E., and Kunst, M. "Psychodynamic aspects of the reading problem," *Am J Orthopsychiatry* 13 (1943): 69–76.

Terman, L., and Merrill, M. *Stanford-Binet Intelligence Scale, 3rd Revision.* Boston, Mass.: Houghton-Mifflin, 1964.

Thorpe, H.S., and Werner, E.E. "Developmental screening of preschool children," *Pediatrics* 53 (1974): 362–70.

Towen, B.C.L., and Prechtl, H.F.R. "The neurological examination of the child and minor nervous dysfunction," *Clinics Dev Med* 38 (1970): 371–79.

U.S. Bureau of the Census, 1960 data, reported in "Economic backgrounds," by R.W. MacMillan, in *Reading for the Disadvantaged*, edited by T.D. Horn. New York: Harcourt, Brace and World, 1970.

U.S. Bureau of the Census. *Low Income Population.* Subject reports, final report PC (2)–9A based on 1970 cencus. Washington, D.C.: Government Printing Office, 1971.

Vandervoort, L., and Senf, G. "Audiovisual integration in retarded readers," *J Learn Disabil* 6 (1973): 170–79.

Vogel, S. "Syntactic abilities in normal and dyslexic children," *J Learn Disabil* 7 (1974): 103–09.

Wachs, T., Uzgires, I., Hunt, J. "Cognitive development in infants from different age levels and from different environmental backgrounds: an explanatory investigation," *Merrill-Palmer Q* 17 (1971): 283–317.

Walberg, H., and Marjoribanks, K. "Differential mental abilities and home environment: a canonical analysis," *Develop Psychol* 9 (1973): 363–68.

Wargo, M.J., Tallmadge, G.K., Michaels, D.D., Lipe, D., Morris, J.J. *ESEA Title I: A Reanalysis and Synthesis of Evaluation Data from Fiscal Year 1965 through 1970.* Palo Alto, Calif.: American Institutes from Research, 1972.

Waugh, K.W., and Bush, W.J. *Diagnosing Learning Disorders.* Columbus, Ohio: Charles E. Merrill Co., 1971.

Waugh, R. "On reporting the findings of a diagnostic center," *J Learn Disabil* 3 (1970): 629–34.

Weber, G. *Inner-city Children Can be Taught to Read: Four Successful Schools.* Occasional papers, No. 18. Washington, D.C.: Council for Basic Education, 1971.

Wechsler, D. *Wechsler Intelligence Scale for Children.* New York: Psychological Corporation, 1949.

Wedell, K. *Learning and Perceptuo-Motor Disabilities in Children.* London: John Wiley and Sons, 1973.

Weinberg, W.A., Renick, E.C., Hammerman, M., and Jackoway, M. "An evaluation of a summer remedial program," *Am J Dis Child* 122 (1971): 494.

Weinberg, W., Rutman, J., Sullivan, L., Penick, E., and Dietz, S., "Depression in children referred to educational diagnostic center: diagnosis and treatment. Preliminary report," *J Pediatr* 83 (1973): 1065–72.

Weiss, G., Minde, K.K., Werry, J.S., Douglas, V.I., and Nemeth, E. "Studies on the hyperactive child. VIII. Five-year follow-up," *Arch Gen Psychiatry* 24 (1971): 409.

Wepman, J.M. "Auditory discrimination, speech and reading," *Elementary School Journal* 60 (1960): 325–33.

Wepman, J.M. "Dyslexia: its relationship to language acquisition and concept formation," in *Reading Disability*, edited by J. Money. Baltimore: Johns Hopkins University Press, 1962.

Werner, E.E., Simonian, K., and Smith, R.S. "Reading achievement, language functioning and perceptual-motor development of 10- and 11-year olds," *Percept Mot Skills* 25 (1967): 409–30.

Whimby, A., and Whimby, L.S. *Intelligence Can be Taught.* New York: E.P. Dutton, 1975.

White, S.H., et al. *Federal Programs for Young Children: Review and Recommendations.* Washington, D.C.: Government Printing Office, 1973.

Wolf, M.W., Giles, D.K., and Hall, R.V. "Experiments with token reinforcement in a remedial classroom," *Behav Res Ther* 6 (1968): 51–64.

Wolff, P.H., and Hurwitz, I. "The choreiform syndrome," *Devel Med Child Neurol* 8 (1966): 160.

Wolff, P.H., and Hurwitz, I. "Function implications of the minimal brain damage syndrome," in *Minimal Cerebral Dysfunction*, edited by S. Walzer and P.H. Wolff. New York: Grune and Stratton, 1973.

Yarrow, M.R., Campbell, J.D., and Burton, R.V. "Recollections of childhood: a study of the retrospective method," *Monographs of the Society for Research in Child Development* 35 (1970): No. 138.

Yule, W. "Differential programs of reading backwardness and specific reading retardation," *Br J Educ Psychol* 43 (1973): 244–48.

Zangwill, O.L. *Cerebral Dominance and its Relation to Psychological Function.* Edinburgh: Oliver and Boyd, 1960.

Zangwill, O.L. "Dyslexia in relation to cerebral dominance," in *Reading Disability*, edited by J. Money. Baltimore: Johns Hopkins Press, 1962.

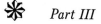 *Part III*

Pediatric Hospitalization

Chapter 12

Efficacy and Effectiveness
of Pediatric Hospitalizations

David S. Mundel, Ph.D.

The next two chapters contain discussions of tonsillectomy, adenoidectomy, and other hospital-based nonprimary care procedures that *may* seem out of place in a
volume on children's primary medical care. This is, however, not the
case; most pediatric hospital admissions are for the same problems
that occupy pediatric primary care providers. As Wennberg and Kimm
indicate, infectious conditions and hypertrophied tonsils account for
55.4 and 53.5 percent of hospital admissions for infants and preschool age children, respectively.[a] For all children less than fifteen
years of age, these conditions account for 47.2 percent of hospital
admissions. Injuries and their adverse effects account for another
14.9 percent of admissions. The infectious diseases most responsible
for pediatric hospital admissions are pneumonias, otitis media, diarrheal disease, and acute bronchitis. These diseases account for approximately 20 percent of all pediatric admissions.

Hospital based nonprimary care procedures need to be considered
in a volume of pediatric primary care because many, if not most,
pediatric hospital admissions result from failures of primary care.
The conditions that result in pediatric admissions could often have
been successfully cared for in a primary care setting if one were available and used; if the primary care practitioner (when used) had correctly recognized the underlying problem, and if recognized, the
problem had been correctly treated and managed. Pediatric hospitalization, even for relatively common and minor procedures, is costly
to the society (in terms of use of scarce medical resources) and to the

---

[a]Based on their studies of Vermont hospitalizations.

patients (in terms of pain, anguish, and in some cases, loss of life). If the primary medical care system were functioning correctly, these costs could be reduced.

These discussions of pediatric hospitalization are also important to our consideration of children's primary care because they reemphasize our lack of knowledge about the effectiveness and efficacy of medical care. As Kimm notes in her review of the clinical studies of tonsillectomy and adenoidectomy procedures, the efficacy of these procedures has never been clearly demonstrated. This uncertainty of medical opinion is confirmed by Wennberg and Kimm's review of the variation in pediatric hospitalization rates across geographic areas. The uncertain efficacy of tonsillectomy, adenoidectomy, and other pediatric hospital procedures leads the two authors to recommend better data collection and more careful and thorough clinical studies of efficacy, a recommendation following those of the authors in earlier chapters. The uncertain efficacy of pediatric hospitalizations also reemphasizes the importance of increasing the effectiveness of the primary care system, in which the treatments for the same problems can be both less costly and less risky.

Chapter 13

Effectiveness of Pediatric Hospitalization: The Case of Tonsillectomy and Adenoidectomy

Sue Y.S. Kimm, M.D., M.P.H.

The combined operations of tonsillectomy and adenoidectomy (T and A) or the single operation of tonsillectomy or adenoidectomy are among the most frequently cited procedures in studies evaluating effectiveness of hospital care. This is because tonsillectomy and adenoidectomy represent a very high proportion of all childhood operations and hospitalizations. Additionally, the efficacy of T and A has never been clearly demonstrated.[a] Perhaps some insights into the nature of the problems associated with assessing effectiveness of hospital care might be obtained by critically reviewing the literature on the controversies surrounding this widely performed and widely questioned surgical procedure. This chapter will focus on the two operations, reviewing basic facts about the anatomy and pathology of tonsils and adenoids (see the appendix), the customary indications for T and A surgery, and summarizing those studies that enable us to estimate effectiveness of surgery in averting serious risks to children's health.

THE NATURE OF THE PROBLEM

Tonsillectomy is a very old procedure whose written record dates back as far as the year A.D. 10 when Celsius spoke with some famil-

[a]Effectiveness in this book is defined as the degree to which the health care system achieves a generally accepted goal. A.L. Cochrane (1972) defines it as "the effect of a particular medical action in altering the natural history of a particular disease for the better." Efficacy, on the other hand, is (in this book) the degree to which diagnostic and therapeutic procedures used in practice can be supported by scientific evidence of their usefulness.

iarity of the operation and described complete removal (Macbeth, 1950). The rise in incidence of tonsillectomy is one of the major phenomena of modern surgery following the development of anesthesia. It is the most frequently performed surgery in the United States and is the most frequent cause of hospitalization of children. In addition to the direct cost incurred in actual consumption of hospital services, there is an enormous indirect cost in terms of postoperative complications such as hemorrhage and other surgical morbidity, significant psychological morbidity, school absenteeism, and deaths.

The following observations were made during a discussion on the incidence of tonsillectomy:

> It appeared from statistics that at the present rates, 25 or 30 out of every 100 children born into all classes of England and Wales would be tonsillectomized before age 14. . . . In the United States, according to one survey, out of every 100 children born, 54% would have been tonsillectomized by their 14th birthday. Twenty years ago about 50,000 tonsillectomies were being performed annually on elementary school children. Had a statistician at that time asked that a large controlled experiment should be arranged by giving and withholding the operation for alternate children and recording their subsequent school medical histories, he would have been met by the usual answer: "If we believe that this treatment is beneficial, then it is unfair to withhold it from one half whilst giving it to the other half. . . . "
> It took a long time to establish or disprove the efficacy of any new form of treatment, even by prearranged statistical studies, *but thirty years was too long to remain in doubt as to the value of a surgical treatment to which a quarter of a population was subjected* (quoted in Glover, 1938).

We may juxtapose these remarks with the transcript of a workshop meeting on T and A:

> A nationwide collaborative, prospective study of the effects of tonsillectomy and adenoidectomy is indicated. This should be conducted at a number of clinical centers in order to achieve suitable geographic and socioeconomic representation and employ a uniform protocol ("Workshop on Tonsillectomy and Adenoidectomy," 1975, hereafter cited as "Workshop").

The first comments were made in London in May 1938. The second were published in May 1975, exactly thirty-seven years later. This may tell us how long it has taken—and may still take—to fill the gap in our knowledge on the efficacy of T and A.

The controversy surrounding the efficacy of T and A has been known since the latter part of the nineteenth century. In 1885, J.F. Goodhart, in a pediatric textbook, said of tonsillar enlargement: "It is comparatively seldom that an operation is necessary, and fortunately so, for patients manifest great repugnance to it. Children grow out of it, and at 14 or 15 years of age the condition ceases to be a disease of any importance" (quoted in Glover, 1938). As an illustration of the magnitude of the controversy, Illingworth et al. (1961) noted that the Quarterly Cumulative Index Medicus in the ten years from 1947 to 1956 listed approximately 1200 papers concerning the tonsil and its removal!

An editorial in the *Journal of the American Medical Association* (Danilevicius, 1975) lamented: "There is hardly any area in which we have more experience and less knowledge than the physiology and pathology of the lymphoid tissue of the throat." And, Hiatt (1975) spoke of "the utilization of precious resources for practices that benefit neither the individual nor society, and that indeed are frequently harmful to both."

Tonsillectomy and adenoidectomy are frequently chosen as classic examples to illustrate these two concepts. First, T and A are currently thought to be of no benefit or of questionable benefit to the majority of recipients of this treatment. Second, T and A consume about $400 million of the "medical commons." Because of this enormous input and a markedly disproportionate output, there is also enormous political interest in the subject of tonsillectomy. This surgery is regarded as a "tracer" model for measuring the incidence of "unnecessary" medical procedures. In addition, when one speaks of the "epidemic" nature of T and A (North, 1968), many physicians suspect accusations of greed against those who hoodwink the public by performing this "useless" procedure. Others feel that this oversimplification may deny surgery to those children for whom T and A would be of definite therapeutic benefit. The whole controversy is further complicated by the current lack of clear-cut scientific evidence regarding the efficacy of the procedure.

Indications for T and A

Tonsils and adenoids have been causally implicated in a variety of childhood ailments for centuries, as evidenced by the long history of tonsillectomy. Therefore, it is not surprising to note that tonsillectomy has at some time been recommended for almost every disease of children and for conditions ranging from mental retardation to bed-wetting.

In discussing indications for operation, Thomas asks: "Can we by scientific test discover the degree of infection or if the tonsil is a septic focus? Extensive reading . . . has convinced me that there is no laboratory test which can help" (1961, p. 397). Nevertheless, the following list, compiled from a literature review, gives some of the indications cited for T and A. They are not carried in order of importance. The first five, however, were the most frequently cited reasons for surgery in a poll on medical practice conducted by the editors and research department of *Modern Medicine* (10 Feb. 1969, p. 77). In this survey, altogether 13,495 physicians responded.

1. Tonsillitis, pharyngitis or upper respiratory infection, chronic or recurrent. The issue here is that both the parents and physicians have problems defining *acceptable* recurrence rates or durations for chronicity. Epidemiologic information on incidence rates of upper respiratory infections in healthy children is often overlooked in defining these terms as reasons for operation.

2. Otitis media, chronic or recurrent. Again, the question of definition of recurrence and chronicity is raised. Additionally, there is a debate on whether or not adenoidectomy alone should be done.

3. Hypertrophy of tonsils or adenoids. Definition of hypertrophy for a specific age is uncertain. If the tonsils are so enlarged that they meet in the midline and the child cannot swallow solid food, there is no controversy. Anything less than this kind of enlargement depends on the subjective impression of the examiner. However, many parents complain of snoring or mouth breathing and are anxious for a remedy.

4. Peritonsillar abscess (quinsy). This is now rare because of the availability of penicillin therapy.

5. Streptococcal complications. Tonsils have been traditionally implicated as foci of infection with streptococci. The efficacy of T and A in eradication of streptococcal infection will be discussed in the following section.

6. Allergy (hay fever or asthma).

7. Bronchitis or pneumonia, chronic or recurrent.

The following eight indications are recommended by a member of the surgery department at a leading U.S. medical school (Baron, 1956).

8. Conduction deafness, with or without otitis media.

9. Suppurative sinusitis, chronic or recurrent.

10. General underdevelopment of the child associated with repeated attacks of adenotonsillitis or excessive adenotonsillar hypertrophy.

11. Chronic or recurrent cervical adenopathy.

12. Speech defects associated with excessive adenoidal or tonsillar hypertrophy.
13. Foul breath due to collection of debris in the tonsillar crypts.
14. Diphtheria carriers.
15. Prophylactically in cases with congenital cardiac defects.

SCIENTIFIC EVIDENCE FOR EFFICACY OF T AND A

In analyzing the studies on the efficacy of T and A, there are several methodologic problems.

Many of the studies were done during the preantibiotic era, when a physician had no appropriate alternative therapy for suppurative infections of the upper respiratory tract and the middle ear. Some of the expected benefits of T and A from that era are no longer appropriate today.

Different investigators had different notions about the benefits of T and A. Therefore, indications for surgery varied widely, and accordingly the benefits also varied. It is difficult to pool the data from different studies to enlarge the data base for analysis or even for comparison.

The follow-up period also varied in different studies. Some studies were for only one to two years. The first, by Kaiser, was based on a ten-year follow-up. If observations are made for only a short period, it is difficult to tease apart the placebo effect of the operation. Presumably, the longer the observation period, the less the placebo effect.

Some studies had rather large numbers of exclusions from their control groups because the investigators felt that T and A was "urgently" indicated. These subjects were thus removed from the study or reassigned to the T and A group. If these "needy" subjects are excluded, the results would be biased toward those for whom T and A may not show dramatic benefits. This manner of exclusion would decrease the power of a study to detect the potential benefits of T and A.

The benefits of surgery were based on both subjective impressions and objective findings. They were not necessarily included in all of the studies. Some of the subjective impressions were based on periodic interviews with parents who might not reliably recall the history. Also, the interviewers may not have been blindly assigned (i.e., they might know whether or not T and A was done) so that bias may have been introduced.

Alternative modes of therapy administered for the control group were rarely specified. Therefore, the control group, despite the standardization for age, sex, and socioeconomic class, may constitute a population with widely varying therapies and concomitantly different outcome potentials.

The ages at which T and A was performed also varied. The age factor may play a significant role in maximizing the benefits of T and A. Many studies did not include age stratification of their results.

Finally, even when there were control groups, they were not true controls. To rule out the placebo effect of the operation itself and to ensure comparability, some sort of placebo surgery (sham operation) would have to be performed. This, of course, would not be feasible, and the question of what constitutes an appropriate control will have to remain unanswered.

The following section is devoted to a critical review of the literature concerning the efficacy of T and A. Only *controlled* studies will be discussed. They are generally more desirable since there is an appropriate comparison group to evaluate whether the frequency of illnesses (in this case, attributable to the presence or absence of tonsils) in the tonsillectomized group is different from that among comparable persons from the source population whose tonsils are intact. Some uncontrolled studies will be listed and cited in the References.

The controlled studies will be further divided into *retrospective* and *prospective* studies. Retrospective studies are based on "looking backward from effects to preceding causes," and the prospective ones "look forward from causes to effects" (MacMahon and Pugh, 1970). In the case of T and A, retrospective studies will be those in which the expected benefits will have occurred before the study. In prospective studies, protocols are designed so as to observe the effects of T and A during the study period. Many of the studies presented on the following pages are mixed types, in that past history of upper respiratory infections, for example, will often be combined with the observed incidence of respiratory infections during the study period.

Retrospective Studies

A.D. Kaiser, 1930, U.S.

Methods. This study is based on two surveys. The first one is a study of 2000 children of high school age, half of whom had tonsillectomy at the age of five or six years. They were examined at the time of surgery and reexamined ten years later. The other half (1000 children) consisted of those for whom tonsillectomy was recommended ten years ago but was not performed. These nontonsillectomized children were matched for geographic, socioeconomic, and racial variables and served as controls.

A similar survey was made on 2400 children three years after tonsillectomy. The results of these two surveys were compared.

Results. There was a definite decrease in the frequency of repeated sore throats; 10 percent in the operated group had this complaint ten years following surgery, whereas 35 percent in the nonsurgery group still had repeated attacks of tonsillitis. The difference was more pronounced in the first three years following surgery. There was a definite reduction in the frequency of head colds in the three-year postoperative period, whereas there was a very slight decrease in the control group. However, at the end of the ten-year postoperative period, the difference between the tonsillectomy group and the controls was not large. At both the three-year and the ten-year examinations, the operated group showed a lessened incidence of cervical adenitis as compared to the controls (7 percent among those operated and 14 percent among the controls).

There were no appreciable changes in the frequency of otitis media, febrile illness, laryngitis, and colds. Bronchitis, pneumonia, and measles occurred more frequently among those operated on.

Comments. The major defects of this study are the long interval between the two sets of observations (ten years) and therefore the reliance on subjective impressions via history. The validity of the incidence estimate by recall is certainly open to question. Also, since it is known that the rate of so-called common infections (such as upper respiratory infections) diminishes with age, age may be a source of confounding bias. Another problem arises from aggregating the three-year follow-up data with the ten-year data. Since differences between the tonsillectomy group and controls were most pronounced in the first three-year postoperative period, one may lose information by grouping the three-year follow-up data with the ten-year data.

G.L. Waldbott and M.S. Ascher, 1936, U.S.

Methods. Tonsils were removed from 433 patients with hay fever and asthma, 228 before the onset of allergic symptoms ("preallergics"), and 205 after allergic manifestations had developed. Both relief of asthma and hay fever and also improvement in conditions other than allergy were compared.

Results. Tonsillectomy resulted in 1.9 percent definite relief in the 205 allergic patients who had allergy before the operation. In the control group of 60 patients, 1.7 percent showed definite relief.

Comments. The control group was not clearly specified. The authors did not define the term "definite relief." The follow-up period was not specified.

J.H. Paton, 1943, U.S.

Methods. This study is based on a record review of 908 girls admitted to boarding school between 1930 and 1939. They were from the upper socioeconomic classes and free from any illness or severe disability at the time of admission. Fifty-seven percent of the 908 girls had been tonsillectomized previously, and 43 percent still had their tonsils intact. The nontonsillectomized group served as controls. The students were examined for cervical adenopathy, for history of otorrhea (draining ears), of "rheumatism," pattern of growth, and incidence of illness during their stay at the boarding school.

Results. The tonsillectomized group was no healthier than the control group on arrival at school and was less healthy in terms of school days lost through illness. Although the operated group suffered less from tonsillitis, they suffered much more from infections of both upper and lower respiratory tract.

Comments. The major weakness of this study is the selection of the two groups, particularly the use as controls of those girls who had not been subjected to tonsillectomy. They may not have been recommended for surgery because they were relatively free of those symptoms attributed to diseases of the tonsils and adenoids. Therefore, the incidence of illness in the control group may represent an unusually low rate.

H. leRiche and W.B. Stiver, 1957, Canada

Methods. A randomly selected sample of 1000 post-tonsillectomy cases, mainly children (854 under age fifteen years), was studied for one year before and one year after the operation. The unit of measurement used was the physician's visit, which included office, home, and hospital calls. For the control group, the investigators selected at random 422 children with the same age and sex distribution as those in the tonsillectomy group and studied the prevalence of respiratory diseases in this group for 1953 as compared with 1954. This period was similar to the period during which the tonsillectomy cases were under observation.

Results. There was a marked reduction in prevalence of acute throat disease in the tonsillectomized group of 706 patients. The rate of physician calls (rate per 1000 cases per annum) was 2392.2 before operation and 503.5 after operation. In the control group, the rate was 658.8 in 1953 and 628.0 in 1954, essentially no change. The average number of physician calls per person in the tonsillectomy group was 3.9 before operation and 1.7 after operation. In the control group, the average number of calls was 1.6 in 1953 and 1.5 in 1954. In the tonsillectomy group, 86.5 percent were ill at one time or another in the year preceding the operation, and 67.1 percent were ill on one or more occasions after the operation. In the control group, 40.5 percent had some form of upper respiratory disease during 1953, and 42 percent had respiratory illnesses in 1954.

There were altogether 135 persons in whom there was no record of respiratory or throat disease before the tonsillectomy. In this group, 57.0 percent had been ill on one or more occasions in the year succeeding the operation. It appeared that this group of 135 persons constitute a particularly healthy segment of the population and that the decision for surgery was probably based on the appearance of the tonsils alone and not on prior history.

An analysis was done to determine what proportion of the tonsillectomized patients benefited from the operation. It was assumed that a patient benefited if calls decreased after the operation, and did not benefit if calls increased. According to these criteria 81.4 percent improved. For otitis media, 68 percent under age five years benefited from the operation compared with 48 percent in the older age groups.

In a group of eighty-one persons with a history of chest infections before tonsillectomy, there was an average of 2.5 calls per patient before the operation, and 0.8 after the operation. The mean difference was 1.7 ± 0.30.

No benefit was demonstrated in cases of allergic rhinitis.

Comments. Analyzing this study, one can say that the number of controls should have been at least equal to the study population. Also the decision to use a relatively objective outcome measure, the number of physician visits, represented a trade-off in which there was a sacrifice of more precise and specific information for objectivity regarding the prevalence of illnesses. The study is weakened by the fact that people will seek a physician's care at different degrees of severity of illnesses. It would also have strengthened the study if the postoperative follow-up period had been longer than one year.

Prospective Studies

J.C. Mertz, 1954, U.S.

Methods. This study is based on a three-year period of monthly surveys of respiratory illness records of families living in two communities in Westchester County, New York. Individual subjects were grouped according to whether they had been tonsillectomized or not. Then the incidence rates of acute respiratory disease were compared between the two groups. The nontonsillectomized group served as controls. Data were further stratified according to three socioeconomic classes (professional-managerial, clerical-skilled, semiskilled-unskilled).

Results. For the age group five to nine years, there was no difference between the tonsillectomized and nontonsillectomized groups. After age forty the incidence of illness among persons with tonsils removed was higher than for persons with tonsils present.

Comments. This appears to be a well-designed and well-conducted study. The major weaknesses are the lack of accompanying objective findings on physical examination (respiratory illnesses are based on history) and the lack of an under-five-years age group.

R. Chamovitz et al., 1960, U.S.

Methods. The effect of tonsillectomy on susceptibility to streptococcal infections was determined in a group of 6974 airmen. This study was undertaken because streptococcal respiratory disease was epidemic in this population and also because adequate clinical and laboratory observations could be made. The influence of previous tonsillectomy on streptococcal disease rates, the clinical course of these illnesses, and the incidence of suppurative and nonsuppurative complications were determined. The population was dichotomized into those with tonsillectomy (2844, or 40.8 percent) and those without tonsillectomy (4130), who served as controls.

Results. In the five-year study period, 18.4 percent of the tonsillectomized group and 19.0 percent of the nontonsillectomized group were admitted with the clinical diagnosis of streptococcal pharyngitis. Of those with tonsillectomy who were hospitalized, 10.9 percent had positive bacteriologic culture, and 13.0 percent of those with no tonsillectomy had positive bacteriologic culture. In the hospitalized tonsillectomy group, 9.2 percent met the serologic criteria (increase in antistreptolysin) for streptococcal infection, whereas 10.0 percent of the nontonsillectomized group met the appropriate criteria. The clinical course was not modified by the presence or absence of tonsils.

Tonsillectomy did not alter significantly the attack rate of acute rheumatic fever as a sequel of streptococcal infections.

Comments. This is a well-designed study with an appropriately comparable control group. Since the population studied is composed of young adults, one cannot generalize these findings to pediatric age groups.

W.J.E. McKee, 1963, England (1963a in References)

Methods. This study had three aims: to assess the morbidity of T and A; to define indications or contraindications for T and A; and to assess changes attributable to T and A. An attempt was made in the study design to overcome the problems of confounding by age and observation bias (by dependence on parental opinion). Criteria for inclusion in the study were standardized as were also the follow-up criteria (by using predefined diagnostic classifications for respiratory illnesses). A two-year follow-up period was used.

Children referred to a surgeon for an opinion on the need for tonsillectomy were divided into three groups.

1. Those for whom "in the present state of knowledge there is an urgent or definite need for tonsillectomy and for whom it would be unethical to defer the operation."

2. Children for whom the surgeon considered that tonsillectomy was not indicated.

3. "Children with symptoms which might be referable to the tonsils and might justify an operation but without urgency" (three or more upper respiratory infections within the past year). Those children in this group who were deemed "unsuitable" for follow-up were excluded.

All children from Group 3 under the age of fifteen (N−413) were accepted into the study, and divided into two categories: 231 for early operation (T and A); and 182 for controls (T and A deferred for at least two years "unless it became urgently needed," when the child was then withdrawn from the study).

Home visits were made by trained nurse field workers who visited in rotation. Each child was visited approximately once every two months. At each visit an itemized questionnaire was completed giving the symptoms and duration of any illness.

Various parameters were measured to compare illness in tonsillectomized and control categories. These were the mean incidence per year of illness in control and tonsillectomized children; mean school loss (days per year); duration of illness (days per year); confinement to bed (days); number of severe episodes; and medical attendances.

Results. There was a statistically significant fall in the incidence of respiratory illness over two years as a result of tonsillectomy. Tonsillectomized children showed a reduction of more than 30 percent when compared with controls, from a mean of 5.0 respiratory illnesses to 3.2 in respect of the first year, and from 3.8 to 2.6 in the second year. The principal source of this improvement was the reduction in sore throats by 82 and 70 percent respectively, for two years. Unoperated children had a statistically higher rate of school loss due to respiratory illness over both years. In the first year sore throats were reduced by 51 percent and in the second year by 36 percent.

The source of this improvement in the incidence of respiratory illness generally was the large reduction in throat disease. Similar benefits from tonsillectomy were found using duration of illness and confinement to bed as criteria for comparison with controls.

Although the effect of surgery on otitis media was not as dramatic as it was for sore throat, a reduction in otitis media followed the combined operation.

The best results of operation were in children under five years of age.

Tonsillectomy did not influence significantly colds, coughs, influenzal disease, behavior upsets, or other nonrespiratory illness (other than otitis media).

Comments. Using subjects referred to an ear, nose, and throat (ENT) surgeon for evaluation of T and A, those with clear-cut indications for T and A and those who clearly did not need T and A were excluded. This reflects a basic bias on the part of the surgeons towards the efficacy of T and A. The group studied was the intermediate group, which was felt to need T and A but not urgently. The assumption is that these are children for whom T and A is of questionable efficacy. Subjects were randomly assigned to two groups: T and A and control. The case-to-control allocation ratio was less than one control per case (231 cases:182 controls). The study could have been more powerful in detecting outcome differences with a greater number of controls. The cases and controls were significantly different for social class distribution ($p = .02$) despite randomization. The age distributions of the two groups were well matched.

Outcome criteria were not measured blindly. Home visitors recorded outcome measures, but no mention is made about attempts at objectivity. The visitors recorded symptoms which were later classified by one doctor into diagnostic categories. No examinations to confirm diagnoses were made.

In the control group, 18.7 percent were lost to follow-up since they were withdrawn to undergo "urgent" tonsillectomy. This introduces bias, but it is a conservative bias in that it would tend to decrease the differences between the T and A and control groups (by removing those controls who have the most symptoms).

This study demonstrates that T and A is of benefit for younger patients and for specified conditions (sore throat, otitis media). It does, however, lack persuasiveness because of the problems mentioned. Factors such as exclusion from the study of the group which would possibly stand to gain the most from T and A (those deemed "urgently in need") would tend to diminish the differences seen between controls and cases. Similarly, use of such criteria as otorrhea for diagnosing otitis media tend to diminish the magnitude of differences seen between the two groups.

W.J.E. McKee, 1963, England (1963b in References)

Methods. This study attempts to compare the influence of adenoidectomy alone with that of the combined T and A operation. The study protocol is essentially the same as that of McKee's first study, save for a few modifications. Two hundred children aged two to fifteen were allocated to two groups randomly. Group I consisted of those children who underwent the combined operation of T and A, and Group II consisted of 100 children who were subjected to adenoidectomy only. The same parameters of morbidity were used as in McKee's study cited on the previous pages. The results of this study were compared with those obtained for tonsillectomized and unoperated (control) children in the previous study.

Results. Throat disease was infrequent after the combined operation, but the incidence and severity of the disease in adenoidectomized children was similar to that in the previous series of unoperated controls. Adenoidectomy alone appeared to have no influence on the occurrence of throat disease.

Otitis media occurred less frequently after either adenoidectomy or the combined operation. Chronic catarrhal conditions occurred less frequently after tonsillectomy with adenoidectomy, but there was no evidence that this group of complaints was relieved by adenoidectomy alone in Group II of this study. Other groups of respiratory disease occurred with similar frequency and severity in children having one operation (A alone) or no operation (the control group in McKee's previous study).

The incidence of complications following operation was twice as high in tonsillectomized children as in those having adenoidectomy alone.

Comments. Since the study design is essentially identical to that used in McKee's previous study, the strengths and weaknesses of the study are the same as those presented in the critique of the first study.

S.R. Mawson et al., 1967, England

Methods. The method of selection was similar to McKee's in that the study group consisted of children who would normally be "placed on the waiting list for routine operation." The investigators excluded those from whom they "could not in good conscience withhold operation" and a group for whom they "could not in good conscience advise operation." Altogether 404 children aged three to twelve were randomly allocated to group X (for operation) and to group Y (postponement of operation up to two years). There were 202 in each group. The two groups were well matched. Pre-intake history was taken prior to assignment. Follow-up was at two-month intervals for two years, usually in hospital clinics and occasionally at home by home visitors. At the follow-up clinic, facilities were offered for diagnosis and treatment of respiratory infections to ensure consistency. The attrition rate amounted to 25 percent in the operated group and 20 percent in the control group by completion of the second year.

During the study period there were "several children" in the control group Y for whom it was considered inadvisable to postpone operation any longer. However, they stayed within the control group after tonsillectomy. Altogether 56 children in the control group required operation.

Results. During the first year, only 3 percent of the X group had more than three attacks (of tonsillitis, sore throat, or cervical adenitis) compared with 21.5 percent of the controls. During the second year 2.5 percent of the operated had more than three attacks, compared with 9.5 percent of the Y group. The effect of the frequency of the attacks is more pronounced in the children between four and twelve.

No significant difference was found in the incidence of otitis media.

There was a greater weight gain in the operated group, especially during the first postoperative year.

Comments. This study is basically a repeat of the study by McKee, so that the critique stated on the previous pages is applicable here. The strength of this study is the randomized trial design, but the numbers of subjects are small. The most bothersome point is the large number of T and A in the control group (altogether fifty-six during the two-year study period) so that the difference between the operated and nonoperated would be masked by the inclusion of the operated children in the control group. Again, there appears to be a bias (for the efficacy of T and A) on the part of the investigators in assuming that there are immediate benefits of T and A when they allowed over 25 percent of the control group to undergo surgery. One is also bothered by no mention as to objectivity of the follow-up.

N. Roydhouse, 1970, New Zealand

Methods. The author states that he uses McKee's methods for the selection of cases, the recording of illnesses, and the use of health visitors, but does not clearly define his methods of analysis. There is one modification in that this study has two control groups: children (matched) with no history of ENT problems and no tonsillectomy, and children on the waiting list for T and A. Twenty-one (of 175) of the most symptomatic children from the waiting list control group were removed to undergo T and A at the end of the first year.

Results. The mean incidence of respiratory illness in the first year in the operated group was 1.88 compared with 3.33 in the group on the waiting list. The incidence in the second group (no ENT symptoms) was 1.42. During the second year, the incidence for the operated group was 1.35, for the waiting group 3.13, and 1.18 for the asymptomatic group. Among respiratory illnesses, sore throat accounted for the difference in the incidence rates of the groups. The mean incidence of sore throat for those waiting was 2.25, for those operated 0.56, and for those asymptomatic 0.34. The difference prevailed during the second year also.

There was no appreciable difference for otitis media. The reduction in the incidence of throat disease was greatest in the two-to-four year age group.

Comments. This study is difficult to analyze since the author did not clarify his methods for analysis of the data. Some of the numbers did not add up correctly.

This study must be interpreted with caution since the shifting of the most symptomatic children out of the group waiting for T and A might have biased the results.

Uncontrolled studies, both retrospective and prospective, were done by: Selkirk and Mitchell (1931); M.H. Bass (1934); H.H. Mason (1934); H.D. Smith (1936); J.H. Johnston and T.W. Watkins (1954); I.J. Wolman (1956); J. Crooks (1957); T.M. Banham (1968); and I.M. Epstein (1937).

The study by Selkirk and Mitchell (1931) was a crossover study in that there was no separate control group, but the same patients before the intervention were used as their own controls by comparing their preoperative complaints with the postoperative ones. A placebo effect can cause significant bias in such a plan, and the fact that the children are three years older at time of follow-up can also confound results in that they may be less susceptible to some of the common childhood infections.

M.H. Bass's study (1934) was based on a questionnaire sent to parents. Only one person, the author, was responsible for the decision to operate and for postoperative follow-up; thus differences of professional opinion were eliminated. Nevertheless, the design is prone to observation bias, and the duration of follow-up was not specified. Of the other studies, the one by J. Crooks (1957) is unusual in that it analyzes fifty consecutive operations on doctors' children. The author hoped in this way to have the benefit of skilled observation. Again, there is the advantage of limiting the operations and clinical examinations to one individual, the author, but is there reason to assume that physicians will be less biased as parental observers than laymen?

The single prospective study in the uncontrolled group by I.M. Epstein (1937) was a crossover design in which children were seen before and after their operations for two years. Observer bias enters again, since the observer knows the subject has been tonsillectomized and therefore may expect and overreport improvement.

EVIDENCE OF THE CONTROVERSY: AREA VARIATION IN T AND A RATES

One approach to examining the issue of effectiveness is to look at the pattern of utilization of pediatric hospital services. What are some of the most frequently utilized hospital services? Is there variation in utilization patterns? If one assumes that there are standardized ways of treating specific conditions, there should not be marked variation (after adjusting for demographic variables) in utilization patterns. However, marked variations exist. These variations may reflect, in part, some of the current controversy surrounding the entire subject of effectiveness of hospital services. One of the most dramatic examples is the marked area variation in rates of tonsillectomy and adenoidectomy.

Various explanations have been offered to interpret these variations. The following is a review of different mechanisms involved in area variation.

Incidence of Diseases
That there may be regional differences in the actual incidence of medical conditions meriting surgical intervention cannot be completely denied. There is a paucity of available information relating the incidence of surgical procedures to the prevalence of the associated disease states. Until there is a reliable data base to correlate surgery rates with the actual prevalence of disease conditions, this particular argument, though not very plausible, remains unchallenged.

Surgical Manpower Supply and Distribution
Bunker (1970) noted that parallel to the twofold higher incidence of surgery in the U.S., there are twice as many surgeons in proportion to population in the U.S. as in the United Kingdom. In a previous study done in Vermont, Wennberg and Gittelsohn (1973) found that in the hospital service areas in Vermont with highest surgery rates there were twice as many full-time equivalent surgeons per 10,000 persons as in the areas with the lowest rates.[b] A study in Kansas (Lewis, 1969) again revealed a strong correlation between appendectomy rates and number of hospital beds available and number of operating physicians in proportion to population.

Systems of Health Care Delivery
Different rates are observed in different systems of medical care. Bunker (1970) notes that within the British National Health Service, the surgeon is a true consultant, seeing only those patients referred to him, and is entirely hospital based. The American surgeon, on the other hand, in addition to functioning as consultant, may also accept patients without referral or may refer the patient himself for surgery, thus "creating his own demand" (Bunker, 1970).

Data from Canada support the view that it is not universal health insurance itself that has led to the observed difference in rates of surgery in England and Canada, but other components of the health care system. Vayda (1973) noted that in Canada there are 1.4 times as many surgeons as in the United Kingdom and twice as much surgery as well. In Canada under universal health insurance, over 95 percent of the population is insured for hospital and medical services, but surgeons are paid on a fee-for-service basis. In England specialists such as surgeons receive a salary and are hospital based. In Canada, surgery is done by both specialists and general practitioners. Vayda's

[b] A corollary to this observation is the twofold difference in common surgery for children one to nineteen between the high and low Vermont hospital service areas (Table 12-6).

study revealed that the national rates for England and Canada are similar for some procedures which are only done by specialists (such as heart-valve surgery, lobectomy-pneumonectomy, and joint arthrodesis) but not for T and A, cholecystectomy, and hemorrhoidectomy.

Prepaid Group Practice versus Fee-for-Service

Studies comparing surgery rates in prepaid group practice and in nongroup practice show that they are generally lower in the group practice population. For instance, data on the hospital experience of federal employees covered under five broad types of voluntary insurance in the Federal Employees Health Benefits Program show that the rate of tonsillectomy with or without adenoidectomy was 10.6 per 1000 covered persons for those with the government-wide Blue Shield plan as compared with that of 4.0 per 1000 persons for those enrolled in prepayment group practice plans (Perrott, 1966). One possible source of confounding bias in this study is that the data compared are not age standardized and may not be comparable.

Data from the Health Services Research Center of the Kaiser Health Plan of Oregon showed that the T and A rate for the Kaiser population was less than half the rate for the comparable age group of Blue Cross subscribers residing in Kansas (Olenick, 1971). A study by Hastings et al. (1970) showed a threefold difference in tonsillectomy rates in a prepaid group health insurance plan as compared with a fee-for-service plan.

A study of surgical admission rates in New York showed that the annual rate under age fifteen years was 33.7 per 1000 population for the Blue Cross-HIP (Health Insurance Plan of Greater New York, prepaid group plan) subscribers as compared with 52.8 per 1000 for Blue Cross-Blue Shield subscribers (Densen, 1958). A later study by Densen showed that the HIP group and a labor union health insurance plan (a fee-for-service plan) had almost identical hospital utilization rates (1962). This finding is opposed to earlier and other studies where fee-for-service plans led to higher hospitalization utilization rates than prepaid plans, particularly in regard to surgery rates.

Why should there be different rates of surgery in the prepaid group practice setting? One may speculate that the care provided with the prepaid group practice may be different, which in turn leads to less need for hospitalization. It is difficult to argue that so-called preventive care (generally assumed to be inherent in the nature of the prepaid group practice because of comprehensive coverage) leads to less frequent occurrence of medical problems such as enlarged tonsils and adenoids or inguinal hernia. In the Kaiser study in Oregon, Olenick (1971) observed that pediatricians within a comprehensive prepaid health care system have about the same amount of patient contact as those in more traditional forms of practice, tend to hospitalize somewhat less frequently, and keep children in for shorter periods.

A study was done in Boston to evaluate the effect of a comprehensive family-focused pediatric program on the health of a selected sample of low-income families (Alpert et al., 1968). This study tested the hypothesis that there should be measurable differences between families who received comprehensive care and similar families who did not. The results showed that within the first six months of the three-year period, the families receiving comprehensive care had a higher rate of hospitalization and operative procedures, most probably caused by the number of necessary procedures found at the time of entry into the program. After the initial six months they had a lower rate of operation. Procedures such as tonsillectomies, circumcisions, and umbilical herniorrhaphies without clear indications were discouraged.

Another reason for the lower rate of hospital services utilization among prepaid group practice populations is the built-in regulatory mechanisms in terms of hospital beds and number of operating surgeons. In this setting hospital admissions and surgical operations are more carefully controlled, which in turn leads to lowered frequency of elective surgery. Klarman (1963) cites lower tonsillectomy rates in prepaid group practice as an example of the conservatism in medical practice that could prevail in the absence of financial incentives to the contrary. On the other hand, it can be argued that in the absence of a fee there is less incentive to perform procedures which may not be absolutely necessary but may be desirable.

There are also arguments that the lowered surgery rates of prepaid group plans do not completely represent the total surgical experience of the subscriber population since some of the group members may seek care outside the plan. In a letter to the editor in the *New England Journal of Medicine*, D.L. Albert (1970) stated that as a physician who formerly worked with the Health Insurance Plan, he could attest that many patients do go outside the plan's medical group for major surgery. Patients in lower-income groups often use New York's municipal hospitals or voluntary hospitals with ward services. Upper-income patients often use HIP for routine care, and for surgery would select a surgeon of their own choice at what they believe a good medical center.

Uncertainty Concerning Clinical Practice

Despite the dramatic expansion of biomedical knowledge during the last half century, there are still sufficient information gaps so that indications for many surgical procedures are far from clear. When the effectiveness of a clinical procedure is controversial, one would expect to see area variations associated with differences in beliefs among physicians concerning indications. The more "elective" the procedure, the more area variation is likely. Hypertrophied tonsils and adenoids, except for a very small proportion of the cases (where there is respiratory embarrassment or, in very rare instances, cardiac failure), cannot generally be considered life-threatening.

J.A. Glover (1938) noted that as early as 1912 there were great local variations in the proportion of children recommended for tonsillectomy. He observed that in 1936 as the provision of medical care increased, these variations did not diminish but actually increased. Glover compared tonsillectomy in geographic districts of England and Wales and pointed out that in 1936 a child living in Rutlandshire was nineteen times more likely to undergo tonsillectomy than one living in Cambridgeshire. A child living in Bexhill was twenty-seven times more likely to be submitted to operation than a Birkenhead child. Glover observed: "A study of the geographic distribution in elementary school children discloses no correlation between the rate of incidence and impersonal factors such as over-crowding, poverty, bad housing, or climate.... In fact it defies any explanation, *save that of variation of medical opinion on the indication for operation.*" The author noted further that large, and in some cases drastic, reductions in the numbers of operations performed on elementary school children in certain areas have had no unsatisfactory results.

The study by Wennberg and Gittelsohn (1973) again revealed that the rate of tonsillectomy showed the widest area variation among the common surgical procedures studied. For instance, in 1969 the incidence in the Vermont hospital area with the lowest rate of tonsillectomy was 13 per 10,000 persons (age-adjusted to the Vermont population) and the incidence in the highest area was 151 per 10,000. A study using five-year aggregate data in Vermont (1969–73) showed the ratio of high area incidence to the lowest area rate as 5.5 (Table 12–6).

A study by leRiche and Stiver (1957) showed a ninefold difference in annual tonsillectomy rates in the different counties and districts of Ontario. The study was based on a six-month survey of tonsillectomies performed among the prepayment plan (Physicians' Services Incorporated, Ontario) population.

Bunker also points out that marked variability in surgical practice in part reflects absent or inadequate data by which to compare operative with nonoperative treatment. He states: "The indications for surgery are sufficiently imprecise to allow a 100 percent variation in rates of operation" (1970, p. 142). In many instances, there is very little information available on the magnitude of risk involved in not operating for many surgical conditions. It is difficult for a surgeon to make a rational decision in the absence of appropriate information. Also, recent malpractice litigation may influence the surgeon to operate when operation might be of borderline or questionable benefit.

Knox (1964) in an article with the provocative title of "How Often Are We Wrong? or the Epidemiology of Doctor Error" says: "We must face the fact that if we had to talk about medicine in terms of what we know for sure, we wouldn't have much to say. . . . It is hoped that it may block the worst clinical sin of all—the selection of one unknown from many to label as the truth" (p. 500).

The Human Factor in Physician's Performance

No one would deny that there is a significant degree of inaccuracy in the interpretation or evaluation of many clinical and laboratory procedures used in medical practice. There is also associated diagnostic error, the extent of which is still little appreciated or known. For instance, the range of observer variability for simple signs of emphysema is known to be 33 to 85 percent (Knox, 1964).

Wood et al. (1972) studied children who had been placed on a waiting list for adenotonsillectomy. The surgeon felt that T and A would be of benefit to these children but was not urgently needed. The waiting time was up to three years and occasionally five years. Out of the 291 children on the list, 217 attended for review. This was undertaken by one of a panel of six pediatricians. The pediatricians judged about half the original group of children to have normal tonsils and lymph nodes, whereas all the surgical case notes recorded some abnormality in either or both.

A test of observer reliability was carried out in the same study. At a joint conference of ENT surgeons, pediatricians, and general practitioners, nine color slides of children's tonsils seen in the review were projected. The audience was given three choices—"discharge," "observe," or "surgery"—as each transparency was shown. To check consistency within individuals, slides 3 and 9 were of the same child as were 5 and 8 of another. With nine questions and a choice of three decisions in each, the chance score would be 3. The average score in this instance was 3.6.

When comparing the four slides of the same two children, the results were:

17 percent of observers consistent and correct in both instances;
46 percent of observers consistent and correct in one instance; and
37 percent of observers inconsistent and incorrect in both instances.

An interesting example of the observer error in indications for tonsillectomy was recounted by Denzer and Felshin (1943) and also by Bakwin (1945). The American Child Health Association surveyed 1000 eleven-year-old school children in New York. It was found that 611, or 61 percent, already had their tonsils removed. The remaining 389 children were then examined in relays by twenty Manhattan school physicians. On the first examination, 174 (45 percent) children were recommended for tonsillectomy. Out of 215 rejected children from this first examination, another 96 children were selected for tonsillectomy when another team of physicians was put to work. This left 119 of the original 389 and these 119 were subjected to a third examination by a different group of physicians who recommended tonsillectomy for 53 children, leaving only 66 of the original 1000 who had not been recommended for tonsillectomy. These subjects were not further examined because the supply of physicians was exhausted!

The Child Health Association study showed that there was no correlation between the estimate of one physician and that of another regarding the advisability of tonsillectomy. One of the conclusions of the study was that the chance of a child's being recommended for operation depended principally on the physician rather than on the child's health. It must be pointed out that nineteen of the twenty physicians participating in the study were willing to pass judgment on whether the tonsils required removal merely on examination with little or no emphasis on history. Also, in this particular study, financial considerations did not influence the physician's decision for tonsillectomy.

Consumer Demand and Secular Trends

As early as 1936, Glover (1938) noted the puzzling phenomenon of a social-class gradient in the incidence of tonsillectomy. He noted that tonsillitis appeared common to all classes of society, but the incidence of tonsillectomy was at least threefold higher in children of the well-to-do. He estimated that about 20 percent of elementary school children were tonsillectomized before the age of fourteen, but 75–83 percent of the students at "one of our most famous public schools" (Eton) had been tonsillectomized before entry at fourteen years of age. The author concluded: "The more fortunate the child in all other circumstances, and the better the opportunities for careful nurture, so much the more is he liable to tonsillectomy" (p. 1232).

In the discussion following Glover's paper, R.P. Garrow said that some of the strange facts presented by the author in regard to the incidence of tonsillectomy might be explained by a psychological factor of great importance: maternal anxiety. Maternal anxiety varied with social circumstances, being greater among the better-off mothers who had fewer children. Garrow felt that this factor alone was sufficient to explain the higher incidence of unnecessary operations (of which tonsillectomy was the most common) in boys than in girls and in the well-to-do as compared with poorer classes.

One can counter Garrow's argument by saying that perhaps the well-to-do had a greater incidence of tonsillectomy because of better access to medical care. However, even if one were to reduce the financial barriers to low-income families, care-seeking patterns are still different in different socioeconomic classes. K.J. Roghmann and R.J. Haggerty in Rochester, New York, compared anticipated with actual changes in health behavior after enrollment in the Medicaid program (Roghmann et al., 1971). Although over 90 percent of the eligible child population in the community was enrolled, little change was observed in service, frequency, and purpose of care. Poor families were still more likely to receive less care, to depend more on public clinics, and to have a higher proportion of illness-related rather than preventive medical contacts. Additional data presented by Roghmann (Haggerty et al., 1975) show that in 1968 in Monroe County, New York, the rate of T and A per 1000 persons under age eighteen years was 18.89 among Blue Cross subscribers, 15.09 for other commercial insurance policyholders, and 5.29 for self-payers as compared with 7.00 for Medicaid enrollees.

Wolman (1956) noted that in the U.S. as in England in the 1930s, tonsillectomy tends to be performed much more often in children whose parents are in the professional and managerial classes. Mertz (1954) noted that in the two communities in Westchester County, New York, the incidence of tonsillectomy was higher in the professional and managerial social class than in the semiskilled and unskilled class, 51.44 percent in the former and 38.9 percent in the latter. This social class gradient may reflect better access to medical care.

In an article entitled "Ritualistic surgery—circumcision and tonsillectomy" Bolande (1969) noted that parental pressure may be a major determinant of a physician's decision to perform tonsillectomy. Additionally, the legacy of misinformation from the past may affect his attitude or help him rationalize his position. "Physicians' willingness to comply with parental demand has institutionalized, and indeed, ritualized, the operation to a considerable extent" (Bunker, 1970, p. 142).

According to the 1975 edition of Nelson's *Textbook of Pediatrics* (Vaughn et al., eds.), the most frequent reason for tonsillectomy and adenoidectomy is probably pressure from parents that something be done about the child with frequent respiratory infections, allergic bronchitis, mouth-breathing, recurrent earaches, poor appetite, or even failure to gain weight. Furman (1959) observed that there are two sources of parental pressure for T and A: wide misconceptions about the need for surgery; and parental feelings such as guilt or frustrated anger. Stool also points out that the parent may see illness in a much different light than the physician who is seeing numerous patients in the community with the same illness and who does not feel the patient is unusual (Stool and Mast, 1973). The inconvenience, expense, and stigma of having a child with multiple respiratory infections are difficult for parents. If the child, in addition, is going through a physiological anorexia, then the relation of snoring, poor appetite, and "large tonsils" may further emphasize the need "to do something."

Whatever the reasons, there are also secular trends in surgery as there are secular trends in other forms of medical therapy. Glover (1938) observed that the tonsillectomy rate remained relatively low for many years during post-Listerian days until after the beginning of the twentieth century. About 1902–1903 a rapid rise accelerated sharply, reaching a peak in 1931. There was then a sharp fall. In 1936 a second rising curve began. Bakwin (1958) estimates that in 1954, one-third or more British children were being tonsillectomized.

A study in Westchester County in New York also showed an increase in tonsillectomy rates (Downes, 1954). Nineteen percent of the study subjects born before 1910 had had their tonsils removed by the time they were nineteen. The second group included persons born during the period 1910–29, and 47.5 percent had had their tonsils removed by age nineteen. The last cohort was those born in the period 1930–48. In this group 56.5 percent had been tonsillectomized by nineteen.

During the past decade, there appears to be a definite downward trend in tonsillectomy rates. Olenick (1971) showed that there was a sharp decline in T and A rates both among the Oregon Kaiser Health Plan subscribers as well as among the nongroup plan population. The decline was approximately 50 percent between 1966 and 1969. Published data on surgical operations in short-stay hospitals reveal that there were 1641.8 T and A per 100,000 persons performed in the U.S. in 1965 (*Surgical Operations in Short-Stay Hospitals*). In 1968 the rate was 1400 per 100,000, and in 1971 there were 1282.6 per 100,000. It is interesting to note that there is no major "breakthrough" reported in the medical literature regarding the pros and cons of T and A, but there is currently a great deal of political pressure regarding the high T and A rates.

COSTS OF TONSILLECTOMY AND ADENOIDECTOMY

Cost of T and A can be direct or indirect. There have been many citations of the direct costs of T and A in the literature (Workshop, 1975; Hiatt, 1975; Illingworth et al., 1961; Bakwin, 1958) but a careful review of indirect costs appears to be lacking.

Direct Cost

The direct cost of the medical services for T and A includes the cost of the operation and of the use of the hospital bed pre- and post-operatively and of other services such as laboratory tests or X-ray.

The total cost to the society, of course, depends on the number of procedures done. If the total is 1,000,000 procedures per year, at approximately $500 per case, the annual cost is around a half billion dollars.

In the United Kingdom there were 200,000 procedures performed at an estimated cost of £3,000,000 in 1969, perhaps £5,000,000 in 1973, for which the Department of Health bears the cost (Workshop, 1975).

Indirect Cost

Foremost among the indirect costs are, of course, the immediate mortality and morbidity associated with the operation itself.

Mortality. In discussing the T and A controversy, Bakwin (1958) observed, " . . . here is a 'disease'—with virtually no mortality, and a therapeutic procedure for it which has a sizable mortality." The number of persons recorded as dying from the operation in the United States during the years 1950–55 varied from 220 to 340 a year according to Bakwin.

In 1968 the Commission on Professional and Hospital Activities reported an average of one death per 16,207 operations (Pratt, 1970).

In a survey of 3617 certified otolaryngologists listed in the Directory of Medical Specialists, the 1447 respondents (40 percent) reported that they had personally performed 6,175,729 T and A (Pratt, 1970). These physicians also reported 377 fatal cases, which is one per 16,381 procedures (0.006 percent). Of these 377 fatal cases, 139, or one per 44,429 (0.002 percent), were attributable to anesthetic causes; 127, or one per 48,627 (0.002 percent), to cardiac arrest; and

11, or one per 55,637 (0.002 percent), to hemorrhage. The problem with this study is the inherent bias in who may be more likely to respond to the questionnaire. Those who experienced higher rates of mortality may not have responded to the inquiry. Therefore, these numbers may represent a very conservative estimate.

In England and Wales in 1965 there were eleven deaths, and seven deaths in 1966, with the estimated incidence of one in approximately every 27,000 operations (Ranger, 1968), lower than the rate estimated by Pratt (1/16,000).

Morbidity. According to Pratt's (1970) survey, 504 catastrophic nonfatal bleeders (requiring ligation of the carotid artery) were reported, a rate of one per 12,253 patients. There were 1496 (one per 4128) delayed bleeders requiring "similar heroic measures." Bleeding sufficient to require five or more units of blood by transfusion was encountered in 538 patients, or one per 11,479 (0.009 percent). There may have been an overlap with those bleeders who required carotid ligation, but it was not examined by this study.

A review of 18,184 T and A in England revealed the incidence of postoperative bleeding to be 0.36 percent.

In Wolman's (1956) survey based on 3441 replies, other "severe" complications included 273 cases of pneumonia, 214 cases of stomatitis, 131 with septicemia, and 241 "other." Although it is no longer a problem, there was an association between bulbar poliomyelitis and T and A as reviewed by Bakwin (1958).

Psychologic trauma can be considerable. According to Wolman's (1956) survey of pediatricians and general practitioners, over 80 percent of the respondents had encountered emotional change of more than two weeks' duration following operation. The most frequent types of postoperative emotional disturbances were night terrors, increased dependence upon parents, hostility to doctors, occasionally enuresis, and asocial or aggressive behavior. Two factors are involved in such reactions. In many instances, an operation for T and A represents the child's first separation from home and his first admission to a hospital. In addition, the child's anxiety state is intensified by his fear of operation.

Mahaffy (1965) studied the effects of hospitalization on children admitted for T and A. He divided the preoperative children into experimental and control groups by random assignment. The experimental group consisted of those children whose parents were given greater attention by the investigator (nurse) to diminish their own anxiety, the assumption being that the less stressed the parents, the more helpful and effective they can be in caring for their child. Outcome measures included vital signs, incidence of crying and vomiting, greater ease in taking oral fluids, and shorter time period between operation and first voiding. The results showed a significant difference between the two groups in all the measured parameters. These were lower pulse rates, lower systolic pressures, less crying in the experimental group.

Jackson et al. (1953) studied behavior changes in 140 children undergoing tonsillectomy. Thirteen children presented behavior changes indicative of emotional trauma. Levy (1945) found in a study of 124 children who had the operation that 25 showed residual emotional disturbances. Half of these children had shown no deviations from normal behavior before surgery. The most frequently encountered types of postoperative reactions were night terrors, fears, dependency, and negativism. Most of the children with night terrors were eighteen months of age or younger.

Opportunity Cost

E. Mansfield (1970) defines opportuntiy cost as: "the cost of producing a certain product is the value of the other products that the resources used in its production could have been used for instead." In other words, what are social costs of T and A in terms of the costs to society when its resources are employed to produce the services involved in T and A?

As Hiatt (1975) noted, the half billion dollars taken from the "medical commons" represents a sizable wedge of the total commons pie. What needed services are not being met because of the allocation of our scarce resources for T and A? Schlesinger (1957) noted that in the study by the American Child Health Association of 1000 school children, the emphasis upon tonsillectomy was out of all proportion to its relative importance as evidenced by the continued presence of extreme physical defects not related to the tonsils. In the tonsillectomized group, 46 percent were found to have uncorrected severe visual defects and 53 percent untreated dental defects.

There is another dimension to the opportunity cost of T and A in terms of utilization of hospital services. One may ask, for instance, how much health manpower is diverted from delivering more "needed" medical care? If there is a real health manpower shortage in this country, is this an efficient use of our manpower resources? What about the hospital beds which may be otherwise used for medical treatment with better payoff?

Loss of Productivity Among School-Age Children. If school absenteeism can be regarded as a form of loss of productivity, then T and A will cost society an additional amount of resources. This factor should be weighed in computing the overall cost of T and A.

RECOMMENDATIONS

Recognize the Problem
To develop a realistic perspective, it is imperative for the medical profession, third-party payers, and the public sector to first recognize the controversy.

Ideally, a carefully designed, large-scale randomized clinical trial should be carried out with blind measurements of defined outcome criteria. In order to obtain a sufficiently large sample size, collaborative studies should be done with uniform protocols so that the data from different institutions will be comparable. Subjects for random allocation might be chosen from children referred for tonsillectomy and deemed appropriate for T and A by a central review board. The follow-up period should be sufficiently long to overcome the placebo effect of surgery. The outcome criteria should include some of the long-term consequences of the illnesses attributable to the presence of enlarged or diseased tonsils and adenoids. An example of this would be monitoring for hearing deficit, since one of the sequelae of repeated middle ear infections is diminished hearing.

Standardize Guidelines for Patient Management
The time has come to clearly define standardized management of patients with problems related to tonsils or adenoids. Carefully set guidelines should be made available at different institutions and to practicing ENT surgeons and primary care physicians. These guidelines should include recommendations for medical management, selection of patients for surgical consultation and surgery, management and duration of hospitalization, and observation for equivocal cases.

Medical Management. It is most likely that many cases of unnecessary surgery occur because some of those patients who could have been potentially relieved by medical intervention alone did not receive optimal therapy. For defined medical conditions related to tonsils and adenoids, protocols should be designed with appropriate treatment recommendations. For example, if a child comes in with an ear infection, what should be the first step? If the initial treatment fails, what then should be the second step? How would one define a treatment failure? Is it someone who did not respond to the first treatment, the second, or the third?

Selection of Patients for Surgical Consultation and Surgery. When should a primary physician refer the patient for consultation—after the first treatment failure, or the second? And when should patients be selected for surgery?

It is clear from the section on "Scientific Evidence for Efficacy of T and A" in this chapter that T and A as a therapeutic procedure does offer some benefits to a select group of patients. For instance, the majority of the studies showed T and A to be beneficial for recurrent tonsillitis or pharyngitis. Adenoidectomy also seemed to play a role in relieving recurrent otitis media. Therefore, despite the persisting question of efficacy, there are some patients for whom T and A is indicated. Criteria for T and A or adenoidectomy alone should be carefully specified.

A review board should be set up at different institutions to ensure that the protocols have been reasonably complied with and also to obtain another professional opinion on the decision for surgery.

Management and Duration of Hospitalization. Appropriate guidelines for specified laboratory tests are needed as a part of the preoperative evaluation and for appropriate nursing and medical care postoperatively.

A study by Heasman (1964) in England showed that the duration of stay for two common surgical conditions (T and A and inguinal herniorrhaphy without obstruction) differed widely. For instance, when four individual hospital groups were selected for further study, Hospital A appeared to routinely discharge T and A patients after three days. Hospital B with a smaller ENT department discharged its cases after six days. Hospital C discharged its cases between the third and sixth day, while Hospital D discharged 50 percent of its cases after one day and 36 percent between five and seven days. There were also wide regional differences. The median duration of stay in Leeds was 2.2 days while in the southwest metropolitan region, it was 5.7 days.

It is useful to remember that the shorter the stay, the less the psychologic trauma of hospitalization and also the lower the total cost of hospitalization.

Observation for Equivocal Cases. The study by Wood et al. (1972) showed that of the 217 children placed on the routine waiting list for T and A, 92 (42 percent) were discharged as needing no further treatment or observation after two separate review evaluations. The waiting time for these children had been up to three years and occasionally five years.

Thus, for equivocal cases where professional opinions for surgery may be equally divided, a period of waiting while under observation appears to be helpful.

Improvement of Primary Care

The primary care physician (pediatrician or general practitioner) has a responsible role in the decision as to whether or not tonsillectomy is necessary. He knows how often the child has had tonsillitis or otitis media and how ill he has been with it. Various studies have shown the importance of medical history as a factor in the decision for surgery. The appearance of the tonsils alone is not a very meaningful guide.

The primary physician also knows the family and is in the best position to alleviate parental anxiety over the child's illness. By reassuring the family that "everything" is being done to help the child, the primary physician can minimize parental pressure as a major reason for tonsillectomy.

The primary physician should also refer the patient to a reliable surgeon for consultation, but the decision for surgery should be primarily his. He should also screen individual candidates for hemorrhagic tendency or cardiac abnormality, since these can lead to surgical complications. He should instruct the parents how to prepare the child for hospitalization to minimize psychologic trauma.

Efforts should be made to help the young primary physician develop mature judgment so that he may try "to replace the security of thinking along well-defined, familiar channels with a new kind of security based on accepting ambiguity, uncertainty and open choice" (Knox, 1964).

Promote Education of the Public

Through magazine articles and news media programs, educational campaigns should be carried out to inform the public about the pros and cons of some of the commonly performed hospital procedures. Without raising the awareness level of the consumer, there will continue to be public misconceptions about many of the commonly performed procedures, evidenced particularly in unrealistic expectations of treatment benefits. One way of coping with the patient's pressure on the physician to "do something" is through education on the effectiveness and noneffectiveness of various medical services.

It is clear by now that there is no ready nor easy answer to the question of effectiveness of pediatric hospitalization. Intellectual openness appears to be essential to arriving at reasonable answers and decisions.

APPENDIX: ANATOMY AND PATHOLOGY OF TONSILS AND ADENOIDS

The complex of lymphoid tissue surrounding the opening of the lower airway includes two faucial tonsils (tonsils), pharyngeal tonsils (adenoids), lymphoid tissue at the base of the tongue (lingual tonsils), and lymphoid tissue on the posterior wall of the pharynx. This ring forms a protective barrier between the mouth and throat and the larynx, trachea, and lungs. In all probability, the lymphoid tissue of the throat plays an important role in the development of immune bodies. In fact, antibody-producing cells of all types are found within the tonsils (Workshop).

The tonsils, because of their location at the portal of entry for many microorganisms, have often been considered the first line of defense against respiratory infections. Microbial agents in the environment come into constant contact with their surface. The tonsils may act as an initial trapping mechanism for a variety of antigens, and it is probable that each infection in the pharyngeal lymphoid tissue stimulates the further protection. R. Thomas (Workshop) states that the function of the tonsil is to become infected with as many pathogens as possible in order to develop the appropriate immunity. He points out that studies reveal that almost every tonsil shows signs of inflammation and that histological studies cannot distinguish between inflammation and "simple hyperplasia." It appears that the tonsil becomes infected soon after birth and remains so throughout life.

The rate of increase of lymphoid tissue is relatively rapid throughout the first decade. At ten years of age there is nearly twice as much lymphoid tissue, including the tonsils and adenoids, as will be present at maturity (Snow, 1971). A childhood excess of lymphoid tissue, as judged by adult standards, may be considered "physiologic" rather than "pathologic" and may be expected to disappear in connection with normal developmental changes during the second decade. In an individual patient, therefore, age plays a role. However, the variation in the size and growth pattern of tonsils and adenoids are not really known (Workshop).

In addition to physiologic changes of growth and development which cause lymphoid hyperplasia (including tonsillar and adenoidal enlargement), pathologic hyperplasia may be due to infection or upper respiratory allergy. It is often difficult to differentiate the role of physiologic hyperplasia of growth and development from the hyperplasia secondary to infection or to allergic conditions. Thomas does so far as to say: "My propaganda has been that the tonsil varies in size; its size is relative to the size of the child's throat. If it is large, it may be doing its work extra well or recovering from an episode of acute infection. Anyway, how do we know that other organs that we cannot see are not also enlarged and should come out too?" (1961, p. 395). He goes on to say that such epithets as "enlarged tonsils" or "enormous tonsils" can only relate to the relative size of the tonsil to the throat. A tonsil may be made to appear large by too firm pressure with the spatula when examining. Absence or under-development of tonsil and adenoid tissue in an infant or young child who suffers from frequent attacks of upper or lower respiratory infections should be viewed with alarm and should raise a suspicion of possible immune deficiency syndromes (DeWeese, 1973).

Acute inflammation of the tonsils is generally a self-limited disease if there are no complications. It is accompanied by severe sore throat, fever, headache, chills, muscular pain, or abdominal pain. Often the lymph glands in the neck become enlarged and tender. Many cases of tonsillitis are thought to be caused by a bacterial agent, the group A beta-hemolytic streptococcus, which is also responsible for rheumatic fever and acute glomerulonephritis. If a bacterial agent is strongly suspected without laboratory confirmation, penicillin is still used for eradicating the organism in order to shorten the course of the disease and also, especially, to prevent the possible complications of streptococcal infection.

When we speak of the "tonsil problem," we generally refer to chronically hypertrophied or infected tonsils due either to recurrent or persistent throat infection. Generally obstruction to swallowing (due to the mechanical blockage from enlarged tonsils) and recurrent or persistent sore throat are the cardinal symptoms.

Infrequently acute tonsillitis or pharyngitis may lead to infection and abscess formation of the tissues adjacent to the tonsils. Quinsy (retrotonsillar abscess) and peritonsillar abscess are uncommon during infancy and relatively uncommon in later childhood. Again, the beta-hemolytic streptococcus is the most frequently involved agent. It has been observed that quinsy is very rare in children whose tonsils have been removed.

Adenoids, sometimes termed pharyngeal tonsils, are masses of lymphoid tissue located in the nasopharynx. They start to regress just before puberty and are usually absent in the adult. Acute infection of the adenoids rarely occurs alone. It almost always accompanies acute tonsillitis. Repeated attacks of acute inflammation of the adenoids eventually lead to adenoidal hypertrophy in many children. When adenoids are enlarged and persist, characteristic symptoms may develop. Nasal obstruction in varying degree is always present, leading to mouth-breathing, snoring, and slightly nasal timber of the voice. Chronic mouth-breathing leads to a typical facial expression due to changes in facial bone configuration. This is called "adenoidal facies," characterized by open mouth, high palatal arch, and pinched appearance of the middle third of the face.

Since adenoids are located near the opening of the Eustachian tubes connecting the middle ear with the pharynx, adenoid enlargement can occlude the orifice of the tube. The most common complication, then, of adenoid hyperplasia is partial blocking of the Eustachian tube, with retraction of the eardrum and fluctuating hearing loss due to impaired drainage of fluid. If chronic infection of the adenoids and hypertrophy are present, recurrent middle ear infection (otitis media) is often present, too. The combination of hypertrophy and chronic infection is the usual reason for recommending removal of the tonsils and adenoids. When adenoid hypertrophy is present without signs of chronic infection of the tonsils, removal of the adenoid tissue is often recommended.

REFERENCES

Albert, D.L. "Surgeons and operations," *N Engl J Med* 283 (1970):49.

Alpert, J.J., et al. "Effective use of comprehensive pediatric care: utilization of health resources," *Am J Dis Child* 116 (1968): 529.

Bakwin, H. "Pseudodoxia pediatricia," *N Engl J Med* 282 (1945): 691.

Bakwin, H. "The tonsil-adenoidectomy enigma," *J Pediatr* 52 (1958): 339.

Banham, T.M. "A survey of over 1000 school leavers who have had their tonsils removed," *J Laryngol Otol* 88 (1968): 203.

Baron, S.H. "Indications for adenoid and tonsil removal in children," *Rocky Mt Med J* Nov (1956): 999.

Bass, M.H. "Results of tonsillectomy in private practice," *Laryngoscope* 44 (1934): 780.

Bolande, R.P. "Ritualistic surgery," *N Engl J Med* 280 (1969): 591.

Bunker, J.P. "Surgical manpower: a comparison of operations and surgeons in the United States and in England and Wales," *N Engl J Med* 282 (1970): 135.

Chamovitz, R., et al. "The effect of tonsillectomy on the incidence of streptococcal respiratory disease and its complications," *Pediatrics* 26 (1960): 355.

Cochrane, A.L. *Effectiveness and Efficiency: Random Reflections on Health Services.* London: Nuffield Provincial Hospital Trust, 1972.

Crooks, J. "Tonsils and adenoids: evaluation of removal in 50 doctors' children," *Practitioner* 178 (1957): 215.

Danilevicius, Z. "When is tonsillectomy indicated?" *JAMA* 233 (1975): 273.

Densen, P.M., et al. "Prepaid medical care and hospital utilization," *Hospital Monograph Series*, No. 3, Chicago, American Hospital Association, 1958.

Densen, P.M., et al. "Prepaid medical care and hospital utilization," *Hospitals* 36 (1962): 63.

Denzer, B.S., and Felshin, G. "The pretonsillectomy clinic," *J Pediatr* 22 (1943): 239.

DeWeese, D.D. *Textbook of Otolaryngology*. St. Louis: Mosby, 1973.

Downes, J. "Changes in the risk of tonsillectomy over the period 1880–1949," *Milbank Mem Fund Q* 32 (1954): 22.

Epstein, I.M. "Factors influencing the results of tonsillectomy and adenoidectomy," *Am J Dis Child* 53 (1937): 1503.

Furman, R.A. "Handling parental pressure for T and A," *J Pediatr* 54 (1959): 195.

Glover, J.A. "The incidence of tonsillectomy in school children," *Proc R Soc Med* 31 (1938): 1219.

Haggerty, R.J., et al. *Child Health and the Community*. New York: John Wiley and Sons, 1975.

Hastings, J.E., et al. "Study: a comparison of personal health services utilization," *Can J Public Health* 61 (1970): 289.

Heasman, M.A. "How long in a hospital? A study in variation in duration of stay for two common surgical conditions," *Lancet* 2 (1964): 539.

Hiatt, H.H. "Protecting the medical commons: who is responsible?" *N Engl J Med* 293 (1975): 235.

Illingworth, R.S. et al. "Discussion—is the removal of tonsils and adenoids necessary?" *Proc R Soc Med* 54 (1961): 393.

Jackson, K., et al. "Behavior changes indicating emotional trauma in tonsillectomized children," *Pediatrics* 12 (1953): 23.

Johnston, J.S. and Watkins, T.W. "Tonsillectomy and adenoidectomy: a re-evaluation of results," *J Pediatr* 44 (1954): 127.

Kaiser, A.D. "Results of tonsillectomy: a comparative study of twenty-two hundred tonsillectomized children with an equal number of controls three and ten years after operation," *JAMA* 95 (1930): 837.

Klarman, H.E. "Effect of prepaid group practice on hospital use," *Public Health Rep* 78 (1963): 955.

Knox, G.S. "How often are we wrong? Or the epidemiology of doctor error," *OSMA Journal* 57 (1964): 494.

leRiche, H. and Stiver, W.B. "1000 cases of tonsillectomy in a prepayment plan: preoperative and postoperative history," *Can Med Assoc J* 77 (1957): 109.

Levy, D.M. "Psychic trauma of operations," *Am J Dis Child* 69 (1945): 7.

Lewis, D.W. "Variations in the incidence of surgery," *N Eng J Med* 281 (1969): 880.

Macbeth, R.G. "Discussion on the tonsil and adenoid problem," *J Laryngol Otol* 64 (1950): 580.

MacMahon, B. and Pugh, T.F. *Epidemiology: Principles and Methods*. Boston: Little, Brown and Co., 1970.

Mahaffy, P.R., Jr. "The effects of hospitalization on children admitted for tonsillectomy and adenoidectomy," *Nurs Res* 14 (1965): 12.

Mansfield, E. *Microeconomics: Theory and Applications*. New York: W.W. Norton & Co., Inc., 1970.

Mason, H.H. "Personal observations on the after-effects of tonsillectomy," *Laryngoscope* 44 (1934): 784.

Mawson, S.R., et al. "A controlled study evaluation of adenotonsillectomy in children," *J Laryngol Otol* 81 (1967): 777.

McKee, W.J.E. "A controlled study of the effects of tonsillectomy and adenoidectomy in children," *Brit J Prev Soc Med* 17 (1963a): 49.

McKee, W.J.E. "The part played by adenoidectomy in the combined operation of tonsillectomy with adenoidectomy," *Brit J Prev Soc Med* 17 (1963b): 133.

Mertz, J.C. "Tonsillectomy and respiratory illness in the population of two communities in New York State," *Milbank Mem Fund Q* 32 (1954): 5.

Nelson, W.E. *Textbook of Pediatrics.* Philadelphia: W.B. Saunders, 1964.

North, A.F., Jr. "An epidemic unchecked," *Pediatrics* 42 (1968): 708.

Olenick, A. "Does comprehensive care make a difference?: pediatric utilization in the Kaiser Health Plan of Oregon," *Am J Dis Child* 122 (1971): 478.

Paton, J.H.P. "The tonsil-adenoid operation in relation to the health of a group of schoolgirls," *Q J Med* 121 (1943): 119.

Perrott, G.S. "Utilization of hospital serviced under the Federal Employees Health Benefits Program." *Am J Public Health* 56 (1966): 57.

Poll on Medical Practice, *Modern Med* 10 Fed 1969: 77.

Pratt, L.W. "Tonsillectomy and adenoidectomy: mortality and morbidity," *Tr Am Acad Opth Otol* 74 (1970): 1146.

Ranger, D. "Tonsillectomy and adenoidectomy," *Lancet* 1 (1968): 1205.

Roghmann, K.J., et al. "Anticipated and actual effects of Medicaid on the medical care pattern of children," *N Engl J Med* 285 (1971): 1053.

Roydhouse, N. "A controlled study of adenotonsillectomy," *Arch Otolaryngol* 92 (1970): 611.

Schlesinger, E.R. "Tonsillectomy: some public health implications," *Health News* 34 (1957): 14.

Selkirk, T.K., and Mitchell, A.G. "Evaluation of the results of tonsillectomy and adenoidotomy," *Am J Dis Child* 42 (1931): 9.

Shah, C.P., and Carr, L.M. "Tonsillectomies: in dollars and cents," *Can Med Assoc J* 110 (1974): 301.

Smith, H.D. "Follow-up of patients eight months after tonsillectomy," *Arch Otolaryngol* 24 (1936): 488.

Snow, J.B. "Current status of the tonsil and adenoid problem," *OSMA Journal* 64 (1971): 47.

Stool, S.E., and Mast, W.R. "Tonsillectomies and adenoidectomies: are they necessary?" *Bol Asoc Med Puerto Rico* 65 (1973): 71.

Surgical Operations in Short-Stay Hospitals, United States—1971, National Center for Health Statistics, Series 13, No. 7.

Surgical Operations in Short-Stay Hospitals, United States—1971, National Center for Health Statistics, Series 13, No. 18.

Thomas, R. "Discussion—is the removal of tonsils and adenoids necessary?" *Proc R Soc Med* 54 (1961): 395.

Vaughan, V.C., et al., ed. *Nelson Textbook of Pediatrics.* Philadelphia: W.B. Saunders Co., 1975.

Vayda, E. "An analysis of pediatric surgery in operation in the U.S.A., Canada, and the United Kingdom," *N Engl J Med* 288 (1973): 527.

Waldbott, G.L., and Ascher, M.S. "The results of tonsillectomy in allergic patients: A follow-up study of 433 cases," *Tr Am Therap Soc* (1936): 82.

Wennberg, J., and Gittelsohn, A. "Small area variations in health care delivery," *Science* 182 (1973): 1102.

Wolman, I.J. "Tonsillectomy and adenoidectomy: an analysis of a nationwide practices," *Q Rev Pediatr* 11 (1956): 109.

Wood, B., et al. "Pediatricians look at children awaiting adenotonsillectomy," *Lancet* 2 (1972): 645.

Workshop on Tonsillectomy and Adenoidectomy, *Ann Otol Rhinol Laryngol* 84 (1975) Suppl. 19, No. 2.

Chapter 14

Common Uses of Hospitals:
A Look at Vermont

John Wennberg, M.D.
Sue Y.S. Kimm, M.D., M.P.H.[a]

The preceding chapter on the effectiveness of pediatric hospitalization built on the common surgical procedure of tonsillectomy and adenoidectomy (T and A) to make its points. In this chapter the emphasis will continue to be on common pediatric disturbances but with somewhat wider scope of disease or procedure considered. Our specific interest will be in the variability of use of hospitals for their treatment—the reasons for variability and the policy implications. We present a systematic analysis of the content of pediatric hospitalizations in Vermont and examine among thirteen geographically defined hospital service areas the extent of variations in case mix admitted to hospitals and in the use of common surgical procedures.

The differences can be large indeed. In the years 1969–71, the age-adjusted rate of tonsillectomy for Vermonters twenty-five years and younger ranged from a low of four to a high of forty-one procedures per thousand per year. It is estimated that 8 percent of residents in the low-rate area and 63 percent of residents in the high-rate area lose their tonsils through surgery (Vermont Cooperative Health Information Center, 1974).

A child may be hospitalized because of the nature of the illness itself; no physician would disagree with hospitalizing a child in a coma from diabetic ketoacidosis or a child convulsing from bacterial meningitis. A child may be hospitalized because the physician the patient contacts feels that the patient has a "hospitalizable" condi-

[a]Dr. Kimm coauthored the first half of this chapter, through "Variations in Use of Resources".

tion as defined by that physician; a second physician, seeing the same patient, might not agree. A child may be hospitalized primarily for nursing purposes to lighten the burden on the mother, who may not be able to cope with the chores of taking care of a sick child. Physicians may hospitalize some patients because parents demand hospitalization. Finally, the hospital may be selected, instead of the physician's office, as the site for diagnostic tests or specific treatment to minimize the direct out-of-pocket costs to the patient by taking advantage of the specific insurance coverage which may reimburse only for hospital services.

The latter part of the chapter reviews available evidence concerning the relative importance of provider and consumer characteristics in determining utilization patterns. The data suggest that the important reasons for variations between neighboring communities include the relative supply of different types of physicians and hospital facilities. But they also include what would appear to be fundamental differences in professional judgment in recognizing illness or in belief concerning the value of specific treatments. Some of the policy implications of this interpretation are discussed, with recommendations for consideration.

CHILDHOOD HOSPITALIZATIONS: STUDY METHODS

Studies at low levels of geographical aggregation, in which the study population is defined empirically by patterns of use of health care, lend themselves to association between local medical care organizations and the per capita rate of use of medical care by the population-at-risk. Lembcke (1959) found extensive differences in pelvic surgery among neighboring communities in Rochester, New York. More recently, population-based data systems covering total resident hospitalization experience have been developed in Vermont and Maine. Analysis of these data has shown extensive variations in age-adjusted rate of use of hospitals for medical as well as surgical conditions.[b]

[b]The data and analyses on which much of this report is based have been developed as part of a long-term health statistic project undertaken in the state of Vermont. This project was first sponsored by Regional Medical Program and more recently by the National Center for Health Statistics and the National Center for Health Service Research. The Cooperative Health Information Center of Vermont has generously contributed the data on which the analyses in "Childhood Hospitalizations: Study Methods" are based. In providing the data CHICV requests acknowledgement of the following specific disclaimer:

The methods developed in Vermont to measure the per capita use of health care have been extensively described in previous publications and are briefly summarized here (Wennberg and Gittelsohn, 1975). Our approach is made possible because of the willingness of all hospitals in Vermont and neighboring out-of-state areas to provide a uniform discharge abstract to the Cooperative Health Information Center of Vermont. Abstracts for a five-year period, 1969–73, available for this study, contain information on the diagnosis, operative procedure, attending physician and surgeon, and the patient's age, sex, and Vermont town of residence. We took three distinct analytic steps: the first to group Vermont towns into hospital service areas, the second to analyze the content of pediatric hospitalizations for children age one month to fifteen years, and the third to obtain admission rates for specific conditions causing admission and for common surgical procedures.

Hospital Service Areas

Like most New England states, Vermont is well situated for small-area analysis of health care delivery. The state is organized administratively into over 250 towns, each with average area of about thirty-six square miles. Geographic areas for study were defined by assigning Vermont towns to a unique hospital service area. A simple procedure was followed: patient records were classified initially by town and hospital, and towns were then assigned to the hospital used by 60 percent or more of patients. Towns assigned to out-of-state hospitals are not included in this study. Sixteen areas were defined. For this study, three areas with populations less than 7000 have been excluded, leaving thirteen areas for study (Figure 14–1). Of the included areas, three have two local hospitals and the remainder one local hospital. Most common procedures are performed at local hospitals, and there is thus a close correspondence between clinical management practices at local institutions and the per capita rate of hospitalization and surgery (Wennberg and Gittelsohn, 1973).

Content of Pediatric Hospitalizations

During the five-year period a total of 63,394 discharges occurred to residents of the thirteen study areas who were between the age of

---

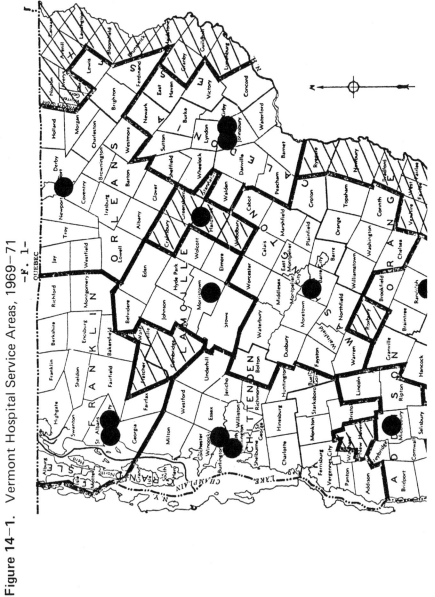

Figure 14–1. Vermont Hospital Service Areas, 1969–71

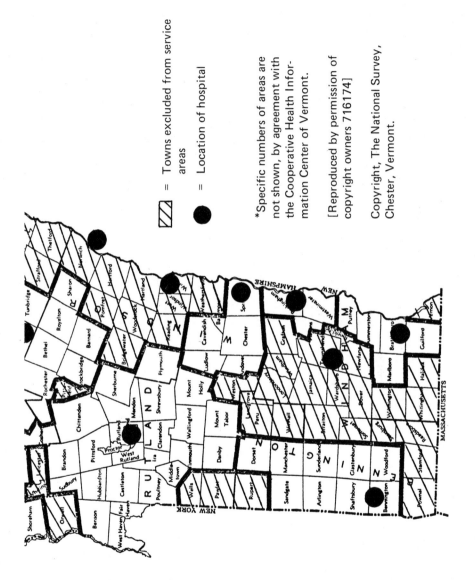

= Towns excluded from service areas

= Location of hospital

*Specific numbers of areas are not shown, by agreement with the Cooperative Health Information Center of Vermont.

[Reproduced by permission of copyright owners 716174]

Copyright, The National Survey, Chester, Vermont.

Table 14–1. Children-Years at Risk and Hospitalizations by Cause of Admission, Vermont Hospital Service Areas, 1969–73[a])

	Area 1	Area 2	Area 3	Area 4	Area 5	Area 6
Number of Children-years at risk ($\times 10^3$)	15.1	25.2	10.5	20.6	31.9	48.0
Number of hospitalizations:						
All causes	1965	2491	1063	1601	2968	3621
Infectious diseases	858	1123	479	611	1141	1035
Injuries and adverse effects	252	415	152	182	393	644
Hypertrophied tonsils	233	131	150	241	411	532
Symptoms and ill-defined conditions	114	104	46	78	105	162
Congenital malformations	67	89	33	83	139	185
Inguinal hernia	39	48	15	48	88	99
Appendicitis	28	42	30	35	101	139
Neoplasms	17	12	4	18	33	47
All other	356	526	151	302	550	772

[a]Excludes children over fifteen years and under one month of age.

one month and fifteen years. These were classified by cause of admission and by primary surgical procedure. We grouped closely related causes to define as many specific conditions as possible. For each area, the number of children-years at risk and the number of cases by condition causing admission are given in Table 14–1.

Incidence of Hospitalization by Area

The 1970 census population for each town (grouped into hospital service areas and multiplied by 5) serves as the denominator for computing incidence rates. The numerator includes all resident hospitalizations (1969–73) regardless of whether in a local or an out-of-area hospital. The rates are therefore estimates of the total incidence. To increase statistical stability, all children between the ages of one month and twenty years are used in computing the rates by areas for specific conditions or procedures. Age-adjustment to the Vermont

Table 14-1. continued

Area 7	Area 8	Area 9	Area 10	Area 11	Area 12	Area 13	All Areas
16.0	28.5	20.8	67.8	72.8	161.2	13.9	532.3
1923	2268	2038	5624	5121	10334	843	41860
595	673	701	2064	1427	3027	246	13980
281	362	258	654	725	1826	125	6269
458	279	378	895	1056	1112	69	5945
95	154	143	281	241	701	60	2284
49	90	116	262	256	636	40	2045
47	67	45	186	214	428	34	1358
69	103	43	145	149	255	41	1180
25	28	27	75	81	146	12	525
300	509	325	1050	970	2173	214	8198

population permits direct comparisons of areas with different age structures, thus eliminating age as a possible explanation of differences. Admissions for pregnancy-related conditions are not included in our analysis. The average number of beds occupied by patients per 1000 population is estimated by dividing the patient day rate by 365.

Statistical Analysis

The expected number of admissions within each area is obtained by multiplying the population in each age group by the corresponding age-specific rate obtained for all areas and summing the age-specific number of cases across all included pediatric age groups. Statistical differences among areas are based on chi-square distributions with one degree of freedom, for which the null hypothesis states that an individual area does not differ from the rate for all areas taken together. The extent to which areas differ for specific procedures or causes for admission are sometimes shown by the coefficient of variations and sometimes by the range between highest and lowest rates. The extent to which variations in per capita use of beds and dollars relate to variations in the incidence of hospitalization or, alternatively, to the length of stay in hospital is evaluated by the "explained variance" or R^2 statistic. It represents an estimate of the variance or difference among the values of one variable which is explained by difference among the values of the second. In calculating the R^2 statistic, the logarithm form of the regression equation has been used.

CAUSES OF CHILDHOOD HOSPITALIZATIONS

During the five-year study period, the average annual rate of hospitalization of children of age one month to fifteen years is 794 admissions per 10,000 (Table 14−2). Infants enter hospitals about four times more often than older children. Three types of admissions— infectious conditions, injuries and adverse effects, and hypertrophied tonsils—are responsible for about 62 percent of pediatric admissions. Among infants and preschoolers, infectious diseases are the most common reason for entering the hospital. Fifty-five percent of infant admissions are for this class of admissions; 5.5 percent are for injuries. Hypertrophied tonsils is an uncommon reason for admission during the first year of life, about 0.4 percent of all admissions. Among preschoolers (ages one to four), tonsillectomies comprise 13.4 percent, injuries and adverse effects 12.2 percent, and infectious conditions, 40.1 percent of all admissions. Hypertrophy of the tonsil is the most common cause for admission for children age five to nine, comprising 26.0 percent of all admissions. For early teenagers (ages ten to fourteen) injuries and adverse effects are the most common reason for admission.

The infectious diseases most responsible for pediatric admission to hospital are pneumonias, otitis media, diarrheal disease, and acute bronchitis. Together these conditions comprise 61.2 percent of infectious illness admissions and account for 20.3 percent of all pediatric admissions. As with all infectious diseases, the age-specific incidence rate is highest in infancy. Diseases of the lower respiratory tract— pneumonia and bronchitis—are the most common infectious conditions in preschool children. However, in younger school-aged children, otitis media is the most prevalent condition (Table 14−3).

Admissions for injuries and adverse effects account for 15 percent of all childhood admissions. Of all admissions for injuries and adverse effects, fractures and dislocations represent 40 percent, head injuries

Table 14–2.   Childhood Hospitalizations by Cause of Admission, by Age Group, 1969–73, Vermont
(Average Annual Rates per 10,000 Children)

Condition	Age in Years				All Children Less Than Fifteen Years of Age[a]
	$<1^a$	1–4	5–9	10–14	
Infectious diseases	1333	306	166	111	263
Injuries and adverse effects	134	90	104	156	118
Hypertrophy of the tonsils	11	102	170	70	112
Symptoms and ill-defined conditions	171	41	28	36	43
Congenital malformations	173	38	28	22	38
Inguinal hernias	114	35	16	9	26
Appendicitis	1	3	21	46	22
Neoplasms	15	11	7	12	10
All others	486	134	114	171	162
All conditions	2438	763	655	632	794

[a]Excludes children less than one month of age.

Table 14-3. Annual Age-Specific Incidence of Childhood Hospitalizations for Infectious Diseases, Vermont, 1966-73 *(Rates per 10,000 Children)*

	Age				*All Children Less Than Fifteen Years of Age*
	Less Than 1	*1-4*	*5-9*	*10-14*	
Pneumonia	299	73	23	11	51
Otitis media	101	39	51	18	41
Diarrhea	225	35	18	22	37
Acute bronchitis	253	40	9	5	32
Acute sinusitis, pharyngitis and tonsilitis	44	23	16	9	18
Acute laryngitis or trachitis	91	32	5	1	17
Oral infections	68	14	10	10	15
Acute upper respiratory infections, unspecified; common cold	115	17	6	3	15
All other infectious diseases	139	33	27	23	35

17 percent, and open wounds and trauma to joints and subcutaneous tissue 10 percent. Adverse effects of drugs, surgery, and other therapy comprise 7 percent, or about 1 percent of all pediatric admissions. In contrast to infectious diseases, the incidence of hospitalization for injuries (particularly fractures and dislocations) is higher among older children. Adverse effects of therapy, however, have a higher incidence in younger age groups (Table 14-4).

Other common reasons for childhood hospitalizations include "symptoms and ill-defined conditions" (5.4 percent) congenital malformations (4.8 percent), inguinal hernia (3.3 percent), appendicitis 2.8 percent), and benign and malignant neoplasms (1.3 percent). The incidence of hospitalization of inguinal hernia, congenital malformations, and symptoms and ill-defined conditions are highest in the first year of life, but occur commonly in each childhood age group. Admissions for appendicitis are most common in the early teenage group, where they represent 7.3 percent of all admissions, with an incidence rate of 46 cases per 10,000 children (Aday and Eichorn, 1972). Appendicitis is rarely a cause for admission among infants.

Table 14-4. Age-Specific Incidence of Childhood Hospitalizations for
Injuries and Adverse Effects, Vermont, 1969-73 *(Rates per 10,000 Children)*

| | *Age* | | | | *All Children Less Than Fifteen Years of Age* |
	Less Than 1	*1-4*	*5-9*	*10-14*	
Fractures and dislocations	35	17	44	79	47
Head Injuries	18	13	21	24	20
Open wounds	6	11	12	15	12
Damage to joints without dislocation	12	8	10	15	11
Adverse reaction to medical treatment and toxic materials	15	14	6	6	8
All other injuries	48	29	11	17	20
All injuries	34	93	104	156	118

Admissions for neoplasms occur at approximately the same incidence rate among each age group.

Variations Among Areas

Table 14-5 shows the age-adjusted rate of admission for each cause of hospitalization for which there were more than 1000 cases during the five-year study period. For most of the conditions there are substantial numbers of admissions in late teenage years, and we have included all persons from one month to twenty years in calculating these rates. Rates are given for each of the thirteen Vermont hospital service areas. Table 14-6 summarizes the variations observed in rates of admission among areas.

The over-all rate of hospitalization of children shows substantial differences among the thirteen areas. The lowest area has an age-adjusted admission rate of 742 admissions per 10,000 children; the highest area is nearly 1.9 times higher: 1387 admissions per 10,000 children. The rates are age-adjusted to the age structure of all thirteen areas. Hypertrophy of the tonsil, infectious conditions (pneumonia, diarrheal diseases, otitis media, and acute bronchitis and bronchiolitis) show the most variation: the ratios of the highest to the lowest area are between 4.2 and 6.0 for these conditions. For each condition the rates in nine or more of the thirteen areas are statistically different from the rate for all areas. For these conditions

Table 14–5. Age Adjusted Incidence of Hospitalization by Cause of Admission, Vermont Hospital Service Areas (Average Annual Rates, 1969–73, per 10,000 Children One Month through Nineteen Years)

AREA	All causes of hospitalization	Hypertrophy of tonsils and adenoids	Fractures, joint dislocations	Symptomatic disorders of unknown cause	Pneumonia	Dysentery, gastroenteritis, diarrhea diseases	Congenital malformations	Otitis media	Appendicitis, "other" diseases of the appendix	Acute bronchitis, bronchiolitis	Head injury, intracranial injury	Inguinal hernia with or without intestinal obstruction
All Areas[a]	892	96	55	45	40	33	33	32	27	25	23	22
1	1387[c]	131[c]	67	78[c]	76[c]	87[c]	37	44[b]	26	70[c]	23	23
7	1340[c]	237[c]	76[c]	64[c]	50	49[c]	30	33	46[c]	59[c]	34[b]	27
3	1137[c]	118[b]	67	52	91[c]	52[c]	25	48[b]	30	65[c]	37[c]	13
9	1058[c]	154[c]	49	66[c]	32	53[c]	46[c]	22[b]	26	41[c]	26	19
2	1041[c]	52[c]	77[c]	43	78[c]	72[c]	31	20[c]	18[c]	72[c]	28	19
5	1032[c]	109[b]	48	37[b]	84[c]	39	36	46[c]	37[c]	33[b]	24	24
8	980[b]	90	58	63[c]	29[c]	33	28	13[c]	38[c]	26	20	22
10	905	113[c]	52	44	59[c]	28[b]	34	54[c]	25	19[c]	20	23
4	894	108	46	41	56[c]	34	34	50[c]	22	27	19	18
6	883	93	66[c]	37[b]	41	26[b]	33	21[c]	35[c]	14[c]	22	18
11	843[b]	121[c]	49[b]	35[c]	29[c]	35	30	12[c]	26	23	23	24
12	743[c]	59[c]	51	43	18[c]	21[c]	34	35	20[c]	12[c]	23	21
13	742[c]	44[c]	56	47	32	19[c]	23	20[b]	32	19	27	21

[a]Ranked by rate of horizontalization for all causes.   [b]Chi-square significant at .01 level.   [c]Chi-square significant at .001 level.

Table 14-6. Variations in Causes for Hospitalization, Thirteen Vermont Areas, 1969-73
(Children One Month Through Nineteen Years)

Condition	Age-adjusted Incidence Rate Per 10,000 Children					
	All 13 Areas	High Area	Low Area	Ratio of High to Low	Coefficient of Variation	No. of Statistical Outliers <.01
All causes	892	1387	742	1.9	36	10
Hypertrophy of tonsils and adenoids	96	237	44	5.4	45	10
Fractures, joint dislocation	55	77	46	1.7	18	4
Symptomatic disorders of unknown cause	45	78	35	2.2	27	7
Pneumonia	40	91	18	5.0	47	9
Dysentery, gastroenteritis, diarrheal diseases	33	87	19	4.6	48	9
Congenital malformations	33	46	23	2.0	18	1
Otitis media	32	54	13	4.2	46	11
Appendicitis, "other" diseases of the appendix	27	46	18	2.6	27	6
Acute bronchitis, bronchiolitis	25	72	12	6.0	60	9
Head injury, intracranial injury	23	37	19	2.0	21	2
Inguinal hernia with or without intestinal obstruction	22	27	13	2.1	17	0

the coefficient of variation is considerably higher than that for all causes.

Other conditions exhibit less variation. Among the lowest are admissions for inguinal hernia, head injuries, fractures and dislocations, and congenital malformations.

COMMON CHILDHOOD
SURGICAL PROCEDURES

Of all children hospitalized between the ages of one month and fifteen years, 46.8 percent undergo a surgical procedure. By far the most common procedure is tonsillectomy: 13.9 percent of all admissions in this age group receive a tonsillectomy—and tonsillectomy comprised nearly 30 percent of all surgery (Table 14−7). Four procedures—inguinal herniorrhaphies, appendectomies, tonsillectomies, and fracture reduction—account for half of childhood surgery. Twenty-two other procedures make up an additional 36 percent. The more common of these (each comprising 2 percent or more of surgery) are: Incision and suture of skin and subcutaneous tissue (5.2 percent), strabismus (3.7 percent), urethral surgery (2.6 percent), teeth extraction (2.2 percent), and traction or fixation of bone for conditions other than fractures (2.0 percent). (Circumcision may seem to deserve a higher place in common procedures. The principal reason that it does not is that it is most commonly performed at less than one month of age.)

Variation Among Areas in Use
of Surgical Procedures

Among the thirteen areas there is a 2.2 fold range of difference in the exposure of children to surgery. The age-adjusted rate in the lowest area is 287 procedures per 10,000 children; in the highest area the rate is 642. Table 14−8 gives the average rate for each of the eight most commonly performed procedures and compares it to the high-area rate and the low-area rate. Their variations are summarized by ratio of high to low.

Of the four most common procedures there are large differences among areas for tonsillectomy. The rates range from 42 to 232 procedures per 10,000 children, a 5.5 fold difference. Nine of the thirteen areas show a statistically significant difference in rates. Appendectomies and in-hospital reduction of fractures show moderate variations among areas. For these procedures there is about a threefold difference between the highest and the lowest areas in incidence. For

Table 14–7. Frequency Distribution and Incidence Rate of the Twenty-Six Most Commonly Performed Surgical Procedures (Vermont Children, One Month through Fifteen Years)

Procedure	Frequency of All Admissions %		Frequency of All Surgery %		Incidence per 10,000 Children
	Each	Accum.	Each	Accum.	
Tonsillectomy	13.90	13.90	29.72	29.72	110.8
Fracture reduction	3.74	17.64	8.00	37.72	29.9
Inguinal herniorraphy	3.09	20.73	6.62	44.34	24.7
Appendectomy	3.00	23.73	6.40	50.74	23.9
Incision, suture of skin and subcutaneous tissue	2.43	26.16	5.18	55.92	19.4
Myringotomy	2.28	28.14	4.88	60.80	18.2
Adenoidectomy alone	1.97	30.41	4.20	65.00	15.7
Strabismus	1.75	32.16	3.73	68.73	13.9
Urethral surgery	1.21	33.37	2.60	71.33	9.7
Teeth extraction	1.03	34.40	2.20	73.53	8.2
Traction or fixation without fracture	0.94	35.34	2.00	75.53	7.5
Muscle or tendon surgery	0.68	36.02	1.46	76.99	5.5
Joint surgery	0.55	36.57	1.18	78.17	4.4
Orchioplexy	0.54	37.11	1.14	79.31	4.3

(Table 14–7. cont'd overleaf . . .)

Table 14–7. continued

Procedure	Frequency of All Admissions %		Frequency of All Surgery %		Incidence per 10,000 Children
	Each	Accum.	Each	Accum.	
Osteotomy	0.52	37.63	1.11	80.42	4.2
Circumcision	0.49	38.12	1.06	81.48	3.9
Tympanoplasty	0.39	38.51	.84	82.32	3.1
Skin graft	0.33	38.84	.33	83.03	2.7
Pylorotomy	0.32	39.16	0.68	83.71	2.6
Umbilical herniorraphy	0.28	39.44	0.59	84.30	2.2
Joint dislocation	0.22	39.66	0.48	84.78	1.8
Intracranial procedures	0.21	39.87	0.46	85.24	1.7
Bladder surgery	0.19	40.66	0.40	85.64	1.5
Ventricular shunts for hydrocephalus	0.19	40.25	0.40	86.04	1.5
Surgical procedures for cleft palate	0.12	40.37	0.26	86.30	1.0
Cosmetic repair of external ear	0.06	40.43	0.13	86.43	0.5
All other surgery	6.34	46.77	13.55	99.98	50.60

Table 14—8. Variations in Incidence of Common Surgery for Children One
Month Through Nineteen Years (Vermont Hospital Service Areas, 1969—73)

Procedure	Age-adjusted Incidence Rate Per 10,000 Children				
	All 13 Areas	High Area	Low Area	Ratio of High to Low	Number of Statistical Outliers .01
All surgical discharges	387	642	287	2.2	10
Tonsillectomy and adenoidectomy, tonsillectomy	96	232	42	5.5	9
Fracture reduction	32	54	19	2.8	6
Appendectomy	29	59	19	3.1	6
Incision, suture skin, subcutaneous tissue	24	52	13	4.0	8
Inguinal herniorraphy	21	27	13	2.1	0
Myringotomy	14	41	3	13.8	8
Adenoidectomy	12	21	4	5.3	5
Repair of strabismus	11	19	4	4.8	3

each procedure, six of the areas exhibit rates that are statistically significant in their differences from the rate for all areas.

On the other hand, the differences among areas for inguinal hernia procedures is considerably less. In no area is the rate of inguinal herniorrhaphy statistically different from the average of all areas. The coefficient of variation is the lowest for all procedures, as is the range of difference from the highest to the lowest area. Among procedures exhibited in the table, myringotomy shows the widest range of difference in use: a thirteenfold difference between the highest and the lowest area.

Among the less commonly employed procedures there are interesting patterns of variation. Ventricular shunts for hydrocephalus and repair of umbilical hernia are illustrative (Table 14—9). Shunt surgery shows little variation among areas, suggesting uniformity in incidence, access to care, and choice of therapy throughout the region. By contrast, umbilical herniorrhaphy shows considerable variation among areas. In Area 11 the observed number of cases was less than half the expected, based on the average for all areas; in Area 5, three times as many occurred as were predicted by the average. Although Area 12 has more than four times as many children as Area 5, only one proce-

Table 14–9. Observed and Expected Umbilical Hernia Repair Procedures and Treatment of Hydrocephalus by Ventricular Shunt (Vermont Hospital Service Areas)

Area	Umbilical Herniorraphy			Ventricular Shunt Procedures		
	Observed	Expected	Chi-square[a]	Observed	Expected	Chi-square[a]
1	7	3.4	3.7	5	2.4	2.9
2	1	5.6	3.7	5	3.0	.3
3	1	2.3	.7	1	1.6	.2
4	6	5.2	.1	0	Na[e]	Na[e]
5	22	7.2	30.2[d]	2	5.0	1.8
6	6	11.3	2.5	7	7.7	.1
7	10	3.7	11.0[d]	2	2.5	.1
8	12	6.6	4.3[b]	8	4.6	2.6
9	4	4.6	.1	5	3.2	1.0
10	29	15.3	12.3[d]	13	10.6	.6
11	7	16.8	5.7[b]	13	11.5	.2
12	17	38.7	12.2[d]	24	26.3	.2
13	2	3.3	.5	0	Na[e]	Na[e]

[a] Statistical differences are based on chi-square distribution with one degree of freedom with null hypothesis that an individual area does not differ from the rate for all areas taken together.   [e] Areas with zero observed cases are excluded.

[b] $p \leq .05$ [c] $p \leq .01$ [d] $p \leq .001$

dure was performed on children under age one year. In Area 5, eighteen children of the same age received the procedure.

Other less common procedures that show no statistical outliers include cardiac catheterization and surgery for cleft palate.

VARIATIONS IN USE OF RESOURCES

Use of Hospital Beds

The differences in use of hospital beds associated with variations in pediatric patient mix treated in Vermont hospitals have been measured. Table 14−10 shows the average number of beds occupied daily per 10,000 resident children, ages one month through nineteen years in four selected Vermont hospital service areas and in all areas. Obstetrical bed use has been excluded from the analysis. The areas selected for display are the two areas (1 and 7) with the highest and the two areas (12 and 13) with the lowest rates of pediatric admission to hospital.

Nearly 90 percent more beds (per capita) are used for pediatric hospitalizations in the highest than in the lowest use area. In the lowest areas, average bed use is about 7.5 beds per 10,000 population in the highest area, average bed use is about 14.3 per 10,000 population. In the lowest areas, 20 percent of beds are devoted to infectious disease conditions (1.5 beds per 10,000). In contrast, the highest bed-use area devotes 38 percent of its beds to infectious diseases and has a bed-use rate of 5.3, 375 percent higher than the lowest use area. In the lowest areas, most beds are devoted to injuries.

Area 7 is markedly higher than the others in use of beds for tonsillectomies. Between the lowest area for this condition and Area 7 there is an 8.8 fold difference for the allocation of hospital resources. Area 7 is also high on bed use for appendectomies and neoplasms.

Intensity of Care Versus Decision to Admit

Are decisions concerning the intensity of care after admission—as measured by length of stay in hospital—or the processes that lead to the decision to admit patients the more important determinant of the observed variations in use of hospital beds? For most conditions, variations in rate of admission rather than length of stay account for most of the variations in use rates (Figure 14−2 and Table 14−11). For all pediatric admissions and for the major causes of pediatric admissions—infectious diseases, injuries, and tonsillectomies—the majority of the variance in inpatient days per 10,000 population among the thirteen Vermont hospital service areas is accounted for

Table 14–10.   Average Number of Beds Occupied per 10,000 Children One Month through Nineteen Years (Areas 1 and 7, Highest Pediatric Admission Rates, versus Areas 12 and 13, Lowest Pediatric Admission Rates)

Area	All Conditions	Infectious Diseases	Injuries	Hypertrophied Tonsils	Congenital Anomalies	Appendectomy	Symptoms, Ill-defined	Neoplasm	Inguinal Hernia	All Others
1	14.30	5.28	3.03	.29	.55	.30	.67	.16	.23	3.03
7	12.52	2.99	2.99	1.32	.41	.70	.52	.36	.20	3.03
12	7.53	1.55	2.11	.24	.53	.25	.38	.19	.11	2.17
13	7.58	1.40	2.68	.15	.28	.38	.37	.13	.11	2.08
All areas	10.57	2.55	2.26	.80	.54	.41	.39	.19	.16	2.41

Table 14-11. Variance in Per Capita Bed Use Associated with Variance
in Average Length of Stay and with Admission Rate to Hospital
(Vermont Hospital Service Areas)[†]

Condition	Incidence of Hospitalization	Length of Stay in Hospital
All conditions	.84	.04
Infectious diseases	.78	.35
Injuries and adverse effects	.56	.05
Hypertrophy of tonsils	.97	.41
Inguinal hernia	.00	.69
Appendicitis	.73	.14
Congenital malformations	.23	.57
Symptoms and ill-defined conditions	.61	.15

[†]Based on logarithmic regression (R^2).

by variations in admission rates. Only for inguinal hernias and congenital anomalies (conditions for which the hospitalization rates showed the least variation between areas) do differences in the length of stay appear to account for more than 50 percent of the variations in hospital facilities allocated for their treatment.

Charge Per Case and Per Capita Expenditure

Variations in rate of hospitalization rather than variations in charge per case appears to be the major reason for variations in per capita expenditure for specific treatments. Figure 14-3 is adapted from studies in Maine and shows the relationship between admissions per capita and charge per case and per capita expenditures. The figure also gives the R^2 statistic. For tonsillectomy and appendectomy, most of the variation in per capita expenditures is related to differences in the decision to undertake the procedure and little to variations in the charges among areas. In contrast, for inguinal hernia (which in Maine as in Vermont shows the least variation of common procedures) the incidence rate shows less importance, accounting for under 50 percent of the variation.

CAUSES OF VARIATION[c]

The use of medical care by an individual depends on his illness and his own behavior in seeking care. Yet studies undertaken in Vermont

[c]The reader is reminded that the sections from here to the end of the chapter were written by J.E. Wennberg. The opinions reflected are his.

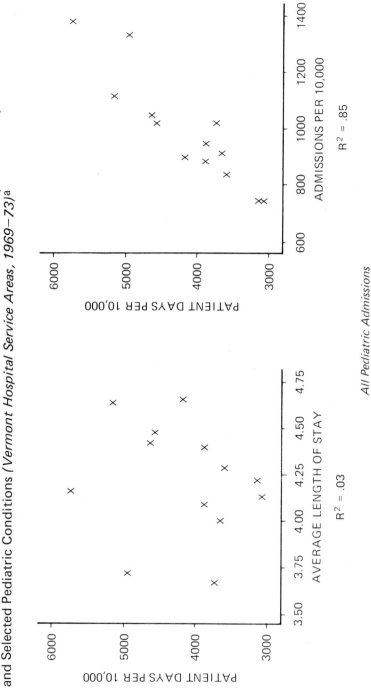

Figure 14–2. Relationship of Length of Stay and Admission Rate with Per Capita Bed Use, All and Selected Pediatric Conditions *(Vermont Hospital Service Areas, 1969–73)*[a]

[a]The *R*² statistic is from the logarithm example of the regression equation.

Figure 14—2. continued

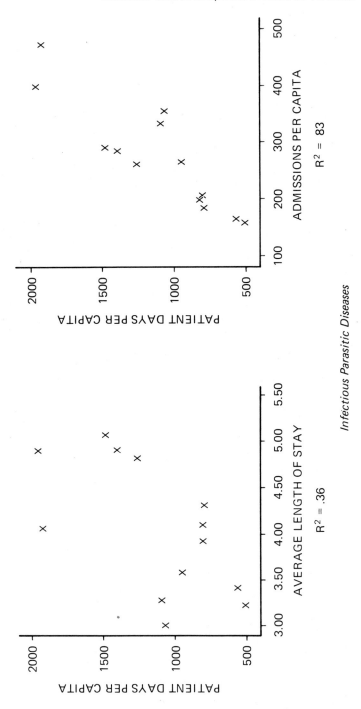

Infectious Parasitic Diseases

Figure 14–2. continued

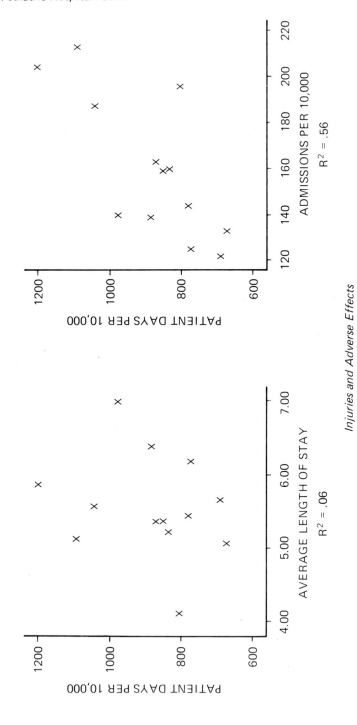

Injuries and Adverse Effects

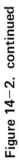

Figure 14–2. continued

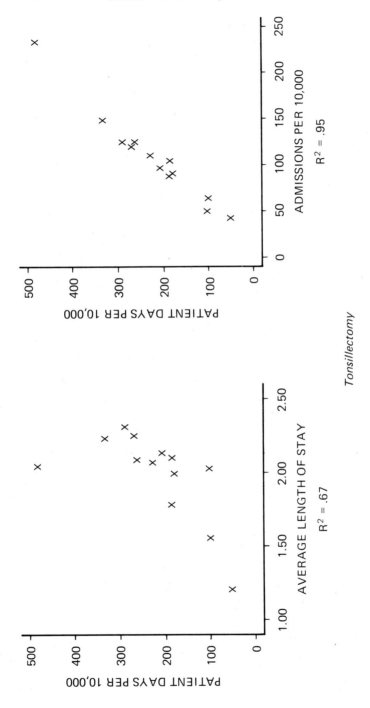

Tonsillectomy

Figure 14–2. continued

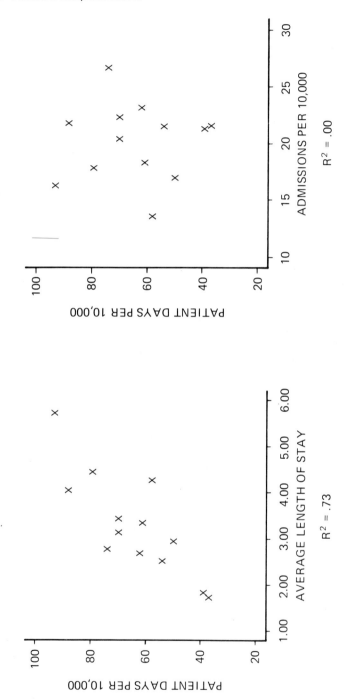

Inguinal Herniorrhaphy

Figure 14–2. continued

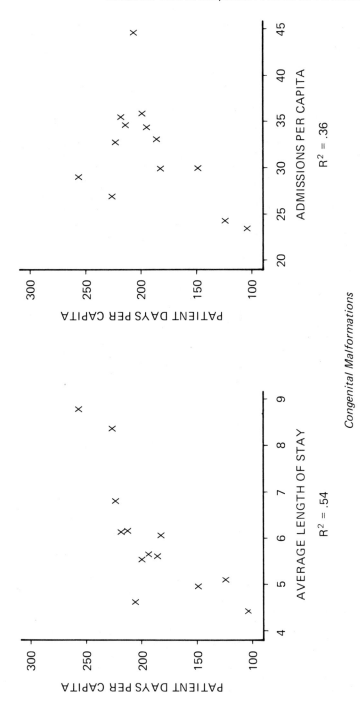

Congenital Malformations

Figure 14–3.   Relationship of Charge per Case and Admission Rate with Per Capita Expenditure Rate for Three Common Surgical Procedures (*Eight Maine Hospital Service Areas, 1973*)[a]

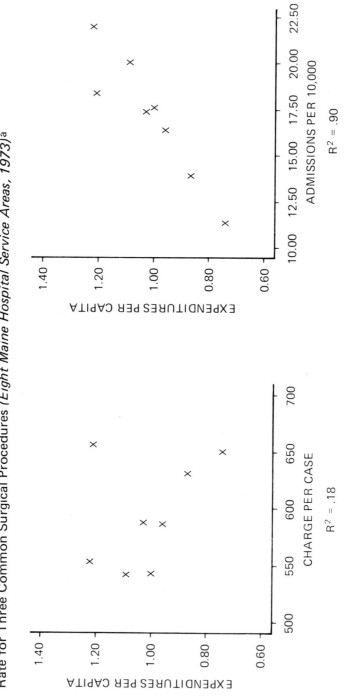

Appendectomy

[a]The R^2 statistic is from the logarithm example of the regression equation.

Figure 14–3. continued

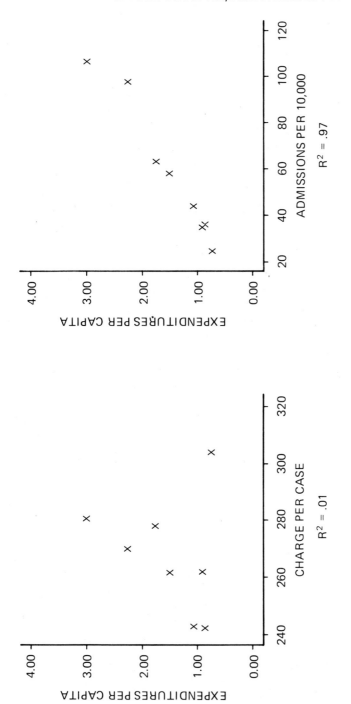

Tonsillectomy

Figure 14—3. continued

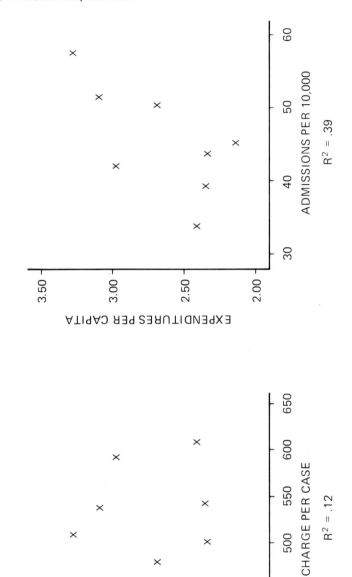

Hernia

on consumer characteristics show that hospital service areas at the extremes of utilization are well matched on characteristics which predict demand for health care among individuals (Wennberg, Fowler and Gittelsohn, unpublished). Further, demand as defined by patient-initiated physician contacts appears to be similar. This evidence has been obtained by sample survey. Based on observed differences in 1969 rates of use of hospital, a household survey was undertaken of residents living in two contiguous hospital service areas, the one with the highest and the one with the lowest age-adjusted rate of use of hospital. These two areas are also the areas ranking highest and lowest in our five-year study of pediatric hospitals (Hospital Service Areas 1 and 13).

The contrasts between these areas are instructive. There are few differences among the residents of the two areas. They report similar illness rates; they have similar demographic and economic circumstances, including the extent of insurance coverage. Further, they appear to contact their physicians in similar proportions on an annual basis and on an episode of illness basis (Table 14–12).

Other studies have suggested the importance of supply of beds and, particularly, physicians. We have found, as have Lewis (1969) and Vayda (1975), that supply of surgeons is positively related to the surgery rate. Yet, although the over-all supply of surgeons may be similar among neighboring communities, surgical workload is not allocated similarly among the various types of surgical procedures. Patterns of variation observed in a recently completed study in Maine illustrate this point (Figure 14–4).

The five largest hospital service areas in Maine are contiguous and large enough so that chance variations are not plausible explanations for patterns of surgery incidence. In three of the areas the over-all rate of surgery is similar. Yet, from area to area the pattern of allocation of surgical technology is different. For five selected procedures, the one performed most commonly is different in four of the five areas.

Remuneration to the surgeon for surgical work is based primarily on time surgeons spend in the operating room (Hughes et al., 1972). There is no obvious economic incentive for physicians to select one procedure over another. Similar patterns of variation in individual procedures were observed among Vermont areas. The variation in use of specific technology appears to reflect differences among physicians in their belief about effectiveness or in their judgments concerning how health care needs are defined.

Uncertainty in Diagnosis. Our studies of variability in procedure rate among Vermont children provide examples of these uncertain-

Table 14–12. Characteristics of Populations Living in Highest and Lowest Hospital Use Areas

	Area 1: Highest Rate of Hospitalization Among Thirteen Vermont Areas	Area 13: Lowest Rate of Hospitalization Among Thirteen Vermont Areas
Sociodemographic characteristics of adults		
Percent white	97	98
Percent Vermont-born	58	57
Percent living in area more than twenty years	47	47
Household economic characteristics		
Percent of families below poverty level	23	20
Percent with health insurance	84	85
Percent of insurance policies, Blue Cross	54	50
Households with regular place of physician care	99	97
Illness levels		
Percent with any restricted days in last two weeks for chronic conditions	4	5
Percent with chronic conditions	22	25
Percent with more than two weeks of bed days in last year	5	4
Access to physicians		
Percent of population with physician contact within year preceding interview	73.4	72.6
Percent of population with episode of illness contacting physician within 2 weeks of interview	26.4	31.5
Percent of females 18 years or older receiving one or more Papanicolou tests within year preceding interview	54.8	63.2

Table 14–12. continued (note)

(Adapted from Wennberg, J., and Fowler, F.J., "A Test of Consumer Contribution to Small Area Variations in Health Care Delivery," to be published in a
forthcoming edition of the Journal of the Maine Medical Association, Number
of adults in interviewed households is 541 in Area 1 and 478 in Area 13: 280
households were interviewed in Area 1, 245 in Area 13. There are no significant
differences between these areas on any of the listed characteristics.)

ties. In the case of appendectomy, the medical literature indicates
nearly universal agreement among the profession concerning the preferred treatment—yet threefold differences are observed in appendectomy rates. This suggests that physicians differ in recognizing the
illness or in their willingness to assume the risk of a false positive
or false negative decision. Indeed, variability in individual physician
performance in the differential diagnosis of appendicitis has been
extensively documented by de Dombal et al. (1975).

Disagreement on Indications. For certain other procedures, the
more likely reason for variation appears to be disagreement on indications for surgery rather than recognition of illness. The value of
tonsillectomy (the most common childhood procedure) has been the
subject of a fifty-year-old debate. While there may be some disagreement on what is an hypertrophied tonsil, the literature review by
Dr. Kimm (Chapter 13) suggests that the major issue is the value of
the procedure. The marked variation in its use among Vermont areas
reflects this disagreement. Umbilical hernia surgery in infants appears
to be a second example of conditions which are easily recognized
but for which there is considerable difference in opinion on the value
of operation.

By contrast, inguinal hernia procedures—which are universally
recommended for this condition in the pediatric age group—show
little variability among Vermont areas. Apparently physicians agree
in recognition of the illness and in their recommendations concerning
treatment. Cleft palate surgery and surgery for hydrocephalus are
other examples.

Physician Choice. The most convincing evidence of the importance
of physician choice as a contributor to geographic variations may be
the changes which have followed after local physicians became aware
of variations. Lembcke (1959) demonstrated changes in the rate of
pelvic surgery among neighboring suburbs of Rochester, New York
subsequent to informing physicians of the rates in their areas and
initiating a peer review process. Per capita rates of hysterectomy
dropped as much as 50 percent following a similar procedure involv-

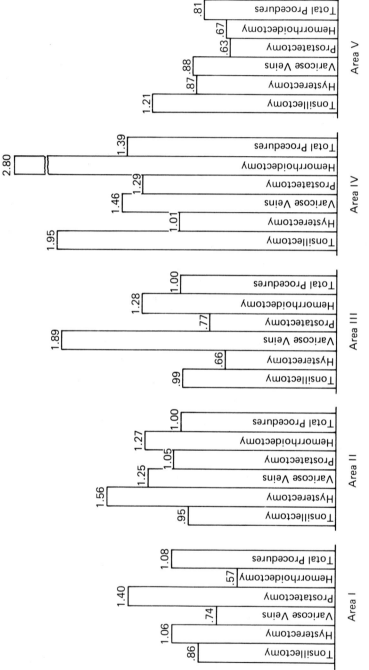

Figure 14–4. The Ratio of Observed to Expected Number of Selected Surgical Procedures Occurring in the Five Largest Hospital Service Areas in Maine

Source: Wennberg, J.E., and Gittelsohn, A., 1975.   Reprinted with permission.

ing communities in Saskatchewan (Dyck, 1975). In Vermont, where the per capita incidence of tonsillectomy has been measured since 1969, a 46 percent drop in rates below the baseline year occurred over three years after variations were reported back to hospitals. The rate of decline in Vermont was considerably higher than nationally. By 1973 the area with the highest rate in 1969 (444 procedures per 10,000 children fourteen years and less) dropped to 11 percent of the baseline year. The accelerating rate of change in this area has been attributed to the adoption of new criteria for tonsillectomy and the initiation of a joint review of all tonsillectomy cases by both pediatrician and surgeon prior to the decision to operate (Wennberg et al., unpublished).

SOME POLICY SUGGESTIONS

The important points of our analysis can be summarized. The incidence of use of specific treatments depends on four considerations: (1) the incidence of illness, (2) access to the medical care system, (3) physician judgment in diagnosis, and (4) physician belief in the effectiveness of treatment. When the variations in per capita use of a procedure or treatment are not explained by random fluctuations, systematic differences in one or more of these facets should be suspected. Among neighboring communities where the populations are apparently homogeneous and the communities defined by patterns of shopping for health care, the first two factors, incidence and access to care, are likely to be more or less the same. Differences in per capita use are thus likely to reflect variations in factors 3 and 4, physician judgment and belief in effectiveness.

A policy interpretation of our analysis is that consensus peer judgment on many of the common practices of medicine does not exist. Therefore, preferred utilization patterns or rates of geographic investment in health resources (particularly the distribution of physicians among specialties) cannot be defined *if the explicit strategy of public policy is to maximize health.* Nor can professionally optimum workloads be defined or consumption equalized among geographic areas on the basis of the relation of health care consumption to health status. In the context of this report, the policy implications of this feature of health care markets cannot be fully explored. I would, however, like to repeat and amplify suggestions I have made elsewhere for reducing physician uncertainty and improving market performance.[d] Some involve actions that are immediately feasible and some require further policy research.

[d] See: Wennberg, J.E. "PSRO and the relationships among health need, elective surgery and health status" in *Preadmission Certification and Elective Sur-*

Establish Regional Data Systems

Regional data systems for small area, epidemiologic analysis of local health care systems should be established throughout the United States and widely used in public and private sector efforts to improve and evaluate health systems performance.

It is not technically possible to evaluate the per capita use of health care without a direct, epidemiologic approach to measurement. This requires a data system organized geographically to coincide with local and regional health care markets. The past decade has seen a rapid, chaotic growth in the number of data systems that collect information on some aspect of use of personal health services. These data systems concentrate on activities of institutions but not on describing the health care received by populations.

The public sector, particularly the federal government, should take the lead to assure the orderly flow of information on performance of local health care systems. As an immediate practical step, the existing Medicare and Medicaid data systems should be adapted for small area, epidemiologic analysis to provide data on variations among local areas on hospital utilization, surgical rates, and reimbursements. The feasibility of this has been demonstrated in Vermont using Medicare Part B data. Medicare data can also be used to estimate total bed supply by area; they should be used in the implementation of PSRO, Certificate of Need Programs and the new federal planning legislation (P.L. 93−641).

As soon as possible, regional data systems describing use of care by all age groups should be established throughout the United States. Subject to reasonable and explicit rules governing confidentiality, statistics on utilization of health services should be considered part of the domain of public health statistics. To educate the public as well as the profession, data on variations in supply, utilization, and expenditures among local areas should be generally available. The policies to rationalize this expansion in extent and concept of health statistics are nascent at best; attention should be given to their development and to the development of a constituency that will see to their implementation.

Reduce Professional Uncertainty

Direct steps should be taken to reduce professional uncertainty by obtaining a second opinion prior to treatment. Clinical trials should

---

gery. Perspectives on Health Policy, No. 2, August, 1975. Boston University Medical Center. See also: Wennberg, J.E. "National health planning goals" in *Papers on the National Health Guidelines*, Volume 3. Department of Health, Education and Welfare, Health Resources Administration, 1976.

also be initiated to obtain direct evidence on the relationship between health care and health status.

As a first step to address the problem of professional differences in diagnosis and recommendations concerning treatment, it is reasonable to adopt a policy of review by a second physician prior to hospitalization and use of surgery. This method has been successful in changing surgical procedure rates among members of union health plans in New York and among children in one Vermont hospital service area. In areas with population-based data systems, I suggest review be restricted to causes of admission and surgical procedures that demonstrate statistically significant differences and, further, that review be restricted to those areas where procedures are somewhat above the mean. For surgery performed on Vermont children, this would include appendectomies and tonsillectomies and umbilical herniorrhaphy but not inguinal herniorrhaphy, cleft palate surgery, or cardiac catheterizations. A review program such as this is a reasonable extension of the PSRO responsibility and ought to be encouraged by third-party carriers and by state insurance commissioners.

In cases where recognition of need or evaluation of treatment remains equivocal, as evidenced by the medical literature, clinical trials should be organized to determine value.

Behind variations are different hypotheses among physicians concerning the effectiveness of care. These hypotheses should be tested.

There are currently few resources available to practicing physicians to conduct such trials and little professional or political pressure to establish an environment where they can be undertaken. This should change. Medical schools and professional societies, particularly specialty accreditation boards, should encourage their members to undertake clarifying investigations.

Assurance of reasonable scientific evidence on the relationship between health care and health status has always been a professional responsibility and will continue to be so. The public sector should improve the circumstances that promote learning and assure that the issue of effectiveness is being addressed. Appropriate funds and incentives must therefore be available. In cases where new health care technology is to be funded by public investments, the purchase of such technologies (such as coronary care units or cancer radiation centers) should be tied to the willingness of the profession to undertake valid trials to establish the effect of the investment.

Public Sector Recognition of
Physician Uncertainty

The public sector should recognize that for many common illnesses ambulatory and hospital care are interchangeable. "Medical neces-

sity" and "need" are often professionally indeterminate. This has important implications for facility and manpower planning.

Facility Planning. In their role as "certifiers of need" for facilities, the states should recognize that professional assertions of need are not necessarily final. They should seek alternative solutions to greater investments in facilities.

When the medical profession itself is uncertain about the proper, optimum use of hospital beds, then the state, as the certifier of need, is in a difficult position. Requests for additional facilities commonly come from areas that are already using hospitals at greater than the rate for the region as a whole. Issuing building permits to such areas will increase the utilization differential between areas. This dilemma needs resolution. Such policies ought to be actively pursued by policy researchers, particularly because the passage of P.L. 93–641 opens up again the issue of how regions should plan for their hospital systems. Alternative solutions to additional construction should be actively sought.

As an example that may be feasible in regions with population-based data systems, a simple extension of the second opinion idea can be suggested. Hospitals seeking additional facilities should be asked to review in detail the per capita rate of use of hospitals in their area by condition causing admission and by surgical procedure. They should also be given comparative data on the rates in neighboring areas. If, upon review, they consider that demographic or other practice circumstances in their area justify the variations, they should ask for a review of their judgment by a panel of physicians from other areas. Alternative suggestions to increased bed supply might be postgraduate education on the indications for specific hospitalizations or a second opinion procedure for specific conditions. Such alternatives should be requested from the reviewing panel of physicians.

Physician Manpower Planning
Because optimum professional actions cannot be defined for many common conditions, optimal physician workloads cannot be specified in advance.

For this reason, it is not possible to determine an optimum number of physicians—either the overall supply or the specialty composition—in terms of health outcome criteria. Alternative policies are needed to guide decisions in manpower training.

Assertions that more or fewer physicians are "needed" cannot be strictly evaluated in terms of health outcome consequences. Improvement in health manpower planning technology along these lines awaits resolution of professional uncertainty concerning effectiveness. However, a strategy to clarify the health outcome value of health care technologies is long-range and iterative. The results of these efforts cannot serve as a basis for contemporary decisions on health manpower needs.

Policy research to find other options is called for. More attention should be given to the effect of different mixes of physician specialists on market performance. Vermont studies suggest two important market effects of pediatricians and general practitioners not performing surgery. When they are in greater supply, (1) use of hospitals, surgery and expenditures are less and (2) those who are unable to contact a physician "when they need to" are fewer.

Thus there is evidence to support the hypothesis that more training of primary care physicians will lead to lower levels of spending for hospitals and less "excess demand" for patient-initiated contacts with the health care system. These possibilities should be thoroughly researched. It may be feasible to plan physician manpower on strategies that will reduce demand for hospitalization.

Private Foundations and the Problem of Effectiveness

Private foundations should promote and support prototype approaches to the problem of effectiveness that can serve as a basis for future public policy.

At the current level of public consciousness, the federal government may not have sufficient flexibility to deal broadly with the effectiveness issues. The opportunities for experimentation afforded by federal programs such as the Regional Medical Program and the Experimental Health Delivery System are gone. The government is currently locked into an effectiveness approach, PSRO (Professional Standards Review Organization), that focuses on issues such as length of hospital stay and avoids the fundamental issue of appropriateness of treatment. P.L. 93−641 places the government in the untenable position of certifying the need for facilities when the medical profession cannot agree on the more fundamental question of how facilities should be used in the treatment of disease.

The possibility that these programs will do nothing to resolve the issues for which they have been invented is serious. It is important to develop alternatives or extensions of the programs and to start on it now. It is particularly important to decide the long-term role of governmental and professional responsibility for effectiveness. Private foundations should play an essential role in promoting professional responsibility in resolving the issue of effectiveness. In my opinion, strategies to resolve uncertainty concerning the value of common medical and surgical practices and to develop more explicit professional responsibility should have top priority.

REFERENCES

Aday, L.A., and Eichorn, R., eds. U.S. Department of Health, Education and Welfare, Health Services and Mental Health Administration. *The Utilization of Health Services: Indices and Correlates.* (DHEW Publication #[HSM] 73–3003) Washington, D.C.: Government Printing Office, 1972.

Cooperative Health Information Center of Vermont, Inc. *See* Vermont.

deDombal, F.T., Horrocks, J.C., Walmsley, G., and Wilson, P.D. "Computer aided diagnosis and decision making in the acute abdomen," *J Roy Coll Physicians Lond* 9 (1975): 211–18.

Dyck, F., Chairman, Committee Appointed to Study Hysterectomies in Saskatchewan. *An Audit of Hysterectomies in Saskatchewan.* Presented at the Annual Meeting of the Royal College of Physicians and Surgeons of Canada, Winnipeg, Manitoba, January 1975, forthcoming in *N Engl J Med.*

Hughes, E.F.X., Fuchs, V.R., Jacoby, J.E., et al. "Surgical work loads in community practice," *Surgery* 71 (1972): 315–27.

Lembcke, P.A. "A scientific method for medical auditing," *Hospitals* 33 (1959): 65–71.

Lewis, C.E. "Variations in the incidence of surgery," *N Engl J Med* 281 (1969): 880–84.

Vayda, E., Anderson, G.D. "Comparison of provincial surgical rates in 1968," *Can J Surg* 18 (1975): 18–26.

Vermont Surgery Study 1969–1971. Cooperative Health Information Center of Vermont, Inc. Burlington, Vt., 1974.

Wennberg, J., and Fowler, F.J. "A test of consumer contribution to small area variations in health care delivery," forthcoming in *J Maine Med Assoc.*

Wennberg, J.E., and Gittelsohn, A. "Small area variations in health care delivery. A population-based health information system can guide planning and regulatory decision-making," *Science* 182 (1973): 1102–08.

Wennberg, J.E., and Gittelsohn, A. "Health care delivery in Maine I: Patterns of use of common surgical procedures," *J Maine Med Assoc* 66 (1975): 123–49.

Wennberg, J.E., Gittelsohn, A., and Soule, D. "Health care delivery in Maine II: Conditions explaining hospital admission," *J Maine Med Assoc* 66 (1975): 255–69.

Wennberg, J.E., Gittelsohn, A., and Shapiro, N. "Health care delivery in Maine III: Evaluating the performance of hospitals," *J Maine Med Assoc* 66 (1975): 298–306.

Wennberg, J., et al. "Changes in tonsillectomy rates associated with feedback and review," forthcoming in *J Pediatr.*